The Experience of Tragic Judgment

Adjudication between conflicting normative universes that do not share the same vocabulary, standards of rationality, and moral commitments cannot be resolved by recourse to traditional principles. Such cases are always in a sense tragic. And what is called for, in our pluralistic and conflictual world, is not to be found, as many would suppose, in an impersonal set of procedures with which all participants could be treated as having rationally agreed. The very idea of such a neutral system is an illusion. Rather, what is needed, Julen Etxabe argues in this book, is a heightened awareness of the difficulty of judgment. *The Experience of Tragic Judgment* draws upon Sophocles' play *Antigone* in order to consider this difficulty and the virtues that attend its acknowledgment. Based on the transformative experience that the audience undergoes in engaging with this play, what is proposed is a reconceptualization of judgment: not as it is generally thought to occur in a single isolated moment, like the falling of an ax, but rather as an experience that develops in and through space and time.

Julen Etxabe is a postdoctoral researcher at the Centre of Excellence in Foundations of European Law and Polity of the University of Helsinki, where he is co-editor of the journal *No Foundations: An Interdisciplinary Journal of Law and Justice*. Julen's research interests include law and humanities, legal theory, rhetoric and constitutional narratives, agonistic democracy, and human rights.

The Experience of Tragic Judgment

Julen Etxabe

Routledge
Taylor & Francis Group
a GlassHouse book

First published 2013
by Routledge
2 Park Square, Milton Park, Abingdon, Oxon OX14 4RN

Simultaneously published in the USA and Canada
by Routledge
711 Third Avenue, New York, NY 10017

A GlassHouse Book

Routledge is an imprint of the Taylor & Francis Group, an informa business

British Library Cataloguing in Publication Data
A catalogue record for this book is available from the British Library

Library of Congress Cataloging in Publication Data
A catalog record for this book has been requested

ISBN 978-0-415-63934-7 (hbk)
ISBN 978-0-415-65718-1 (pbk)
ISBN 978-0-203-07732-0 (ebk)

Typeset in Garamond
by Cenveo Publisher Services

For Jim and Mónica

We shall not cease from exploration
And the end of all our exploring
Will be to arrive where we started
And know the place for the first time

T. S. Eliot

Contents

Acknowledgements

I want to thank all the people and the institutions that have contributed to the actual shape of this book. The initial spark originated in Brussels, first during my studies at the European Academy of Legal Theory and, then, as a researcher at the Facultés Universitaires Saint Louis. I am grateful to Joxerramon Bengoetxea, Scott Veitch, Juha Karhu (f.k.a. Pöyhönen), and François Ost for their invaluable advice at these initial stages of the project, and for opening my mind to it.

A substantial part of this book was written in Ann Arbor, where I spent eight years as member of the larger community of the University of Michigan and the stimulating environment of the Law School. I would like to express my deep gratitude to the Fulbright Commission in Spain for enabling such a life-turning experience. In Michigan, I benefited from rich interdisciplinary dialogue as a Hunting Family graduate fellow at the Institute for the Humanities, and from teaching both at the Great Books Honors program led by Dr Cameron at the Department of Classical Studies, and at the Department of Romance Languages and Literatures. During all those years, I enjoyed the company and conversation of a great many friends, too many to mention here. Warm thanks go to Carrie Wood, Manuel Chinchilla and, above all, Gareth Williams and Cristina Moreiras Menor, whose generosity and intellectual honesty continue to inspire me.

The last push for the book was made in Helsinki, at the Center of Excellence in Foundations in European Law and Policy Research funded by the Academy of Finland, which has afforded me the resources and the peace of mind to complete the manuscript. I would like to thank all my friends and colleagues in Helsinki for putting up with my continued interest in Greek tragedy and the challenges it presents for modern law.

To say that no word can properly convey my gratitude does not begin to do justice to the single most important influence in my academic life, a person without whom this book could not even be *imagined*. James Boyd White has seen this book through from its infancy to its current completion. Most surprisingly, he managed to do so even before I could! I thank Jim for his intuition and enormous confidence, which he has entrusted and shared with me.

Though undoubtedly the person who has read, criticized, discussed, debated, and suffered this book the most is Mónica López Lerma, who has always worked beside me in Brussels, Ann Arbor, and Helsinki. Mónica's own research interests have pushed me to expand the range of readings and authors that transpire in this book, and I have benefited greatly from her ability to separate the wheat from the chaff, both in law and life. Finally, I also want to thank my parents and brother for their encouragement, support, and patience throughout the entire process of writing this book.

***

Parts of the book have already appeared elsewhere. Chapter 1 appeared with a different introduction and closing sections as "The Legal Universe After Robert Cover" in *Law and Humanities* 4 (2010). Chapter 3 appeared in a similar form as "Tragic Incommensurability and Legal judgment," in the *Canadian Journal of Law and Jurisprudence* 24 (2011). A few pages of Chapter 5 appeared in "What do the Poets Know about Democracy? A Case Study in Law and Literature," in Bart van Klink and Sanne Taekema (eds), *Law and Method: Interdisciplinary Research into Law* (Mohr Siebeck, 2011). A few pages of Chapter 4 appeared as an independent article entitled "Antigone's Nomos" in *Animus: Canadian Journal of Philosophy and Humanities*, vol. 13 (2009). I wish to thank them all for allowing me to republish the materials here. Lastly, I am indebted to Gary Watt for helping me with the design of the cover, and for drawing it stirringly, as a dilemma facing the audience.

Introduction: *Antigone* and the experience of legal judgment

> The loss of standards, which does indeed define the modern world in its facticity and cannot be reversed, is a catastrophe in the moral world only if one assumes that people are actually incapable of judging, that their faculty of judgment is inadequate, and that the most we can demand of it is the correct application of familiar rules from already established standards.
>
> (Hannah Arendt)[1]

The two guiding ideas of this book are not difficult to state plainly. The first is that the audience's experience of judging a tragic conflict – of which I take Sophocles' *Antigone* as paradigmatic – is akin to that of the legal judge facing a hard case between two conflicting normative universes. The second is that to reflect critically about this experience, about what it demands and entails, helps to develop the skills and aptitudes necessary for the practice of legal judgment – without easy automatism or indoctrination. If I were to leave it at that, these statements would contain nothing necessarily surprising or new: even though the analogy between theatrical audiences and judges is not often made explicit,[2] it has been often noted that Greek tragedy, as performed in Classical Athens, fostered a kind of civic education or *paideia* closely related to the exercise of democratic citizenship.[3] On the other hand, legal scholars working with a humanistic perspective have advanced the argument that literature and the arts in general have lots to teach legal practitioners.[4]

This book goes beyond these (more or less established, more or less accepted) lines of inquiry and demonstrates, on the basis of a reading of Sophocles' *Antigone*, not only that tragedy constructs its audience as a citizen who is also a judge, but how exactly it accomplishes this task, providing, at the same time, a repertoire of gestures, attitudes, and affective registers for performing this role responsibly. Among other things, I show that in order to lead the audience to enact its role as audience, the play requires every member to perform myriads of judgments that are integral to understanding the play and to the discharge of the duties of both citizen and judge.

Among the capacities and dispositions needed for engaging with and judging the tragic conflict, in addition to openness and receptiveness to differing points of view, I stress the ability to locate our own position, as members of the audience, within a continuously shifting narrative that constantly modifies it – a process that entails the ability to operate in, but also *through* and *within*, space and time. Time in particular is not only crucial, but crucially absent in most accounts where judgment is thought to take place in a vacuum of universal laws and general principles. Even in accounts of judgment avowedly *situated*,[5] time itself is often understood as a background condition that *itself* does not change, hence rendering it static and largely inoperative. The best way to have a sense of time's flow is to plunge directly in it and become attuned with its *movement*, which requires reflexive attention to our own shifting position within the drama's gradual unfolding.[6] The experience of judging tragedy is therefore woven around a series of displacements and motions, both spatial and temporal, that must be identified and acted upon, all of which enable audiences to define and assess their relative positions and stands on the issues with greater understanding and sensitivity to context.

The engagement I describe is necessarily called for by an incommensurable conflict such as the one dramatized in the *Antigone*, which is similar in kind, I suggest, to what in legal theory is called a "hard case" – defined provisionally as a case of conflict between two norms of equal validity at the same time and place, each of which provides in its own right an authoritative answer to a legal issue of substantial complexity. Contrary to those who would relegate these cases to the "corners of law,"[7] I argue that the way a given legal system responds to hard cases, concerned as they often are with the most pressing and contested issues in society, illuminates the normative universe in its entirety, just like metals reveal their latent properties under extreme conditions.

Finally, I illustrate that a phenomenological account of the audience's engagement with the tragedy – which requires detailed and sequential analysis of the play – provides a vocabulary and a language for the analysis of law and judgment that is richer than those currently found in the literature on legal adjudication in general.[8] To develop this language, and the capacities for judgment it calls into existence, is vital, I believe, for the sustained practice of democracy and the exercise of legal decision-making in the pluralistic age we now inhabit. This task demands, fundamentally, a complete reconceptualization of judgment not as something that occurs in a single isolated moment, like the falling of an ax or the pressing of a button, but rather as an elongated experience woven around multiple relationships and trajectories that generate thick constellations of connections. The hope is that this view of judgment generates thick layers of expression and webs of interconnected practices that can be communicated and interpenetrated across languages, cultures, and ideologies. Naturally for all this, more than my simple statement is needed. But before I outline the rest of the argument, I would like to say a few words about what attracted me first to the *Antigone* and why I think it provides an incomparable window on the phenomenology of law and legal judgment in a hard case scenario.

I

The origin of this work lies in a preoccupation with normative conflicts of the serious and vital kind famously put forward by Isaiah Berlin and others.[9] The issue that concerned me initially was how to justify judicial decisions in cases of deep normative conflict, namely in cases where the participants do not share the same standards of rationality, the same vocabulary, or the same normative commitments (due to differences in culture, religion, ideology, social predicament, and so on). For example, how is it possible to justify – indeed to think about and to conceptualize – cases in which one of the contenders does not accept the jurisdiction of the court, the validity of the norms to be applied, or the rules and principles of the legal system that is supposed to adjudicate the issue? The standard line of argument at the time did not directly contemplate this hypothesis – in it the legal system figures as a neutral framework in which conflicts can be played out without itself ever being put in question. But this explanation is question-begging, as the conflict concerns not just the content of primary norms and principles, but the very rules and principles structuring the discussion (i.e. the meta-rules). Accordingly, we no longer have one single legal system that functions as an umbrella for all kinds of disputes, but rather multiple, alternative legal universes, where no system can claim to be superior to the other (except by political domination). In this vein, for example, James Tully has demonstrated how the language of modern constitutionalism has been unable to integrate, and has actually precluded, the legal claims of aboriginal people from being properly heard by (i.e. having a legal hearing in) the dominant constitutional framework.[10]

To a higher or lesser degree, it appeared to me, procedural theories all failed to take normative conflict seriously. For, even when normative pluralism became accepted in a limited sense, the usual answer proposed criteria of rational acceptability that could be inter-subjectively argued and accepted by a reasonable person (e.g. reasonableness, consistency, coherence).[11] Of course this kind of argument runs against the fact that what is reasonable for one party is often unreasonable for the other, that the parties do not always behave "reasonably," and that one can be perfectly consistent yet a consistent fool (let alone cruel, or insensitive to others).

To be sure there existed an alternative approach, which entailed accepting that every such decision is always irredeemably political (as opposed to purely legal), and to be understood as part of the language-games in which each of the participants seeks to impose his or her own self-interested criteria by means of superior strength or force. This explanation, although not far from the truth in important ways, did not generate a more productive avenue. In fact, by depriving us of the possibility of distinguishing between different kinds of political action it unwittingly empties this word of all meaning, for "if everything is political, then nothing is."[12] Here again, the problem is not that every legal decision contains a gap that is to be filled by political, ethical, even existential considerations – that much, to me, is certain – but that we still need a language in which to distinguish between decisions that may in some way be justified from those that cannot (however subject to variation and contestation).

A confluence of happy circumstances made me rediscover Sophocles' *Antigone*. One was Werner Jaeger's seminal work *Paideia*, which opened for me a world, distant in time yet surprisingly contemporary in outlook, of Greek thought before Plato and Aristotle. A second factor was my encounter with the work of James Body White, who made me realize the radical literariness of law – its roots in peoples' imagination and narratives – and the urge to explore the creative, personal, and non-objectifiable aspect of law that I found wanting in legal theory. A third circumstance was the close proximity with the work of François Ost and Philippe Gerard, whose brilliant analysis of the play pushed me to study it in more depth, paying closer attention to its ambiguities, tensions, and legal implications. Could the *Antigone* serve in this way as a point of departure of a different kind of approach not yet attempted in the legal literature, using the conflict between the two contenders as a framing device?

The clash between Antigone and Creon seemed to exemplify better than I could imagine (or find in the case law of any jurisdiction) exactly the kind of conflict at once absolute and incommensurable that was at the heart of my concerns. As I began to understand it, the conflict was not so much between distinct Hegelian *spheres* of life (family and religion on the one side and politics and the state on the other), but rather between *entire normative worlds*, each constituted by contradictory considerations of family, religion, and community, with alternative visions of the good, the right, and the just.[13] From this perspective, Antigone and Creon both fight for the supremacy of the same symbolic space, which each wishes to dominate at the expense of the other.

In this, the play offers a "real" as opposed to an ideal speech situation, where characters speak with anger, mistrust, and prejudice, and use emotionally charged language and identical terms of value not to communicate and reach an agreement, but as weapons to crush each other. Here rationality is not shared, nor can we presume a horizon of common intelligibility. The play also demands constant involvement from the audience, being emotionally invested in the characters' fates, empathizing with one point of view and then with another, and then again shifting positions or modifying them according to the arguments of each side. All this is quite different from the model of detached, impersonal, and objectifying form of judging that was the standard in legal studies.[14] Finally, the *Antigone* is structured like a legal trial, with two agents in clear contention over one specific legal issue, other characters playing the part of witnesses (providing factual evidence, speaking on behalf of one of the contenders, providing hearsay or expert testimony), and the chorus of Theban elders acting as a collective actor and jury on the stage, while the audience is placed in the role of judge or tribunal having to adjudicate the conflict. To be sure, the *Antigone* is much more than the clash between the two protagonists. The *Antigone*, more clearly than any other tragedy, is a choral play that functions like a polyphony of voices and points of view that enrich and complicate any easy identification with one single character or legal perspective. All this I thought could illuminate an interdisciplinary study into the character, praxis, and judgment of deep normative conflicts.

But there was still another reason, more powerful than the rest, which I only intuited at the time but later would acquire a more prominent role in my thinking. This is that, while the incommensurable conflict between the two contenders is indeed real and leads to an experience of aporia, the impasse seems gradually overcome when in the last instance Antigone's legal position prevails over Creon's initial decree that forbade it. The puzzle was and still is: how can we possibly understand *both* the aporia of judgment *and* its eventual resolution as part of the same experience of judgment? This opens up the analysis to a temporal dimension that must be interrogated, as it may hold the key for the way prejudices and fore-understandings can be challenged and eventually transcended.

This project also gave me the chance to approach law in a different way, not in terms of rules and regulations or a set of social policies and institutional arrangements, to which law is often unjustifiably reduced, but in terms of characters, voices, performances, gestures, images, symbols, perceptions, and rhetoric, which would open the door to the full phenomenon of law as a *lived experience* that I aimed to comprehend, and which seemed incomprehensibly absent in dominant accounts of law.

II

But what connection is there between Athenian tragedy and law (both ancient and modern)? In *Myth and Tragedy in Ancient Greece*, Jean-Paul Vernant and Pierre Vidal-Naquet write that the true material of tragedy is the social thought peculiar to the city-state, and in particular the legal thought that it was then in the process of transformation.[15] As a result, everyone who approaches tragedy has to become a legal scholar of sorts, coming to grips with the "verbal and intellectual equipment, categories of thought, types of reasoning, the system of representations, and the modalities of action and of agency" that comprise both tragedy and law.[16] Still, this is only preliminary, the authors warn us, because "legal thought will not shed any light directly upon the tragic text as if the latter were no more than a transfer from it."[17] This is so, on the one hand, because tragic poets deliberately exploited the ambiguities, fluctuations, and incompleteness of this legal vocabulary, which is how the word "nomos" (law, custom, rule, convention) can be used with precisely opposite connotations by the two protagonists (Antigone and Creon).[18] On the other hand, because tragedies generally represented a world that was distant in space and time from the historical Athens, theatrical audiences of the city Dionysia were used to customs and traditions quite different from their own. Indeed, it is not often sufficiently stressed that Athenian audiences had to imagine a distant land and time that did not correspond to Athenian standards and that they were very much conscious of watching a work of fiction.[19] Thus the relationship between the Athenian audience and the world of the tragedies is potentially as complex as our own relationship with their world and with the world of the tragedies: they too had to negotiate their way through a world that did not accurately represent their own.

In this regard, the task is not to recreate an idealized (fixed, homogeneous, and inalterable) concept of an "original audience" that could guide our own reading of the text. The ideal of an original audience – like its legal correlative in the idea of the original meaning of the Constitution or the intention of the Framers – cannot be used as an *independent* variable, since it cannot be construed separately from a dynamic reading of the text that it is supposed to help us understand. This is not to say that historical specificities do not matter or are to be discounted. To be sure, tragedies resonated profoundly with Athenian culture, social institutions, family structures, and so on, and the "perceptual filters" of the historical audience must be incorporated in any sound interpretation of the play.[20] However, the text itself modifies the audience's assumptions and expectations, forcing their re-evaluation in the course of the performance.[21] To put it simply, it is not that the Athenian stops being an Athenian when going to the theater, but that he/she is invited to adopt different habits of mind for the duration of the play. What must be explained then is not what the historical audience or the "average theater-goer" was supposed to think or to react according to a prior set of values or principles, but rather *how they were invited to position themselves* in regard to what they were watching – as indeed we still are invited to position ourselves, with regard to a work of art that still resonates in our own world. Instead of an original audience, then, I prefer to speak of an implied (or implicated) audience, which is constructed through the interaction of invited responses and reactions that crystallize in the text – in which we can, with all our differences and historical circumstances, all participate.[22]

As a result, a mere historical analysis of the legal institution of burial and honoring the dead in Ancient or Classical Greece will not exhaust the meaning of Antigone's particular performance, or reveal its significance in the context of the drama. In order to understand Antigone's action of burial one must understand the entire legal universe that makes it meaningful (its symbols, myths, and narratives) within the imagined society in which this action figures as meaningful. All this forces the interpreter to go back to the tragedy itself and to the world that it helps to construct, which creates its own symbolic geography in the audience's imagination.

Take the law of the gods that Antigone is said to obey. Obviously, there is an easy connection to be drawn with the Aristotelian doctrine of natural law as it will be explained later in the book. However, if her law embodies a law of nature obvious for all to see, why are not other characters equally compelled to act in the same way and even dare to criticize her? Can we even postulate a divine origin for these laws when "no one knows when these laws came to be" (457)? If we also consider that Antigone is not endowed with prophetic vision like Cassandra, nor can she read the birds of augury like Teireisas, what is her authority to declare such laws? More puzzlingly, if such general law of burial is supposed to admit no exceptions, why does she utter a final speech in which she seemingly qualifies its alleged universality by restricting it to her last brother but not to her (hypothetical) husband or child (905–7)? Arguably Antigone's law cannot be pinned down to a single or simple formulation, but rather follows a complex trajectory that needs to be traced from start to finish. That is, one must develop a way of reading the play that accounts for its evolutions and shifts of meanings and articulations, through the gradual unfolding of events in which her legal claim takes shape and can eventually succeed.

This in turn requires a legal theory to help us to understand a law that is constantly evolving. To begin with, we must abandon the presupposition of a legal system with clear and pre-established rules, structured around well-defined hierarchies, sharp separations between law and morals, fact and value, is and ought, and where a sovereign power issues norms of general character to all the citizens. In its place, we must imagine a law that is enlivened by the myths and narratives that make it meaningful and the language that lends norms their full expressive force, enabling individuals to argue, modify, change, appeal, or defend these norms, and to persuade others about their interpretation, validity, and pre eminence. We are to conceive of a law constructed rhetorically, by way of conversations and exchanges, often of a polemic nature, with others; a law that is structured in no systematic design, without clear separation between the "legal" and other realms of human activity (ethics, politics, aesthetics); where every fact is always a statement of value (as when Antigone defines Polyneices as a "brother," i.e. not a traitor).

Beyond the strict confines of the *Antigone*, such a view compels us to see every law, of every kind, not as something that can be created once and for all in a single sovereign act, but through a complex interplay of related acts and speeches, constantly changing its forms to better adapt to its environment and the contexts of its use and the desires and aspirations of its users. In saying so I wish to make no conceptual claim about the essential properties or "nature" of law of the kind attempted by the field of general jurisprudence, as if we could somehow transcend our historical condition and provide a-historical and universal concepts of law. Rather, my claim touches on the habits of perception that form anyone's experience of law; that is, the perceptual lens with which any person, at any given time, can approach, perceive, and understand a phenomenon which has as diverse and multiple manifestations as law. Thus it would not be fatal to object that "the Greeks" (or

Sophocles, or his audience, or Antigone herself) would not have understood law in the way I suggest we do in this book. It suffices that this view of law helps us to visualize certain aspects about normative phenomena of the play that do remain obscured by rival theories of law. This particular and contingent frame enables us to place under the same rubric similar though not always identical normative phenomena occurring at different geographies and historical times, without claiming to have discovered their unifying essence. I do suggest, nevertheless, that this "tragic vision of law" is actually pertinent for the pluralistic age of diversity in which we now live, where phenomena such as legal fragmentation, state-less legal regimes, normative pluralism, and transnational law make it necessary to rethink all our inherited legal categories in serious and fundamental ways.

III

Indeed, tragedy testifies not just to a bygone historical era. In our midst we find nowadays a variety of legal conflicts we can very well call "tragic." By this I mean cases where there is, as between Antigone and Creon, no unitary and harmonious system of law (or equivalent philosophical construction) that can serve as a neutral framework to arbitrate the dispute. Think, for example, of the conflict between Israel and Palestine (or China and Tibet, India and Pakistan, Turkey and Kurdistan). Or think, less virulently, of cases over historically disputed territory, over the rights of native and indigenous people, and over the constitutional status of regional and infra-state legal communities which do not see their claims properly recognized by the state constitution. Or yet again, take the example of religious or cultural symbols, which have come to the fore in recent years particularly in the European context. For instance, should women who wear the burka be prohibited from doing it publicly? Which and whose principles should be relied upon to decide on the matter? Does the burka symbolize a prison for women? All women? Even those who wear it voluntarily? And what does "voluntarily" mean? Can someone voluntarily waive her rights to personal freedom and autonomy? Or does autonomy speak precisely in favor of allowing anyone to wear what she wants? (Are even "autonomy" and "freedom" pertinent categories to frame the issue?) What is/are the "meaning" or meanings of wearing this attire? From which perspective can and should this be ascertained? Which of those meanings should be taken as "salient" and with respect to what segment of the population?[23]

The answer to this pluralistic and conflictive world is not to be found in a supposedly neutral set of procedures that all participants could rationally agree. The very idea that a language can be found in which everything can be rendered harmonious – a universal language into which every particularity can be adequately translated – is illusory. To seek such procedures is also undesirable, as it seeks to transfer the responsibility of judgment to impersonal entities, which do not possess the nimbleness to adjust to the changing circumstances, or to situations where the framework itself is the source of conflict. What the situation seems to be demanding is, rather, a heightened awareness of the difficulty of judgment, hence heightened appreciation of the capacity for judgment and of the activities that can develop it. What is needed as well is the development of a language of criticism beyond the reiteration of worn-out dichotomies like judging according to reason or to emotion, according to objective or to subjective criteria, according to rules or to intuition, according to general standards or to arbitrary discretion. The notion that we must be either able to judge with formal rules and generalizable standards or else yield to the imponderables of passion and "judicial gastronomy"[24] is not just simplistic, but it ignores a full array of practical abilities and faculties that humans possess, as Hanna Arendt writes in the introductory quote.

Like Arendt herself, who sought to unearth Kant's unwritten political philosophy in his writing, not on history, but on judgment[25] (and without accepting Arendt's own view of the political as a separated sphere or Kant's theory of judgment developed in his Third Critique[26]), I too believe that judgment holds the potential for a true sense of the institutional and the normative. This is so provided that we understand institutions genuinely as practices of social communication – and not as concrete embodiments in organizational structures and arrangements. Instead of providing the framework or architecture, judgment seeps in the cracks of intellectual devices that ambition teleological closure, carving out spaces of dissent where a plurality of voices can contest their meanings. Further, judgment holds the key to radical innovation and newness, for in every judgment there lies the potential to alter the conditions for understanding both the institution and its constitutive norms – henceforth shifting the direction of the whole enterprise. Within the plural worlds we all inhabit or are able to imagine, judgment generates experiences that are transversal and multi-perspectival, opening up what legal theorists Marie Claire Belleau and Rebecca Johnson have analyzed as "noetic spaces."[27] In all this, there is an implicit political philosophy that will remain largely in the background, of writers in the tradition of agonism and radical democracy such as Jacques Rancière, Chantal Mouffe, Iris Young, Sheldon Wolin, James Tully, William Connolly, and others.[28] To invoke judgment in this context is therefore also to think of tragedy as the stage for democracy.

IV

The lack of clear standards does not relieve us of the responsibility for judgment, which may cause uneasiness. Indeed, judgment affirms the value of that which is chosen, but in doing so it may close the door to other valuable options. Perhaps, then, judging is an inherently tragic endeavor, planted with a seed of remorse, regret, and occasional guilt. But just as Isaiah Berlin urged us to accept that we cannot have everything in life, learning to make and to *own* our judgments is part of being human. As John Caputo writes:

> We must judge even if we do not know how to judge. That is where we are. Life does not ask if we are prepared and it does not have the decency to wait until we are ready. Even though we lack criteriology, a law of laws, we are still not dispensed from judging. We are from the start before the law, forced to act and choose, to judge and respond.[29]

For far too long legal theory has sought in vain to achieve certainty by relying on rules and principles that would constrain the work of interpretation and limit the dangers of arbitrariness and bias. Thus judgment has often been treated as a suspect category and relegated to a black box that cannot be accessed. A different prejudice arises from a certain (post)modern sensibility, where judgment is associated with forms of domination, exclusion, and boundary-setting that work on behalf of the law that inflicts pain and suffering on those who are subject to it. Yet another roadblock comes from the notion that judging something or someone presupposes a position of superiority – a sentiment well captured in the ethical maxim "do not judge and you shall not be judged."[30] Therefore, before advancing any further, it is important to define our topic, since some of the issues hinge on how we understand the term "judgment."

When we judge something we often say that we are taking a stand on something,[31] which is why judgment often takes a sense of finality. In other words, when passing a judgment we say that we are taking or affirming a position on a given topic or issue. Judgment as it will be defined in this book refers properly not to the quality of the object being judged (i.e. "this object is good or beautiful"), but to the *relationship* between "I" and this "object" (as in "I relate to this object in such and such a manner"). The most natural relation is the one between the subject who judges and the object being judged (e.g. "I consider this relationship to be over"). But to be sure, this object can also be another person (e.g. "I felt John was being quite rude") and even our own selves, as when we make a reflexive judgment (e.g. "After what happened yesterday, I can't bear to look at my face in the mirror"), or when I suddenly realize than an opinion maintained for many years no longer represents me.

Judgment, I would like to suggest, is more than the affirmation of something, i.e. "I judge this to be the case." Rather, it is a matter of positioning, perspective, and timing. Thus to judge something is a kind of "moving relationship" that a person establishes with a given object (or person), as in "I realize now that I stand in such and such a manner in relation to that case," where all the elements of this relationship ("I," "realize," "now," "such and such manner," and "that case") are being defined in the very act of pronouncing the judgment. In such a way, judgment can be viewed as the activity of establishing relationships and motions between the subjects and the objects of judgment.

This view of judging must be distinguished from maintaining a judgmental attitude. Judging as described here presupposes a willingness to remain open and to reconsider all the elements of the relationship (its subject, its object, its place, its time). This may be caused by reflection, for example, or by the intervention of a third party who gives us a perspective not previously considered. Sometimes we may consider that the moment is not ripe to reach certain conclusions, or to get carried away by first impressions. By contrast, a judgmental attitude is characterized by a much more rigid and inflexible position, as well as by a certain rashness to pass verdicts without proper understanding. As a hierarchical form of relationship, too, a judgmental attitude assumes its own superiority, which often leads to judgments that are self-righteous, patronizing, and performed with a sense of entitlement.

When making a judgment we establish relationships and perform motions that are of a spatial and temporal nature. Concerning the former, some are more immediate and direct than others, as when I listen directly to a person and identify closely with him or her, whereas others are indirect and mediated, for example through the influence of other people or my own prior personal background on the issue. By spatial relations, then, I mean the distances, interstices, and mediations that lie between the subject and the object of judgment. On the other hand, judgments also have a temporal dimension, as when a given issue awakens our recollection, desire, or urgency to act. When I judge something in anticipation, for example, I see an object not in its present form, but as it may later appear if the conditions of my actual judgment come true. Anticipation is thus a way of relating temporally to the object before me, as I bring the future to bear on my present considerations and perceptions about it. Likewise, a given judgment can look back to an object in retrospection, or forward prospectively, and therefore judge the same object differently depending on that motion. Hence, this temporal dimension can be perceived as a kind of motion with which a person approaches an issue and be described in the trajectory it forms when it is expressed, which is not always linear and can go in several directions at once (e.g. in spirals, cyclically, or recursively), acquiring depth, richness, complexity.

As a form of relationship, judgment is also a matter of attitudes or dispositions. Therefore a judgment can be timid, trusting, or confident; it can be respectful and tactful, or authoritarian and insensitive; it can be deferential to the judgments of others, or mindfully ignorant about them; it can be engaged and committed or else detached and aloof; it can be responsible and aware of the consequences, or hide behind the wall of rules and regulations. Judgments are often not simple and flat, but multi-layered and complex, sometimes expressing more than one value, as when they express clear ambivalence; sometimes they can incorporate contradictory points of view, as when a judgment accepts the truth of both sides.

Judging as I am describing here is not on a separate realm from our everyday activities. When we enjoy a movie, when we hear a story from a friend, when we give and receive advice, when we articulate a point of view or engage in political discussion, these all are instances that require activating such capacities, though naturally some judgments are more important than others. But clearly judging is not the privilege of judges, juries, and those who hold jurisdictional offices, for it falls directly in line with private and public lives, roles, and responsibilities.

V

How does this relate to the experience of theatrical audiences and the judge? I have already suggested that tragedy invites its audience to adopt the role of the judge. It is important to realize, however, that for this to be the case the audience must be actively implicated in the construction of a position that is far from being passive or neutral, which is why the conventional qualities associated with good judging (impartiality, detachment, disinterestedness, abstractedness, generality) do not adequately represent good judging in the drama. This is important and not always sufficiently stressed. At the level of the society represented in the play, Antigone is merely a subject in the legal order dominated by Creon, who acts in representation of the sovereign (statist) power (ignoring the anachronism for the moment). By the time Antigone articulates her legal argument denying the validity of Creon's decree, however, Creon no longer figures as the personification of "the law." Instead, he begins to be seen as a party to a conflict in which he is no more entitled to dominion than his counterpart. Thus the audience assists in the creation of a different "order of law" from the one that is represented, which is the register at which the audience's judgment operates.

The realization is crucial. Whereas in "the court of King Creon" (the law represented in the drama) Antigone has neither voice nor representation; in the court that is being constituted or enacted symbolically by the audience Antigone has as much a voice and standing as does he. For the conflict to be fully deployed, in fact, the audience is to constitute this triangular structure where Antigone and Creon are the two parties of a trial conducted between equals, despite all their differences in gender, status, age, and power. The audience acts as the guarantor of the symbolic structure in which the incommensurable conflict can take place and be properly staged. As it shall be shown in Chapter 1 this too is the role and position that a judge must construct when facing a hard case, without relying in the prerogative of jurisdiction as a matter of course, or aligning the jurisdictional office with the powers that be.

In the *Antigone*, the moment of incommensurability leads to an impasse where judgment seems impossible and no road to justice can be traversed. To understand one party is to deny the other and both have claims that need attending. Their conflict illustrates what Isaiah Berlin called a conflict at once absolute and incommensurable, where both Antigone and Creon make mutually exclusive demands that cannot both be satisfied. Modern readings of *Antigone* have stressed that no shortcut can be devised to sidestep its aporetic structure.

Nevertheless, the tragedy does not conclude in the enunciation of the conflict between the two main characters, but advances towards a resolution by which Creon's decree is finally annulled and the burial properly performed. In a gradual reversal of positions, Antigone, who as a young female under the care of her uncle was without legal standing at the outset, begins to gain normative traction until she becomes a fully-fledged legal actor whose claim ultimately prevails (even if she has to die for it). Inversely, Creon slowly but surely begins a process of disintegration in which he loses all the support he may have had in the beginning, sure as he was of himself. Thus, whereas in the beginning one might think that the claim of the *polis* comes from Creon's mouth, it is highly unlikely that one could say the same thing in the end where Creon does not speak for the *polis* at all – although it would be wrong to deduce from here a rule of universal application.

This transformation extends to the audience and to its normative perceptions: many in the audience may have accepted prima facie Creon's right to declare the law over the life and death of a "traitor," but no one in the end can fail to notice the shortcomings and disastrous consequences of his rule. Thus we start, as the audience, from a position where political leaders have wide latitude to decide over the life and death of their subjects, but we would not comprehend anything if, as a result of our engagement with the play, the former presuppositions were not severely tested and modified.[32] *Something has happened to us* and to our understanding of the law that must be accounted for. Such transformation, which is not covered by the Aristotelian formal concept of *peripeteia* or reversal, arguably coincides with the experience of judgment occurring not at the level of the dramatic action, but in the audience's field of perception – the stage where law is not simply represented but *enacted* by the mutual interaction between audience and stage. This complex experience, which I hope to illustrate with a detailed and sequential reading of the *Antigone*, must be followed through and traced without collapsing it into a flat *ex post facto* narrative that dilutes the dilemmas and uncertainties of judging. Instead, we must develop a way of reading that enables us to account for these transformations as they are occurring.

By talking about an "experience," I want firstly to characterize it as something that happens to us, that is that affects and has an effect upon us, upsetting expectations, challenging assumptions, confirming certain intuitions, crushing others, constantly pushing us to reflect about the complex issues and dilemmas it presents.[33] This experience presupposes a willingness to participate and engage with the drama, but once we constitute ourselves as members of the theatrical audience, some of these effects tend to operate somewhat "against our will," which does not mean that we are mere passive receptacles of whatever the play wishes to imprint on us. Quite the opposite, in fact: experiencing tragedy to the fullest demands a continuous effort not to lose ourselves in the simple pleasures of contemplation, and that we remain cognizant and ultimately responsible for all the judgments that the tragedy is inviting us to make – as captivated, but not captive, members of the audience.

As a result, the experience of tragic judgment is not the result of rules, standards, or criteria that could be systematized or learnt simply in a book (not even this one). Judgment is more similar to an art, impossible to lock into a set of operations that could be memorized and applied mechanically without further personal effort. As a process one must undergo, moreover, all the stages that form the experience must be followed, in the sense that one cannot skip them in order to go directly to the end and obtain the same "result." Indeed, an experience requires a learning period that must be gradually interiorized before it can be turned into a competence one might later rely on in different circumstances and situations. Such "education" is neither automatic nor guaranteed, nor are the necessary consequences of all kinds of engagement, but it *can* be learned and nurtured, I hope to show, by means of undergoing the experience that I try to exemplify in my own reading of *Antigone*. Your experience will be different to mine, but it will be an experience, nonetheless, to which I hope you can relate and learn to identify in your own reading.

Against Robert Cover, who believed that the interpretation of literature and law were two radically different activities that could not (and should not) be compared, I argue that the capacities and skills required for judging both are actually the same, even though the implications of the two contexts differ. The audience and the judge (either as an individual or as a member of a collective body) are both faced with narratives and normative universes that they must approach without losing their capacity and independence of judgment; they must both confront their own prejudices and moral standpoints, operating from within a narrative structure – the tragic play in one case, the legal proceedings in the other – that is continuously moving in ways that cannot be anticipated. The audience and the judge alike must perform their respective tasks to their best of their abilities, within the constraints of the interpretive context, guided by their own understanding and assessment of the materials available to them, and following their own desire to be just. Both activities run towards an end, and that end is justice.

VI

As for my own approach to the play, what I provide is not so much a reading of the *Antigone* as much as a way of reading it. That is to say, I offer not an interpretation of the *Antigone* (at least not initially), but rather an understanding of how I think the play is to be read – what kind of engagements the text invites us to perform – if some of those meanings are to arise in the first place.

What I hope to describe is an activity, explored to the fullest of its possibilities, which can never be done in practice in exactly the same way and which should therefore always leave ample room for individual expression and variances in performance, just like there are many ways to play the flute or the piano. But within the contours of the activity I believe it is possible to give an account of how to perform it in some ways better than in others. In doing so, I do not seek a predictive model of the sort attempted by social scientists, but a kind of practical knowledge that cannot be detached from the personal experience that it entails. Your *Antigone* and mine will be different, and our judgments will differ too, but both you and I will be faced with similar dilemmas and demands from these characters, which will force us to engage in a similar activity of judgment. These capacities, and not any particular interpretation, are the real concern of this book.

For this purpose, I try to replicate the conditions of an audience that sees the play represented before their eyes from start to finish – imaginatively attempting to visualize its performance. To adopt such a perspective, for instance, without jumping ahead of the narrative and reading it backwards, is important for the deployment of certain dramatic effects, unexpected reversals, and surprising turns of events, and fundamental, as a result, for the way characters, actions, and events are being judged. As such these conditions are constitutive of the experience of judgment and must be configured (and reconfigured) each and every time we read or engage with the text, regardless of how often we have done it already, or how long it takes us to read through the text.

Naturally, I am also a *reader*, that is I have the benefit of being able to go through the text as many times as needed – not unlike a judge may go back to the transcripts of the trial or the text to be interpreted as many times as necessary. In addition, my understandings are the result of many readings, in fact of many years of reading, which have naturally enriched, modified, and often subverted many of my earliest assumptions. But no matter how many times one has read a text – or a judge has heard a similar case – we must be ready to re-live the experience every time we are confronted by it again, in fact open to be surprised by the newness of the case and ready for a fresh judgment, as every case provides the opportunity for reconsidering all the premises. This is indeed the expectation of every claimant that appears before a court of law: that his or her case will receive full attention from the court or judge and will not be dealt with in a bureaucratic and mechanistic fashion.

Some may object that this is an impossible task to do with a text as steeped in tradition as is the *Antigone*, having received the attention of a great many thinkers in the past. What I propose to do is not to read the play as if none of these writers had written before – this would be presumptuous and wrongheaded – but rather to engage with it as they themselves had to at some time or another. The final aim of this exercise is to feel that we are not speaking with borrowed language, but with a language that we have earned and learned how to use.

Finally I should say that in choosing Sophocles' text I do not wish to make any argument about the origin of law or the Western psyche, nor do I wish to grant any foundational value to the myth that the *Antigone* dramatizes,[34] nor do I speculate about the beginning of language and the grammar of conflict.[35] My argument is rather that the *Antigone* exemplifies, better than any other cultural artifact I am aware of, all the complexities of judging normative conflicts in tragic contexts. Thus the *Antigone* serves at one at the same time as a paradigmatic *stage* for the conflict, as a framing device or *lens* through which to observe legal judgment, and as a *reflecting mirror* that stares back at our own activity of judgment. Perhaps, one might think, I could have chosen a different text.[36] To be honest, I doubt I could have found another with the same exploratory force.

VII

This book steers its way from within and at the margins of law, legal theory, classical studies, literary criticism and philosophy, not fully inhabiting one single domain but wishing to make a singular contribution to each. Its structure intertwines an in-depth and sequential reading of Sophocles' *Antigone* (in three acts) with a corresponding set of chapters of legal and philosophical inquiry. The argument develops gradually, just like the tragedy, and is meant to replicate in its own unfolding the experience of understanding and judging tragic conflicts. Although one could read each part separately, the book forms an interconnected whole that cannot be understood without reading it from beginning to end, in the precise order in which it is arranged. The form of the book is thus an integral and essential part of my argument and richer than any of its parts in isolation.

In the first chapter, I reconstruct the jurisprudence of Robert Cover, whose philosophy of law can rival, and provide a rich alternative to, the dominant theoretical perspectives of Hans Kelsen, H. L. A. Hart, and Ronald Dworkin. Distinctive to his approach is the emphasis on narrative and language as the key to the normative aspect of law and to its constant becoming. This aspect of law is the key to law's phenomenological existence, that is to the way individuals and collectives live and are bound by their law. The rich amalgam of language, myth, and narrative that forms Cover's notion of law (or "nomos") improves upon dominant conceptions, and it helps us to access the various manifestations of law that are present in the tragedy (i.e. the legal worlds of the various characters). This vision of law will accompany us throughout, particularly the description of "hard cases" as clashes between contrasting normative worldviews, each of which would provide their own "right legal answer" to the issue under consideration (the burial of Polyneices). Considering that Cover was weary of pushing the analogy between law and literature too far, in the final part of this chapter I provide a rejoinder to that kind of criticism.

Equipped with these tools, Chapter 2 offers a close textual examination of the various normative positions concerning the burial of Polyneices in the initial part of Sophocles' play. First, Ismene's and Antigone's opposite reactions to the prohibition reveal, among other things, contrary conceptions of the obligations of family, gender relations, and the authority and legitimacy of the new ruler. Likewise, Creon's legal prohibition of the burial expresses ethical and political demands that in his mind justify the decree. In this way, I try to make explicit the cultural, historical, and political presuppositions that inform the issue of the burial and its prohibition. This chapter closes with the main confrontation between Antigone and Creon, in which Antigone rejects not just the decree but Creon's authority to issue it. This is not a conflict of spheres or individual norms, but between *entire* normative worlds and over the *entire* realm of law. Their legal battle puts images, principles, values, and symbols, as well as the manner of arguing them, all at stake, each as colored by the distinctive personalities and attitudes of the two main characters. Antigone and Creon find no mutually acceptable grounds to frame their conflict and they each remain unflinching in their claim of the self-evident supremacy of their own *nomos*, making their clash at once absolute and incommensurable.

Chapter 3 reflects on the implications of accepting such incommensurability and wonders about the stakes and the tasks involved in cases such as these. Drawing on, but beyond, the work of authors such as Isaiah Berlin, Joseph Raz, David Wiggins, Jean-François Lyotard, and Jacques Rancière in the areas of social practices, life-choices, clash of values, and political disagreement, the chapter arrives at a crucial distinction between two types of incommensurability: on the one hand, the case of an individual who faces a vital (sometimes tragic) choice between incommensurable options; on the other hand, the situation of a third person who must adjudicate an incommensurable conflict between two parties – which is the precise situation faced by the audience. In the former case, both alternatives make equally compelling demands upon the individual, but the person retains the privilege of favoring either of the options. In the latter case, the equally legitimate claims of both parties must be upheld as a matter of right, and hence the judge cannot discriminate between the two. I argue that the latter leads to a situation of aporia where it becomes impossible (yet nonetheless necessary) to render a just legal verdict.

Should this lead us to conclude that judgment itself ought to be suspended? Resisting this conclusion, Chapter 4 approaches the conflict anew with the help of other characters and voices that illustrate diverse alternatives and possibilities for judgment. For example, when Haemon brings the report of a group of citizens who are silently praising Antigone's action, the audience is invited to challenge Creon's earlier assumption that the citizens' loyalty rested exclusively with him. Similarly, Antigone reveals a more socially aware side of her, which leads the audience to recollect the extent of her sacrifice and the reasons behind it, projecting it into her actual situation of solitude and desperation.

Chapter 5 analyses these various shifts of perspective as what I call "spatial relations" of *identification* and *disidentification* between the stage and the audience. The former enables audiences to get "under the skin" of the characters and identify with their worldviews. In the opposite direction, the latter relations generate a "distancing effect" which separates the audience from one-dimensional and simplistic identifications. Through successive processes of identification and separation, then, the audience is able to judge the issue from various "spatial distances," now from close proximity, now from farther away. After distinguishing in detail six spatial relationships that are at work in the *Antigone*, I show that identical categories of judgment apply in the hard case scenario of the Jehovah's Witnesses who refuse to accept a blood transfusion that could save the life of their sick child.

This chapter is framed as a response to Plato's well known attack on the poets, which argues that the *pathos* of poetry prevents the production of any kind of responsible *logos*. The argument can be recast as the modern debate about the appropriate relationship between law and literature, as well as the merits of a humanistic approach to law and legal education. An adequate response to the philosopher demands, fundamentally, the reclaiming of judgment as central to the experience of tragedy. I demonstrate how such judgments are made possible in the *Antigone*, and how they can be understood also to apply in a hard case scenario, hence providing training essential for the pluralistic and agonistic public sphere in which we now live.

Chapter 6 closes the reading of the play, which shows Creon's total destruction as a father, husband, head of the family, and political leader. Looking back on it, Creon enacted a decree aimed at distinguishing the brother who honored the city from the one who betrayed it, after a war instigated by a family quarrel that almost devastated the land and enslaved its people. In deciding so, he acted not out of personal gain or interest, but consistently with what he thought would best exemplify, preserve, and honor the values of the community. The decree itself was apparently within his purview, not obviously beyond his jurisdiction, and gathered the assent of a representative body of citizens as a way of legitimation. Now we know that as a result of defending his decree Creon has destroyed his family and, the opposite of what he intended, not benefited the city but actually endangered it. In the end, all the support that Creon had in the beginning vanishes and the audience recognizes that Creon's decree should be nullified and Polyneices buried. This presents an obvious but important question: how is it that a conflict that seemed unsolvable in principle has been finally resolved in a way that vindicates Antigone's position and, more intriguingly, in a way that the audience too can perceive it as naturally justified?

The concluding chapter tackles this critical question and, completing the argument started in Chapter 5, analyses in detail the necessary "temporal motions" involved in this judgment. This will enable us to see the play in a whole new light, trying to trace the genealogy of Antigone's law. Sometimes the audience performs judgments as a form of what I term *prospection*, where the audience profits from the fact that it knows more than the characters do, whereas other judgments are made in *retrospection*, when the audience looks backwards in order to assess what has already happened. After distinguishing six such temporal motions at work in the play, I turn once again to the case of the Jehovah's Witness parents faced with a mandatory blood-transfusion that could save the life of their child, and suggest ways to justify an eventual resolution by attending to the former temporal dimensions, for time is indeed essential if judgment in the law is to become just.

Chapter 1

A window on the normative world

> We inhabit a *nomos* – a normative universe. We constantly create and maintain a world of right and wrong, of lawful and unlawful, of valid and void. [. . .] No set of legal institutions or prescriptions exists apart from the narratives that locate it and give it meaning. For every constitution there is an epic, for each decalogue a scripture. Once understood in the context of the narratives that give it meaning, law becomes not merely a system of rules to be observed, but a world in which we live.
>
> (Robert Cover)[1]

The idea that law consists of a set of rules emanating from a sovereign power is so ingrained in our ways of thinking about the law – from professionals to ordinary citizens, from legal academics to those who touch upon law in other fields – that trying to shift that habit of perception in the reader may appear a daunting, if not a vain, endeavor. I propose to begin this imaginative task with the help of legal historian and theorist Robert Cover, who urged us to view law neither as a set of institutional rules and principles nor as a set of policies and mechanisms for social control, but rather as a narrative prism through which we observe and filter the world of right and wrong, valid and void, good and bad. From this perspective, law is best described not as a *system*, but rather as an extremely rich and malleable set of expressive and argumentative resources that comprise all aspects of the normative life of individuals and communities.

To give further content to this statement is my object in this chapter, with the aim of establishing an alternative to dominant ways of thinking and talking about the law that will also enable us to approach fruitfully a play that is as eminently "about law" as is the *Antigone*. The rich amalgam of language, myth, and narrative that form Cover's notion of the normative universe will help us to understand the legal worlds of Antigone and Creon as analogously constituted. This will I believe produce a richer and more precise understanding of the play than the usual categories of written/unwritten, natural/positive, mortal/divine, kinship/state would do.[2]

In this chapter we shall see that the normative universe acts like a force field affecting the reality surrounding it, and that just about anything that passes through its filter of perception will be charged juridically and become legal. We shall also see that the normative universe, while preserving some constitutive elements, is in a constant process of becoming. In this it reveals both flexibility and fluidity on the one hand, and constancy and solidity on the other. Further, we shall see that norms are constructed through a process of simultaneous engagement and disengagement that makes law an extremely personal and subjective experience, though it retains its form as a general and objectified legal text. This analysis will help us to approach certain key interpretive issues of the play – for instance, how to assess the legality of Creon's decree at various moments of the play, and how to read Antigone's diverse normative articulations of her position without canceling any of them. These judgments will require a critical engagement with the play in later chapters, to which the present one is meant as a preliminary.

This initial chapter is also meant to create and reflect in its own configuration the general architecture of the process of adjudication in contexts of deep normative conflict. Thus from the original idea of the normative universe we shall move to consider a plurality of self-legitimating normative worlds that live side by side in a given territory. This will produce a map of the social cosmos that reveals the paths that "insular" and "redemptive" trajectories traverse, not unlike some of the characters of *Antigone*, sometimes to points of conflict between them. This will lead us directly to consider the context of adjudication and to Cover's analysis of "hard cases," which will clarify both stakes and the difficulty of judging any such conflict.

In using Cover's lens to approach the *Antigone*, I do not mean to imply that his analysis would fit that play perfectly. The play, as literature often does, resists categorization in significant ways. For example, the social cosmos of the *Antigone* is far richer than Cover's analysis would suggest and it deepens the problem of incommensurability in a way that Cover does not contemplate. In other words, this is a real investigation, where the theoretical framework helps us to approach the object of study, but the object in turn requires us to modify our presuppositions. In the analysis that follows I build upon Cover's vision of the social world where the State and the courts are conceded no logical or normative priority, and argue that the *Antigone* creates a similar world in which the members of the audience, both ancient and modern, are given the task of ultimate judgment. This imaginative tour de force will lead me to argue, against Cover himself, that the emotional and intellectual abilities required for judging tragedy are not essentially different from those required to judge a legal case. Therefore, even though I follow in Cover's footsteps, my real aim is to trace not Cover's work, but the activity of judgment – in both tragedy and law.

1.1 *Nomos*: a normative world

One of Cover's most original insights is that law should be understood not as a system of rules or a set of rules and principles, but as a normative universe or *nomos*, which comprises (and organizes) the whole of the normative resources and activity that are immanent in any society or human collective.[3] In contrast to the famous sophist distinction between *nomos* and *physis*, here the law is not imposed upon the individual, as it were externally, but comes naturally through a process of acculturation and is learned gradually from childhood. Once internalized, it becomes part of the psycho-social structure of the individual's universe as much as do the physical phenomena of mass, energy, and momentum.[4]

The best way to imagine the workings of the normative universe is to think of it not as a system (in its mechanistic, enclosed, and finished patterns), but rather as a kind of language (open-ended, flexible, and constantly evolving). This language is much richer than the image of law as the syllogistic application of rules would have us think, for it provides the entire arsenal for a full and flourishing normative life.[5] Contrary to popular view, the greatness of a legal tradition is not to be gauged by the consistency and predictability of its system of laws, but rather by the possibilities of expression, argument, and judgment that its language allows. To be a competent speaker of this language requires more than knowing how a particular concept or precept is *used* and connects with others; significantly, one must know how it is *charged*, that is the heavy load of symbols, connotations, and values it carries with it.

To illustrate this point, Cover offers the example of the law of inheritance in the Bible: on the level of legal precept, the rules that regulate the institution of inheritance seem clear and unproblematic. They state, for instance, that the oldest son will succeed his father as head of the family.[6] However, such a simple rule is made problematic by the narratives in which it is embedded and which flatly contradict it. Particularly interesting is that whenever the rule of inheritance is undermined, the story associates it with the workings of the divine hand. Therefore, to understand the law of inheritance in the Bible, or as Cover puts it, to be an inhabitant of the biblical normative world, is to know not only that this rule can be overturned, but that God's will is likely to be behind the overturning of this specific rule. Therefore, no legal precept can be properly understood without the narratives in which it is embedded, and these are often tumultuous, full of contradictions, and not clearly defined.

Some may want to believe that the positivistic framework of the modern state has overcome the mythical foundations that enliven the biblical world. But every legal system, Cover argues, must conceive itself in one way or another as emerging out of that which is itself unlawful.[7] This always entails a narrative, often in the form of a myth, to explain how the law came to be. In the *Antigone*, it is easy to perceive the mythical undertones in Antigone's appeal to the immemorial unwritten laws, but it is not so often noted that Creon's political authority depends on his kinship with Cadmus, the mythical founder of Thebes (who killed the dragon and planted its teeth in the ground). Athenians too were fond of the myth of autochthony and of the idea they were sprung directly from the earth. This was no mere "poetic embellishment," for it was used to claim inalienable rights over the land to which they were naturally born.[8] Regardless of the differences in the foundational act and the device used to explain it (the dragon's teeth, the immemorial laws, the original position, the State of nature, the Founding Fathers, or the positivistic *Grundnorm* and the rule of recognition), law can never escape the narrativization of its origin and of its source of legitimacy.[9]

"Narrative" is an important term of art that merits some pause. The proper way to discover its meaning is not through the customary dichotomy between fact and fiction, but rather through the one between fact and value: Cover places narrative in the context of the latter dichotomy but only to overcome it. For Cover, fact and value – narrative account and normative assessment – are inextricably linked. As he says, every prescription (norm, covenant, value) is placed within a narrative that explains it and gives it meaning. In turn, every narrative (be it historical or imaginary) is insistent in its demand for its prescriptive point, its moral. Narrative is in fact the act of "imposing a normative force upon reality," which Hayden White refers to as the "moralizing effect" of narrative.[10] In other words, narrative gives reality a shape, direction, plot, and characterization that it would otherwise lack, and in doing so, it models reality after the attributes of its rhetorical construction and the world of value implied in it.

This assertion may worry those who think of law as purely objective, and believe that the scientific description of law requires that it be extricated from the realm of values.[11] But upon consideration, it simply brings to legal language what we always suspected was true of language in general, namely that every description is colored by the type of relationship we establish and want others to establish with what it is we are describing (for instance, by adopting an ironic, sarcastic, or critical tone). Moreover, those worries should not obstruct one's view of Cover's major contribution: considering that the act of narrating adds the element of value to the world of fact, narrative traverses (and allows us to traverse) the seemingly unbridgeable gap between fact and value. To say it differently, by connecting a given reality with its normative significance, narrative is the bridge that connects the world of the *is* with the world of the *ought*. Regrettably, this critical contribution to legal philosophy has gone largely unnoticed. Still today the world of law is largely thought to be that of the "ought," completely different from that of the "is." All this creates an insuperable dilemma for legal positivism that cannot explain – except as the result of acts of pure will – how it is possible for social practices to become norms.[12]

Cover's response is ingenious in its simplicity. First of all, to the twofold ontological distinction between "is" and "ought" he adds a third category of being, the "might be." This is not just an artifice. In fact, it can be said to have its roots in Aristotle's metaphysics, for whom things are not just how they actually are, but how they will be if they reach their *potential*, or, one could say, how they *might be.* The reinstatement of this third ontological category of norms enables Cover to verify the link between *is* and *ought* and to mark the transition from a given state of affairs to its desired transformation. As the bridge linking a given concept of reality to its imagined alternative,[13] law is neither fully *here* in the realm of social reality nor *there* in the realm of pure normativity. Law partakes of all three of these categories at once, for of every norm one can reasonably say that the norm *is*, that it *ought to be*, and that it *might be.* Therefore, "to live in the legal world requires that one know not only the precepts, but also their connections to possible and plausible states of affairs. It requires that one integrate not only the 'is' and the 'ought,' but the 'is,' the 'ought,' and the 'what might be.'"[14]

The former does not mean that every vision, no matter how ludicrous, can automatically become part of the *nomos*. At the very least, the fact that every vision must be articulated through language and inserted into socially constructed narratives demands that they be made intelligible to others first. In this view, too, those who are not able to adjust their visions to their surroundings, including the predictable patterns of behavior of other actors that may oppose them, lose their grip on the legal reality (as Antigone has often being accused of doing). Therefore, far from an allegedly "unencumbered *nomos*," it is more appropriate to think of every *nomos* as being part and parcel of a complex and wider cosmos that it attempts to, but cannot fully, control.

The structure of the *nomos* is not to be imagined as a pyramid in which each norm is validated by its immediate superior until we reach the highest normative step of the ladder.[15] The picture is rather one of an enmeshed web of narratives around a possible, plausible, and desirable state of affairs, which are stored and brought to life by the usual processes of memory and recollection. Such a conceptualization would help to ease some of the well-known problems associated with the pyramidal model.[16] For one, it would serve to acknowledge the existence of very real normative sources – i.e. soft law, informal regulation, *contra-legem* customs, non-official practices, extra-legal arguments – that are not acknowledged by, and therefore escape, the shadow of the pyramid. Secondly, the static nature of the pyramidal model is unable to explain legal change except as a result of deliberate and willful action. In contrast, the normative universe is in a continuous process of *becoming*, and hence changing, for every new articulation of its "constitutive cells" brings about a new reconfiguration of the whole body. From the resources that are available at any one moment several different reconfigurations are possible, which are never perfectly consistent with each other. The non-identity of the various possible reconfigurations is in fact what makes renewal possible, which occurs through a process of generative mutation that provides both stability and change. The fact that the nomos is in a constant process of becoming forces us to speak of law's concrete *location* as well as its *direction* (or trajectory).[17]

The characterization of law as a system of rules rejects the existence of antinomies, inconsistencies, gaps, and lacunae. In contrast, the normative universe can harbor many potentially contradictory norms and, for the most part, allows for their peaceful coexistence, suggesting the possibility (not contemplated in the pyramidal model) of several contradictory supreme norms at the same time and in the same place.[18] For instance, both Ismene and Haemon appear to find ways to harmonize two contradictory fundamental norms (i.e. loyalty to the citizens and loyalty to the family). Moreover, the mere existence of a gap does not create the need to fill it. The normative universe can have holes and be incomplete, for it is subject to the same lapses and imperfections as ordinary processes of memory and recollection.

One important question from a practical perspective is how it is possible, if the normative universe is not a system, to know whether a given norm belongs to it or not. In other words, how are we to identify a valid law and distinguish it from what is not? This issue is also important in reading the *Antigone*. For example, how do we determine whether Creon's decree forbidding the burial of Polyneices is legal or not? Is the fact that there seems to be almost universal support for the practice of burial enough reason to declare the decree forbidding it to be illegal? Is it by contrast sufficient that the ruler of the city declares it to be the law to accept it as such? Or does Antigone's appeal to the immemorial laws of burial invalidate the decree? Positivist legal theory argues that every legal system sets forth predictable rules to decide the validity of a particular law with conclusive character, for example by way of the rules of recognition and habilitation.[19] By contrast, the normative universe contains no fixed and a priori criteria to decide whether a given norm belongs to it or not. Naturally, it is unrealistic to question the general validity of a given source in certain contexts, e.g. a formally enacted statute in a court of law (unless of course the case requires doing precisely that because the statute is claimed to be unconstitutional or to have exceeded its jurisdiction). The statute of the legislature could be challenged, however, if the case were to arise in a tribal court. On this view, the doctrinal question of what the law *is* in a given situation is not a proposition that can be answered in a true or false fashion. To make a valid legal claim is rather a matter of argument that can be more or less compelling, and this depends on different audiences and contexts (what might persuade a first instance judge may not persuade the Supreme Court, and vice versa). The limit of a valid legal claim is hence set by the imagination of the speaker and the persuasiveness of the claim (i.e. the ability to frame the legal argument in ways that can be accepted by others as valid). As a result, practical decisions of validity are reached on a case-by-case basis and according to rhetorically tailored criteria of relevance that are contingent (because they depend on temporal and spatial considerations), heterogeneous (because they are not enclosed in any list of permissible sources), and evaluative (because they depend on judgments).

In the case of the *Antigone*, this means that there is no set of external facts determinative of the validity of Creon's decree. Rather, that judgment of validity (or not) is to be determined by the (con)textual response of the community enacted in the play, formed both by the characters that inhabit it and by the audience that watches it. Interestingly, the answer may vary depending on the moment of the play at which we find ourselves. In the beginning, there may be good reason to support the validity of Creon's decree which seems to have been enacted by the legitimate authority, and the citizens of the Chorus do not object to it. By the end of the play, however, the opposite may in fact be concluded. As we shall see, the temporal dimension is an essential element of judgment that demands considering the norms in their duration, in changing contexts, and not in single isolated moments.

A second related issue has to do with the relationship between the normative universe and the outer, non-legal environment, which is essentially this: when the *nomos* enters into contact with the external world, or, to put it differently, when the rest of world is filtered through the normative lens of the *nomos*, the latter acts like a magnetic field with the capacity to *charge* it juridically. In addition to being "a world in which to live," then, the normative universe is also the prism or pervasive filter through which the rest of the world is perceived (and assessed).[20] As a result, when objects, events, or actions, existing in the outer world enter the scope of action of the normative universe – i.e. for one reason or another they *become* relevant – they are impregnated with the normative force of that *nomos*. This means that just about anything can become legal at a given point (when it falls within the law's area of influence), but not that everything *actually* does (because the law's field of perception is limited). In distinction to the autopoetic theories of Luhmann and (to a lesser extent) Teubner, the division between legal/illegal is never sharp and crispy, but fuzzy,[21] which turns law into an essentially porous entity, distinguishable from, and yet permeable by, its exterior.

A third and final issue has to do with the felt need to distinguish law from other normative realms, especially from morality. This question is often framed as whether morality is a necessary requirement of law or whether law can exist separately from it. As this debate has traditionally been conducted between juspositivists and jusnaturalists – the former saying that an unjust law is still *legal*, the latter that unjust law cannot be *properly* called law – I find the controversy tiresome and not particularly illuminating.[22] As this story is often told, the point seems to have been finally settled by Hart, who circumvented the dilemma by arguing that a legal rule may still be legal even though too iniquitous to be obeyed or applied.[23] However, one cannot but wonder how empty a concept of law is that requires neither obedience nor application. Cover enters this debate to state the obvious (and perhaps for that, all the more in need of being said): "If there existed two legal orders with identical legal precepts and identical, predictable patterns of public force, they would nonetheless *differ essentially in meaning* if, in one of the orders, the precepts were universally venerated while in the other they were regarded by many as fundamentally unjust."[24]

This argument does not lead, on the other hand, to the automatic invalidation of a law judged to be unjust. For example, what the organs of the State declare to be the law may be enforced *as* law, regardless of what the addressees think about it, for "[s]urely a law may be successfully enforced but actively resented."[25] However, when a law is perceived as being unjust by the addressees and touches fundamental aspects of their lives, such a law will likely be greeted with rejection and, in some cases, with active resistance, which may affect its future enforcement or application (here the example of Antigone's disobedience is a case in point). In some cases, the validity of the law may be put into question in court, where it may be nullified. This argument shows that the real debate should not be about an abstract category of legal validity, but about the diversity of meanings, and the divergence in judgments, created out of the same legal threads and materials by various actors in diverse contexts.

This line of thought suggests several things. First, every legal context is imbued with, and will be necessarily affected by, the *tacit moral judgment* of the people that utter, receive, and use the law.[26] Second, depending on these various judgments, the *same* rules can look either unjust, or just, or both. Third, the way the law is viewed (and this includes how it is viewed morally) may end up affecting all the aspects of that law, including its interpretation, application, adjudication, enforcement, and ultimately its validity. And fourth, the real issue seems not one of determining whether an unjust law may be *valid*, but what it means to declare a law to be unjust, and how this declaration affects the subsequent life (or becoming) of such a law.

There may still be differences between law and morality, but not in the alleged lack of coercive power of morality (as in Kelsen), or the presence of secondary rules (as in Hart). (One needs only to remember the Spanish Inquisition to realize that morality can be as coercive, enforceable, and structurally complex as the most coercive, elaborate, and immoral of the legal systems, if not more so.). On the other hand, it is not accurate to say that law and morality each regulate separate aspects of life, say the matters of the State and of the family respectively. (We will see how the claims of Antigone and Creon are both legally as well as morally grounded.) Perhaps one distinction is that morality need not be enforced to remain in place, whereas a law that is not enforced may lose its legal force (e.g. through desuetude). Moreover, there seems to be less toleration of a gap between individual beliefs and the demands of morality, whereas the law leaves more open spaces for individual disagreement. Finally, the question with morality is whether it is *right*, while with law the question is whether it is *legal* – which has consequences on the way arguments on both realms are framed. These differences aside, an important conclusion appears to be that every argument of legality carries an implicit moral judgment within it, and, vice versa, that an argument of morality perhaps may carry also a claim for legal recognition.

1.2 The construction of norms

Legal theorists still debate what exactly makes a legal norm a *norm*, that is what marks the transition from a given provision found in a legal instrument to a fully-fledged norm capable of modeling human conduct.[27] The debate is not about what it is that makes the norm effective (what makes individuals conform their behavior to its dictates), rather it is about what it is that makes it *binding* (what makes individuals accept it as mandatory). Clearly, the fact that the legal utterance emanates from the legitimate authority does not explain how that authority is originally bestowed, nor why individuals yield their conformity to the provisions emanated from it. In the view of the normative universe expounded here, a mere legal provision is not automatically endowed with actual normative force by reason of its being inserted in an official legal instrument or, alternatively, in a body of cultural practices, customs, and/or traditions. The shift from a legal provision into a norm begins with interpretation, which is an act by which the interpreter attributes a certain meaning to the given provision and decides how it should be read in the concrete circumstances.

However, interpretation is only the first step in the creation of norms. More important is the personal act that Cover calls *commitment*. Commitment can be defined as an act of personal engagement with the legal precept by which the individual affirms its meaning as it pertains personally to him or her.[28] Through the act of commitment, the individual accepts that the provision as it has been interpreted exercises binding influence upon him or her. Thus, while interpretation particularizes the meaning of a given provision, commitment is the subjective act that turns the content of that interpretation into a *norm* proper, for it determines what law is and what law shall be.[29]

The statement that commitment "determines" the normative aspect of the law is not metaphorical. Cover offers an example in the form of an anti-slavery group, the Garrisonians, who, using the dominant hermeneutic techniques of the day, interpreted the American Constitution as being favorable to slavery. Despite their public antagonism towards such a proposition, this interpretation of the Constitution "agreed" with that of Chief Justice Roger B. Taney, who declared that the Constitution required the return of runaway slaves to their owners.[30] But the Garrisonians were not committed to the principle of obedience to the Constitution that Taney took for granted. For them, a Constitution that permitted slavery could never be binding and ought not to be obeyed.

To be sure, the Constitution – as interpreted by Chief Justice Taney – was still in force in the rest of the territory and could be enforced against the Garrisonians who resisted it (though as it happened not for long). But from within the normative universe of the Garrisonians, the Constitution was felt as an externally imposed precept and not as a norm in the full sense of the term. In the normative universe of the Garrisonians, the American Constitution (at least in what concerned slavery) was not a valid norm.

This argument can be fittingly transposed to the fictional world of the *Antigone* too: it may be said that Creon's decree forbidding the burial of Polyneices may be "legal" in the territory of Thebes, but for Antigone and the normative universe she embodies, even if it can and will be used against her by Creon, the prohibition is *not* a valid norm. Earlier we saw that the question of legality may receive different responses at various times and contexts; now we see that the answer may be different too depending on the normative filter we apply to it (depending on the *nomos* from which we see the rest of the world).

Nothing said thus far should be interpreted as claiming that the realm of law is "merely subjective." In fact the very idea of commitment implies by definition that we are committed *to something* other than ourselves. In the juridical field, that which we are committed to obeying is posited as (an external object of) the law. The process of positing an external object of law is what Cover calls *objectification*, and with it, the full structure of norm-generation is finally revealed: "[This] entails the disengagement of the self from the 'object' of law, and at the same time . . . an engagement to that object as a faithful 'other.'"[31] As a result, the formation of normativity occurs through simultaneous engagement and disengagement, in a cycle that spins continuously in the opposite directions of commitment and objectification.

The analysis can be taken further than Cover takes it by breaking down each motion into two logical sequences, if only as visual representations of a non-linear process. In what concerns the motion of commitment or subjective engagement, the initial legal utterance or *provision* must be *interpreted* as establishing a *demand* which lacks normative force until the individuals *commit* to it and make it properly a *norm*, in the following logical steps: (1) provision; (2) interpretation; (3) demand; (4) commitment; and (5) norm (Figure 1). In the opposite direction, the committed norm is objectified as an external precept to which individuals owe obedience as law, in the following sequence: (1) norm; (2) objectification; (3) precept; (4) obedience; and (5) law (Figure 2).

Presented in this way, each sequence is the perfect mirror of the other. Provision, interpretation, and demand are mirrored by norm, objectification, and precept, respectively, whereas the commitment prior to the norm mirrors the obedience owed to the law. The culmination of each sequence gives a point of stability to legal meaning: in the moment, the commitment to the norm is unreserved and the law is obeyed. But this stability may be non-lasting: the norm reached at the end of the process of commitment will be challenged in unforeseen circumstances and turn into another provision (to be reinterpreted again). In turn, the law that exacts obedience will have to respond to different circumstances and warrant a variety of norms.

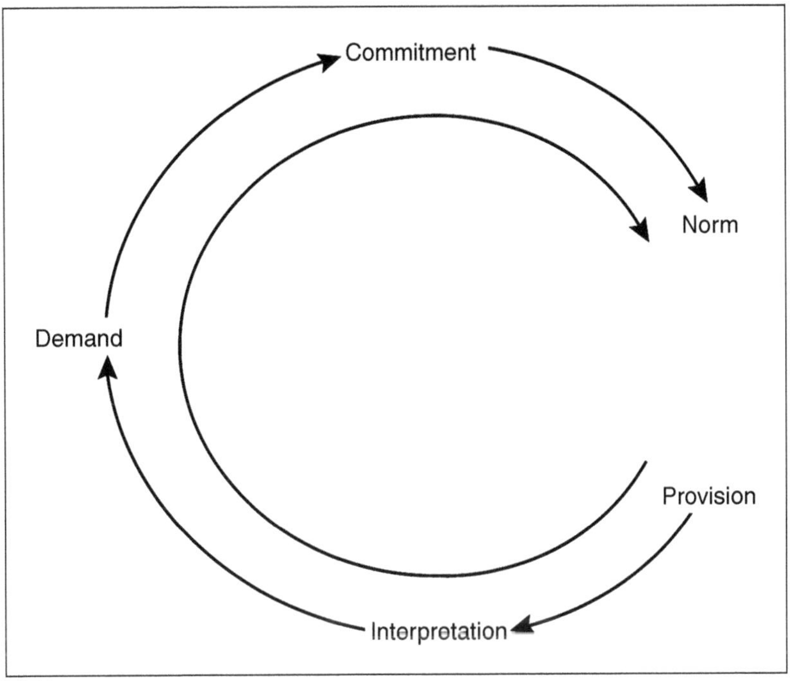

Figure 1 Process of commitment.

This essential variability can be observed in Antigone's law as well. At the moment of her discussion with Creon, Antigone expresses her commitment to her brother, and the norm that obligates her to bury him, in the form of an objectified law that is general and apparently unconditional (447–57). Nothing in her speech prepares us for the revelation, in her last moments, of a different norm that includes only her brother, but not her hypothetical husband or child (905–7). For the most part, authors lament Antigone's departure from the unqualified and universal validity of the unwritten laws, and regard her statements as a normative contradiction.[32] Against these views, I will argue that what we find instead is Antigone's articulation of a norm that singularizes her commitment and adjusts the law to the changing circumstances.[33]

This cycle allows for moments of apparent stability in which law is endowed with the characteristics of determinacy, abstraction, and generality often attributed to law. And yet consider how, under different conditions, the

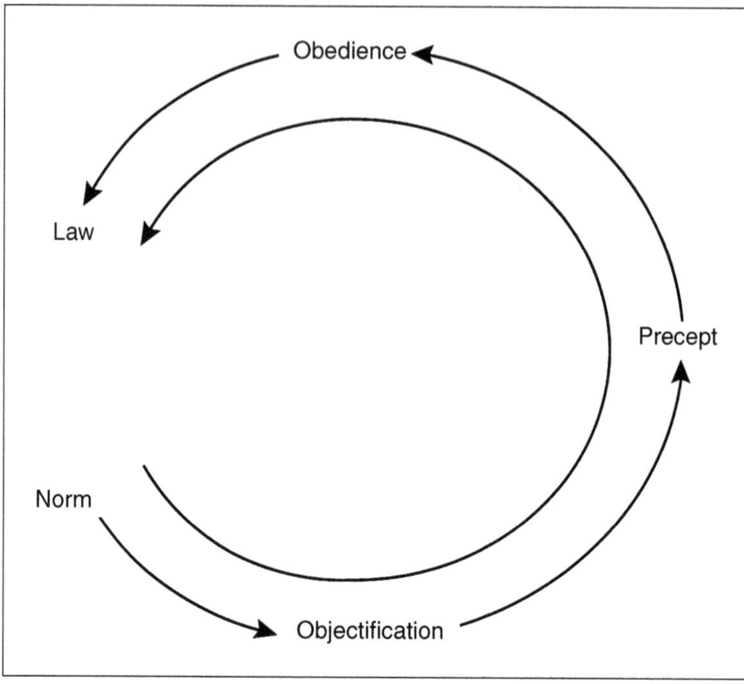

Figure 2 Process of objectification.

same genetic code can yield significantly modified normative determinations – like various states of water – without altering its basic composition. The formation of legal meaning must be thought of as a never-ending cycle spinning around opposite motions of commitment and objectification, which make the whole process unstoppable and in constant flux (Figure 3).[34]

Two final remarks will help us to explain the transition from one motion to the other. As presented in Figure 3, it can be seen that both sequences share the common space of the norm. This is because the norm is doubly constituted by the subjective or internal element (the belief of being bound by it) and the objective or external element (the behavior that the norm commands). In the transitional moment, the norm suffers the *mitosis*[35] of its constitutive cells and splits in two: the subjective or internal element gives way to the aspect of the norm that is to be objectified into a legal precept. Conversely, the law that demands obedience is to be made specific in the concrete situation. This demands that the general and undetermined law

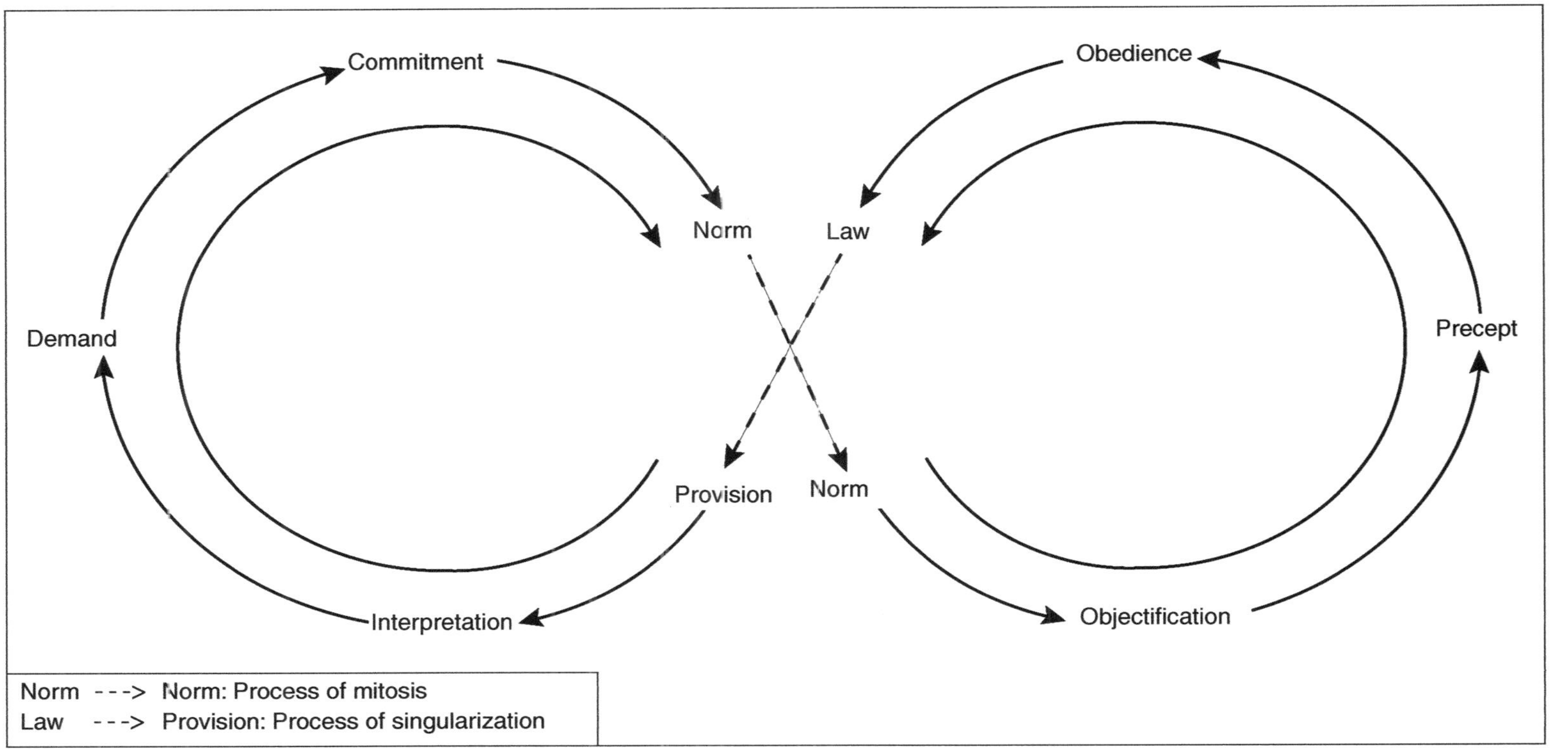

Figure 3 Formation of legal meaning.

follow a process of *singularization* or individuation by which the particular legal provision (or a group of them) is selected as applicable to the present case. It is important to realize finally that both moments of transition occur through the medium of narrative: narrative helps, on the one hand, to give verifiable content to the purely subjective element of the norm, and, on the other hand, to provide the textual basis for the interpretation of legal provisions. Thus narrative is the bridge that connects the subjective and the objective dimensions of legal meaning, and brings the world of material reality in contact with our imagination.

1.3 Mapping the social trajectories

Every plural society is populated by innumerable heterogeneous entities. Cover draws a distinction between two ways of interacting with the rest of the *nomoi*. The first he calls *insular*, the second *redemptive*, attending to the way each group comes to terms with the "ontological reality of the other."[36] Although Cover focuses on social groups or communities, I prefer to speak of insular and redemptive *trajectories* instead. This choice of words is meant to stress a sense of directionality by presenting them in terms of tendencies or propensities rather than as fixed and stable attributes. These trajectories are meant to describe the way different normative universes understand and conceive their relationships with their exterior. As ideal types, neither insular nor redemptive trajectories are ever found in pure form in reality, but I hope they will illuminate important aspects of *Antigone*.

Firstly, *insular trajectories* are those with the tendency to generate some sort of autonomous island free from external encroachment and thus draw a "boundary rule" that delimits the borders of their world and separates it from others.[37] Although insularity does not entail hermetism or total isolation from the outer world, these trajectories characteristically draw a circle around themselves that prevents unwanted intrusions while permitting a rich normative development in the space left open. That is why the principle of insularity is both constitutive and generative, that is it constitutes an open space free from interferences and, at the same time, it serves as the autonomous source for the creation of norms.

Cover draws from historical and legal scholarship to illustrate how, from time to time, some social actors utilize well-known legal instruments to create and emerge as self-legitimating normative universes, often incorporating explicit rules and precepts to assure the self-referential supremacy of their own norms.[38] For example, he mentions how nineteenth-century utopian communities used freedom of contract to ground their insularity and assert a right to law-creation and enforcement with respect to social relations. What matters, however, is not the concrete legal instrument utilized – whether it be freedom of contract, liberty of association, free exercise of religion, or corporation law – but how it grows to become the center around which the normative universe stands (the boundary rule separating the inside and the outside).

The meaning of this "boundary rule" differs greatly depending on which side of the wall we happen to be on. From the point of view of statist doctrine, a simple way to interpret the space left open for the insular activity is through the lens of the liberty of association, which is the easiest way to recognize such private sphere of autonomy. However, to assimilate this norm-generating capacity to the doctrine of associational rights is, according to Cover, to assume the perspective of the State official looking out:

> This norm-generating autonomy might be formally granted in charter language. It might be implicit in a principle of religious liberty, freedom of contract, or protection of property. Typically, however, communities with a total-life vision, a nomos entirely of their own, find *their own charters* for the norm-generating aspects of their collective lives.[39]

Furthermore, such insular nomic entities do not need the State's permission or recognition to exist and to generate their own activity, because "the State's explicit or implicit acknowledgement of a limited sphere of autonomy is understood from within the association to be the State's accommodation to the *extant reality of nomian separation*."[40] From the perspective of the modern liberal state, the existence of such norm-generating activity may appear to be merely an unimportant accommodation of a limited principle of autonomy, but from the perspective of those who believe and act upon their premises, it may well be "the axis on which the wheel of history turns."[41]

Secondly, *redemptive trajectories* are used by those whose sharply different visions of the social order require changing not just themselves, but the social world in which they live. While insular narratives want the rest of the world to leave them alone, redemptive ones want the world to become like theirs. The term "redemptive" bears a heavy weight of meaning, but it may be appropriate considering the deep emotional, social, and cosmological connotations that it carries with it. Redemptive narratives set out to liberate persons and the law and to raise both from a "fallen state."[42] Accordingly, they postulate: (1) the unredeemable character of reality as we know it; (2) the fundamentally different reality that should take its place; and (3) the replacement of the one with the other.

As an illustration, Cover takes the example of the radical constitutionalists during the anti-slavery era.[43] In a manner diametrically opposed to that of the insular Garrisonians – who believed that the Constitution upheld slavery and that, therefore, it ought not to be obeyed – radical constitutionalists declared that no word could be found in the Constitution that authorized the practice of slavery. It is not that the radical constitutionalists were unaware of historical and legal reality, but rather that they chose to embrace a vision "in which the entire order of American slavery would be without foundation in law."[44] Radical constitutionalists hoped to transform the constitutional order to reflect their vision opposing slavery, and therefore an alternative like the Garrisonians' acceptance of the "official meaning" of the Constitution seemed almost a dereliction of duty: their redemptive ambition could not content itself with finding a safe haven for runaway slaves – as may have been the case of the Garrisonians – but necessitated instead the full power of the State to destroy, altogether, all safe havens for slave owners.

As one can immediately perceive, the strength of such an interpretive move is, at the same time, its major weakness. For the radical constitutionalist view to cohere, "its adherent must either give up his connections with what is the case, including the predictable patterns of behavior of other actors, or give up the vision."[45] The more they distance themselves from the realm of social reality and the predictable behavior of other actors, the more likely they are to inhabit the realm of "mere utopianism," i.e. the world without (legal) influence.[46] But redemptive trajectories may be extremely rich in upsetting and helping to overcome stagnant tendencies in society, rendering them susceptible to amelioration and change. For example, in spite of the short-lived historical experience of the radical constitutionalists, their efforts were extremely productive in promoting an egalitarian streak in the Constitution, "extending the range of constitutional sources to include at least the Declaration of Independence."[47]

The idea of people trying to redeem the world to reflect their particular view of heaven may produce some understandable uneasiness. In particular, not everyone is likely to share their absolute sense of urgency, approve of their acts of martyrdom, or welcome the mandatory evangelization of their ideals.[48] This is why it is important to remark that redemptive trajectories may not be as inflexible and uncompromising as they appear at first. As long as they seek to inspire and influence the broader social and political world, they cannot remain impassive to the legitimate concerns of those others who do not share their beliefs, especially when those others have the will and the strength to oppose them.[49] Not only must these trajectories take into account the possible reactions of other actors, including violent ones, but in cases in which such a reaction effectively ensues, they must undergo a second hermeneutic process to decide how to respond by reconstituting their original norms. Thus, even though narratives of redemption may seem particularly prone to "impel a man . . . to rise up in arms against any law whatever that he happens not to like,"[50] texts of resistance "are always subject to an interpretation process that limits the situations in which resistance is a legitimate response."[51]

The typology elaborated by Cover can illuminate our reading of the *Antigone*. Using his terms we can ask, for example, whether Antigone's disobedience can be better described in terms of an insular or a redemptive trajectory. According to the former, she wishes only to be let alone in order to bury her brother in peace; according to the latter, she would also want to change the convictions of the *polis* to reflect hers. Without wishing to foreclose the terms of the debate yet, it is interesting to note that Antigone will definitely undergo a "second hermeneutic process" in her final farewell speech, precisely as a response to the opposition she has encountered throughout.

On the other hand, just as Cover does not claim his typology to be exhaustive, the micro-cosmos of the *Antigone* shows a wider variety of trajectories than those contained in the insular-redemptive dichotomy. For example, in the figures of Ismene and Haemon we find trajectories that can be called rather *transactional* or cooperative. And, the old and wise seer Teiresias traces another trajectory that can be called *authoritative* or commanding. Moreover, characters may trace several different trajectories depending on the context and their interlocutors. Notwithstanding these limitations, there still is one significant aspect that the analysis in terms of insular/redemptive trajectories brings to light, namely that when a third-party adjudicator faces a conflict of such a nature, the judge must decide either to accept the redemptive vision or else to reject it, and cannot avoid the responsibility for doing either.[52]

1.4 The pathos of judgment

In Chapter 7 of *The Concept of Law*, H. L. A. Hart famously argued that, due to the open texture of language there were cases that could not be clearly subsumed under the terms of a rule. To these, he opposed other cases in which the language of the rule clearly specifies the conditions that must be present for it to apply. The latter he called clear or paradigmatic cases; the former are those we know as hard. For instance, Hart explained that it is clear that the rule prohibiting vehicles in the park applies to motor vehicles, but it is less clear whether it applies equally to an electrical motor car. Hart believed that hard cases arise because they fall within the zone of penumbra of rules, where his view was that judges could simply use their discretion to fill in the gaps. But he also thought these exceptional cases, believing that most of the time language left no doubt as to which cases were meant to fall within its scope and which were not.[53]

Against this canonical view, it has been sometimes argued that the distinction between easy and hard cases is itself not an easy one,[54] and that the dividing line is blurry and not fixable in advance.[55] Furthermore, it is also argued that the source of hardness is to be found not in *semantic* reasons, but in *substantive* or other *pragmatic* circumstances.[56] For one, Ronald Dworkin believes that "a hard case is a situation in the law that gives rise to genuine argument about the truth of a proposition of law that cannot be resolved by recourse to a set of plain facts determinative of the issue."[57] Concerning hard cases, several questions must be distinguished. First, we want to know *when* we are in front of a hard case. Second, we want to know *why* it is that the case is hard.[58] Third, we ask *what* the task ahead of the judge is in a hard case, and fourth, *how* she ought to proceed in judging it. In sum, a theory of hard cases must respond to the *when*, *why*, *what* and *how* of these cases.

Hart argues that there is a hard case when the law is unclear, and the case is hard because the language of the rule does not clearly specify whether it falls within its scope or not.[59] Dworkin thinks differently: that we face a hard case when decent arguments can be advanced for competing interpretations of a legal point, and that the case is hard because the disagreement is substantive, as opposed to merely conceptual. As to the *how*, Hart suggests that judges can use their discretion, while Dworkin denies this and says they must at any rate proceed to find the best law that there is.[60] Notwithstanding their notable differences, both Hart and Dworkin agree that the task of the judge (the *what*) is to reinstate the unity or integrity of a law that is perceived as having been compromised.[61]

Opposing both, Cover offers a fresh and insightful perspective. In his view, the true problem in hard cases is one not of lack of clear or settled law, but one of too much law. That is, the issue is one not of indeterminacy, but of multiplicity.[62] In Cover's view, the origin and justification of courts lies not in the need for law, but rather in the need to suppress it, an argument that is well-grounded in myth and history. For example, in Aeschylus' *Oresteia*, the mythic foundation of the oldest Athenian court, the Areopagus, is the result of the conflict between two bodies of laws, the one invoked by the Erinyes and the other by Apollo, one of which must be supressed.[63] Likewise, the historical justification for having one "supreme" court is precisely to produce uniformity out of diversity.[64] As a result, the task of such a court is not simply how to apply the law, but to decide, more radically, which law to apply and which law to kill off.

Cover's particular take on the issue of hard cases is connected to his understanding of the legal cosmos as populated by multiple self-legitimating normative entities, each of which provides its own legal response to every issue of substantial complexity. Cover's plural and essentially contested legal cosmos demands a radical relativization of law which accords no logical or normative priority to the political structures of the State. Consistent with this approach, he argues that we must posit the nomic integrity of each of the laws in conflict and recognize that, for each normative universe, the norm articulated *is* the right legal response.[65] A failure to do so, Cover warns, is to fall victim to the hubris of presupposing the hermeneutic superiority of one perspective over another, or to confuse the reality of legal meaning with the status of political domination. Thus, for Cover, a hard case arises *when* to a single question of law that needs adjudicating there are opposing *nomoi*, each providing its own "right legal answer." In the case of the conflict between Antigone and Creon, this is to say that, barring other inconsistencies, the two antagonistic norms concerning the body of Polyneices may be right from their own legal perspective.

The conflict is hard *because* we are dealing not with divergent interpretations of a given unclear or unsettled legal provision, but with holistic sets of corpuses, myths, and narratives that consider their own *nomos* to be supreme and are ready and committed to maintaining it.[66] The issue then is not how to square the disagreement with an allegedly compromised legal system, but how to choose between two competing systems of law, which is clearly not just an interpretive question. The conflict becomes *inter* – and not just *intra* – systemic. This entails that there is no neutral and agreed upon "concept of law" with which to square an answer for the conflict between Antigone and Creon.

Framed in this light, it is easier to see why Cover does not think that what is at stake – the *what* of hard cases – is how better to reinstate the lost unity of the legal system, as both Hart and Dworkin agreed. Nor is the choice one between accepting the judicial articulation of values or the looming void of nihilism.[67] Rather, the fundamental question is how to preserve a sense of legal meaning in spite of the inability to ground the killing of the law in the pretense of an objective and superior hermeneutics.[68] In more striking terms, the *what* of hard cases is how to create value out of the death of law.[69] How this might be achieved while engendering *justice* – or, in the language we have learned to use, the *how* of hard cases – is, perhaps, the central question that this book seeks to explore and detailed attention will be devoted to it in the chapters that follow.

To conclude with Cover, the task requires, first, denouncing the much extended practice of "judicial helplessness" (i.e. the argument that judges have no other choice but to "follow the law" no matter what) and the underlying rhetoric and strategies of concealment:[70] despite the strong ideological charge implied in the function and the practices of conflict resolution, "[t]he judge rarely concedes that these underlying questions are even at issue."[71] Under the pretext of applying mere technical rules, the judge is able to ignore the stakes involved in the adjudication of deep or hard normative conflict, or else to expel them to some extra-judicial non-legal limbo outside their purview. The seemingly innocuous maneuver allows the judge to camouflage inter-systemic adjudication – the killing off of law – and to present this task as a more or less difficult maintenance of intra-systemic consistency – the clarification of law.

Instead, Cover urges judges to develop an independent hermeneutics that would not defer to the hierarchy of the political structures, but would put the construction of legal meaning above it.[72] This would open the way for a more aggressive yet articulate judicial review that would be grounded on the judges' "committed constitutionalism."[73] In this task, the authority of judges can only rest on the articulation and the quality of their jurisdictional claims and their opinions, which make their *nomos* look more like that of the rest of the normative universes of the world.[74]

What separates this view from the standard defense of judicial review is that Cover would have judges act upon such committed constitutionalism only if there is a plurality of *nomoi* ready and able to oppose the judges' law.[75] In this view, the judicial articulation of principle is not sufficient to strike a balance between alternative worldviews, which can only be assured through the interplay of heterogeneous perspectives and forces that keep each other at bay. Justice would result then from the result of tensions between mutually effecting narratives, each of which could speak and act as they see fit in the face of contrary ones.

The need to see the matter not only with the eyes of the judge improves the analysis of hard cases, and is particularly pertinent to the *Antigone*, where the legal conflict cannot properly be understood from the sole perspective of Creon. However, Cover's analysis presents also some shortcomings that I will briefly mention here, but will develop at length in following chapters. One is that if the adjudicators are committed only to the development and articulation of an independent hermeneutics, there is no incentive for them to pay attention to the laws of the parties in conflict and, abusing their position, they may reach a decision that falls short of justice. If judges must articulate their own narrative without submitting to the hierarchical ordering, this must incorporate a self-reflective mechanism that would put a critical mirror to their personal commitments. Secondly, the adjudicators must show the ability to penetrate within the normative worldviews of the parties, while being able to reflect critically on these claims and their own responses to them. This attitude of *concerned reflexivity* enables him or her to see things from within each of the perspectives while maintaining a symbolic triangulation with them.[76] Thirdly, to perform this activity to the best of one's abilities (as opposed to doing it poorly) the adjudicator must let his or her preconceptions be tested against the particular demands of the concrete situation. Out of this engagement, the adjudicator weaves not an independent, but an *inter*-dependent narrative that connects the many and sometimes inconsistent threads of the case. Fourthly and finally, an honest engagement with the hermeneutics of judgment assumes taking the risk of being transformed by it, often in ways that could not have been predicted. Therefore, judging these kinds of conflicts is to accept taking a journey the destination of which may not be known in advance.

In what follows I will develop these arguments with the help of a close and detailed critical reading of Sophocles' *Antigone*, on the assumption that this tragedy can illuminate problems in the judicial sphere similar in kind to the ones I have been discussing with the help of Robert Cover. This assumption may encounter two sorts of initial objections. On the one hand, my choice for tragedy as a template for legal judgment can be questioned considering that, as many have argued, tragedy requires not judgment, but the suspension of it. Since this argument depends on a reading of tragedy, I will wait until after we have done some of that work to answer it directly, which I will do in Chapter 5. There I respond to the sharpest and more sustained criticism of tragedy itself, that of Plato in *The Republic*. We shall see that at the core of Plato's critique there is the idea that tragedy works precisely to deprive individuals of their critical faculties, that is of judgment. The success of my argument requires showing that it does not. A second objection may be made to the analogy between legal and literary activities of interpretation and judgment. One of the most forceful expressions of this criticism is made, interestingly enough, by the same Robert Cover in various well-known pieces. Since Cover's critique could undermine my endeavor before it could even begin, I must respond to it directly now.

1.5 Judgment in tragedy and law

The view of law outlined above, a view that will be embraced throughout, takes law to be a sort of literature, or rather literature *of a certain kind*. In what follows, I will be using Sophocles' *Antigone* as a window on the issues raised in this chapter, namely those of alternative normative worldviews, their likely conflict, and the challenge of adjudicating between them. That law has a lot of the theatrical can hardly be contentious. The world of law is inhabited by characters dressed in peculiar clothes, wearing robes, gowns, and wigs; as in theatre, there are scripts about when each character is supposed to speak or be silent; there are codes about how one is supposed to act and talk; and there are cues as to when one should intervene and for how long. The truth of law must also be *staged*, that is performed in a particular time and place, for a particular audience, with a particular setting and *mise en scène*. No wonder that historically, as Peter Goodrich recounts, law courts were often called "theaters."[77] The genre of this particular theater of ours will be neither comedy nor farce, but tragedy. The claim is not entirely original either. This is what the Old Athenian – representative of the State – has to say about law in response to the tragic poets seeking their reinstatement into Plato's imagined state:

> Most honored guests, we're tragedians ourselves, and our tragedy is the finest and best we can create. At any rate, our entire state has been constructed so as to be a 'representation' of the finest and noblest life – the very thing we maintain is most genuinely a tragedy. So we are poets like yourselves, composing in the same *genre*, and your competitors as artists and actors in the finest drama . . .[78]

The project of combining the study of law with that of literature in the broadest sense has given rise to an important scholarly movement. Nowadays, law and literature – or *law and humanities* as I rather call it – can be said to be a firmly established discipline with its own specific journals, devoted monographs, annual conferences, and international symposia, and it is increasingly being incorporated into many law school curricula, in the US, Canada, Europe and beyond. However, Cover himself is wary of assimilating law with literature. Already in *Nomos and Narrative* he criticizes interpretative theories such as Ronald Dworkin's, among other things, for not paying enough attention to the institutional constraints of the *legal* – as opposed to the literary – interpreter.[79] But it is in another well-known article, "Violence and the Word," that Cover distances himself from a body of scholarship that places meaning at the center of law or has more generally, a humanistic approach to law.[80] To summarize briefly the points relevant for our present discussion, he argues that interpretation in law has (real) and painful incidence in the world. Through law people are sentenced to jail, disposessed of their land, evicted from their houses, or even sent to their deaths. These are not pure hermeneutic activities, but actions that have immediate and tangible, sometimes even dramatic, consequences in the outer world. Thus, to treat law as literature – let alone to put literature at the core of law – is not only misleading, but dangerous. (We will come back to this later.)

Despite his attempts at severing ties, Cover's own relationship with *law and literature* is not that simple.[81] On the one hand, he seems fascinated by the literariness of law and the multiplicity of forms it allows; on the other hand, he is skeptical of pushing the analogy too far. Speaking not about all kinds of literature but about the particular case of tragedy at this point, I will explore where the analogy between law and literature might be said to break apart. By digging into the source of Cover's own ambivalence I hope to be able to say something meaningful about my own approach to the subject.

There are several dimensions in which law and literature can be thought to part ways. The first obvious candidate is the distinction between fact and fiction, reality and fantasy. Tragedy is fictional in the sense that the events it recounts, the characters it portrays, the storylines it follows need never have happened, or even if they did, they are purposefully and carefully re-enacted to serve the ends of the fiction itself. Nevertheless, it is also true that such fictional enactment does create *a* reality that must be considered as such. In fact, I would argue that only if and when we take the enacted world *as* real that we become susceptible to the full experience of tragedy. Moreover, the reality of tragedy exceeds that of the world being depicted and reaches out to the "real" world: real is the occasion for the festival; real are the prizes awarded to the winner; real are the fines for those who made Athenians cry or suffer excessively;[82] and more importantly for our present purposes, *real are also the emotions and the cognitive processes that they generate in the audience*. In fact, Aristotle included some of these effects, pity (*eleos*) and fear (*phobos*), as essential attributes of tragedy.

It is also worth noting that almost invariably tragedians did not make up but made use of stories of their own distant past. These stories were borrowed from the audience's oral tradition, mythological lore, and, in a very real sense, their history. For this reason it was virtually impossible for the poet to flatly contradict well-known *facts*. For instance, Homer could no more make the Trojans win the war, or Sophocles have Oedipus not kill his father and marry his mother, than Thucydides could alter the course of the Peloponnesian War. Poets had to work within the parameters that their (collective) epistemic framework imposed upon their (individual) creativity. Hence, one needs to be guarded against uncritically assuming that tragedy is, unlike law, only fiction. And the reverse is true about the law, for example a student brief or an academic or lawyerly restatement of the law, which is "made" and hence also "fictional."

A second major contrast, it could be thought that literature lives in the realm of the unruly and unconstrained whereas law inhabits the realm of the rule-bound and constrained. In this view, the legal interpreter is bound in a way that the literary interpreter is not, for the latter is free to choose and recreate the world she reads at will. Although generalized, I believe this argument misconceives the nature of literary interpretation, for here too the reader is subject to the *rhetorics of the text*[83] and faces many other forms of institutional constraint.[84]

This is not to say that the literary reader has no leeway in interpretation. At the very least, the interpreter does always incorporate his or her own point of view into the object under interpretation. (Not unlike in law, I would point out.) But there is always something before our eyes to be interpreted. The literary interpreter thus begins with something (a text, an image, a situation, an emotion, a motive) that she then tries to understand herself and make understandable to others, in her own words. This means that the literary reader submits herself to what Gadamer calls the logic of the question and answer.[85] The text is a question to which the interpretation is an answer, which in turn poses another question that will have to be answered, and thus successively. This cyclical logic encapsulates the hermeneutic act, thereby creating the boundaries within which interpretation can operate. Conversely, legal interpretation is indeed bound to certain authoritative sources and materials, but the indeterminacy of legal language, the multiplicity of authoritative materials, and the irreducibility of each perspective do always leave room for selection, shaping, choice, and, in that respect, freedom. Therefore, each law and literature has sources of constraint as well as of freedom.[86]

One might still want to stress the difference in the types of constraint in both cases: police, jail, armies on one side, universities, intellectual communities, or publishers on the other; also, the difference in the consequences of breaking the standards of interpretation: jail, eviction, or even death in case of law; demerit, lack of influence, or academic ostracism in the case of literature. But the differences in the types of constraint and consequences only reflect differences in the *milieu* where interpretation takes place, not in the hermeneutic *activity* itself: in both cases, the constraints are to be incorporated and made part of the object of interpretation.

A third possible cleavage is suggested by the dichotomy between word and action, thought and deed. Unlike poets, critics, and artists, Cover suggests that judges (as paradigmatic cases of legal interpreters) not only say, but *do* things. Their interpretations are not just words or thoughts, but deeds or actions-in-the-world. Law, unlike literature, he thinks, must be capable of transforming itself into action.[87] Once again, clear-cut as this distinction first appears, philosophers of language and rhetoricians have taught us "how to do things with words," and elaborated on the performative and constitutive effects of language.[88] Tragedy in particular presents a challenge to its placement in the category of "words," for it cannot be severed from the movements, gestures, dances, and songs that enliven it, nor can the words of the characters be divorced from the behaviors and actions that accompany them. Not without reason Aristotle said that tragedy is, above all, action.[89]

But perhaps I am just quibbling with words. Clearly what Cover means is that law has a direct and immediate incidence in the world that literature does not have. This is so, he says, because law has the *conditions for effective domination*, that is the structural arrangements to turn its wordy mandates into effect.[90] It is true that literary interpretation – say my interpretation of the *Antigone* – has not the same direct and immediate consequences as the interpretation of a judge or a jury in a law court. Yet this is not due to a logical chasm between both interpretive activities, but to the different status of each interpreter: the same result would obtain, I suppose, were I to demand obedience to my *legal* interpretation of the American Constitution.

Most importantly, the conditions of domination of which Cover speaks are subject to contingent historical processes. In other times and places they have been known to favor actors – be they prophets, seers, theologians, philosophers, quacks, or priests – that nowadays we would categorize merely as "speakers" – some would say charlatans. Also, there were times in which the interpretation of a literary (i.e. non-legal) text judged to be incorrect or heterodox – say of the sacred text – could end up with the interpreter in jail, if not worse. Arguably then, that (State) law has the machinery for its effective implementation is not a conceptual truth about law, nor does it separate it from literature. It must be kept in mind that the things judges command are done not *by* them but *for* them; in other words, for these things to get done an act *other* than the judicial interpretation is required. This means that there is a logical gap between judges' words and the kind of actions (loss of property, liberty, death) Cover has in mind, and furthermore, that the causal chain that links judges' words and such deeds can be broken. Cover considers this argument, but argues that modern legal systems have institutionalized an array of mechanisms for this problem never to arise. However, the fact remains that there is a logical gap between the words of judges and their conversion into action. As it turns out, to say that judges *do* things or that their words *are* actions is also metaphorical, in a way no different from literature. If we are to accept the fact that law does not live only in its official statements, we must also accept the fact that many normative universes will lack the conditions to turn their *nomos* into full effect.[91]

Cover insists, however, on the fact that law deals in the terrain of physical pain, suffering, and death, all of which makes literature look in comparison like quite an inoffensive activity indeed. Further, he worries that those who put the emphasis on the literariness of law ignore or systematically downplay law's violence, and the unbridgeable wall that it erects between those who do and those who suffer it. Here, I will not take issue with the assertion that law operates under the shadow of violence. Nor will I contend – but in fact will often make the argument myself in regard to discursive, dialogic, and coherentist theories of law and politics – that there is a tragic limit to the level of agreement that can be reached through the process of rational discussion. But all this ought not to lead us to the conclusion – somehow implicit in Cover's argument – that a humanistic approach to law is naturally inclined to be dismissive of these issues. Cover appears to think that to place literature at the center of law leads to idealizing the commonalities of values and shared understandings that law allows. However, whatever else is true about tragedy as a literary genre, tragedy connects us with extreme experiences of anguish, suffering, pain, and death, which actually produce the kind of meanings tragedy is said to have – and these meanings are essentially conflictual.

On the other hand, it is not at all clear what practical benefits derive from disconnecting the naked and physical acts of violence from the linguistic and imaginative operations that make it thinkable and possible. To limit violence to its pure naked expression runs the risk of making violence impermeable to analysis, and to leave us without arguments for criticizing or even opposing it.[92] As the "torture memos" of the lawyers for the Bush administration for prisoners at Guantánamo manifest, even more criminal than the acts of torture themselves are the words and the fictions of the lawyers who supported them.[93] The fact that law acts with violence would make it more important, not less, to read and criticize these "words." At the end of the day a reasonable way to interpret Cover's argument, perhaps, may be not as an outright dismissal of the whole law and literature enterprise, but as a warning against some tendencies towards sentimentalizing it.[94] If that is the case, engaging with tragedy may prove to be a salutary antidote.

Nothing in my argument should be interpreted as saying that law and literature are the same thing or that judging tragedy is exactly like judging a legal case. The only point of the analogy that I ask the reader to accept for the moment is that the hard cases as described in the previous section show similarities to the legal case presented in the *Antigone*. In both cases, there is a need to engage with the parties and their disparate claims and understandings of law, and to judge them with justice.

My interest lies in sorting out the emotional and intellectual processes that are at the heart of this activity, and I offer my own reading of the *Antigone* as an example of it. Such a goal demands close and detailed attention to the phenomenology of judging, of the kind that often eludes more empirically oriented studies on decision-making which take the activity of judgment for granted. In doing so, I aspire neither to the universality of mathematic demonstration, nor to the flawless and beautifully crafted designs of social scientists. What I offer instead is a kind of practical knowledge that cannot be detached from the personal experience that it entails, but that can nonetheless be put to good use, as well as perfected, by anyone who has the mind and the desire to take it further.

Chapter 2

Antigone, Part I: Beginnings

In the beginning we will encounter a language, a culture, and a *polis*, a distant land and geography, foreign rites and institutions, and a legal issue of tragic dimensions. We will encounter a family of brothers and sisters, fathers and mothers, uncles and nieces. We will hear the arguments of a political newcomer and ponder about the ambivalent nature of man and human progress. We will see holistic *nomoi* bloom and forms of life grow. Many unexpected things will slowly but surely be revealed; others will remain undisclosed. In all this we will constantly be making judgments about law and justice, good and evil, right and wrong, sometimes in anticipation of judgments still to come.

2.1 Antigone and Ismene at the palace gates (lines 1–99)

The first words are those of Antigone:[1] *"Oh, my own dear sister* [koinon autadelphon], *which of the evils that come from Oedipus will he* [Zeus] *fail to accomplish while we still live? No, there is nothing painful . . . I have not witnessed." Antigone wants to know whether her sister has heard the latest public proclamation* [kerugma] *(8) that the new ruler* [strategos] *(8) has made to the whole city. Ismene has not heard anything new, she says, not since she learned that her two brothers died at each other's hands. Antigone tells her that for Eteocles, Thebes' champion, Creon has ordered the most honorable funeral rites, according to justice and proper custom* [dikaiai kai nomôi] *(24); but for Polyneices, he has decided his corpse must be left unburied and unwept to be prey to birds and dogs. Moreover, the penalty for whoever transgresses the orders will be to be stoned to death. This is the time to show, Antigone tells Ismene, whether her nature is noble or she is rather the worthless daughter of their parents. Certainly Creon has no right to keep her from her own.*

Ismene thinks that it is reckless to act against what has been ordained for the whole city,[2] *and begs Antigone to reconsider. She recalls the dreadful death that came to their father, who perished hated and ill-famed after striking out both his eyes; to their mother, who ended up hanging herself; and now to their brothers too, killing each other on a single day. Ismene suggests that worse will happen to them if they act against the law* [nomou biai] *(59). She reminds Antigone that they are only women, and they cannot fight against men and those who rule from power, to whose wills they must submit. She begs forgiveness from the dead, since she is under duress, but she will obey those in authority.*

Antigone rebels against this reasoning. She alone will bury her brother, if need be. She tells Ismene that she can be the kind of person she has decided to be. If she dies in the act, Antigone claims, what an honorable death that will be, and how sweet it will be to rest with her own. At any rate, she owes more to them, and for a longer time, than to the living. She says to Ismene, "[go ahead] *and dishonor the laws the gods hold in honor."*

She means no dishonor to the dead, Ismene assures Antigone, but it is not in her to act against the citizens [biai politôn] *(79). Afraid for her sister, Ismene begs Antigone at least to keep her deed a secret. Antigone refuses: She will hate Ismene all the more if she does not proclaim what Antigone is about to do to the world, the result of which can bring no worse than an honorable death. "Go if you must," Ismene concludes, "and know that your act is senseless* [anous], *but "rightly loving the ones you love"* [tois philois d'orthôs philê] *(99).*[3]

It is difficult to imagine a more compact beginning. All the main elements of the tragedy (the relationship of the sisters, their family history, the mutual dead of their brothers, the prohibition of the burial of Polyneices, the grounds and reasons for disobeying or obeying the law, the risks of doing so) are already delineated in the conversation between the two sisters. Antigone begins with words of closeness and proximity, trying to enlist Ismene's support to bury Polyneices, but by the end of their dialogue they have grown quite apart. This is a *defining* moment: Antigone challenges Ismene to show what she is made of and, after it becomes clear that Ismene is not going to help her, she retorts: "be the kind of person you have decided to be" (71). By the end of their dialogue, Antigone and Ismene prove to be two distinct individuals, with different perceptions about their own lives and roles in society, their family history, and the gendered and political constraints they now face.

The play does not begin with Creon's personal announcement of his decree, but rather with Antigone explaining it to Ismene, which predisposes the audience to see the issue through the normative lenses of the two sisters. Antigone explains that whereas Creon has granted Eteocles the proper rights of burial ("according to law and justice"), for Polyneices he has announced publicly his decision that no one shall bury him or mourn his death, and threatens with death anyone who disobeys that decision. We are not told what exactly justifies such harsh treatment of Polyneices – for Antigone and Ismene what Polyeneices did or did not do is inconsequential – and the scene centers around the way the decree affects the sisters and how they each respond to it, rather than on Creon's reasons for it.

Antigone refers to Creon's decree as a "proclamation" [*kerugma*] and, unlike Ismene, does not use the ordinary term for law (i.e. *nomos*) to refer to it. Some read negative connotations in Antigone's choice of words,[4] but this is not necessarily so. In fact, the term "kerugma" is a politically neutral term that applies to democratic and autocratic proclamations alike,[5] and it may well be that "there was no way other than by proclamation that Creon's edict could have been promulgated."[6] Likewise, the term *strategos* that Antigone uses to refer to Creon does not mean that, in that capacity, Creon did not have the authority to make a decree. As Mark Griffith explains, "an Athenian *strategos* on campaign could issue a *kerugma* on his own initiative (even one invoking the death penalty)."[7]

At first glance, the decree possesses the formal characteristics of law: it has been uttered publicly by the person who possesses the authority in the city, it addresses and imposes obligations on all citizens, and it establishes a clear sanction for cases of breaches.[8] Edward Harris argues that Creon's decree lacks the generality and future applicability of laws because it is directed mainly at one person, Polyneices.[9] However, this can hardly be the case since Polyneices is dead and cannot be the addressee of the law. Creon's decree is actually addressed to all citizens (7, 28–35) and Polyneices is singled out as its object of application because, according to Creon, he falls under the category of a traitor. Thus Creon's decree can be rewritten as a general statement for future cases as well: "if anyone buries a traitor. . . he/she will be sentenced to death," which is similar in form to the Athenian statutes provided by Harris as examples of general laws.[10] These formal characteristics notwithstanding, the decree impinges upon a very delicate issue such as the obligation of burying one's dead, which foreshadows the conflict in Antigone's determination to resist it.

For Antigone, the exposure of Polyneices' body to be torn apart by scavenger birds and dogs is an intolerable outrage, and, in announcing her intention not to stand idly by, she reacts like the typical Homeric warrior who must rescue the bodies of his fellow soldiers from the enemy. The sentiment appears understandable, even without the poetic and cultural background. As H.D.F. Kitto notes: "What Sophocles relies on and presents again and again is the sheer physical horror, the sense of indecent outrage, that we all feel. . . at the idea that a human body, the body of someone we have known and maybe loved, should be treated like this."[11]

Ismene does not seem to feel less of an abuse, but perhaps as just another in a long chain of abuses that she must endure, as she has done in the past. Thus the two sisters draw opposite conclusions from the same wretched family history. Ismene wants Antigone to bear in mind the terrible destinies of their family members: their father's death, hated and ill-famed, after striking out both his eyes himself; the suicide by hanging of their mother, Oedipus' wife and mother as well; and now the death of their two brothers, who killed each other on one single day. Ismene relies on this family history to convey that their own death will be the more terrible, now that they are alone, if they act against the law [*nomou biai*] (59).

The same family history gives Antigone all the more reason not to put up with any more abuse and to stand up for her lost family. Creon's decree has varying meanings for each: whereas for Antigone Creon's decree is the final act of injustice, the last straw, that must be resisted come what may, for Ismene the decree is to be added to the long list of sufferings of equal magnitude with which she must learn to cope. Antigone's first and foremost duty is towards her brother and to burying him, expressed in terms of love, loyalty, and honor; Ismene, with identical relations and therefore obligations towards the dead, adduces extreme duress to excuse her behavior and the gendered constraints imposed upon her, but she additionally expresses the positive value of obeying those in authority and their laws (59, 66, 79). While Antigone thinks she must act regardless of the opposition, Ismene fears the consequences and wants to act within the boundaries of the "possible," which is a reminder of Simonides' expression "not even the gods can resist necessity."[12] Through Ismene, we encounter a certain male-dominated culture in which women are expected to be submissive, which Antigone rejects.[13]

Antigone defends the burial as a long-standing practice that accords both with justice [*dike*] and legal convention [*nomos*] (24–5), and that it is honored even among the gods (77). Ismene does not dispute these assertions, but finds herself unable to break the law [*nomou biai*] (59) and act against the authority of the ruler [*tyrannos krate*] (60) and the citizens [*biai politôn*] (79). Ismene makes the logical jump of equating the will of the ruler to the will of the city (44, 59, 79), and it appears that, for her, whatever the ruler decides is law.[14] Antigone does not equate the will of Creon to that of the citizens, and considers the decree as issued particularly *by* Creon (31) *to* the citizens (27). In her mind, she is not acting against the *polis*, but only against Creon. Moreover, Antigone does not accept Ismene's commitment to the laws of the *polis* as a genuine reason, but rather as a pretext for not performing her obligations of *philia* – the obligations towards her family. Antigone expresses her duty in terms of loyalty and the failure to act in terms of betrayal, and accuses Ismene of dishonoring the dead. Ismene wishes no dishonor, she says, but finds it impossible to overcome the enormous constraints. Her obligations to the dead are not nullified by her inaction – she actually begs forgiveness from them – but she must obey, and cannot rise above, the city. The two sisters share the *commitment* to the norm that imposes performing the burial rites for the dead brother, but only Ismene is committed to a principle of obedience that Antigone does not accept.

Furthermore, Antigone shows no concern for the death sentence attached to the disobedience and focuses instead on the essential nobility of such an act. She knows Creon will accuse her of committing a "crime," but she denies him the right to nullify her family obligations. Ismene worries about the risks that the burial entails, thereby focusing more on the value of life and its preservation. Antigone further shows that she is not afraid when she begs Ismene to *proclaim* her deed to all [*pasis kêruxêis*] (87), in terms that remind of, and reverse, Creon's "kerugma."[15] Antigone's intention to publicize her defiance demonstrates not just her boldness of character (in contrast to the shyness of Ismene), but also, and more importantly, her determination to turn the apparently private matter of burying a family member into a public and hence political act, with concern for the whole *polis*.

By the end of the dialogue, the distance between the sisters becomes insurmountable. Antigone resents Ismene's "cowardly" choice and reiterates her determination to fight for her loved ones until her strength fails. In turn, Ismene remarks upon her sister's fiery heart, her love for the impossible, and her "senseless" act. Still, Ismene seems to be genuinely concerned for Antigone and her last words reflect a certain ambivalence of judgment: Ismene suggests admiration for the sentiments that inspire Antigone's action, if not for the action itself.

This ambivalence may reflect the audience's own: Antigone's commitment to her brother and to his proper burial may awaken some level of sympathy in the audience (especially since they are not told exactly what Polyneices has done to deserve such harsh treatment), but the open and frontal challenge to the city's law she wishes to undertake (and to make public) may appear no less shocking to them than it does to Ismene – considering in particular fifth-century attitudes on gender relations and authority.[16] From this perspective, Ismene's arguments about the obedience owed the city and its laws appear in principle more "sensible" than the directly confrontational character of Antigone's position. In this way, the sisters' exchange presents a real dilemma for the audience to ponder, which will have to be considered from different angles as the drama advances, and cannot be sidestepped by recourse to a priori legal categories or norms that could settle the dispute. The play presents the hypothesis of a clash of commitments in the figure of a young woman and sister committed to burying her brother in spite of the decree that forbids it. Antigone privileges the obligations of *philia* with the argument that the city has no right to deprive her of her own. In this sense, the play poses an interesting question: is there a limit to the loyalty that the city can demand from its citizens and subjects?

Some authors wish to foreclose the debate, arguing that an Athenian audience would have considered the issue of burial as a universal norm that admits of no exception.[17] This conclusion cannot be accepted for various reasons. The actual mutilation of bodies was, if not the norm, at least a frequent occurrence in the Homeric poems, where the winners of battle make great efforts to strip the bodies of their enemies and increase their honor [*time*]. This suggests, first, that the obligation of burial was not all-inclusive, but fell exclusively upon the warrior's friends; second, that enemies were neither obligated nor *expected* to perform the burial; and third, that the latter felt no great reverence and feared no ritual pollution from the contact with them.[18] Certainly the sentiment appears to have shifted by the fifth century – the exposure of the body was no longer considered "appropriate" and was increasingly perceived as barbaric (i.e. un-Greek). At this time, it was usual for the winners of battle to offer a truce to the losing side to recover their dead, a practice known as *anairesis*. Thus the Athenians were able to argue against the Thebans who did not offer such a truce that they were acting against the "established law" (Thucydides 4.97–8) – although naturally the Thebans disagreed as to what the law required.

The Theban denial of burial of the seven Argive captains, and the Athenian intervention as champions of their right of burial, became the source of several tragedies,[19] and became a favorite also among the Athenian nationalist rhetoric (e.g. Lysias 2.7–10; Isocrates 12.168–74; and Herodotus 9.27), which shaped and relied upon it for its own ideological purposes, as Vincent Rosivach has argued.[20] However, it is difficult to say with certainty when this nationalist *topos* became established,[21] and it cannot be excluded that it was influenced by the tragedies themselves.[22] In fact, Philip Holt argues that the story is "probably an Athenian invention, counter to a tradition which had the Seven buried, apparently without opposition, at Thebes."[23] There is also the issue, as Helene Foley points out, that in the *Antigone* "we are not dealing directly, as in the Attic funerary topoi, with a conflict between Thebes and Athens, but with a conflict within Thebes."[24] Polyneices is not a foreigner whose body can be returned to the foreign enemy, because Polyneices is one of their own.[25]

Moreover, real-life refusals and failures to perform burial rites continued to occur in fifth-century Athens. For example, in 430 BC, the Athenians captured six ambassadors from various Peloponnesian states and without giving them a trial or allowing them to say what they wished to say in their defense, put them all to death and threw their bodies into a pit.[26] Although it is clear from Thucydides' account that the actions of the Athenians were contrary to custom, he reports that the Athenians regarded this action as "legitimate retaliation" for the way in which the Spartans had been behaving. More to the point, the law prohibiting the burial of traitors in Attic soil was in place at the time (e.g. Themistocles was denied burial in Attica due to his suspected treason[27]), and the ill-treatment of their bodies by the state could continue after their death, even by public decree.[28] Therefore the legal situation surrounding the burial and its prohibition is to be understood in dynamic and not in static fashion, for norms are embedded in narratives that are malleable and open to reinterpretation.[29] As Holt puts it:

> Whatever the letter of the law, the *principle* that burial could be denied to particularly egregious offenders was established in people's minds well before Sophokles' day, and it stayed in their minds well after. Given sufficient provocation, it could be awakened and put into action in general laws or in sanctions against people or families in particular cases.[30]

This should tell us something about the ontology of the legal norms concerning burial, which is too sensitive an issue to remain settled in clear and predictable rules. The situation can be analogized to the biblical rule of primogeniture already described in Chapter 1. Whereas the rule that the oldest son must succeed the father is defined in no uncertain terms in *Deuteronomy*, such a simple precept is surrounded by a rich array of narratives that flatly contradict it – often connecting the subversion of the rule with divine intervention. Likewise in the case of burial, a hypothetical provision stating clearly that burial of traitors is forbidden has to be understood in the context of the narratives in which burial is either factually prevented or else performed in violation of it, adding depth and *charging* the meaning of the rule. Thus it cannot be a total coincidence that when Thucydides speaks of the law prohibiting the burial of traitors he does so precisely in the context of its disobedience and breach – when Themistocles' family brought his bones back and buried them secretly in Attica.

Beyond the lack of uniform historical record and the general malleability of legal precepts, the central objection to the attempt to settle the issue by attending to Athenian law is that fifth-century Athenians' practices are certainly not the *decisive* factor. As Helene Foley says, "[t]he Athenian audience was used to being nurtured by poetry with an ethos that did not correspond fully to its own. . . [And] did not expect literature to mirror in any obvious way its own reality and ideology."[31] The contemporary sensibility filters the information that the audience hears and watches, but the standard by which practices and customs are considered "normal" is set not by contemporary Athenian ones, but by those that the audience imagines to occur in Thebes at the legendary time of the dramatic action. The *Antigone* takes place not in contemporary Athens, but in the legendary past of the Homeric world, before the Trojan War, where the exposure of bodies was much more common. The Athenian audience, no differently than modern audiences, would have to jump imaginatively to this distant land and time, where very different social norms and cultural practices were thought to apply. As a methodological point, then, the interpreter cannot pretend to "fish for the correct legal answer" in Athenian law, because learning the law of the *Antigone* requires progressive internalization of the norms pertinent to the play, which often challenges, modifies, surprises, or transforms the audience's assumptions. Thus, when the tragedy has just begun, the audience may still want to see the drama develop further before making definitive judgments.

2.2 *Parodos*: first entrance of the Chorus (lines 100–55)

In their first song the Chorus, elders of Thebes, remember the dreadful war that has almost devastated the seven-gated city which now sees the sun, the brightest light. The Chorus reminds us that the foreign man from Argos,[32] *raised by the contentious quarrel of Polyneices, flew over the land loudly screaming like an eagle, with many weapons and helmets, and spears that longed for their own blood. But Zeus, who hates the boasts of a proud tongue the most, saw him advance with the arrogance of flashing gold, and the fire he hurled smote him who was already hastening to sing victory. And he fell down, shaken, the torchbearer . . .*

The Chorus recalls the seven captains posted at seven gates, seven against their equals . . . but only the two wretched brothers stood against each other, and both perished, brother slain by brother. But now, Victory has come, to bring joy and forgetfulness of these wars, and they dance and sing the livelong night, to the Bacchic god who rules Thebes.

The Chorus, a collective body formed by Theban elders close to the ruling family, makes a solemn entrance showing their concern for the *polis* and its well-being. It would be simplistic to associate them with the Athenian demos or with the poet's voice. The Chorus is an elusive character whose role and function must be decided in each particular instance. Sometimes, especially during the dialogues, it is just another character advancing opinions that are conditioned by their age, status, and role in the city. Other times, especially during the odes, it adopts a more general voice that reflects on the wider implications of the drama (though still preserving their personal characteristics and limited vision).[33] Thus the Chorus is both inside the dramatic action and somewhat detached from it, showing the capacity to distance itself from the actions and to offer reflections of a general nature. In order to keep these various roles separate, I will refer to "the elders" when they act as another character and reserve the term "Chorus" to refer to the collective body that sings in the choral odes.

The ode tells the story of the fratricidal war that almost brought the city of Thebes to the ground, but that, almost miraculously, has been averted at last. The Chorus' song expresses both terror and joy, mixing images of light and destruction, often in the same metaphors (light, sun, golden shields, fire, torches), as if the anxiety and fears were still too vivid in their imaginations. If the opening scene focuses on the reaction of the two sisters to Polyneices' unburied corpse, the Chorus of Theban elders focus now on the dangers that the foreign army led by Polyneices brought to Thebes – the spears of destruction and the blazing fire with which he threatened his own city.

Polyneices, as the head of the Argive army, is associated with an eagle that spreads his wings over the city and comes to devour it, with his jaws wide open and the spears longing for blood.[34] The Chorus vividly describes that Polyneices was forced out before his jaws could be sated with their blood and the city set on fire. The Chorus' impassioned description of their anguish and of the gory details of the city's impending destruction helps us to picture Polyneices and his "contentious quarrel" [*neikeôn amphilogôn*] (111) negatively.[35] Likewise, the allusion to the boastful soldier who was about to sing victory when he was struck by lightning (which the poetic tradition identifies with Capaneus) does not eliminate but confirms the parallelism with Polyneices, who also had inscribed on his shield the threatening words "I will set the city on fire" in golden letters.[36] This narrative does not contradict, but in fact prepares for Creon's label of Polyneices as a traitor, ignoring other poetic traditions in which Polyneices may have had a legitimate claim to the throne.[37]

Now that the immediate dangers have been prevented and Thebes seems finally saved, the Chorus wishes to leave the past behind: it is time for celebration and to visit the temples of the gods with all-night dances, in honor of Dionysus, patron of the city.

2.3 Creon, new King of Thebes: inaugural speech (lines 155–222)

The elders announce Creon's entrance as the new King, and he speaks with the solemnity required by his recently acquired kingship. He has summoned the council of elders because they are, and always have been, loyal to the royal line and he expects the same loyalty. He claims it is impossible to know any man – his nature [psuchên], *thought* [phronêma], *and judgment* [gnômên] *– until he has proven himself in the exercise of rule and law. In his view, the person guiding the city must reach for the best counsel without faltering, and those who shut their mouths for fear of consequences are the worst of all; second, anyone who puts a friend* [philon] (184) *before his country – he rates him as nothing. He calls Zeus to bear witness that he will never hold his tongue in fear, nor praise as friend* [philon] (187) *anyone hostile* [dusmenês] *to this land, for the city is the ship that helps citizens to sail safely and to make friends* [philous]. *These are the principles* [nomois] (191), *Creon claims, which make the city great.*

In accordance with these principles, Creon has made the proclamation concerning Oedipus's two sons. For Eteocles, who excelled in battle for the city, due honors and proper funeral rites will be paid. For Polyneices, who came from exile attempting to burn the ground of his native city and enslave its citizens, shameful punishment will be meted out: his corpse will lie exposed, unburied and unlamented by anyone, to feed the birds and dogs. In Creon's appraisal, bad men shall never surpass good men in honor, but those who are loyal to the city will be honored in life and death alike. The Chorus concedes that it is up to the one in power to decide about the living as well as the dead.

Creon's confident and reassuring inaugural speech has the majestic, somewhat pompous tone of a political newcomer who wants to make a fresh start after the war, but who must establish, at the same time, his own connection with the past. First of all, he relies on the hereditary principle as the legitimate source of his claim to power. His kinship with the family of Oedipus[38] serves him in order to establish and justify his government. In this light, he summons the closest allies of the former government, the elders of the Chorus, to ask for the same support and loyalty they have shown in the past. The Chorus' support will certainly help Creon further establish his authority and legitimize his kingship, and thus he asks them for a chance to prove himself in the art of government, since no man can be truly known before he does so – reminding us of the aphorism "ruling will show the man" attributed to one of the seven wise men of antiquity.[39]

Creon's attempt at establishing his own authority shapes the need for his principles to be compelling before his audience. Creon reverses Antigone's priority of *philos* over *polis* by assuring not only that the loyalties established within the *polis* are more important, but that the city actually builds the ties of friendship [*philia*] and makes them altogether possible. Creon hits a further patriotic chord when he promises that he will put the safety of his country first, and wishes to demonstrate his resolute character by assuring that he will not deviate from the best policies [*boulematôn*] for fear of any sort. Creon calls on Zeus as witness to this oath, demonstrating his allegiance to and confidence in the gods of the city. The metaphor of the *polis* as the ship holding the citizens together is a cultural commonplace,[40] as are the grounds for the distinction between friends and enemies, on which he bases his decision.[41]

Creon's anxieties to prove himself as a worthy political leader may lead him to overstate these allegiances, but the sentiments expressed are not far from Athenian patriotic self-image. Creon's words are echoed in Pericles' portrayal of the ideal of Athenian democracy in his *Funeral* speech, and cited approvingly by Demosthenes in a legal case involving high treason.[42] I cannot therefore agree with Kitto when he says that "ordinary Greek sentiment would certainly reject this as a political theory."[43] Contrarily, being part of a common patriotic lore, it is unlikely that Creon's speech would be greeted with normative disapproval.[44] This does not require us to posit a uniform and homogenous concept of democratic ideology that could be used as an external yardstick to settle the argument. As Foley argues, "it seems sensible to assume as a critical principle that Athens was in reality populated with citizens with different and changing views and that democratic ideology, which itself contains contradictions, was hard to apply consistently."[45] Yet democracy remains ingrained in the play as an important socio-cultural and political presupposition in the sense elaborated by Simon Goldhill, not as a set of fixed principles and values, but rather as a form of engagement with it that activates an "ideal of citizenship."[46]

Parallel arguments can be made in regard to the "proclamation" that is presented as the logical consequence, the denial of burial to Polyneices. The fact that Creon himself is willing to say he has "proclaimed" [keruxas] (192) his decree suggests that this word has no especial negative connotation and in no way is deprived of legal status.[47] After praising Eteocles' sacrifice for his country, Creon describes Polyneices in the most treacherous terms as someone who came back from exile in order to bring his native city and its temples to the ground, and to drink the blood of his people and to enslave them; (he makes no reference to another version of the legend in which Polyneices and Eteocles were supposed to share the throne in alternate years and Eteocles failed to yield it when the time came).[48] This description accords well with the Chorus' previous depiction of the bloodthirsty eagle that wished to gorge on their blood and set the whole city on fire. That Creon can speak of

Polyneices as a traitor appears justified, and, as we have seen, traitors were denied burial in Attica according to Attic law.[49] Similar and even harsher treatments for the bodies of traitors are known to Xenophon[50] and prescribed by Plato in the *Laws*.[51] Implicit in the prohibition is the idea not only that the city can retaliate against those who like Polyneices raise an army violently against it, but that the person who dares to attack his own land has, for that very reason, forfeited the right to be buried in it.

In preventing anyone from even mourning Polyneices and lamenting his death, Creon may exaggerate his zeal beyond what Attic law prescribed for these cases (presumably burial could take place somewhere else), but as the person now in charge both of the family and of the city-state, the decision about the burial may fall under his authority.[52] It is still not clear how imposing this severe punishment on Polyneices serves to increase the city's overall well-being. But there is no reason to doubt that he believes to have the best interests of the city in mind, which in his view demands rejecting any inkling of nepotism and making an example out of his own family.

Since Creon's decree appears not without some justification, I cannot share the confidence of authors who, at this stage of the tragedy, are able to determine that Creon's decree is clearly illegal and would have been perceived as such unanimously by the audience.[53] At this early stage of the tragedy such a conclusion appears hasty, not simply because the law in Athens prescribed similar measures for traitors. More importantly, Creon has not yet fully demonstrated the extent of his experience in government – the standard he sets for himself and judging him properly – which requires observing the full range of his activities as ruler, including how he resolves the controversies that arise out of his original resolution, how he interacts with other characters and defends his arguments further, and how well he is able to respond to the arguments of others.

Furthermore, the Chorus concedes Creon the right to decide about the matter of Polyneices' body as he sees fit, which invites the audience to accept it, as not evidently beyond his jurisdiction, and in no fundamental contradiction with the elders' religious sentiment. Notably, the elders of the Chorus have been prominent actors in Theban politics for quite a long time – before the arrival of Creon, they first honored the throne of Laius, then of Oedipus at his height and later of his children too (164–9) – which makes it reasonable to take their views as a more or less reliable (though contestable) barometer of the normative assumptions of the community. The fact that they refuse to carry out Creon's orders themselves (215) may give the audience pause to reflect on their genuine opinion – are they implicitly raising doubts about it? – but, by the same token, the gesture grants them a measure of independence of character that precludes treating them as mere puppets of Creon. At any rate the elders confirm that they will not disobey an order which carries a death sentence attached to it, underscoring the seriousness of the offense.

2.4 The guard enters the palace (lines 223–331)

Interrupting their train of thought, one of the guards posted to watch the body suddenly enters the palace. After many circumlocutions that denote the gravity of the news he brings (and his fear that it may cost him his life), the guard explains that without any of the guards having done or seen anything, someone laid dust on the body of Polyneices and performed the proper rites. Creon cannot believe what he is hearing: "What man [tis andrôn] *has dared to do this?" he asks. The guard responds they could see no trace of pick or mattock, no chariot wheels, no human signs around the body, other than the dust that covered it, as if someone had tried to avoid the pollution of the unburied body.*

The elders, still in amazement, wonder whether this could be the work of the gods. Creon retorts in anger that the gods cannot show concern for those who came to destroy their temples, their land, and their laws [nomous]. *"Do you see the gods honoring evil men?" Creon asks. No, he says, there is another explanation: a group of men in the city* [poleôs andres] *who find it hard to abide by his decision and refuse to bend to his rule have bribed the guards. Creon declares there is no institution so ruinous as money. It destroys cities and homes and corrupts noble minds, forcing them to commit the most shameful acts. As he still reveres Zeus, he swears that if the guard does not bring him the doer soon, death for him will not suffice, and he will be strung up alive, and thus learn how ill-gotten gains ruin more than they save.*

The ingenuity and resourcefulness of the guard contradict Creon's depiction of him as a born chatterbox. The guard's witty and caustic remarks are driven by his immediate interest in self-preservation, but in so doing, he demonstrates that intelligence and wit are not the property of the ruler class. He comes to the palace fearing for his life, swearing he has nothing to do with what happened, or knowing anything about it. He presents himself as the unwilling bearer of bad news, and minimizes his offense as causing pain only to Creon's ears. This presentation of events casts any potential retaliation by Creon in a negative light: having done nothing wrong, he does not deserve to be penalized – after all, he is only the messenger. This reasoning cleverly plays down his professional failing: he was stationed to guard the body and, for whatever reason, he has not performed his duty and Creon has a right to be angry at him.

The guard's description of the untouched ground and the lack of traces indicates that Creon's designs for the body have been thwarted – there is no sign that beasts or dogs have torn the body – and it has the additional effect of surrounding the whole incident in a shroud of mystery. To the elders the lack of human traces suggests the possibility of divine intervention. For the audience who has already heard of Antigone's plans this hypothesis has no more basis in fact than does Creon's supposition about the malcontents that have bribed the guards. Still, the elders' readiness to entertain this possibility indicates their predisposition to treat the issue of burial (and its denial) as a matter that concerns the gods, which is an aspect of his decree that eludes Creon.

Creon is absolutely convinced that the gods could not have lent a hand for Polyneices who came to burn down their temples, and he offers a much more "natural" explanation for what happened: a group of malcontents in the city refuse to abide by his decision, which suggests that his position is still vulnerable and his authority not sufficiently secured. Similarly unfounded is Creon's accusation of bribery, which underscores his general mistrust and limited imagination about human motivation.[54] Creon speaks of money as the only factor driving political opposition, whereas Antigone has let the audience know in no uncertain terms that there are other, more important reasons for wanting to oppose it. Creon's partial blindness to the full implications of his decree extends to his patriarchal conception of the social sphere, unable to entertain that a young woman, and not a *man* (248), may be behind the deed.

In his favor, Creon himself does not embrace a profit-driven morality, and none of his actions are motivated by it. His long-winded harangue against the corrupting influence of money and how it destroys cities and men alike can be faulted as extemporaneous. But in terms of the values it espouses, it resembles the complaints of Solon, one of the founding fathers of Athenian democracy of the older generation, about the seductive power of money and the dangers of greed for good government and democracy.[55] This enables Creon to cast himself in the role of a "man of principles" and an incorruptible leader.

2.5 First *stasimon*: Ode on Man (lines 332–75)

Next, the Chorus intones what is known as the Ode on Man: "Many wonders there are but nothing more wondrous than man" [polla ta deina kouden anthrôpou deinoteron pelei]. *He sails the sea through the windy storms and swelling waves; he ploughs the Earth, oldest of gods, unwearied and immortal, from year to year. He snares birds and wild beasts, and with his nets he captures fish; master of cunning, he tames bulls, goats, and horses bend under the yoke. Speech, thought, and political wisdom he has taught himself* [edidaxato]. *He also provides shelter against the frost and the rain. He meets nothing in the future without resource; only from Hades has he found no escape; and yet he has found cures for terrible diseases. Skillful beyond belief, he possesses ingenious dexterity* [to mêchanoen technas], *which guides him now to evil, now to good. The Chorus concludes: when he respects the laws of the land* [nomous chthonous], *and the justice of the gods* [theôn dikan] *that he has sworn to uphold, he is high in the city* [hupsipolis]; *but outcast from the city* [apolis] *is he with whom the ignoble consorts because of his recklessness. "May he who does such things never sit by my hearth or share my thoughts!"*

The depth and ambivalence of this Ode makes it particularly fascinating. Traditionally, the Ode has been interpreted as a hymn to the glory of man, and to his technical and intellectual achievements.[56] It has also been remarked that the story of progress from savagery to civilization owes much to Protagoras the Sophist, as it is recounted in Plato's *Protagoras*.[57] In a mythical form, Protagoras explains that the acquisition of the practical arts such as hunting, agriculture, and architecture allowed them to stay alive and survive, whereas the art of politics, evenly shared among all men, allowed them to create communities and establish cities.[58] Critical readers such as Charles Segal, however, have noted that the glorification of man's achievements is only apparent,[59] and underneath the seemingly smooth path of human accomplishments there hides the danger and the risk of mischief and transgression.

Man is defined through an intentionally ambivalent term, *deinos*, which is that which at once terrifies and fascinates. According to a famous reading of Heidegger, the ode as a whole is not the narration of man's increasing development from savage to civilized, but an inquiry into the very nature of such *wonder* – which is to be found in man's essence or beginning.[60] This condition already presupposes man's ontological duality. As C.M. Bowra says, "he has in himself such possibilities for good and for bad, for order and destruction."[61] In other words, his very potentialities (his intellect, cunning, and resourcefulness) are the source of his own terrible and captivating nature. Therefore, even though the Chorus' account shares much of the elements of Protagoras' myth – the mastery of agriculture, hunting, fishing, language, and political life – it is doubtful that they share the optimistic outlook emanating from that foundational myth.[62]

The Chorus mentions positive aspects of man's technological inventiveness, such as his ability to provide for food, shelter, and health, which culminate in the ability of establishing political institutions and social interactions through language and political wisdom. At the same time, the Ode describes man's relation with his natural habitat as one defined by control, manipulation, and the somewhat aggressive imposition of his own will over matter. Thus the birds are snared, the animals are yoked, the fish are trapped in nets, and the earth is ploughed and worn away. The description of man's achievements as an act of encroachment on the natural world casts into shadow the Protagorean idea of seamless progress and, more importantly, suggests the potential for abuse, through the very same qualities that make for those accomplishments (i.e. now turned to good, now to evil).

Likewise, in Protagoras' myth, political virtue descends originally from Zeus, but afterwards the exercise, practice, and improvement of this virtue is the result of an individual process of learning in the context of the political and familial communities, with the implication that human beings are henceforth autonomous in political matters. By contrast, the Chorus refers to external limitations imposed by the laws of the land and the justice of the gods, which oversee normative behavior as immanent forces at play for the whole society. This further challenges the sophistic view of a *man-measured universe*, for it is precisely by adopting such a perspective – and the temptations for self-aggrandizement that go with it – that man is led to forget and transgress those limits, and ultimately, to be brought low and become cityless (*apolis*). The Chorus thus reasserts the value and the precedence of the *polis* (over the autonomous individual), understood here not in the concrete historical manifestation of the Athenian democracy, but rather as the site of human interactions that transcend a particular cultural or historical arrangement, and which allows human beings to pursue joint ventures that overcome their natural limitations and essential fragility.

The Chorus ends by expressing the wish that men who forget their limits and act recklessly may never share their hearth and their thoughts, wishing to distance themselves from those who think they are above good and evil and do not respect these laws. It is not clear to whom the Chorus refers at this moment. On the one hand, the reckless behavior points directly to Antigone, who had announced from the beginning her intention to defy the law of Creon (now ruler of Thebes and high in the city) and had been accused of boldness by Ismene. In this sense, the ode might be read as a reflection, in highly abstract poetic style, on the mysterious circumstances surrounding the burial and the breach of law that the guard reported. On the other hand, however, Creon's explicit desire to assert control and bring the opposition under his yoke (292–3) may resemble *that* man about whom the Chorus wonder, who has learned to put a yoke about their necks (350–2). If the Chorus' words can still be understood as praise for man's civilizing accomplishments, there is an underlying thread and warning behind the apparent. The call for weaving together diverse normative commitments alerts us also to the importance, and yet the difficulty, of doing so.

2.6 Antigone and Creon: the clash of *nomoi* (lines 376–525)

The Chorus is shocked to see Antigone escorted by the guard: has she really been caught in the folly [aphrosunêi] *of disobeying the King's law* [Basileiois nomois]*? The guard confirms that Antigone has been arrested while trying to bury Polyneices' corpse. He explains how, after returning to his post, he and the rest of the guards brushed off the ritual dust that lay upon the body, leaving it moist and naked, and in order to avoid the smell, sat on a close hill to watch. There they stood until after a sudden storm of dust, they caught a glimpse of her: she was groaning and cursing those who had done the act, crying like a bird when she saw her empty nest robbed of her young. When she saw the body laid bare she cursed those responsible, and with her hands she poured a threefold libation over the body. The guard seized her and charged her with what she had done earlier, and now she denied nothing.*

Creon addresses Antigone directly, who keeps her face towards the ground: Do you admit it? Antigone says she did it, and will not deny it. Creon asks whether she was aware of the proclamation forbidding it. Of course, says Antigone, since it was public. And yet she dared to break these laws [nomous]*? Antigone responds that neither Zeus above nor Justice below enacted such laws* [nomous[63]] *among men, nor did she think his proclamation was strong enough, mortal as it was, to override the unwritten and unfaltering laws of the gods* [agrapta kasphalê theôn nomima]*. They are not in existence from day to day, but live forever, and no one knows where they originated. She* *did not intend to incur that penalty from the gods for fear of any man. She knows she would die eventually, but if she dies before her time, she deems it a profit* [kerdos], *for death is a gain for those who, like her, live a life of misery. Besides, how could she have failed her brother, her own mother's son? If Creon deems her a fool for that, he will prove to be a fool himself.*

The elders comment on her fiery spirit, wild daughter of a wild father who has not learned to yield before adversity. Creon says that the most stubborn wills are soonest bent. Her act of transgression is pure insolence, made twice insolent by glorifying in it, and swears that he is not the man, but she is, if Antigone can enjoy that kind of power and get away with it. In fact neither she nor her sister will escape death, for Creon has seen Ismene in the house as if she harbored some dark intentions.

Antigone tells him to spare her the talk, because nothing he says is sweet for her, as nothing she says pleases him. There is no nobler glory than burying her brother, she assures Creon, and says that the elders too would share her view if they did not have their mouths shut in fear, which are the prerogatives of tyrannies. Creon replies that none of the Thebans thinks as she does and asks her whether she is not ashamed of differing from them. "{T}here is no shame in burying a brother." Creon replies that Eteocles was also her brother: Is she not dishonoring Eteocles by rating both equally? For Antigone the brothers are equals, for who can assure that such distinctions apply also in Hades? For Creon, an enemy [echthcros] *is never a friend* [philos], *not even in death. Antigone replies, "I am not to join in hate* [sunecthein], *but in love* [sumphilein]."[64] *And Creon: "Love if you will and join them in death: while I'm alive, no woman will rule over me!"*

The preceding scene displays the tragedy's major dramatic force, where all the political, ethical, and religious principles confront each other in the battle between the two main characters. When the guard enters the palace for the second time, he admits that he has broken his oath never to return again, but expresses his joy at being freed from the threat hanging over his life (393–5, 400–1); he also feels sorry for bringing suffering to his friends (438), but justifies it on account of putting his life out of danger. The breach of two fundamental ethical principles – keep your oaths and help your friends – does more than cast him as an amoral hedonistic individual as Mary Whitlock Blundell describes him;[65] the guard's natural interest in self-preservation and all-too-common valuation of life above anything (and everything) else, sharpens, more pointedly, the contrast with Antigone's position.

Authors have wondered, perhaps excessively, about the fact that Antigone comes back to bury her brother for a second time.[66] The guard explains that after Creon's admonition he brushed off the ritual dust and left the body, once again, exposed. This reproduces the original conditions and the outrage that justified Antigone to act in the first place, and it is only natural that she must repeat what has been undone, for, as Griffith argues, "the uncovering of the body amounts to a renewed dishonor."[67] Antigone's reaction upon discovering the body, like that of a "bird when she sees her empty nest robbed of her young," displays both affection for her brother and indignation against those responsible for the outrage of leaving him exposed.

The guard's narration of the storm gives an aura of the supernatural to the whole situation, but when the dust settles Antigone is caught red-handed. When questioned Antigone denies nothing, which is unnecessary since the guards saw "with their own eyes" how Antigone sprinkled dust and poured three libations (402, 404–5, 429–31). Creon nevertheless wants to make sure, asking her whether she was aware of the decree that forbade the burial. Once again, Antigone's refusal to deny the charge confirms her responsibility.[68]

The ensuing debate between Antigone and Creon, one of the most celebrated in Attic tragedy, has been framed as enacting the conflict between family and state,[69] human and divine law,[70] written and unwritten law,[71] particular and universal law,[72] law in effect and ideal law,[73] law and justice,[74] *nomos* and *phusis*.[75] However, any attempt at putting either Antigone or Creon at one side of a strict dichotomy is misleading. Antigone and Creon do not inhabit different and separate spheres (i.e. family and religion on the one hand, the state and secular authority on the other), but rather share – and struggle over – the same normative space that they each define differently.

As Victor Ehrenberg has argued, Antigone's defense of the "unfaltering and unwritten laws of the gods" is the first time, in our knowledge, that this expression was ever used.[76] This is important to stress because, by the late fifth and fourth centuries, the "unwritten laws" was a fairly common expression, which included, among others, the proper rites for the dead, respect for parents and hospitality towards foreigners, and the worship of the gods.[77] Antigone's appeal to the unwritten laws has been enormously influential in shaping later historical developments, most notably in connection with the Aristotelian and Thomistic traditions of natural law. Thus Aristotle claims the support of Antigone to defend his notion of a universal and natural sense of law and justice, not dependent upon any particular agreement between individuals.[78] However, Herodotus, contemporary and friend of Sophocles, would question that such notion applies to the rights and obligations of burial, which are heavily dependent upon particular customs and conventions. Therefore to avoid the evident risk of over-determination requires us here to consider Antigone's claim in its own right.

According to Griffith, Antigone makes largely a negative claim (with no fewer than nine negatives in 450–62) and "her concern is not to distinguish and define the limits of secular authority, nor articulate a coherent set of religious or political principles, but simply to defend the deeply-felt convictions that her brother and the gods below *must* be honored, come what may."[79] In a similar vein, Bernard Knox writes:

> Antigone's appeal is not general but specific. She is not opposing a whole set of unwritten laws to the written laws of the *polis*, nor is she pleading the force of individual conscience or universal and natural law. She is

> claiming that the age-old customary rites of mourning and burial for the dead, which are unwritten because they existed even before the alphabet was invented or the *polis* organized, have the *force of law*.[80]

Both Griffith and Knox stress the fact that Antigone may be less interested in presenting a coherent set of principles and values than in defending her obligation to bury Polyneices. However, in trying to preserve an area of (negative) liberty free from Creon's intrusion, Antigone is also doing something else. Antigone's expression is the formulation (orally and performatively) of an ancient tradition, which fixes in time how this tradition should be interpreted in the case at hand. In doing so, Antigone is actively helping to transform the precepts, narratives, and memory of the long-practiced and unwritten laws of burial. Thus, whatever that customary law might have been before or after, it does not and *cannot* remain the same after Antigone's particular act of instantiation. As it has been explained in the previous chapter, Antigone undergoes a process of *objectification*, by which her initial, largely intuitive commitment (her refusal to comply with Creon's orders and bury her brother instead) is constructed as legal precept with the authority and force of law she must now obey.

Antigone's appeal to the unwritten laws, shaped by her individual character and particular form of expression, aims thus to obtain legal recognition in the political realm currently dominated by Creon. Accepting Antigone's claim would entail not just accepting the singular rule that imposes the burial of a family member, but also the worldview she represents. Most radically it would mean to accept the right of a young female – as such with no rights of citizenship – to speak the law authoritatively for the *polis*. Antigone's purpose might have been *insular* in origin, but in objectifying her initial intuitive commitment and claiming the force of law for it – and doing it in public and later glorifying in an act performed deliberately against an explicit prohibition – she implicitly argues that the norm as she interprets it ought to bind not just her but also the entire community, including Creon. This is, no doubt, a grand *redemptive* ambition.

Creon referred to the *polis* as primordial and the point of origin of all civilization and law, assuring his audience that it alone makes all friendship (*philia*) possible. Antigone does not so much deny the value and authority of the *polis* as bring to light an undercurrent of prior bonds and obligations that connect humans to other humans and to their place on earth. Antigone alludes to other narratives and myths of origin to defend the age-old customary obligations of *philia* (in her meaning, family) that are antecedent yet presupposed in the continued life of the *polis*. This vision of the *polis* is no longer hierarchical and dependent upon the fear and submission of its subjects, like Creon's metaphor of the ship and its commander suggests. Rather, the *polis* and its norms are rooted in the human bonds and the relationships that presuppose them, and these are brought to life and preserved by the personal conviction and respect of all citizens (which should include young women as well).

Antigone's defense of these obligations has an added cosmological dimension that points to the interconnectedness and mutual acknowledgment between mortals and gods. Her formulation, "no one knows whence or when they were established, for they just came to be" does not allow us to be precise about the exact origin of these age-old customs – as Philip Nonet has rightly pointed out, it would actually be incorrect to say that they are "divine" in origin[81] – but they nevertheless remain certain in the obligations they impose, none the less binding because they are unwritten. To say with Antigone that the laws of burial are *theôn nomima*, then, does not entail that they are issued by the gods, but rather that the gods *stand behind* them or even that they *sanction* them, in the sense that they are concerned with keeping them in place. Here, too, to say that these laws are sanctioned by the gods gives the performance of burial an aura of extra-legitimacy that her action alone lacks.

Antigone accuses Creon of having exceeded his jurisdiction; as a mortal, he is overstepping into a realm that far exceeds his authority. Antigone ridicules Creon's puniness and insignificance, his ontological limitations and finitude as a human being, by comparing his decree with the long-lastingness of those laws that precede him and that will continue to exist even when he dies. In her view, Creon's decree is a transgression of such ordering of time and, for that reason, invalid. Still she knows that Creon has the power to put her to death – just as the radical constitutionalists of the anti-slavery era recognized that the Constitution as interpreted by Chief Taney could be used against them.[82] But if Creon has still the power to decide over life and death, Antigone denies him the privilege of defining the meaning of either term. Death is no longer the threat that led the guard to betray his friends and break his oath never to return again. Antigone is committed to maintaining her *nomos* even if it means to cut her life short, which means something altogether different for her. When she dies – she is a mortal, after all, and she has not forgotten it like Creon seems to have done[83] – her death now will bring her nothing but a "gain" [*kerdos*]: not as Creon understood it as monetary profit, but as Antigone redefines it, in the sense of honor and praise.

Antigone's assertive, even bold, attempt to redefine the language and the value-terms of her society entails a formidable challenge to Creon and to the worldview he represents. The fact that a woman would dare to speak the law and to thwart the authority of the political leader – calling him a "fool" no less – is certainly extraordinary. It is no wonder that the elders of the Chorus comment on her "fiery" and "unyielding" character. Moreover, Antigone cannot point to anything other than her own judgment as "proof" that the *polis* has no authority to declare that law to her. She might want to present her obligation to bury Polyneices as embodying the will of the gods, but in the absence of a direct link with divinity – Antigone does not receive the law like Moses, nor does Zeus impose it by decree – her appeal to the unwritten laws of the gods is a matter of persuasion and argument, and not of self-evident truth (except, perhaps, for Antigone). As Statis Gourgouris explains, in Ancient Greece "there is no divine court of law and in Athens no priests ever presided as judges or legislators, [which is why] 'divine laws' have as guarantor and interpreter the political *krisis* (judgment) of individual citizens." Thus "the unwritten and unfailing *nomima* of the gods literally 'revert' to human customs; they are reabsorbed into the realm of traditional communal practices from which all law emerges, as Plato himself acknowledges (Laws, 793a)."[84] This, in turn, raises the question of Antigone's epistemology – how did she have access to such laws – and whether the audience will share the same understandings.

Creon is certainly unimpressed and concedes no normative status to what she says. To his eyes, Antigone's gloating on her defiance of the settled laws [*nomous . . . prokeimenous*] (481) is a childish act of insolence that must be corrected and brought under the bridle. As a result, he appears more intent on disciplining Antigone than on defending the "reasonableness" of his own decree and how it is supposed to protect the *polis*. For Creon it is mainly a matter of personal pride: as head both of the state and of the family he finds it appalling that his niece would dare to disobey. Antigone's act of insubordination – surely aided by her sister Ismene, he believes wrongly[85] – must be severely punished. Consequently, he does not make much of the accusation of tyrant that Antigone raises against him. He harbors no doubt that the elders are on his side and that Antigone is alone in her ways of thinking, which the elders never disprove.

Not until their final, turbulent exchange does Creon point out the apparent contradiction of defending one brother while dishonoring the other. Polyneices is not Eteocles and pretending that they ought to be valued similarly is to commit a fundamental injustice on the one who died for his country. Polyneices is a traitor who betrayed his own country and the *polis* has the right to do with his body as it sees fit. This is not to oppose religion or the traditional practices as such: for him, and he has firm grounds in his culture to believe it, both the legal classification and the appropriation of the body of a "traitor" is for the *polis* to make, especially when it touches upon the body of one who came to destroy and dishonor their land and temples. In doing so, he acts on the further assumption that it is right to harm one's enemies as part of the conventional morality and principles of justice criticized by Plato in the *Republic*.

There is no need to inquire whether Polyneices could legitimately claim the throne of Thebes and protest the label of "traitor." Antigone does not deny the accusation, because for her this piece of information is irrelevant: a *philos* is always a *philos*, no matter what he has done, or been accused of having done.[86] Moreover, the distinction Creon wishes to maintain between the two brothers is inoperative after death and does not hold for the obligation she wants to uphold: once in Hades the two brothers are essentially equal, and honoring Polyneices with a proper burial does not entail Eteocles' dishonor. Arguably, Antigone acts upon a new ethics of *philia* which turns inoperative the distinction wanted by Creon – an act of "hate" she defines it – more proper for the battlefield.

Antigone and Creon find no mutually acceptable grounds to frame their conflict and they each remain unflinching in their claim of the self-evident supremacy of their own *nomos*. In their all-or-nothing battle for "the crown of rightness," there is no such thing as a compromise, only grandiose victory or ignominious defeat. Their dialogue enters now into a violent spiral of mutual accusations and reproaches that makes it even doubtful to speak of a *dialogue*, for the participants do not seem to have a common object or show any concern in reaching agreement. Rather, each party is interested in gaining points and in knocking the contrary down. Thus a word from one triggers a response by the other that does not properly respond to the accusation but strives to annul it. Their conflict becomes all-pervasive as it illustrates incommensurable outlooks on friendship and enmity, family and *polis*, love and hate, life and death. For Antigone, the duty of burying a family member trumps every other consideration, and claims it will bring her nothing but praise from the body of citizens. For Creon, the interest of the *polis* demands keeping the distinction between friends and enemies alive, and he thinks Antigone's disobedience threatens the very foundations of the community. Antigone deems this distinction the result of hate and she aims to defend love [*sumphilein*]; for Creon, this kind of love can only lead to death. For Antigone, dying honorably is better than living in misery; for Creon, death is misery, with death we lose it all.[87] Their antagonism and mutual antipathy could not be deeper. Antigone sums it all up well when she assures that nothing in Creon's words pleases her, and nothing in hers pleases Creon (499–501).

In the absence of an adequate language that would enable them to approach each other, their *final vocabularies*, to use an expression of Richard Rorty, remain unbridgeable.[88] This would seem to justify an analysis in terms of parallel worlds that are condemned never to meet each other. The temptation is, then, to declare both views irreconcilable and not follow through with the discussion. But, there are points of intersection among them. Hence, they both admit implicitly that the opinion of the citizens matter. They each in fact believe that the citizens are on their side, for they read differently the non-committal attitude of the Chorus at this time: whereas Creon interprets the absence of opposition as an unequivocal sign of "approval," Antigone interprets it as a result of "fear," and thinks they would actually agree with her if they were to speak freely.

This example signals the importance of coming down from the conceptual level of binary oppositions and abstract principles to the terrain of their *evolving performance*, the diachronic and contextual experience that builds and makes possible the judgment of tragedy and every other conflict in law. This also marks the need for the audience not to be dulled by the immediacy of the fight and to listen more carefully and with a heightened sensitivity. For instance, is the audience to take literally Antigone's claim that she will welcome her death as a "gain," or is it more likely to think of it as her pointedly defiant way of letting Creon know that she is not afraid of his threats? Likewise her comment, "I am not to join in hate, but in love" (523), often taken as a remark that describes Antigone's character, serves rather to defend the essential nobility of her action, in contrast to Creon's "hateful" decision. In other words, the characters' words and actions cannot be separated from the concrete rhetorical circumstances in which they are uttered and the purpose they serve in context.

As to the legal conflict, Creon's decree imposes the negative obligation to abstain from burying Polyneices, while the dead body imposes on Antigone the positive obligation of performing the burial. Conventional legal theory speaks of a legal antinomy that it would be the task of the legal system to resolve. This is precisely the role of old maxims of hierarchy (*lex superior derogat inferiori*), temporality (*lex posterior derogat priori*), and particularity (*lex specialis derogat generali*). Faced with two distinct normative universes, however, these traditional mechanisms do not apply, for there is no neutral system of law with which to square the answer and resolve the antinomy. Which of the laws is superior? Which posterior? Which more particular? It may be that Antigone's law is "eternal," yet it comes logically after Creon's decree; it is general (i.e. universal) and yet particular (i.e. referring to the specific case of Polyneices); and it may claim to be superior to Creon's decree, yet, coming from a non-citizen, it is inferior to the rule emanated from the leader of the city. In other words, there is no uncontested frame of reference to settle the issue, just as there is no "objective" practice of burial against which to measure the adequacy of either *nomos*. The situation is not one of a gap in the law that it is the task of the judge to fill in, but rather one of a hard case in the sense described in the previous chapter. There is not an absence but rather an excess of law, where both Antigone's and Creon's respective *nomoi* claim to provide an authoritative legal answer to the case at hand. Antigone and Creon become thus parties of a legal conflict the exact nature of which we must now try to comprehend more fully in the following chapter.

Chapter 3

Incommensurability and judgment

In the legal battle between Antigone and Creon, images, principles, values, and symbols, as well as the manner of arguing them, are all at stake, colored by the distinctive personalities and attitudes of the two main characters. Antigone and Creon find no mutually acceptable grounds to frame their conflict and they each remain unflinching in their claim of the self-evident supremacy of their own *nomos*. The situation is not one of a gap in the law that is the task of the judge to fill in, but rather one of an *excess* of law, where both Antigone's and Creon's respective *nomoi* claim to provide an authoritative legal answer to the case at hand, and no overarching and agreed upon system of norms exists that can frame and resolve the dispute. A judge confronted with adjudicating the conflict between these two irreconcilable and mutually exclusive positions can find no a priori satisfactory solution to the case.

Such conflict resembles contemporary debates about abortion, gay marriage, and euthanasia; quarrels between parents arguing bitterly in a custody battle; public and constitutional disputes about the relationships between federal law and state law, EU law and national law; and many political conflicts around the world: Israel and Palestine, Armenia and Turkey, Tibet and China, India and Pakistan, Serbia and Kosovo. The issue in such disputes is often about the meaning of a single or a few words (i.e. "marriage," "life," "interest of the child," "territories," "genocide," "sovereignty," "self-determination"), and here as there, accepting the claims of one of the parties entails the rejection of the other.

With the hope that such conflicts can be solved through rational discussion, modern theorists accept normative pluralism as a given and try to build a framework that would allow participants to reach agreements by the logic and the force of the better argument.[1] The aim of these models – philosophical constructions that owe their universal assent to culture-transcending validity claims – is to create a "neutral grammar," within which individuals can openly and freely discuss their conflicting viewpoints.[2] According to Jürgen Habermas, the aim is to generate "subjectless forms of argumentation," unaffected by the particular singularities of conflicting worldviews and able to reach society-wide agreements.[3] This entails privileging rational arguments over other kinds of (poetic, metaphoric, and emotional) expressions. Among these, law and constitutionalism are reserved a prominent place as concrete embodiments of institutionalized processes of rational discussion.[4]

But cases like the one dramatized in the *Antigone* permits us to question our faith in such models.[5] For one thing, the participants do not appear to understand each other, or do so just enough to oppose each other with stronger force. Secondly, they often invoke emotional and deeply charged language, unassailable myths, and overarching narratives which are not possible to excise without excising at the same time the materials that enliven the conflict and make it meaningful to the participants themselves. Thirdly, every such conflict has explicit or implicit forms of coercion lingering in the background and these power-inequalities necessarily affect the quality and the conditions of the debate. Fourthly, no fundamental grammar exists that can frame the conflict in a neutral fashion, because the very frame of the discussion is in dispute. Finally, conflict is often most virulent precisely over the conditions and terms of engagement – about how they are to be set in place, understood, and implemented. In this way, the hope that law can provide a neutral institutional framework for channeling conflict is disputed at the very marrow by a tragedy like the *Antigone* in which law is *anything but* neutral and precisely that which constitutes the core conflict between Creon and Antigone. All this forces us to take seriously the depth and severity of these kinds of incommensurable conflicts, which present some characteristics that are hard to account for in the procedural models. In this chapter I aim to elucidate the stakes of incommensurability in modern contexts.

Not every conceivable case of incommensurability is as starkly tragic as the case between Antigone and Creon; indeed the term incommensurable can be understood in various ways. For example, philosophers like Joseph Raz take the term to mean that some things cannot be mutually compared,[6] whereas others use it to advance the slightly different argument that some things cannot be put on a common scale.[7] Still others use it to mean that the evaluation between different conceptual schemes, forms of life, or cultures is impossible.[8] But it is also true, as in *Antigone*, that incommensurability can consist in the fact that the participants speak different normative languages, based upon values that cannot be reduced to a single and common value. One of my purposes here is to distinguish various situations in which we can speak of incommensurability, often in ways that resemble each other, in the general areas of values, life choices, social practices, moral dilemmas, and so forth. Concerning the legal sphere in particular, my focus will not be on the kind of "tragic choices" that the law must sometimes make – for example, whether the defense of the environment must yield on occasion to economic interests, or whether cost-benefit rationality and market criteria are appropriate for the allocation of dialysis machines.[9] Rather, the focus will be on conflicts between mutually exclusive and irreconcilable positions where the law offers no guarantee of a legally correct and unitary answer.[10]

Keeping the conflict of the *Antigone* in the background, I will proceed, first, by exploring incommensurability in the sense in which Isaiah Berlin originally understood it, which is, to my mind, the most lucid modern description of the phenomenon. Berlin will additionally help us to establish a working definition of incommensurability as a conflict of ends equally valuable and ultimate and where choosing entails inevitable sacrifice. On this basis, I will extend the discussion to similar (though not identical) concerns about social practices and constitutive incommensurabilities (Raz), ethical dilemmas and forms of life (Wiggins), phrase regimens (Lyotard), and political disagreements (Rancière). These authors do not all necessarily contemplate the same phenomenon, but I find it useful to bring them together in order to open the discussion to a broad array of possibilities that the term "incommensurability" suggests. In this way we shall arrive at a crucial distinction between two types of incommensurable situations: on the one hand, the case of an individual who faces a vital (sometimes tragic) *choice* between incommensurable options; on the other hand, the situation of a third person who must adjudicate an incommensurable conflict between two parties – a completely different thing. I will argue that both the audience of the *Antigone* and the judge in a legal case face the latter but not the former situation.

3.1 Berlin and the incommensurable clash of ends

If there is one person indelibly associated with the idea of incommensurability, it is Isaiah Berlin, who, perhaps more vigorously than anybody else before or after, pursued the thought that not all ends in human life are mutually compatible.[11] In his most celebrated example, negative liberty (the lack of obstacles in one's path) conflicts with positive liberty (the ability to create the conditions for meaningful choice). These are not two different interpretations of a single concept, or one concept mistakenly masquerading as two, but two profoundly divergent and irreconcilable attitudes to the ends of life. In arguing so, Berlin was reacting against a whole tradition of philosophical, political, and economic thought which postulates that the ends of rational beings must of necessity fit into one single, all-embracing, and harmonious pattern; that conflicts among them are due solely to the clash of reason with the irrational, or with the insufficiently rational; and that consequently, when reason is used appropriately, conflict – and so all tragedy – is avoidable.[12] For Berlin, such a frame of mind was as dangerous intellectually as it was politically, because "when ends are agreed, the only questions left are those of means, and these are not political but technical, that is to say, capable of being settled by experts or machines, like arguments between engineers or doctors,"[13] which would lead ultimately to the impoverishment of public life.

Berlin never denied that the application of skill or knowledge could, in many cases, lead to satisfactory solutions. Rather, he opposed the idea that an a priori correct and conclusive solution could always in principle be found.

In his view, if the claims of two ends "prove incompatible in a particular case, and if this is an instance of the clash of values at once absolute and incommensurable, it is better to face this intellectually uncomfortable fact than to ignore it, or to automatically attribute it to some deficiency on our part which could be eliminated by an increase in skill or knowledge."[14] The implications of Berlin's position are abundantly clear: "[I]f . . . the ends of men are many, and not all of them are in principle compatible with each other, then the possibility of conflict – and of tragedy – can never be wholly eliminated from human life."[15]

My interest here is not to defend Berlin's philosophical conclusions, but to inquire further into the notion of incommensurable conflicts – what Berlin calls the clash of values at once absolute and irreconcilable – with the purpose of adding depth to our reading of the *Antigone*. The first thing to notice in Berlin's original conception is the gravity of the occasion he imagines. The use of expressions such as "profoundly divergent and irreconcilable," "clash," "absolute," "ultimate," and "incompatible" makes it clear that Berlin is pointing out situations of serious, often vital, importance. Secondly, Berlin insists that these clashes are between ends, not between ends and means, or between means mistakenly masquerading as ends. Considering them as "ends" entails that they cannot be simplified to some other more basic or elemental "units" of value, fulfilled by any other goods, or reduced to each other. This also entails that there is no appropriate rate of exchange by which they can be traded with other goods, nor a common denominator to cancel each other out without loss. Berlin's argument goes against the principles of cost-benefit rationality, which treats all values – including human life – as "preferences," and therefore as fungible within the same ratio of exchange.[16] As far as the individual goes, both ends are equally final.

A third general observation is that incommensurability is a particular instance of a conflict that arises not in the abstract, but in a concrete and particular situation. What is more, the conflict of ends must be experienced as real, not just as a hypothetical or *notional* possibility.[17] An example may help. Some definitions of incommensurability would argue that Shakespeare's *Hamlet* and Mozart's *The Magic Flute* are incommensurable, because neither of them is better than, worse than, or equal to the other.[18] However, we do not usually think of *Hamlet* and *The Magic Flute* as being in conflict, which suggests that, unless such a conflict is artificially created, there ought to be no incommensurability between them. It would be different if a fire were set in the only library that holds the original copies of both these works, and only one of these two masterpieces could be saved. Then you might want to say that you were confronted with an incommensurable choice, because having to decide between two sublime works of art, choosing either one would mean that the other would be irremediably lost.

This is not to say, however, that the incommensurability lies simply in the circumstances, which would dilute the point Berlin is trying to make. In his original and straightforward expression, the clash between positive liberty and negative liberty lies in the very disposition of these two ends mutually to collide. Thus, while positive liberty wants authority to be placed in its own hands, negative liberty wants to curb authority as such. For Berlin, negative and positive liberties are two different and mutually non-reducible types of liberty, both necessary to the area of experience commonly referred to by this name. Even though they are both necessary for understanding "liberty," their respective demands cannot be simultaneously upheld, and the individual who wants to keep both is pushed in opposite and mutually incompatible directions. What gives Berlin's example its distinctive flavor is that such reductionism appears to follow from a logical pursuit of either of the ends.

It can be said, as a fourth general observation, that the relationship between these two concepts of liberty is marked by, what may be called, a *dialectical negativity*, where the two ends are connected by the same, albeit inverse, area of experience. The dialectical negativity that defines the relationship between the two incommensurable ends derives from a doubly-paired claim that each makes. The first one is a *claim of exclusion*, which is a claim to counter or, more precisely, to exclude the demands made by the other. The second one is a *claim of totalization*, that is to take over, single-handedly and at the expense of the other, the whole and same field of experience. In sum, although the two ends, positive and negative liberty in Berlin's example, must be thought to share the same semantic or symbolic space, each aspires to expel the other from it to occupy it fully on its own.

This pushes me to make, finally, the counter-intuitive claim that incommensurability is more likely to exist between things that one has reasons to compare. One would not likely speak of incommensurability, because there is no reason to compare, between Picasso's paintings and the speed of light. By contrast, *Hamlet* and *The Magic Flute* are likely to be found in the same (burning) library, on account that they share a comparable epistemic and symbolic space, and only one can be saved.

To sum up thus far, Berlin's conception of incommensurability implies a serious conflict of ends, each of which makes demands of an absolute and incompatible nature that cannot be simultaneously upheld. No intellectually satisfying, harmonizing pattern can be devised to save both. As Berlin argues, separating his views from those of J. S. Mill, "the very notion that a pattern must in principle be discoverable in which they [human ends] are all rendered harmonious is founded on a false a priori view of what the world is like."[19] What interests me here is not so much the epistemic status of Berlin's own assertion (whether he is speaking as an empiricist, a metaphysician, or a pragmatist[20]), but what it means to accept it. Berlin assures us that incommensurability is – as is tragedy in general – a *fact of life* and that there is nothing we can do to avoid it or eradicate it altogether.[21] We must therefore learn to live with it, for "the need to choose, to sacrifice some ultimate values to others, turns out to be a permanent characteristic of the human predicament."[22] In the context of incommensurability, choice entails sacrifice.

To acknowledge incommensurability as part of the human condition has notable implications for the realms of choice, human agency, and rationality. Berlin warns that incommensurability excludes hard-and-fast, clear-cut rules to guide our choices. Nor can the decision be arrived at in mechanical or deductive fashion. In such cases, says Berlin, conditions are often unclear and principles incapable of being fully analyzed or articulated. Therefore, in seeking to "adjust the unadjustable," individuals must follow "the course of conduct which least obstructs the general pattern of life in which [they] believe," hoping in the end to justify their decisions only by their coherence with that pattern.[23]

Berlin's understanding of the term rationality is ambiguous.[24] On the one hand, Berlin does not think that concrete choices can be reached by the kind of deductive computation often associated with rationality; on the other, he wants to preserve a sense in which these decisions can be reached in a manner that is consistent with individuals' overall way of thinking and being. Therefore he surmises that we can stand firmly behind these choices as those most fundamentally and characteristically our own. Just as metals show their true properties when subjected to extreme conditions, our ability to steer our way under extreme circumstances reveals our moral fiber. This does not make things any easier. For Berlin, to be rational and to remain rational in those situations requires both the agony and the anguish of choosing, and yet the maturity to accept those choices.[25] Insofar as one is capable of moral judgments, he concludes, to be rational is to make choices and to learn to live with them.[26]

Before we bring Berlin's insights to bear on the *Antigone*, let us conclude with a preliminary definition. In Berlin, incommensurability comes to mean a *serious conflict of ends equally valuable and ultimate, each of which makes mutually exclusive and totalizing demands upon the individual, where rationality requires choice and sacrifice, yet offers no guarantee of a principled and satisfactory solution.*

3.2 Raz and the constitutive incommensurability of social practices

In *The Morality of Freedom*, Joseph Raz wishes to defend a credible and useful concept of incommensurability against the utilitarian or consequentialist belief in the comparability of all values, and argues for the *constitutive incommensurability* of certain social practices (e.g. institutions, professional activities, and so on).[27] According to Raz, the enjoyment of many social practices entails refusing to make them commensurate (i.e. comparable[28]) with certain other values or goods as a qualification for enjoying them (hence the constitutive character of this type of incommensurability). Further, Raz argues that the belief in incommensurability is part of the symbolic capital of some practices, and therefore "the refusal to trade one option for the other is a condition of the agent's ability successfully to pursue one of his goals."[29]

Raz uses the example of friendship and money.[30] According to the argument, the enjoyment of friendship entails that one refuses to put a monetary value on it, or else fall short of it. As Raz says, "we know that not everyone is capable of having friends, or any relationships involving companionship. The capacity to have such involves interest in other people, empathy with them, and other psychological attributes."[31] He continues: "Those, for example, whose single-minded pursuit of a career led them to put a price on any human association, lose the capacity for friendship."[32] Therefore "[o]nly those who hold the view that friendship is neither better nor worse than money, but is simply not comparable to money or other commodities are capable of having friends."[33] "Here," states Raz, "failure of commensurability is a success."[34] As one critic explains it, "[t]o come up with reasons that could compare friendship and monetary value could only be done, so to speak, at a price: in this case, the loss of the ability to participate in the institution of friendship."[35] This gives meaning to Raz's enigmatic summation: "Incommensurability speaks not of what does escape reason but of what must elude it."[36]

Raz's take on rationality deserves closer inspection. On the one hand, he thinks that reason is unable to guide choice because both options are rational pursuits, and the reasons for one option are incommensurate with the reasons for its alternative. As a result, neither option can be said to be more rational than the other. For instance, "[p]eople who say, 'For me money is more important than friends' are neither mistaken nor do they commit a wrong. They are simply incapable of having friends."[37] That is, choosing money over friendship incapacitated them from engaging in the institution of friendship, "but they did not, just by doing so, act against reason."[38] On the other hand, rationality is still useful, because the reason given for the chosen option, while incommensurate with the reason for its alternative, shows at least the value of the options finally chosen.

Concerning this choice between incommensurable options, Raz wishes to deny the consequentialist argument according to which the individual's final choices can be always re-interpreted as implicit judgments on the comparative value of the different options. For example, the very person who denies that one can measure the value of friendship in money is often willing to sacrifice a friendship for a job which takes him to a different part of the country. So, the consequentialist argument goes, he is in effect trading a friendship for money, and by extrapolation its rough monetary value can be established. According to Raz, however, this conclusion may be disputed. He concedes that when people are forced to choose they will, at the time of choosing or subsequently, come to hold views concerning the comparative value of these options. But, he asks, do these views reflect their previous beliefs, or are they new beliefs acquired under the impact of the forced choice? In Raz's view, if one takes seriously the people's earlier refusal to compare the value of the different options, one must conclude that the test *changed* rather than revealed their valuations. In other words, the choice indicates not an antecedent comparative value of the options, but rather a change in the agent's judgment. This is why the individual, having made certain dramatic choices, may feel that he or she will never be the same, and refer to it as an occasion of "loss of innocence."[39]

Moreover, Raz argues that the "a priori commitment to commensurability" – the idea that the commensurability of the options can always be established in principle – can lead to a "distorted" description of the situation.[40] For instance, on parting with one's spouse for a job, one is tempted to say that in fact there is a price put on the company of one's spouse. But such a description does not capture (and even betrays) the meaning that the decision has for the individual making the choice, who would be indignant if someone were to suggest that he or she is putting a price on his/her relationship with his/her spouse.[41] The refusal even to consider a monetary exchange is part of the conventional meaning of marriage, and simply to ignore this symbolic significance is to misrepresent the individual decision.

Raz's concept of constitutive incommensurability permits us to identify several important features. First of all, a temporal dimension: the fact that a final choice between incommensurable options may be eventually resolved does not mean that the incommensurability was not there to begin with, or that it can be wholly neutralized always in principle. As Raz suggests, the a priori and the a posteriori moments of incommensurability may represent different judgments of value, and the two must be considered separately, without invalidating the earlier moment with later rationalizations. Secondly, Raz argues that it is important to capture the symbolic meaning of the moment of the choice, without distorting the meaning of this particular juncture with interpretations after the fact. This suggests the need for the interpreter to understand the internal motivation of the individuals facing the incommensurable choices and to describe their actions and decisions as they *themselves* would find them acceptable, without imposing an external interpretative framework that does not do justice to their views. Thirdly, Raz's argument suggests that choices among incommensurable options occur within forms of rationality that are themselves incommensurable, and where there is no single and unifying concept of reason that can measure which one of the alternatives is more or less "reasonable." (This leads us to consider the possibility of plural or alternative forms of rationality, each with its own distinctive ways of arguing and valuing argument. Even further, these forms can be tragically opposed to each other, as in the case of the *Antigone*, where accepting one form of rationality entails the automatic rejection of the other.) Finally, Raz captures something essential in the individual's refusal or unwillingness to make certain things commensurate with each other. However, I would introduce the distinction that the former is not properly a refusal to *compare*, but rather a refusal to compare *according to the same metric or unit of value*. In the example between friendship and money, many people do (rationally, I think) rank friendship above money, and do not refuse to compare the two.[42]

What most people would refuse to do, however, is to put friendship on a monetary scale and measure it according to a monetary value, which is a very different thing. Rather than incomparability, I think, what the example suggests is (a) that there is no single or unitary metric under which both options can be weighed *and* (b) that if and when an individual tries to create or claim such a metric, certain impossibility (or incommensurability) arises. The incommensurability in this sense arises from the refusal of *co-measurement*, that is from the principled denial to measure the two options according to the forms of rationality proper to only one of them.

3.3 Wiggins: tragic dilemmas and forms of life

I propose to advance now in a different but important direction with the help of David Wiggins.[43] Wiggins claims that individuals often do find rational means to choose and compare among incommensurable options. Some of these choices are made according to criteria such as the "overall choice-worthiness" of one option over the other, or in cases of difficult life choices, "in the light of our overall practical conceptions of how to be or how to live a life."[44] Yet this is in no way to say, in the same way Berlin argued, that these decisions are easy or uncomplicated, and are free from anguish, pain, and even error. Indeed there are what Wiggins calls "tragic dilemmas," in which not only is there no correct, unitary, projectible way for the individual that is pressed to choose, but even if she does choose, and this pushes us a little further than Berlin, there is no guarantee that the choice made will find "an accommodation that we can accept or live out."[45]

Wiggins recalls the example of Sartre's student in World War II, who sought Sartre's advice in deciding either to fight for the resistance against the Nazi occupation and to avenge the death of his brother, or else to stay at home as the only solace for his deeply afflicted mother.[46] As Sartre explains it, the case presents two different modes of action (a concrete and immediate action of help that benefits one individual, and a more general action for the benefit of a national collectivity but more easily frustrated), and two different types of morality (one based on sympathy and personal devotion and charity, and another wider in scope but of less concrete grounding). On the other hand, Sartre claims that no ethical system seems to offer an unequivocal answer as to what to do. Christian morality says things like "love your neighbor," or "choose the hardest way," but Sartre asks, "to whom does one owe the more brotherly love?" and "which way is the hardest?" Also, Kantian morality says to treat persons not as means but as ends in themselves, but in this case, opting for staying at home, thus treating filial duty as an end, may entail treating those who are fighting for the Resistance as a means, and vice versa.[47]

According to Wiggins, in such cases it is a mistake to suppose that rationality can be confected from the thin threads of plain consistency; if anything, he adds poignantly (and pertinently to describe the characters of both

Antigone and Creon), too much emphasis on consistency only makes practical unreasonableness worse. Indeed, each of the options validates one form of life, but in doing so it frustrates another, which may be unbearable. This is why Wiggins suggests the need to reinterpret rationality as "the disposition, episodically exercised . . . to prefer . . . an act or a belief or an attitude in the light of the standards of evaluation and normative ends and ideals that is the substantive work of evidential, axiological, moral, and whatever other reflection to determine"[48] Here, as in Berlin, rationality is transformed into a sort of general ability to discern the stakes of the choice, and to adopt that option more in consonance with one's own overall pattern of life.

This redefinition of rationality opens up a space for the agent's ability to navigate through incommensurable options. At the same time, however, it gives us pause to reflect about its limits, especially as this ability is tested in the world of tragedy. First, it is clear that any eventual decision not only springs from our whole being, but determines the kind of person we will become. However, one is not always able to predict the full consequences of the decisions (in Sartre's example the student feared that his choice to join the Resistance might be diluted by being assigned a menial task in an office), nor to comprehend the significance they may later acquire in life. Thus, even in Wiggins' loose sense, rationality seems to be informed, as the chorus of the *Antigone* will remind us later, by man's radical blindness to the future and embedded in the same context of uncertainty.

Secondly, so far we have assumed that individuals *know* or are capable of knowing the social forms they are to choose between. We know (or have the ability of knowing) what friendship is and what it entails, what obligations, mutual expectations, satisfactions, and worries it brings about and calls for. Some forms of life, however, entail long-lasting, life-learning experiences that one may not be able to discern so clearly. I am not thinking of cases in which the forms of life in question are not available to us anymore, either because they are too distant to our current practices or forever lost in the tides of history (e.g. one can longer choose to be a medieval templar). Even among the various forms of life that one has the possibility of encountering in real life, any eventual decision about them is subject to rationality's cognitive limits as to the kind of life each would afford us, the benefits it would bring, and the sacrifices it would require. (Think, for example, about becoming a professional cello player or choosing to move to a different country: one can never know what these "choices" will mean in the long run). Thus Antigone may courageously advance in the beginning that she is not afraid to die and welcome her death-sentence as a "gain," but once she faces the harsh consequences of her decision, she may reach a different conclusion about the worth of life and the meaning of her death. And the same can be said about the claims made by Creon, for example, about the family.

Finally, following Raz, we have seen that rationality is exercised within modes of valuation proper to the specific social forms in which the agent already participates. These forms establish what is to count as a valid reason, an authoritative assertion, or an argument that is off the mark and misses the point. The issue is whether, and how far, forms of life in which we are already immersed foreclose the consideration of alternatives that are incommensurable to them. This is the case of Sartre's pupil who, by the mere fact of seeking Sartre rather than a priest, made a kind of commitment beforehand to the advice he was to receive. If so, there is some real question as to our ability rationally to consider forms of life that are not just alternative, but, in the context of incommensurability, mutually exclusive to the ones upon which we already stand. Once we accept the form of life represented by Antigone – and all the values, the commitments, and the worldview that go with it – is there not a risk that we are automatically prevented from equally considering those of Creon and Ismene? If so, what is the assurance to say that our choices were "rational" to begin with? Can we be certain, as both Berlin and to some extent also Wiggins pushed us to accept, that we can stand firmly behind those choices?

3.4 Lyotard's differend and the incommensurability of judgment

Trying to unravel this blind spot in the argument may yield a deeper understanding of what is at stake in a tragic conflict such as the one presented in the *Antigone*. I propose to begin with the help of Jean-François Lyotard's alluring concept of the "differend"[49]:

> As distinguished from a litigation, a differend [*différend*] would be a case of conflict, between (at least) two parties, that cannot be equitably resolved for lack of a rule of judgment applicable to both arguments. One side's legitimacy does not imply the other's lack of legitimacy. However, applying a single rule of judgment to both in order to settle their differend as though it were merely a litigation would *wrong* (at least) one of them (and both of them if neither side admits this rule).[50]

In addition to lacking an appropriate rule of judgment for both parties, a differend is further distinguished from litigation by the lack of a common procedure to channel their conflict, and hence of an adequate remedy to redress the harm being done. This distinguishes a wrong [*tort*] proper to the differend, from regular damages [*dommage*]. As Lyotard says: "Damages result from an injury which is inflicted upon the rules of a genre of discourse but which is reparable according to these rules. A wrong results from the fact that the rules of the genre of discourse by which one judges are not those of the judged genre or genres of discourse."[51] Moreover, "the nature of the tribunal that must pronounce upon the case is itself the object of a differend."[52]

Lyotard gives several illustrations, for instance the impossibility of proving the existence of the gas chambers to the satisfaction of a holocaust denier historian whose burden of proof would only be met by a direct eyewitness. Or the impossibility of testifying to the communist character of the Ibanskian society in Zinoviev's novel *The Yawning Heights*, for either you are a communist and accept the determination made by the party, in which case there is no need to testify, or else you do not accept the determination of the party and testify, but then cease to be a communist. Examples in which the logic of the system does not allow, or rather precludes, certain claims from being articulated can be multiplied, for instance in the cases of indigenous people under a system of oppression and colonization, ethnic minorities under a system of slavery and apartheid, or, from a different perspective, wage laborers under a capitalist system which treats labor as a commodity.[53] Therefore the differend is marked by absences: of a common language between the parties; of a common procedure to channel their conflict; of an equitable rule of judgment; of an adequate remedy to redress the wrong; or of an agreed-upon tribunal. The differend is the deficit, remainder, or leftover of these encounters.

The first thing to remark in Lyotard's definition is the use of legal terminology. By speaking about litigation, parties, cases, rules of judgment, damages, injury, etc., Lyotard gives the issue an unmistakable legal flavor. What interests me most about this *juridification* is that, almost imperceptibly, it brings to light the symbolic structure of adjudication which had been absent before. If, thus far, we have spoken of an individual confronted with a choice between incommensurable options, the picture now enlarges and reveals a third party called to adjudicate a conflict between (at least) two parties. Secondly, Lyotard assumes that the person confronted with such a task does not want to do wrong, or to wrong anyone. We may say, in other words, that the person faced with the task of adjudicating such an incommensurable conflict is committed to justice (to doing justice or to avoiding its opposite).

The combination of these two elements – the symbolic structure of adjudication and the commitment to justice – provides the groundwork for a supplementary distinction between two types of incommensurability, beyond Lyotard's differend. Thus we can distinguish between the *incommensurability of choice* and the *incommensurability of judgment*. The key factor in this distinction is the disparate normative grip that each of the rival options holds on the one making the decision (choice or judgment). In cases of *choice* both alternatives make equally compelling demands upon the individual, but the latter retains the *privilege* (in the technical legal sense) of favoring either one of the options – as I favored friendship over money, or Sartre's student decided to seek him out rather than a priest. On the occasions that Wiggins labeled tragic dilemmas, the need for a choice may generate a deep sense of anxiety and anguish in the individual, but the person making the choice cannot be properly accused of committing an injustice. Here, it makes all the sense to recall Sartre's maxim "we are condemned to be free." In contrast, in cases of *judgment*, the equally legitimate claims of both parties must be upheld as a matter of *right*: discriminating against one of the parties is failing to uphold the commitment to justice, that is to wrong and to do wrong. This too is the situation of those holding the jurisdictional office. The institutional position of the judge forces him to posit that each of the parties in conflict is equally entitled to and deserving of justice.

Note also that the psycho-social structure of these two types of incommensurability differs. In the context of choice, the frame of mind of the individual is marked by anxiety, anguish, agony, and the like.[54] There is the deep psychological uneasiness of coming to terms and living with the consequences of one's choices. In contrast, the incommensurability of judgment forces us to move beyond, say, the existential wonderings of a Hamlet to an altogether different sphere of justice, the realm of obligations, duties, burdens, conscientiousness, and accountability, where the judge must deploy a vigilant and scrupulous care for the concern of both parties. Significantly, she must move within a justificatory scheme that accommodates not only the internal dilemma, but its external justification, marking the transition from the *morality of choice* to the *responsibility of judgment*.[55] This allows us to make a further distinction between *moral dilemmas* (applicable to the context of choice), and *incommensurable conflicts* proper (applicable to the context of judgment).

Different, too, are the consequences of any eventual decision. Following Berlin, we said that choosing between incommensurable options entails the sacrifice of the option not chosen. He also argued that choosing is inherent to rationality and being human. However, a third party confronted with an incommensurable conflict would be actively responsible for doing wrong, that is of infringing the rights of one of the parties, which cannot be equally rationalized. That is, a judgment that inevitably wrongs one of the parties cannot be justified, as Berlin would have us do, with appeals to rationality. Should this lead us to conclude that in the context of incommensurability judgment ought to be suspended?

This stance has a certain appeal and resonates strongly in some intellectual circles.[56] However, once we acknowledge that the conflict is *real* and not an artificially created hypothetical, we are no longer afforded that option.[57] By shutting our eyes to it we cannot make the conflict disappear, turn the claims of both parties less demanding, or diminish the need and the urgency to do it justice. Furthermore, both the decision to make a judgment and the decision to defer judgment are, in a true sense, judgments. Just as every omission is a form of action, refusal to decide is itself a decision, which generates its own unwanted consequences and beneficiaries. Either *by* us or *for* us, judgments will be made, and there is no certainty that suspending judgment will result in an increment of justice or in a correlative diminution of injustice.

Putting the issue like this should help us to take a different direction than Berlin. Berlin, I believe, was right in his intuition that human beings are often faced with decisions between ultimate ends, not all of which are compatible with each other, and which require necessarily the sacrifice of some. Where I believe he slipped is in linking such necessary action to the demands of rationality, for no rational argument justifies doing wrong to any of the parties in conflict. If judgment remains necessary, I would suggest this necessity is linked to the pragmatics of *action* (and the corollary demands of justice), but not to human rationality. Judging between incommensurables remains actually a *tragic necessity*, because even though there is no certainty that there will be any gain by acting, there is no other alternative but to try.

In the sense given to it now, this type of incommensurability does not stem simply from the absence of common language, procedure, rule of judgment, remedy, or agreed-upon tribunal, but from the necessity of judging these encounters justly in spite of these absences. The incommensurability of judgment points towards the legal and ethical impossibility of rendering justice to both parties simultaneously. This gives us a clue to separating the incommensurable conflict from the differend: whereas the differend refers to the deficit, residue, or untranslatable remainder of the encounter, the incommensurability expands over the totality of the encounter, and encompasses its whole structure of signification.[58] Equally important, this incommensurability refers properly not to the deficit in the communication between the parties – although this may be part of it as well – but to the predicament of a third party who is faced with the twofold task of comprehending and presiding over it.

Rebranding Berlin's original conception, then we could reformulate the incommensurability of judgment as: *the juridical impossibility of adjudicating a serious conflict between two equally rational and legitimate parties, each of whom makes mutually exclusive and totalizing demands that must be respected as a matter of right, where the pragmatics of action requires judgment, yet where the latter is no guarantee of an increment of justice.*

3.5 Rancière's disagreement and the staging of the conflict

Before confronting the *Antigone* directly, we should undertake a final step with the help of Jacques Rancière's concept of disagreement [*mésentente*]. According to Rancière, disagreement is not the conflict between one who says white and another who says black. Rather, "[i]t is the conflict between one who says white and another who also says white but does not understand the same thing by it or does not understand that the other is saying the same thing in the name of whiteness."[59] Disagreement must therefore be distinguished from misconstruction, which implies that at least one of the parties in conflict does not know what she is saying through ignorance, dissimulation, or delusion. Nor is disagreement a simple misunderstanding, which stems from the imprecise nature of words. Disagreement has nothing to do with more or less transparent or opaque linguistic contents, but instead with what it means to be a being that uses words to argue, where there is a dispute over the object of the discussion and the capacity of those who are arguing about it.

Disagreement does not reside in the linguistic mismatch of phrase regimens and the untranslatability that these yield (as in Lyotard), nor is it well contained within an ideal-speech situation where participants are able to reach inter-subjective agreements through the logic and force of the better argument (as in Habermas' theory of communicative action). This is so because, "[b]efore any confrontation of interests and values, before any assertions are submitted to the demands for validation between established partners, there is the dispute over the object of dispute, the dispute over the existence of the dispute and the parties confronting each other in it."[60] In fact, "[i]n any social discussion in which there is actually anything to discuss . . . the place, the object, and the subjects of discussion are themselves in dispute and must in the first instance be tested."[61] The polemical situation of disagreement often involves situations in which one of the parties refuses to recognize one of the features of the disagreement (its place, its object, its subjects). The primary concern of disagreement is therefore a dispute over the existence of a dispute, over the status of those that are parties to it, and over the stage in which their disagreement can be played out.[62]

Rancière offers the historical example of the revolt of the Roman plebeians, their retreat into the Aventine Hill, the ambassadorship of Menenius Agrippa, and the eventual return of the plebs to order recorded by the Roman historian Livy.[63] Rather than focusing on Livy's account, however, Rancière follows Pierre-Simon Ballanche's retelling of this tale, in which the Roman historian is criticized for being incapable of understanding the plebeian uprising as anything other than a revolt devoid of all meaning. Ballanche's imaginative rewriting of this historical event focuses instead on the discussions between the senators and the speech acts of the plebs. By centering the quarrel over the issue of speech itself, Ballanche performs a "restaging of the conflict" in which the entire issue involves finding out whether there exists a common stage where plebeians and patricians can debate anything.

The position of the plebeians is straightforward: they deny that there is anything up for discussion for the simple reason that the plebs are not entitled to representation and *cannot* speak. Faced with this kind of opposition, the plebeians perform a series of speech acts that mimic those of the patricians and pronounce speeches, consult their oracles, and elect their own representatives. In doing so, the plebeians claim a place in the symbolic order of the city in which they do not yet have any effective power. According to Rancière, all this has the unexpected consequence that, when Menenius Agrippa is sent to deliver his famous speech against their revolt, that very gesture raises them to the category of equals (even when Agrippa's speech wishes precisely to deny them that status). The Roman Senate, composed by wise old men in

Ballanche's story, is forcefully led to conclude that since the plebs have now become creatures of speech, there is nothing left to do but to talk to them.[64]

In Rancière's view, Ballanche's staging of this "paradoxical community" – paradoxical because there was no community prior to its being staged – "cannot be identified [as in Habermas] with a model of communication between established partners concerning objects and ends belonging to a common language."[65] This does not mean, in the other direction, that the stage is "reduced [as in Lyotard] to the incommunicability of languages, [or to] an impossibility of understanding linked to the heterogeneity of language games."[66] The choice between the enlightenment of rational communication and the murkiness of inherent violence or irreducible difference is a false dichotomy. For him, the real dilemma lies not in the fact that people speak "different languages," but in the need for "creating a stage [between people who speak different languages] on which . . . the conflict can be played out."[67]

Rancière offers further historical examples. During the trial of the revolutionary Auguste Blanqui in 1832, the judge asked him to state his profession and Blanqui replied that he was a "proletarian." The magistrate immediately objected to this response arguing that to be a proletarian is not a profession. The judge's reaction sets up Blanqui's proverbial declaration: but "it is the profession of thirty million Frenchmen who live off their labor and who are deprived of their political rights!" After this response, the judge then agreed to have the court clerk list proletarian as a new profession. As Rancière explains, everything turns on the single word "profession": for the magistrate, profession means job, trade, or occupation, and in this sense it is clear to him that the term proletarian does not designate any such occupation. Blanqui gives the term profession an altogether different meaning. For him, the term proletariat does not designate a determinate body of people, but the collectivity that is unaccounted for in the ordinary political process and that, as such, exist only in the declaration in which they are named as a class deprived of political rights.

Another example is offered by Jeanne Deroin in 1849, when she presented herself as a candidate for a legislative election in which she could not run because women were not allowed to do so. In presenting herself up for election, she demonstrates the contradiction within a universal suffrage which excluded her gender from any such universality. Jeanne Deroin's performative demonstration reveals the subject "women" both as necessarily included in the sovereign French people enjoying universal suffrage and equality before the law, and yet as simultaneously excluded from it. This goes beyond the simple denunciation of an inconsistency within the system, suggests Rancière, for it further stages the contradiction that lies at the heart of the French political community in a bold attempt to reconfigure it as a whole. It is this newly formed "community" which alone makes possible the expression of an injustice that could not have been denounced before.

Rancière wonders whether it is not necessarily the case, then, that this description already presupposes some level of understanding between the parties, prior to the staging of their disagreement. If so, could it not be argued, along with Habermas, that the interlocutors share at least the principles of an inter-subjective or common grammar that could enable them ideally to reach a potential agreement? Opposing this conclusion, Rancière argues that, while all interlocution supposes some sort of comprehension of its content, it does not necessarily presuppose a horizon of *shared* understanding. For example, that a command is understood by an inferior does not entail that the person uttering the command and the person carrying it out share the same understanding of the command, or even of what it means "to understand" it. One way to interpret the ordinary sentence "Do you understand?" actually denies the need for "understanding" anything at all. The false interrogative could be then rephrased as follows: "There is nothing for you to understand; all you have to do is obey." Therefore, even if carrying an order successfully implies some level of understanding at both ends of the command, there might still be a gap between two accepted meanings of "to understand," each of which establishes the type of "success" appropriate to it.

Where the assumption of understanding is in question, says Rancière, "it is necessary to simultaneously produce both the argument and the situation in which it is to be understood, the object of the discussion and the world in which it features as object."[68] This entails a peculiar platform of argument: "[T]he . . . subject that gets included on it as speaker has to behave as though such a stage existed, as though there were a common world of argument – which is eminently reasonable *and* eminently unreasonable, eminently wise and resolutely subversive, since such a world does not exist."[69] This often involves using the threads and the materials that already exist in that culture albeit with a different meaning, and creating for them, as a result, an altogether different context. In the example of the French worker, Blanqui uses the language of human rights already inscribed in the Declaration of Rights of Man to demonstrate that the dominant social practices are exclusionary of that language. Yet such a "demonstration" is always both an argument and an opening up of the world in which the argument can be received and considered as such. In this task, Rancière suggests that there can be no strict division between a rational order of argument and a poetic or metaphorical order of language, for they are "at the same time rational arguments and 'poetic' metaphors,"[70] "at once arguments and world openers."[71] In situations of disagreement, the utterances of a speaker are oftentimes "stolen" and ironically tossed back at their authors with distorted meanings to say something that was previously unsayable. This is precisely the way Antigone is able to transform Creon's language of gain [*kerdos*], friendship [*philia*], and enmity [*echthra*] and use it against him. Therefore the logic of demonstration is indissolubly an aesthetic of expression.[72]

Since the dispute must always be won on the pre-existing conditions and the constantly re-enacted distribution of heterogeneous languages, assessing it often involves the participation of a voice in the third person, most notably in the form of public opinion. Rancière calls this intervention the "objectifying function of commentary,"[73] which is discursively enacted in the form of the "they" that each of the parties appeals to in defense of its respective positions.[74] This "they" is not a fixed position external to the discourse, but a function of the speech that can be used interchangeably by every speaker, with the main function of making apparent the situation of disagreement.[75] As a result, "[t]he play of the third person is essential to the logic of . . . discussion, which is never a simple dialogue."[76]

In sum, disagreement occurs out of the encounters between heterogeneous worlds, which are nevertheless able to express themselves *as though* inhabiting a common world of argument. This common world does not pre-exist the concrete manifestation of the conflict, which is why the staging of the disagreement is generative, perhaps, of possibilities that are only thinkable in the narrative configuration in which they are articulated. For example, Sophocles' text – like Ballanche's rewriting of Livy's story – enacts a conflict between Antigone and Creon that could not have been possible, in that exact form, in either Thebes or Athens, where it is hardly imaginable that a young woman could have claimed to replace the law of the political leader with a law of her own. This does not mean that the conflict *itself* does not exist prior to its staging, as could be inferred from Lyotard's differend.[77] Still, it is Sophocles' text which makes possible that the clash between Antigone and Creon might be represented as a conflict between two alternative and equally compelling normative universes.

Rancière's analysis is helpful in visualizing the various dimensions at play in the staging of the incommensurable conflict between Antigone and Creon. First, there is the level of their dispute and the kind of arguments and gestures they each must make in order to be considered parties to a conflict. Second, there is the dimension of the conflict that addresses the audience as a third party to this conflict (both *in* the play – i.e. the body of citizens that both Antigone and Creon think are on their side – and *of* the play, both ancient and modern). Third, there is the textual level which imagines this conflict for the first time (a conflict which would have been unthinkable in either Thebes or Athens). But there is a further, and most fundamental, passage involved in the activity of understanding Sophocles' narrative. Even though Rancière does not say it explicitly, this further staging involves not the parties of the dispute, nor even Sophocles's representation of it, but the aesthetic sensibility of those of us who are now observing and trying to comprehend the incommensurable conflict between Antigone and Creon. This fourth and final dimension brings back to our own writing the responsibility of re-enacting, without diluting it, the incommensurable conflict within Sophocles' play.

3.6 Incommensurability, *Antigone*, and law

The conflict between Antigone and Creon is a clash of *nomoi* at once absolute and incommensurable, where each of the sides maintains equally ultimate and mutually incompatible demands. Theirs is not an abstract conflict between family and religion on the one side, and law and civic authority on the other. This description would assume two perfectly delimited camps in advance, irrespective of how this conflict is played out in practice. But parties do not pre-exist the particular conflict, for they are uniquely constituted by it. As Rancière explains, "[p]arties do not exist prior to the conflict they name and in which they are counted as parties."[78] In the case at hand, the prohibition of burying Polyneices' body generates the occasion on which Antigone and Creon construct their respective normative worlds, not in the abstract, but in response to that particular situation. Each position is informed by their individual characters and worldviews, wherein Antigone and Creon hold contradictory views about the meaning of family and filial duty, the aims and purposes of the ethical life and the *polis*, the strictures of friendship and enmity, the grounds for love and hate, and the boundaries of life and death.

It would seem at first that Antigone does not want any part in the dealings of the *polis*, but simply to be let alone to fulfill her duty towards her unburied brother. Similarly, Creon seems to be concerned only with the task of government and civic authority. Accordingly, the canonical view of this play since Hegel is that each character wants to inhabit his or her own particular area: Antigone, the area of family and family relations; Creon, that of the state and its institutions. Such a reading, however, is complicated by the undeniable fact of their encounter, a real and actual clash that demonstrates some point of intersection. This intersection, which obstructs the view of incommensurability as represented by two parallel lines, functions rather as the principle of attraction around which the parties deploy an arsenal of arguments, images, and symbols. On a closer inspection, then, it can be observed that Antigone claims the force of law for her own law, and that Creon's decree clearly extends to the familial and religious realms. Arguably, the two fight for the supremacy of the normative realm: the area of experience concerned with lawful and unlawful, just and unjust, right and wrong. This shared ambition to impose their law as *the* law for the entire city forces them to clash inevitably.

Their clash displays the *dialectical negativity* proper to incommensurability, where each party wishes their views to prevail to the exclusion of the other's. Listening to Antigone, one gets the impression that her concerns for her brother are the only ones that matter, and that we ought to disregard Creon's without loss. The same is true about Creon: he believes his principles to be exhaustive and self-sufficient, and does not leave room for those of Antigone. Moreover, each denies the other the capacity or legitimacy to be a party to the conflict. Creon denies Antigone, as a young and female member of his own family, the capacity to speak authoritatively on matters of law and civic duty. In turn, Antigone denies Creon the legitimacy to rule on a matter that oversteps his authority and to issue a decree prohibiting the burial of her brother. Lastly, each speaks as the perfect embodiment of the community and its laws. Thus both make claims which are exclusionary (of the other's) and totalizing (of the normative field).

Antigone and Creon clash over the same normative field that they each would define differently, in fact, using the same terms of value although with completely different meanings. Their dispute about the meanings of *philia* (which for Creon entails friendships established within the *polis* and for Antigone the love for one's loved ones and the family); the underlying principles of the *polis* (the strict obedience to its appointed leaders or the interpersonal bonds that antecede and make it possible); what constitutes a "gain" (Creon's monetary value or Antigone's desire for honor and glory); what counts as a proper act of "enmity" (either Polyneices' treason or Creon's own prohibition to bury him); and, to be sure, what counts as proper *nomos* (Creon's decree or Antigone's unwritten laws) – none of these is a simple question of semantics. They are rather expressive of alternative worlds of value and heterogeneous languages.

Antigone and Creon "understand each other" just so that they can oppose each other, mixing both rational and poetic language *as though* they inhabited the same world of argument. This barely perceptible common stage does not allow us to posit a shared horizon of common understanding between the two. Here understanding is clearly not shared. Least of all can we describe them as participants in a dialogue with the purpose of reaching rational, or any other kind of, agreement. If anything, they show the dangers of a strict adherence to rationality. Antigone and Creon *despise* each other and use their reasons not as a means towards better comprehension, but as weapons to crush the other.

And yet, they both can be said to have "reason" on their side and there is some level of rationality embedded in their positions. One must understand what it is to see the body of one's brother exposed and feel the grievance of being formally prohibited from taking any action. Still, treason is not lightly to be condoned in the aftermath of an internecine war instigated by it and hence Creon's position is not without merit. As Berlin would have insisted, to downplay their disagreement as the result of a deficiency in rationality is not to take conflict seriously enough.

Interestingly, the *Antigone* instantiates the distinction established between the two types of incommensurability. Antigone, the character, faces no incommensurability of *choice*, no dilemma whatsoever as to what she must do and where her loyalties should reside. She is absolutely certain that her decision to bury Polyneices is right, despite Creon's prohibition. So is Creon: there is no doubt in his mind that he is acting in the best interest of the *polis* and that he has the support of both the citizens and the gods. In contrast, Antigone's sister Ismene can be said to face an incommensurability of *choice*. For her, the duty to bury a dead family member and the obedience owed to authority make equally valid and compelling demands. She not only faces the anxiety of choosing, but also the realization that the choice she is actually making may be too hard to accept or to live with, all of which leads her to request "forgiveness" from her loved ones.

In turn, the audience is confronted with an incommensurability of *judgment*, for it is in the position of judging a conflict between two incommensurable parties, each of which is right in its own terms. This is not to claim a false equivalency between the two parties, for there are clear inequalities in the positions of Antigone and Creon. The two are equal only as parties of a conflict that is made possible only in Sophocles' text and by the audience trying to comprehend it. To become a member of the audience, that is to adopt the position (and the responsibilities) of the audience, compels one to act *as if* he or she were committed to both, that is to comprehend and to be just to both. Paradoxically, the more one tries to comprehend each party, the more one is distanced from the other; the more one penetrates the conflict, the more one realizes the severity and depth of it. At this point, judgment appears unjust when possible, impossible when just. The incommensurability of judgment refers to this moment of inapprehensible simultaneity, not just to the deficit or remainder, but to its entire structure of signification.

Trying to find a shortcut to this fundamental dilemma, for instance by arguing that Creon's decree was wrong *ab initio*, trivializes the tragedy, and hence cripples our ability successfully to experience and to engage with it to the fullest. The a priori commitment to commensurability in this case falls short of comprehension, for it prevents the argument of each party to be deployed, the stakes to be raised, their implications known, and the contradictions and potential inconsistencies unveiled. The audience, which is the judge of the legal conflict, must therefore construct the position of each of the parties in a way that reveals this incommensurability, prior to and before rendering any kind of definitive judgment.

Acknowledging this incommensurability and the moment of impasse it brings with it is not the end of judgment, for the tragedy does not conclude with the clash between the two protagonists. The play shows developments and transformations that will force us to re-evaluate this position, and which might enable us, in time, to unglue the current situation of impasse. This will lead us to observe, in the following chapters, different *spatial relations* with and among the characters (for example, in the next encounter between the two sisters, the failed dialogue between Haemon and his father, and Antigone's final lament), and to identify various *temporal motions* through which judgments are being performed along with the narrative progression of the drama. As I will show in Chapters 5 and 7, these various spatial and temporal dimensions are part of the experience of judging, not just in the *Antigone* but in every legal conflict, and must be incorporated in any account of this activity.

This leads us to some final considerations about the general implications of incommensurability for law and legal judgment. First, for Antigone's argument to become a valid and respectable legal claim with the audience, it is necessary for her to make a remarkable imaginative effort, which allows her to *invent* the memorable expression about the "unswerving laws of the gods."[79] Therefore the incommensurable conflict provides the opportunity for generating new and sophisticated legal language which was inexpressible before. This act of "rendering visible the invisible" can help the critic to identify blind spots in the system and spaces in need of social reform, which is why giving voice to the incommensurability can have potentially transformative effects. Second, but equally important, upon the risk of remaining deaf to the kind of wrongs, injustices, and inequalities that cannot be properly articulated in the current state of affairs, the staging of the incommensurability requires the vigilant and timely intervention of an audience that will *recognize* the incommensurability. Finally, the incommensurability of judgment increases the judicial concern of not knowing how to decide, and yet having to do so. This would perhaps lead to a different style of judging, guided by the virtues of humility and reflexivity (concerning one's own authority to speak), capacity to listen (concerning the voices and narratives of others), and personal responsibility (concerning the object of judgment). Before an incommensurable conflict, principles such as Dworkin's "one right answer" seem not just misguided, but unhelpful.

Chapter 4

Antigone, Part II: Transitions

This will be a time of introspection and uncertainty. Questions will be asked more than answered, problems raised more than solved. We will feel Ismene's affection for her sister and the Chorus' impending sense of disaster. We will consider Haemon's defense of his bride and the primeval force of Eros. And we will walk along with Antigone, lonely, wretched, and forsaken, to inquire, with the Chorus in the end, what the tragedy keeps in store and cannot be anticipated.

4.1 Ismene comes forward (lines 526–81)

When Ismene enters the scene, Creon asks her about her involvement in the offense. Ismene answers that she did it, if her sister agrees to it. Antigone says that justice will not allow it, since Ismene refused to help her and she has no regard for those who love only in words. Ismene begs her sister not to reject her and to let her die with her. Antigone tells her not to lay claim to something she has not done. Her own death will suffice. Ismene asks, What kind of life is left for her, deprived of Antigone? "Ask Creon," replies Antigone, "your concern is all for him." Ismene feels hurt, and asks what pleasure Antigone derives from it. Antigone says that doing so hurts herself as well. Ismene insists on offering some help. Antigone says "{S}ave yourself!" and states *"{Y}ou chose life, and I chose death" (555). Ismene responds that she did not remain silent, and Antigone, "some think you are right and sensible* [kalôs . . . phronein], *others that I am" (557). They can both be equally faulted, says Ismene. "Take heart," concludes Antigone, "you are alive, but my life has been dead long ago"(559–60).*

Creon, who has not intervened so far, cannot overcome his perplexity, declaring that one sister has suddenly lost her senses whereas the other was born that way. He then says that Antigone is as good as dead. Ismene asks whether he is about to deprive his son of his bride. Creon says his son can find "other fields to plough." And Ismene: "Not as fitting for both." After a few more remarks from both sides, the Chorus[1] *intervenes: It appears that her* [Antigone's] *death is already decided. Creon agrees with the elders: "Yes, by you and me!" (577). Creon orders the guards not to let any of them loose, because even those who are bold try to escape when they see death closing in.*

In this scene, there are three actors on the stage instead of two, which is Sophocles' own innovation according to Aristotle.[2] This not only intensifies the speed and agility of the exchanges, but it allows the audience to observe the interchanges through the eyes of each interlocutor, as well as through those of a third person who watches and responds to this interaction. Such an additional perspective enriches the perspectives of judgment, for it enables audiences to assess how the words of the characters are being interpreted by, and affecting, this third party.[3] The scene is constructed in two halves: the first with Antigone and Ismene as interlocutors and Creon (and the Chorus) as their audience; the second with Ismene and Creon as interlocutors and Antigone as their audience.

The last time we saw Ismene and Antigone together, the two had parted ways dramatizing a sharp separation. Ismene wishes now to bridge that distance by coming closer to her sister. She offers to share responsibility for the burial and to be a fellow traveler in her sister's voyage of suffering. Speaking the language of sisterhood and emotional intimacy, Ismene's words demonstrate her generosity of spirit and heartfelt sentiments for Antigone. From this perspective, then, Ismene cannot be treated as merely "the hero's foil,"[4] for she represents an alternative way of understanding and framing the tragic conflict.

However it may doubted whether Ismene's normative position has shifted in any significant way. Ismene may speak of not being "ashamed" to share her sister's lot and express longing to share her honor, but she does not have the strong sense of pride and the conviction that animated Antigone. Certainly, Ismene's passive acceptance of punishment does not amount to an expression of a new legal argument. Ismene recognizes that she tried to dissuade her sister until the end (which suggests that Ismene may still keep some reservations about the whole incident), and that the two of them can be equally "faulted." Here, the use of the word *hamartia* (558), which conveys the idea of transgression and trespass, entails the admission of a breach (against the laws of Creon?) that Antigone is not willing to make. For Ismene and Antigone alike the burial is an appropriate way to honor the dead, but Ismene does not claim that Antigone was necessarily right in everything she did, or that she sees things eye to eye with her. Despite her best intentions, Ismene's advance does not impress Antigone as having sufficient normative standing. In order to lay claim to the honor, it is necessary to perform the deed and to defend it as a requirement of law and justice. Measured against both standards, Ismene's proposition to share the blame falls short.

This does not make Ismene's sympathy for her sister – and her desire to comfort her – any less real. Thus Ismene is understandably hurt when Antigone accuses her of being on the side of Creon and of showing concern only for him. Ismene cannot endure, and criticizes Antigone's effort to turn her down. Ismene's reproach has an unexpected effect in Antigone, who does not want to hurt her sister either. Antigone's hostility gradually recedes and now she attempts to assuage Ismene: just as Antigone has come to terms with the path she has chosen, Ismene should not suffer over hers. Antigone appears to have accepted her sister as she is, and not as she would like her to be. She cannot expect Ismene to think and act contrary to her own view of the world, against her *bios*. In the end, she admits something she would have never acknowledged before: "[S]ome approve your wisdom, others mine" (557). Ismene too understands that the path that Antigone has chosen, painful as it is, is for her sister to decide. Although the scene thus ends in separation, this is a kind of distance based on a newly found respect for each other. Their earlier, mutually insular trajectories thus come into contact not through agreement, but through the acceptance of each other's different normative choices.

This subtle but significant transformation completely eludes Creon, for whom the language of mutual appreciation between the sisters remains foreign. Creon cannot fathom why Ismene wishes to share the penalty for something in which she has not participated and he responds in a way that empties Ismene's gesture of all meaning. He concludes that Ismene must have gone mad (while Antigone was mad long ago). Such a response is likely to create a dissonance between Creon and the audience, as the latter is able to understand, in a way that Creon simply cannot, the emotional and normative complexities of the scene.

Such dissonance creates also a space for the audience to perceive Creon's coldness of character, underscored in the second half of the scene in his dialogue with Ismene (for Creon, Antigone is already dead and there is no need to address her). Here Ismene reveals something we did not know before. Antigone is betrothed to Haemon, Creon's own son.[5] Ismene's defense of Antigone and Haemon's "fitting relationship"[6] reveals an aspect of Antigone that may have gone unnoticed, and we are now in the position to grasp the extent of Antigone's sacrifice: in order to defend the right of her dead brother, Antigone must forgo a good marriage and the prospect of creating a new family and having children with Haemon. Creon is unmoved. In his mind, Antigone's act of defiance means she is a "bad woman," and to imagine a woman like her as a daughter-in-law is inconceivable. The audience could expect that Creon would not be persuaded by such an argument, but his coarse response "there are other fields to plough" shows particular insensitivity, and does not take notice of how this decision may affect his son. Creon reaffirms Antigone's death sentence, and believes that nothing has changed. But for the audience, the fact that Antigone and Haemon are betrothed reveals another aspect of the decree to consider, namely that beyond its effects on the two sisters, the decree may have broader and unpredictable implications.

4.2 Second *stasimon*: disaster returns again (lines 582–625)

With Antigone and Ismene both off the stage, the Chorus intones an enigmatic and somewhat somber song about the evils that threaten the descendants of the Labdacids and the house of Oedipus. The ode has two sets of strophes and antistrophes that I reproduce somewhat loosely:[7]

Fortunate [eudaimones] *are those whose life never tastes of evil. Once a house is shaken by the gods, no part of ruin* [atas] *is wanting, from generation to generation; like the swell of the deep sea, when the roaring wind from Thrace drives blustering over the water, and the groaning cliffs repel the smack of wind and angry breakers. In the House of the Labdacids, I see* [horômai] *how ancient sorrows rise again; disaster is linked with disaster, some god shattering them, and they find no deliverance. There gleamed a shimmering light on the last of the royal blood of Oedipus; but Death comes again with blood-stained ax*[8] *of the infernal gods, and hews the sapling down, aided by the "folly of reasoning"* [logou t'anoia] *and "fury of mind"* [phrenôn erinus].

O Zeus, what mortal power can quell your power? Neither the all-snaring sleep, nor the unwearying years can overcome you, but throughout time, ageless, you rule in the radiant splendor of Olympus. For today, and in all past time, and through all the time to come, this is the law: "[T]o none among mortals shall nothing great come without disaster." Hope [elpis] *springs high, and to many a man Hope brings comfort. Yet to others she is nothing but fond illusion. Swiftly they come to ruin, as when a man treads unaware on hot fire. For it was a wise man that first said: To the man whom gods will ruin, one day shall evil seem good, in his twisted judgment: He comes in short time to fell disaster.*

Somewhat bewildered by the dark turn of events, the Chorus engages in a general reflection about the events they are witnessing and the tragedy that is being unraveled before their eyes. The Chorus' song stages and gives form to the kind of questions that the audience itself may be asking about the dramatic action. The ode is thus prompted by the concrete dramatic events and as a response to them, but it turns into something deeper that conveys a far-reaching tragic vision. It has been remarked that the ode depicts a cosmology and moral universe that reverberates with ideas of Solon, Aeschylus, and Hesiod, and as such is profoundly rooted in the poetic tradition.[9] However, these ancient ideas find new and concrete manifestations in the Chorus' keen observations, as the vision zooms in and out from the dramatic action.[10]

In the first strophe, the Chorus reflects on the (mis)fortune of being struck by disaster, as exemplified in the house that, once shaken by the gods, finds no release from generation to generation. Unlike Aeschylus' universe of hereditary curses,[11] no moral justification is needed nor offered here for the gods to shake a house. The gods' influence is better understood as the embodiment of powerful forces beyond man's control, like the swelling deep sea and the Thracian wind. A house shaken by these elemental forces is lifted as a dark cloud of mud is heaved from the bottom of the sea, only to be smashed against the wall of disaster. Disaster, then, as tragedy in general, is the solid wall against which mortals crash, like the groaning cliffs breaking the waves blustered by the wind. The ultimate causes for it remain unknown and largely irrelevant: only their felt presence is certain.

Indeed, in the second strophe the Chorus uses a verb of perception (*horômai*: *horaô* = to see) to state that the newborn shoot of the House of Oedipus is being chopped off. This is not so much an inquiry into what is causing it as a statement about the situation they *observe* and the anticipation of the consequences they already *see* coming. Antigone, as the last shoot of the Royal House, could have been able to escape the cycle of destruction that razed House Oedipus and destroyed the lives of Oedipus, Yocasta, and their two sons Eteocles and Polyneices. But this glimmer of hope is short-lived, and is being cut off like the branch of an old tree. The nether gods seem at work again, this time aided by the "fury of mind" and the "senseless reasoning" already witnessed on the stage. As Gerald Else argues, the external forces are therefore internalized in the attitudes that can be observed in the *phren* [mind] and the *logos* [reasoning] of the individuals.[12]

Without clearly attributing these traits to anyone in particular, the third strophe shifts again to a general plane and brings the perspective of Zeus, unconquered by the otherwise irresistible forces of sleep and old age. Compared with the relative puniness of mortals, the image of Zeus as reigning supreme throughout all time confers stability and order to this universe of apparently unruly forces. The Chorus concludes by reaffirming the law, stated as an immanent law of reality, that nothing too great comes to the life of mortals without its accompanying ruin. This introduces the ideas of measure and cosmic balance in the universe, in the same way that the Ionian philosopher Anaximander explained the eternal cycle of life as a continuous process of atonement according to its own rules of justice.[13] The Chorus reaffirms the "natural" tendency of things to balance each other out over time, and to bring low excess, transgression, and the overstepping of boundaries as also Solon, the famous Athenian lawgiver and poet, had forewarned.[14]

From a mortal's perspective, there is still something fortuitous, almost random, in the way tragedy strikes and spares no one. Absolutely everyone can have a blow of disaster, without warning and at any moment, irrespective of how much foresight or intelligence they apply to prevent or anticipate it. Mortals can be comforted in the hopes that they have done everything possible to avert the strikes of fortune. But they may end up being crushed despite their best plans, in which case their hopes result in nothing but fond illusion.[15] Ultimately, however, the fact that disaster can crush the innocent and guilty alike does not eliminate moral responsibility, which is the essential part, for those who mistake wrong for right are to tread on hot fire sooner rather than later. The ode thus ends with an invitation for the audience to keep an eye on every action and to be ready to judge them according to their merit. Even in the worst of circumstances, the justice and injustice of every action must be assessed, if mortals are to learn anything at all. The ode thus functions at two levels, first by presenting a world of distant and incontrollable forces of nature, and then by bringing these down to the level of the characters and their respective behavior.

From a closer distance, the Chorus appears to ponder on Antigone's fate. Her daring breach of Creon's laws may lead her to be crushed, as the "angry breakers" are smashed against the cliff of disaster. Any hopes that Antigone may be spared hang from a thread, now that the ax of death is ready to fall. Creon has accused Antigone of being "mad" (using the same word Ismene used to define her act as "senseless" [*anous*] in the beginning), and the Chorus' admonition about the fury of mind and senseless reasoning may apply to her, as having precipitated her own fall.

Nevertheless, the audience may not entirely agree with Creon's judgment, since he failed to perceive the slight shift in the position of Antigone, who has come closer to understanding and respecting Ismene. Moreover, the two sisters agree that the burial of Polyneices is an honor owed the dead, which Creon ordained to keep above the ground without their dues. Finally, his arguments against Ismene are anything but sensible, without consideration of how his decision may affect his son. Therefore, even though the ode remains vague, there may be elements to consider whether it might not be Creon's lack of awareness which can eventually lead to treading on hot fire.

4.3 Haemon: son and groom (lines 626–780)

The elders observe the entrance of Haemon and wonder: "Is he angry at the fate of his bride-to-be and grieving at the baffled hope of marriage?" Creon asks his son whether he has come in rage against him, or as dear [philoi] *to his side. Haemon replies "I'm yours"* [sos eimi] *and assures that no marriage will ever be as highly valued as his father's guidance. Haemon's words reassure Creon, who says the best parents can wish for is to beget obedient children, so that they can requite their enemies and honor their friends. He tells his son never to be robbed of his senses* [phrenas] *for the sake of a bad woman. Therefore, Haemon should cast Antigone away as an enemy, for she is the only one among all citizens who dared to rebel and did so openly. His principles are clear: "Show me the man who knows how to rule his household well and I'll show you someone fit to rule the state." Only those who know to be disciplined, like the soldier in battlefield, will one day be able to give commands, but anarchy destroys families and cities. The Chorus admits that unless they are led astray by their old age, Creon seems to have spoken sensible words.*

Haemon confirms that good sense [phrenas] is *the best gift bestowed on mortals, and although he cannot say that his father spoke without reason, other people might be reasonable as well. Haemon reports the rumor that the city is mourning for the girl's fate on account of actions which are noble, as she was trying to prevent her brother's body from becoming carrion to birds of prey and dogs. "Does she not deserve a golden crown?" Haemon reports. He begs Creon not to remain close-minded, for the tree that yields to the flood is the one that retains its branches, whereas the unbending one perishes. To be born with absolute wisdom would be ideal, but failing that, the next best thing is to listen to good advice. The Chorus points out that the two should learn from each other, for true things have been said on both sides.*

Creon is skeptical about a young beardless boy teaching him good sense and accuses him of pleading for wrongdoers; Haemon denies it, and adds that all Thebes shares the same views. Creon, indignant: "{I}s it now for Thebes to teach me how to govern?" Haemon responds: "{W}ho is behaving like a boy now?" and points out that there can be no polis *of a single man. Creon counterattacks: "{I}s it not said that the* polis *belongs to its ruler?" And Haemon: "You would be a fine ruler over a deserted city." Creon, trapped, accuses his son of taking a woman's side. With both characters uninhibited, their dispute enters a spiral of reproaches and accusations. At its climax, Creon shouts that no matter how his son argues, he will never marry that girl while alive. "Well then," warns Haemon, "if she dies, her death will destroy some other." Perceiving that as a threat, Creon threatens him back, after which Haemon exits in rage.*

The elders fear that he is liable to do anything. "Let him go," says Creon, and adds, "but he shall not save those two girls from death!" (768–9). "Both of them?" the elders ask. "You are right," Creon stands corrected, "not the one that did not touch the corpse." As for Antigone, she will be led where no man treads, and there she will be buried alive with food enough to protect the city from pollution [miasma]. *Perhaps there she can be spared from death, or else she will learn, too late, that it is labor lost to concern oneself with things in Hades.*

This dialogue between father and son is one of the most vibrant and politically charged of the play.[16] Their exchange contains two clearly separate halves: the first, an example of civility and diplomatic talent; the second, anything but respectful and subtle. In the beginning, when Haemon confirms his loyalty to his father, Creon is naturally reassured. Creon sees children as an extension of their parents and the world of friend and enemies inherited from them. Therefore Haemon's role and obligation as a good son is to follow on his father's policies, which entails rejecting and casting Antigone away as an enemy. Her public disobedience justifies her punishment to be set as an example, for the entire city, of the way Creon governs his own family, neither driven nor softened by personal considerations. These principles reveal his idea of a well-ordered society. The good citizen, like the good soldier, must stay put and obey orders, which suggests that Creon assimilates military strategy into the act of political governing.

Decidedly conventional, Creon's ideals of discipline, order, and obedience – and the hierarchical view of society they embody – are not far off from the morality of an older generation,[17] as the elders of the Chorus confirm "unless they are led astray by their old age." Embedded in the language of war that has just ravaged the country, Creon recalls the old aristocratic ideals of Spartan discipline. Creon envisions the possibility of slow changes, for those who today are young will in time occupy positions of leadership, but these do not alter the fundamental fabric and constitution of society. Creon's sociopolitical realm is composed of fixed and binary categories – citizen/ruler, father/son, old/young, men/women – that define each person's location within the community. This includes gender relationships in particular, for women must know their role as "subordinates" and cannot claim an equal station to men. In his hierarchically structured society, he has given himself a place defined by his status as ruler, paterfamilias, mature citizen, and man, and he classifies the world around himself accordingly. His static conception of his *character* (his conception of himself, the world, and social interactions) turns every attempt to make him reconsider into a direct attack on his person. In his view, any slight revision or adjustment of his position would be admitting defeat, as dishonorable as retreat in the middle of battle.

Despite Creon's limited capacity to recognize anything beyond his rigid conception of the world, there is something he understands quite well, and this is the extent of Antigone's defiance. Creon identifies correctly that Antigone did more than break the law (as defined by Creon); additionally, she wished to enact a norm to replace the laws of the city with a law of her own. To make matters worse, Antigone dared to do so in public, so that all citizens could witness it. If Creon cannot remedy the situation, his authority as he understands it (including his manly pride) is in danger of being shattered.

Haemon must gather all his diplomatic composure in order to defend his position without unnecessarily unnerving his father. He confirms that good sense is indeed the main excellence of human beings, but this entails more than merely being able to make a decision and to have the determination to carry it through to the end. Redefining Creon's meaning of the same term, to be "reasonable" for Haemon entails being able to identify one's mistakes and to rectify them in time. Haemon's dynamic conception of human interactions and the family help him reconcile his own interests with those of his father and to present them as mutually beneficial. In contrast to Creon's top-down and rather authoritarian view of government, Haemon shows a more horizontal understanding of authority and democratic politics, perhaps an expression of a generational shift. For Haemon, the wise exercise of authority entails a more open and inclusive politics, which takes into account other perspectives and voices. Since humans are inherently fallible, real wisdom consists in being open to learning from others. From this point of view, his father's firmness and determination are transformed into obstinacy and stubbornness, as futile as the tree that tries in vain to resist the force of the flood, or the captain who does not slacken the sails and ends up capsizing the boat. Interestingly, the elders have words of praise for his speech and urge Creon to "learn" [*mathein*] from them, thus endorsing Haemon's key term.[18]

Behind this apparently harmless advice, however, Haemon hides a stinging defense of Antigone. In support of his argument he brings the rumors [*phatis*] of an indeterminate number of citizens who oppose Creon but are afraid to speak their minds before him. This is not, in fact, the first time we hear from an indeterminate body of citizens that oppose Creon and murmur against him in secret (even though the possibility was disregarded when Creon had first raised it in 289–91). Haemon relies on his relative social invisibility to report these rumors, according to which Antigone does not deserve to be punished but rather to be crowned in gold. Judith Fletcher likens such rumors to the public clamor or *thorubus* by which the Athenian demos expressed their collective approval or disapproval.[19] But how reliable are these "rumors" and how should the audience take them?[20] Aristotle had already remarked that "Sophocles makes Haemon speak for Antigone before his father by using the device that others are saying what he is saying."[21] There is no need to agree with the philosopher to realize that Haemon could very well be suspected (certainly by Creon) to be hiding his own opinions behind those of the citizens. Gerald Else for example talks about Haemon's "identification" and "total acceptance of Antigone's ideas," where even his diction raises some doubt as to whether he is merely "reporting" or expressing his own mind.[22]

Still, Haemon's challenge pushes the audience to wonder about the social legitimacy of Creon's decree. Creon does nothing to appease these doubts, as he takes no notice of Haemon's report about these "rumors" and instead accuses his son of being too young to teach him any lesson, of defending wrongdoing, and of being on a woman's side. We need not take everything he says at face value. For example, when Creon asks, rhetorically, "[S]hould the city tell me how I am to rule?" (734), the authoritarian remark is immediately followed by Haemon's response, "[W]ho speaks now like a boy?", which suggests that he does not recognize his father in them (i.e. this statement does not do justice to Creon). Still, Creon's exclusive defense of his position as ruler indicates that he is increasingly confusing the interests of the city with his own. If Creon had promised that "rule will reveal the man" (175–7), such a rule progressively reveals a man who is prone to authoritarianism and fits of anger. His demand for unquestioned obedience endangers the family more than it protects it, as it has caused irreparable damage to his relationship with his son. After Creon threatens to kill Antigone in Haemon's presence, Haemon assures his father that he will not set eyes on him again. In the end, Haemon's opening statement "I'm yours" is completely nullified, for he can no longer be counted as one of his father's *philos*.

After Haemon's wrathful exit, the elders point out sparingly that Haemon is liable to do anything in such furious state of mind, but remain conspicuously silent as to the central issues of the debate, perhaps maintaining a calculated ambiguity that does not commit them much. Still two sudden and major changes occur. First, Creon decides finally to liberate Ismene, who was not responsible for the burial.[23] Second, the punishment of Antigone changes from public stoning to being buried alive with food enough to keep her alive. Several hypotheses may explain the change of punishment,[24] but as far as Creon goes, he claims to be protecting the city from pollution – maybe from the physical contact with Antigone.[25] Be that as it may, the change in method has the effect of leaving Antigone's destiny in her own hands.

4.4 Third *stasimon*: the power of Eros (lines 781–800)

The Chorus moves from the central issues of the debate and considers instead the uncontrollable power of Eros (and Aphrodite):

Love invincible in battle, who falls upon men's herds[26] *and spends the night upon the soft cheeks of a girl, and ranges over the open sea and in the shelters of the pasture-land . . . None among the immortals can escape you, nor among the mortals, and he who is possessed by you becomes crazed.*

You make the mind of the just unjust [dikaiôn adikous phrenas]. *It is you who have stirred this quarrel between men of the same blood. Victory goes to she who sits on the throne among the greatest authorities* [tôn megalôn thesmôn], *nothing can resist this invincible desire* [himeros], *golden Aphrodite holds her play and no one can overcome her.*

The idea of Eros as an uncontrollable power that blinds both humans and gods is a commonplace in Greek lyric tradition, at least since the *Iliad*.[27] Here, after the heated quarrel between father and son, the elders of the Chorus offer a retroactive explanation of what they have witnessed and assume that Eros must lie behind it. The chorus refuses to make a political statement or interpretation of the conflict between father and son, but attributes the bitter quarrel to the *manic* influence of Love. The latter is defined as a mighty power that sits among the greatest powers on earth and subdues both mortals and gods in its maddening path, extending its sovereignty over land and sea.

Arguably the Chorus is thinking about Haemon's love for Antigone, which may have pushed him over the edge of sanity. According to this, love may be the cause for Haemon to lose his *phrenes* – the possession that he himself defined as the most precious gift (684–5), and to stir the controversy with his father. Dominated by love (a force so strong that it is capable of wresting the minds of the righteous aside from justice), a naturally obedient young man such as Haemon may have set aside his duties as a son. Notwithstanding this interpretation, the Chorus' words can serve paradoxically as a sort of excuse, for whatever Haemon might have done to offend his father was done under the influence of Eros, which absolutely no one can resist.

Many commentators reject the Chorus' interpretation, denying any influence of Eros in Haemon as if to acknowledge this influence would automatically nullify Haemon's arguments against his father.[28] But to blame love for stirring the quarrel between father and son is natural enough, as love stands between father and son as the wedge of opposite allegiances impossible to repair, once the father obliges the son to cast his love away. Love in fact makes apparent Haemon's incommensurable dilemma between mutually exclusive loyalties that cannot be both observed without choice and sacrifice. The issue then is not *whether*, but *how far* the influence of love can discredit Haemon's central arguments about the injustice of Creon's behavior and the rightness of Antigone's position. Even if Haemon had acted under the influence of Eros (e.g. when he exits the scene in total dispossession of his temper and severing all affiliations with his father), the description would say absolutely nothing about Creon's decision to prohibit the burial or about Antigone. In other words, the Ode leaves untouched, because it remains deliberately silent about, the main legal dispute between the two, retiring to the safe ground of aphorisms and codas known of old.

As a result, the Ode provides no commentary on Creon's increasing authoritarianism and says nothing about Haemon's damning allegations of the citizens who oppose Creon. Instead, it raises the suspicion of love as an influencing factor with the curious effect, for the audience, of having to consider whether love may have clouded Haemon's judgment and tainted his reliability as a witness. By inviting its audience in this way to consider a factor that may have eluded them before, the Ode generates a "distancing effect" that pushes audiences to take a step back and re-evaluate retrospectively whatever sympathies and conclusions they may have reached earlier.

4.5 Antigone's farewell march (lines 801–943)

When the elders see Antigone approaching, they no longer can restrain their tears. Antigone addresses them: "Behold me, citizens of my native land [patrias politai] *as I make my last journey." Antigone is to depart from life, she says, without the wedding that was her due, nor songs being sung for her in marriage. The elders reply that, uncrowned with glory,*[29] *she alone among mortals is to walk to her death by a law set unto herself* [autonomos]. *Antigone compares her story with that of Niobe, who was transformed into a rock and suffered the saddest of deaths. The elders reprimand her for setting herself so high, for Niobe was a goddess and she is only mortal. Still, they claim it is great glory for mortals to share the lot equal to gods.*

Antigone feels mocked and invokes the entire city [ô polis], *the rich men of the city* [ô poleôs andres], *the fountains of Dirce and the grove of Thebes. At least she can call them all to witness under what laws* [nomois] *(847) she is being driven, unmourned by friends, towards her terrible ordeal. The Chorus responds that, advancing to the extreme of daring, she stumbled upon the altar of Justice. They also wonder whether she might not be suffering from some fault of her parents. Antigone replies: "{Y}ou have touched on a thought most painful to me, the fate of my father . . . and the whole of our destiny, that of the famous Labdacids". The elders reply that the piety she showed is a noble kind of respect, but she showed none in transgressing the authority of those who hold power. "Your own self-willed passion* [autognôtos orgas] *has destroyed you". Creon intervenes to cut short her laments and orders the guard to lead her off as soon as possible.*

Addressing now her deep-dug prison, she remembers her father, mother, brothers, and all their deaths, and how with her bare hands, she poured libations on their graves. She regrets the price she has to pay only for showing reverence to Polyneices. And yet she was right to do it, and she will be judged by those who are wise [phronousin eu] *(904). Antigone declares that not even if she were the mother of children, not if her husband were dead and rotting, would she have acted against the citizens* [biai politôn] *(907). For the sake of what law* [nomou] *(908) does she say this? If her husband died, there would be another husband for her, and there would be a child from another man if hers were lost; but with both her parents dead in Hades, no more brother can ever be born. She honored him, Polyneices, by such a law* [nomoi] *(914), but Creon judged it to be wrong. She concludes: "If this is the pleasure of the gods, I will know it once I suffer; but if these men are wrong, may they suffer nothing worse than what they are inflicting upon me at present".*

The Chorus interprets her words as coming from the same winds of wild passion. Creon orders that she be taken away. Antigone utters her last words: "Ancestral city of the land of Thebes and the gods of my forebears," she invokes all of them, "Look, rulers of Thebes, upon the last of the royal house, what things I am suffering from what men, for having shown reverence for reverence!"

When Antigone enters the stage (probably in shackles) the elders remark that they are being carried away from what is proper[30] and cannot refrain from crying for the girl. Their initial remark sets the tone of the entire *kommos*, in which they combine sincere affection and sympathy for her suffering, with a more detached and less enthusiastic stance towards her actions. This reaction helps to modulate the audience's as well, in which the sympathy for Antigone's suffering is to be made compatible with a critical assessment of her actions.

Antigone had declared that she would welcome death as a gain (462), but now she confronts the crude reality of her choice. For the first time, she expresses the human cost of her decisions and wants the citizens "to look" at it, inviting them to witness the sense of loss and sacrifice she is now experiencing. Antigone presents herself as another Niobe, in her mind, a symbol of a person unjustly punished by the powers that be. Her complaints have an unmistakably legal flavor, as the plea of someone who wishes to bring attention to the particularly sad circumstances of her punishment and, by the same token, to the cruelty of the person who sanctioned it. This *witnessing* to which she invites her audience takes the symbolic form of a trial in which she presents herself as the victim of Creon's injustice.

But the elders of the Chorus fail to react as she had hoped. Instead of accepting Antigone's description, they reprimand her for setting herself so high and adduce that it was her commitment to her own law that put her there. Even though they are able to appreciate her reverence towards her loved ones, they also point out that she has nevertheless transgressed authority, driven by her own strong-willed passion. Throughout the *kommos*, then, the elders try to find an adequate distance between themselves and the girl. They combine traces of genuine sadness for her misery in their desire to offer her some level of comfort, with a more critical and censorious attitude towards her action. Antigone, however, only registers the chords of reproach in their voice and feels utterly abandoned by all, demonstrating that she does not want their compassion, but their (normative) acceptance. Having failed to gather their support for her cause and to turn the tables against Creon, she conveys her total and utter desolation.

Antigone's charged lament is abruptly interrupted by Creon, who cannot wait to get rid of her. Creon's hurried expression is unmitigated in its coldness, as if he were not emotionally attuned to what is happening on stage. His insensitivity to his niece's suffering appears at odds with the subtle and nuanced interaction established between Antigone and the Chorus, and by this channel with the audience. The effect of having Creon watch the *kommos* and then respond as he does, Simon Goldhill explains, "not only affects an audience's view of the King, but also works to isolate him from the action . . ."[31]

Creon's words mark the transition to the second half of the scene, Antigone's last attempt at self-explanation. In a long speech, Antigone tries to offer a reasoned argument to justify her action one last time. Antigone defends her action against the charges that she was trying to impose a law on her own (i.e. being *autonomos*), that she acted in breach of authority and justice, was driven by self-willed passion, and showed reverence for a family so "tainted" that it was not worth, perhaps, the price Antigone is willing to pay for it. Antigone responds by reaffirming that she was right to act as she did, even if she had to act in spite of the will of the citizens, and provides a *nomos* or legal argument to prove it. Antigone assures that she would not have felt entitled to defy the citizens for a husband or a child, but that she only would do so on behalf of her last brother.

Antigone's argument has caused great controversy and there is no easy way to explain it.[32] Her words are certainly strange: what does Antigone mean when she says that she would not have done the same thing for a husband or child? Can it be that, as Richard Jebb famously argued, "she suddenly gives up that which, throughout the drama, has been the immovable basis of her action – the universal and unqualified validity of the divine law"?[33] Moreover, why does she make the distinction between brother on the one side and husband and child on the other? In the story of Herodotus from which Sophocles may have borrowed this passage,[34] the wife of Intaphernes was given the choice of saving the life of one of her family members who had been sentenced to death by the Persian King Darius, and she chose to save her brother. However, Antigone has no husband and children to choose among and she cannot save those who are already dead. Finally, is Antigone recognizing the validity of Creon's decree by equating it with the will of the citizens?

In order to untangle these questions, it is necessary to situate the argument in the context of her conversation with the Chorus. When the elders make it known to her that they do not necessarily approve of her actions, for the first time Antigone confronts the possibility of acting not against the arbitrary decree of a tyrant, but against a representative body of citizens whom she cannot equally disregard. It is not that she now recognizes them as a new source of authority, for Antigone did not hesitate to use their opinion against Creon when she thought it was favorable to her (509). What is different now is her sudden perception (whether justified or not) that they may oppose her on the merits of her case. Antigone can no longer ignore that, while fulfilling sacred duties, she may have transgressed the laws of the political community.[35] It is only at this point that her disobedience of the laws of the citizens can crystallize in her mind. (Since she denied the validity and legitimacy of Creon's decree to impose any restriction, in her eyes there was no valid and legitimate law to disobey before.) And to this alone she wishes to respond, for Antigone still thinks her action was right in the eyes of "those who think wisely" (904), despite having acted "against the will of the citizens" [*biai politôn*]. In claiming the binding force of law for her argument, therefore, Antigone is formulating what she thinks is (or should be) a socially validated or legitimate norm that justifies her *disobedience*, in the hope that it will be judged so, if not by all, at least by those citizens with good enough sense to understand her claim.

This is not an easy task for Antigone. After all, she is doing something quite exceptional, perhaps even subversive, for her time and place: as a young woman she is claiming the right to act against the body of citizens and their laws, and argues that her audience should accept her *nomos* instead. To convince the audience of the legitimacy of her action, Antigone must persuade them that her disobedience does not challenge the rule of law generally, and that accepting it does not risk permanent confrontation between the *polis* and the family. She does so by introducing the contrasting case of a husband or child (the closest analogy she can think of), aiming to show both the exceptionality and the limits of the case she actually presents.

Her reasoning here is logically similar to what rhetoricians call *a fortiori* argument. If she is able to demonstrate that her claim does not reach the case of a husband or child, she is demonstrating that it certainly does not extend to every conflict between family and *polis*. And thus, using a paradoxical yet meaningful argument according to Aristotle,[36] Antigone distinguishes only what the particular situation forces her to distinguish (i.e. if the burial were not forbidden, the distinction would have been unnecessary). Antigone concedes that even if her husband and child had died, the *polis* had forbidden their burial, and their bodies lay rotting in the ground, not even then, would she have claimed to have acted *legitimately* against the laws of the city – which is not to say that the obligations owed a husband or child are less demanding than those owed a brother.[37]

Arguably, the circumstances that make her disobedience on behalf of a brother more legitimate are explicitly connected with the death of their parents and the impossibility of renewing the family. Walter Lacey explains that in the Greek patrilineal society (which is the one represented in the play as the succession of Eteocles and Polyneices by Creon demonstrates) the death of the last brother would often mark the destruction of the entire house, for women could not continue the family on their own.[38] Accordingly, Antigone sees herself as the "last of the Royal House" (941) and the Chorus too has pointed out earlier that Antigone is "the last root in the house of Oedipus" (600). Such an extreme situation (the extinction of the whole family Oedipus) makes this case unlike any other, in fact so unique and exceptional a circumstance that it is the only case, in Antigone's present view, that warrants her disobedience.

In contrast to the former case, Antigone could marry and help to create *another* family, a possibility implied by the husband and children she imagines herself as having (905). This new, second family with her husband would presumably grow free from the fatalities besieging the house of Oedipus, and it could outlive (and this must be noted with care) the potential loss of some of its members. That is, I believe, the main thrust of her argument: if she were to constitute a *second family* with her husband, the death of either husband or child would not replicate the same circumstances (the death of a spouse could be cured by marriage, the death of a child by a new birth), in which case her action against the citizens would not be legitimate.

Antigone's *nomos* is not to be interpreted as an abandonment of the unwritten laws she defended in the beginning, for she is in fact reaffirming her determination of law above the will of the citizens. Nor is Antigone choosing, like Intaphernes' wife, which members of the family to bury (or save). And certainly, she nowhere equates the laws of the city to the will of Creon. In context, Antigone's argument is meant to set the conditions in which an individual can claim legitimately to defy the laws of the city (and to prevail over them). In other words, Antigone attempts to re-define the normative realm by bringing to the public eye what a given society fails to recognize as the law (but nonetheless ought to), according to principles and values that can be recognized by that very society. This is the implicit claim Antigone makes in branding her argument a *nomos* and submitting it to the scrutiny of the "wise citizens." In doing so, Antigone is pushing the boundaries of what is "possible" and *performing* the role of a citizen; a conscientious act of resistance[39] that seeks to transform the society around her attending to principles that are immanent to it. Antigone's performative action is similar to Electra's in the example chosen by Nicole Loraux, when she refers to her female companions with the term "citizenness" [*politides*], employing the improbable and surprising feminine noun.[40] Thus audiences are invited to reassess Antigone's gesture and to grant her some largely unrecognized measure of political awareness and consideration.

However, Antigone does not wait for the elders' reaction. By the end of her speech, she appears to give up all hope, as if she no longer expected the vindication of those next to her on the stage. The dramatic effect of Antigone's plea, which seems to have fallen on deaf ears within the play, is to put the audience in the position of the person who can still hear and judge what she says and does. In particular, Antigone's admission that she has acted "against the will of the citizens," but that her action is still right in the eyes of "those [citizens] who think clearly" has the effect of splitting the concept of citizenship into various possible constituents, not necessarily coinciding with those present on the stage, but extending to those members of the theatrical audience that are to enact or embody the role of the wise citizens that are supposed to approve her claim. In fact her last words ("if I am wrong . . . but if they are wrong . . .") alludes to judgments still to be made on the correlative merit of the main two characters, which shall put Creon, as Antigone has always wanted, on trial.

4.6 Fourth *stasimon*: besieged as others (944–987)

When Antigone is being taken away, the Chorus recalls stories of other legendary characters that also suffered terrible fates. Structurally, the ode is composed of two pairs of strophes and antistrophes which I paraphrase:

Even Danaë had to exchange the light of the day for a brazen chamber where she was bent to the yoke. Yet, she was of noble family, oh my child, and was treasurer for Zeus's golden-flowing seed. The Chorus announces: "wondrous is whatever that is allotted" [moiridia tis dynasis deina]*: Neither wealth, nor battle, nor fortress, nor ships can escape it. Yoked, too, was the hot-tempered son of Dryas, King of Edonians, because of his mocking fury held prisoner by Dionysus in a rocky cave, where his terrible madness* [manias] *drained away. At last, he came to know the god whom he had infuriated with his taunting tongue, for he had tried to stop the maidens, provoking the anger of the Muses who love the flute.*

Also in the Thracian place called Salmydessus, Ares witnessed the cursed blinding wound inflicted on the two sons of Phineus by his fierce wife, robbing the sight of their vengeful eyes by her bloody hands and a sharp shuttle . . . As they pine away they were lamenting their affliction, children born of a mother unhappily married [Cleopatra]. *She was by birth a princess of the ancient line of the Erectheids; raised in distant caves among the winds of her father Boreas,* [she was a] *child of the gods. Yet she, too, was besieged by the long-lived Fates, oh my child.*

This Ode has been called, with good reason, one of the most enigmatic and disconcerting of all of the extant Sophoclean Odes.[41] The Ode consists only of mythical material which is notoriously difficult to interpret.[42] The thematic link(s) among the narrated stories is tenuous at best, and its connection to the dramatic action appears particularly vague and ambiguous.[43] Still, the main problem seems to be the apparent emptiness of its moral, for the Chorus' attempt at consolation may seem, in the context of the drama, a vacuous lesson for Antigone. This notwithstanding, I will try to show that the Ode is more illuminating once we move from the narrative level of the characters to that of the audience - its expectations, hopes, and fears.

The Chorus begins by comparing Antigone with Danaë, who also had to "exchange the light of the day for a brazen chamber," when her father Acrisius imprisoned her because an oracle had foretold that her son would kill him.[44] She too came from an honorable house and even was impregnated with the seed of Zeus,[45] which did not shield her from suffering. Some authors evoke the story in which Perseus, Danaë's son by Zeus, ended up killing up his grandfather Acrisius, who would stand for Creon. Thus, Robert Goheen suggests "that the underlying implications of the first strophe are favorable to Antigone but ominous to Creon."[46] However, this conclusion is doubtful because the sources stress very much the fact that Acrisius' death was accidental (not a vindication).

In the next strophe, the Chorus remembers the story of Lycurgus. As the Chorus recalls it, Lycurgus had opposed the god Dionysus with a mad tongue and was punished with imprisonment, where his madness drained away. On an apparent level, imprisonment is what links the stories of Lycurgus and Danaë, for he too had been imprisoned by Dionysus for opposing him. But the motives involved appear so at variance that many have wondered whether both stories are in fact comparable.[47] Some authors have suggested a closer connection between Creon and Lycurgus, and allude to the version of the myth in which Lycurgus killed his son in an act of maniac seizure provoked by the god.[48] However, the latter seems more likely another version of the myth,[49] because the Chorus' reference to Lycurgus madness or "*mania* is made in the context of its cessation through imprisonment."[50] The last story, that of Cleopatra, is the most unclear. The text does not give us much detail about the background story, but most authors agree that Phineus had repudiated Cleopatra due to his second marriage, and the new wife blinded Cleopatra's two children.[51] The connection between this story and Antigone's own are not easily established. Winnington-Ingram suggests that the Chorus' remark about the 'cursed blinded wound' implied that the children brought a curse upon Phineus and his wife, which would presage Creon's own punishment.[52] However, Griffith warns against it.[53] This time again, the emphasis appears to be on suffering.[54] As the Chorus reminds Antigone, being the child of a god did not exempt Cleopatra from being struck by the Fates too.

On a narrative level, the only thing that all three stories have in common is noble ancestry – a princess, a King, and the daughter of a god – suffering an unexpected blow of fortune. Other suggested motifs, such as imprisonment,[55] or child-parent hostility[56] are not common to all. But, one might wonder, should a "deeper" connection even be sought? Structurally, the ode follows the pattern of Dione's speech to Aphrodite in the *Iliad* after being wounded.[57] Dione exhorts her child Aphrodite to endure (*tlê*), just as the Chorus wants the "child" Antigone to endure.[58] As Burton argues, exhortations of these types are a "fixed element in Greek literature," and one of their features is the "often very tenuous point of contact between the examples chosen and the detailed stories and personalities of the people exhorted. Only a very general similarity at one or two points is required."[59]

Concerning its connection with the dramatic action the Ode is sung after Antigone's final lament and while she is being led away to her tomblike chamber. At this moment, with Creon following at a close distance, the elders address Antigone directly calling her "oh my child" [*o pai pai*] once at the beginning (949), and once [*o pai*] at the end (987), thus closing and encircling the Ode. They do so by comparing her lot with three other mythological figures, all of whom descended from families of nobility and high social standing [*geneai timios*], which did not immunize them against the blows of misfortune. The Ode thus connects with Antigone's precedent complaints about her undeserved and unmerited lot. In her final lament, Antigone insists on presenting herself as the victim of wanton cruelty. She stresses many times the exceptionality of her misery, unbearable because she has to suffer it unwept, friendless, and unwedded. Her being the last member of a wretched family, among whom she is "the saddest of all" (895), reinforces the same feeling. In this regard, her last words are demonstrative: "Look, rulers of Thebes, upon the last of the royal house, what things I am suffering from what men" (939–41). The Chorus responds by pointing out that other characters with no less noble blood in their veins also suffered terrible blows of fortune, just as when Antigone compares herself to Niobe. Danaë, Lycurgus, Cleopatra, all of them came from well-respected houses and ancestors, and yet in one way or another, for one motive or another, all of them experienced terrible ordeals. Putting Antigone's lot in mythological perspective underscores her claim to distinctiveness and produces a humbling effect, even though the elders also point out that there is something comforting in sharing the lot of people of great repute (cf. 836–8).

While the Chorus' attempt at consolation may sound a bit hollow, things become more intriguing once we move from the narrative level of the characters onto the world of expectations, hopes, and fears of the audience. Indeed, the audience is eager to know what may happen to Antigone after her imprisonment. One could think her fate is sealed, especially after Creon said that her sentence would be carried out, but, as far as Creon is concerned, what happens to Antigone in that cave is entirely up to her. Absolutely anything can still happen. The poet greatly benefits from his audience's natural sense of anticipation. By comparing Antigone's fate to what happened to three different mythological figures, the audience is invited to speculate and to project those stories onto Antigone's own. Will Antigone, like Danaë, be visited by Zeus while imprisoned? Will she finally have to face her errors, like Lycurgus? Will she suffer as did Cleopatra? At this moment in the drama, the audience lacks the ability to foretell what only the future can clarify. If, on the one hand, the poem stimulates the free flow of ideas by inviting us to draw parallelisms with the mythological stories (and to project them onto the action and the characters), on the other hand, the tersely embroidered mixture of stories frustrate any sense of clarification about their future. The fact that the circumstances surrounding fatality diverge so much in all three mythological stories (combining innocence and culpability, deserved and undeserved punishments, and no clear assignment of responsibility) prevents using them as predictors or indicators of future moral judgments.

But what about the apparent emptiness of the Ode? At the precise point where Antigone's (and soon also Creon's) *moira* seems to start taking shape, the Chorus reflects upon the wondrous things allotted, *whatever* they are.[60] The flavor of this word *moira* (literally "lot, portion, or share," and which has nothing to do with what we moderns call ordinarily fate and that the Greeks lacked[61]) is to be understood as the gradual and progressive individuation of one course of events among potentially infinite ones. In the tragic context, the "taking shape" of one possibility among the wide-open range of alternatives occurs only as events unfold in their timely sequence. Only then does *moira* become "necessary," not because the outcome was somehow "fated" from the beginning, but because all other alternatives have been exhausted by former choices and courses of action.[62] My argument is that, by locating the relative position of human beings in the broader scheme of things no one can master or control (i.e. the *moiridia*), it becomes a profound reflection on human finitude. Just as man was defined ontologically as the most wonderful creature of all (332–3), man's existential predicament is equally wondrous.

As the Ode advances, man's capacity to grasp his destiny is constrained by the radical blindness with which mortals confront it. And yet, his inquisitive nature pushes man to look for answers beyond that which can be intelligibly known. Pushed by the relentless urge to look ahead, yet constrained by the natural limitations before the unforeseeable, the two motions define, surprisingly enough, the audience's motions as well. The inquisitive impulse is demonstrated by the audience's desire for anticipation, as evidenced by the critical impulse to see the destiny of Antigone and Creon foreshadowed in the mythological stories of the Ode; the limits of comprehension in the inability of the audience to prefigure with certainty what the characters' lots will eventually look like. The former sets the imagination in motion, the latter holds it back. The most remarkable poetic achievement of the Ode is that the audience replicates in his or her own experience the situation of man's existential quandary. A pure act of self-consciousness then (not the gnomic expression of the Chorus) reveals both man's relative position before the *moira*, and the audience's precise location or *inhabitance* of the tragedy. Whatever lies ahead, the play imposes this realization upon its readers, trapped – like man – in a tragic world not of their making. Not until the soon-to-come prophetic utterances of Teiresias will the audience begin to see clearly through all this fog of uncertainty.

Chapter 5

Acts of reading, acts of judgment

> Let us freely admit that if drama and poetry written for pleasure can prove to us that they have a place in a well-run society, we will gladly admit them . . . And we should give her defenders, men who aren't poets themselves but love poetry, a chance of defending her in prose and proving that she doesn't only give pleasure but brings lasting benefit to the human life and human society. And we will listen favorably, as we shall gain much if we find her a source of profit as well as pleasure.
>
> (Plato, *The Republic*, X, 607c–e[1])

We are finally prepared at this point to consider fully the main idea of this book, which is that tragedy (at least at its best) educates its audience in the process of judging difficult or hard conflicts. In this way I invert the suggestion made by Hans-Georg Gadamer of taking legal interpretation as a model for the rest of human sciences, and propose instead the experience of judging tragedy as exemplary for legal judgment.[2] The heart of my position is that the engagement with the tragic performance elicits certain kinds of emotional and cognitive capacity in the audience (creative imagination, affective and empathetic engagements, critical distancing, perspective-taking, self-reflexivity, and re-dimensioning) that are central to the activity of judging – including judging in the law. Tragedy does this by stimulating its audience to consider the equal claims of mutually incompatible positions, and then by calling upon us all to assess them from varying and multiple perspectives that change through space and time. In doing so, it helps to develop the kind of skills and attitudes necessary for judging the tragic conflict with increasing proficiency in the course of the drama, just as legal trials are designed ideally to perform.[3] To bring to consciousness the operations of the mind involved in *experiencing tragedy* (i.e. the experience of watching, responding to, and being affected by tragedy) can, in this way, lay the groundwork for a phenomenology of judging in a hard case situation, where the conventional attributes of detachment, disinterestedness, abstraction, and generality do not adequately represent (and even mislead as to) the attitudes and dispositions required in these situations.

In Chapter 1, Robert Cover helped us to explain that a hard case is not produced simply by unclear or unsettled law, but rather by (at least) two conflicting laws governing the situation, with no single and agreed upon referent to provide an answer. The adjudication of hard cases requires more than judicial clarification, for one of the laws in conflict may be inevitably crushed by this judicial action. For Cover, justice in such a setting comes not from more or less disingenuous attempts to tame judicial discretion (e.g. by pretending to make the judges' role more "rule-bound" or "restrained"), but rather from a constant struggle of forces where each *nomos* is allowed to speak and act as it sees fit in the face of contrary commitments from others.

Despite its merits, several concerns remain about this approach, which gives the judge no incentive to reach out to those whose *nomos* it is about to crush. This may fall short of justice in another sense, for it may lead to the rigid and inflexible defense of a particular normative view. In addition, there is the risk that a judge is so fixed in his original commitments that he does not see the need for undertaking a fresh and serious consideration of the conflict, as every new legal case deserves. This is why a theory of adjudication must provide mechanisms to assure that the judge's preconceptions and prejudices are tested if the decision is to be considered part of the legitimate exercise of authority, and not based on personal preferences or simple bias.[4]

Throughout the book my claim has been that tragedy can help us in that task. Relying on the motions and displacements required in judging the positions set forth in the *Antigone*, in this chapter I begin to develop a view of the activity of judging that goes beyond current models of narrative coherence in judicial decision-making, and incorporates the multi-voicedness and the agonistic nature of the tragic stage. Far from the self-image of the "unmoved" and impartial arbiter often found in the authoritative language of many national and international courts, tragedy constructs an implicated audience that constantly moves from one position to another, and which must learn to cope with shifting loyalties between contrary perspectives, while reflecting critically about them all. From the engagement with the tragedy an idea of good judgment (or "judging well") will progressively emerge out of the concrete experience of reading and responding to the tragic performance. My argument is of course not that all audiences are meant to react in the same way.[5] But the play does construct certain "spaces of judgment" that can be identified and shown to guide audiences in a certain direction, without completely determining the content of their judgments that must remain open. The main goal of this chapter is to identify these signposts and to show how they can inform the activity of legal judgment.

At this juncture, a critical reader might still harbor some doubts about the pertinence of this comparison: are we not perhaps falling into a certain aestheticization by comparing the "illusion of the theater" with the "real practice" of legal judgment?[6] In what sense are we entitled to use literature to illuminate the activity of legal judgment?[7] In this chapter I respond to these questions by taking on Plato's challenge after his well-known expulsion of the poets from his ideal *Republic*.[8] Plato's critique is more insightful than it is often taken to be, and paradoxically rather sensitive and sympathetic to poetry in general. Plato himself is unable to find a way to harmonize his undeniable love for poetry with his philosophical interest in the promotion of civic virtue and justice, and takes the painful (and hesitant) step of demoting the former from the eminent position in which it was previously held.[9] Nonetheless, he entertains the idea that his arguments may be misguided and invites his audience to prove him wrong. Nothing would satisfy the philosopher more than to be persuaded that poetry can make a positive contribution to the *polis* and human society.

The purpose of what follows is neither to give a comprehensive account of Plato's views on poetry and mimesis,[10] nor to account for the old quarrel between philosophy and poetry,[11] nor to inquire about the political implications of the banishment of the poets.[12] Rather, it is to defend the potential of tragedy to educate its audience into the kind of judgments that are needed in a hard-case scenario. Even though it is important to bear in mind that tragedy[13] fulfills many different "functions" (including a purely escapist one), to acquit poetry fully from Plato's charges – and certainly to defend the claims that I am making about tragedy – it is necessary to show that poets can bring "knowledge" to their audience; that the emotions poetry generates are not irrational or mindless reactions; that the effects it produces in the audience are not unsuitable from the perspective of citizenship; that enjoying the tragic spectacle does not require abandoning the capacity for judgment; and that the kind of experience it offers can be a source of education for the citizen, the statesman, and even the philosopher.

Certainly one needs no justification to engage with tragedy, but the question imposes itself more prominently in the disciplinary context of law where literature is potentially undermining of the perceived autonomy, predictability, and internal coherence of law. Indeed the Platonic critique, or a simplified version of it, remains quite influential in law schools and some legal circles, where literature is often associated uncritically with the subjective, emotional, and deceptive world of appearances and entertainment. Therefore, my response to the philosopher hides an ulterior and decidedly more contemporary objective, for the argument can be recast as a debate about the appropriate relationship between law and literature, as well as the merits of a law-and-humanities approach to law and legal education. In my effort to offer a justification for such an approach, I deal with side debates about the role of emotions in legal judgment, the pertinence or not of particularly sensitive narratives (e.g. victim impact statements) in trials, and the value and role of literature for the legal profession. Ultimately, I aim to demonstrate against Plato and his modern counterparts that the tragic engagement provides training essential for the pluralistic and agonistic public sphere in which we all live.

5.1 The challenge of Plato

Plato begins his attack in Books 2 and 3 of the *Republic* with the kind of stories (*mythoi*) children are told when growing up. Plato views poetry – at this point we may rightly say "storytelling" – as the first and main vehicle for the transmission of cultural, behavioral, and emotional patterns in the education of children. His assumption is that these are not just "stories," for at that impressionable age, when the minds of the listeners are young and tender, not only are they easily imprinted, but lasting impressions are left in the child's psyche. Unlike adults, who may have the ability to disregard or take distance from them, infants do not have this ability, and are therefore more readily suggestible to these influences. Thus, not only do stories have the power to mould the minds and characters of infants, but "opinions formed at that age are usually difficult to eradicate or change."[14]

Plato worries especially about stories of characters with high social standing or pedigree, for they are likely to be taken as paradigms of excellence for children to imitate. For example, he says, when young men listen to passages in which famous men, reputed heroes, or gods are given to inconsolable lament, "they [children] are hardly likely to think this sort of conduct unworthy of them as men, or to resist the temptation to similar words and actions" (388d). Plato suggests that passages that might interfere with the healthy intellectual and emotional growth of children should be eliminated from their education. Alternatively, attempts ought to be made to encourage children not to take these stories too seriously (388d), so that the patterns of conduct or models they foster do not become culturally validated. If children grow to accept these actions as exemplary, Plato says, they are all the more likely to rationalize their own misdoings as "doing merely what the first and greatest of the gods have done before."[15] In other words, he fears that seeing how these apparent role models behave, it is likely that "they [children] will be lenient to their own shortcomings."[16]

Noteworthy in Plato's attack on storytelling is the recognition of its enormous influence. In their ability to celebrate heroes, to prescribe cultural models, and to sanction social aspirations and ideals, stories provide a repertoire of normative thought and action, a lexicon of moral and ethical judgment, and a range of emotional and moral responses that constitute the child's mental universe. Once internalized, these habits of perception are difficult to uproot or to modify. Moreover, the characters portrayed in these stories often have an exemplary nature, which is reflected in the children's behavior. Children learn to admire and to imitate the behavior of the characters portrayed in these stories, which makes Plato wary about the kind of examples they receive. Whatever we may think about Plato's measures and ideals, the underlying pedagogical idea is no different from what is currently implied in rating systems in the film industry,[17] or in criticisms of the behavior of certain actors, politicians, sportsmen, and public figures as being "bad role models." Certainly, cautionary tales against the negative influence of all-pervasive means of cultural transmission – e.g. stereotypical, chauvinistic, or xenophobic attitudes conveyed through products of mass consumption – remain quite strong among us.

After dealing with children's literature, Plato shifts the focus to the kind of poetry that is enacted or dramatized. This ranges from theatrical performances (where the individual must impersonate a given character and play out that role), to representations that require the imaginative and vivid re-creation of the poetic universe (including the reproduction of music and ambient sound, e.g. thunder or dog barks). What these performances have in common is that the individual performer is required to leave his or her own persona behind in order to embody and convey to others the character, emotions, and setting appropriate to the represented object. Even the declamation of lyric or epic poetry, as described in other Platonic dialogues such as *Ion* or *Phaedrus*, requires one to memorize the words and platitudes of another person, to adopt her tone of voice, gestures and poise, and, in short, to re-live and re-create the world of the story one recites. For our present purposes, Plato's description finds a correlative in the judge who would be required to "walk in the shoes" of the characters to be judged – of which he disapproves and I will try to defend.[18]

Plato warns that this kind of activity makes the individual assume certain habits of perception that, if prolonged in time, can become second nature. The assumption is that such "inhabitance" performs a subtle transformation in the person by acclimating her, almost imperceptibly, to this new "character." Except perhaps when this is done for the sole purpose of amusement, Plato thinks that this may cause "cumulative psychological damage."[19] This seems to go beyond the unsuitability of certain role models. More subtly, Plato appears to suggest additionally that the depersonalization or disembodiment inherent in this activity (requiring the actor to forget him or herself in order to embody the character) may end up merging the actor's personality into the many roles played.[20] From this perspective, then, the role does not just permeate the character but replaces it. The inherent loss of personal identity (its substitution for the myriad roles played) may end up having an unsettling effect on the individual. This sums up quite well Plato's initial concern with poetry, which centers on its effects on the individual character. Plato worries about the continued exposure and habituation to certain patterns of conduct, models, and roles, either for the child's personal growth and development, or for those who abandon their own self for the benefit of the role they play. Pointedly, this is not a moral, but an *ethical* concern, for it addresses not "what we ought to do," but rather "who we are to become."[21]

Plato's interest in poetry is renewed in the concluding section of the *Republic*. This time, he comes back to it with a sharpened, take-no-prisoners attitude, targeting tragedy with specific intent.[22] His attack has three broad themes. The first has to do with the epistemic grounds of the poets; the second with the part of the human mind which poetry targets and stimulates; and the third, the most daunting and damaging of all, with the enchanting fascination created in the audience, and the paradoxical experience of enjoying and even praising the poet who is able to transport us to a place or state of mind we would be otherwise ashamed to display. Plato's ultimate goal is to establish the priority of his philosophical *paideia*, which forces him to confront the social prestige of the poets in the society for which he writes. Without bearing in mind this cultural presupposition – for poets had a status at least comparable to that of the best statesmen, legislators, and generals – it is hard to grasp the impulse behind Plato's argument.[23]

Plato challenges the social prestige of poets by discrediting two powerful social conventions: one, that poets are *creators* of paradigms of human excellence; two, that they are *knowledgeable* about them. Therefore, he asks: "What is it that poets really *do*?" and "What is it that poets really *know*?" Regarding the first assumption, Plato asserts that poets do not really create anything – they simply try to depict or reflect reality with more, or less, success. The label of creators, *poietes*, is deceptive then, because their skill entails not creation (*poiesis*), but merely an ability to render or imitate reality as faithfully as possible (*mimesis*).[24] The thing that poets do is, therefore, not the thing itself, but only something that looks like it. As for the second presupposition, Plato points out that being able to depict things with verisimilitude does not presuppose knowledge of the things themselves. Indeed, it is perfectly possible to make a plausible description of how an arch or a bridge is built without actually knowing how to build an arch or a bridge. Thus, when poets deal with technical or specialized knowledge such as medicine or shipbuilding, we had better defer to those who really know the craft without crediting what poets say about it. Concerning human excellence, the apparent familiarity with which poets speak about these matters does not give them the expertise that a practitioner of a given instrument is said to develop about it.[25] Thus, even when poets speak about matters of human excellence – the topics about which they are reputed to be masters – we must always exercise our right to cross-examine them in order to ascertain whether they are in fact knowledgeable about it.[26]

In addition to being neither creators nor knowledgeable about human excellence, Plato asserts that, worse still, they are not even interested in any of that. In his view, poets are interested solely in the quality of their own representations and their own perfection (e.g. in making them more moving and dramatic), but not in the object behind the representation, i.e. in improving the reality underlying their depictions. Otherwise, Plato says, we would expect to find a Homeric school of thought like the one left by Pythagoras, concrete legislative measures like those of Solon in Athens or Lycurgus in Sparta, or practical technical devices like those designed by Thales. The absence of any such ascertainable legacy confirms the fact that poets prefer to stick to their make-believe world rather than to promote the betterment of humankind. In sum, how is it possible for anyone to argue that poets can make a "lasting contribution to society" when they have neither the capacity, nor the expertise, nor the intention of doing so?

Plato continues his criticism by shifting attention to the part of the human mind that poetry appeals to and stimulates. This more subtle critique comes after having explained the tripartite division of the human psyche into the reasoning, the spirited, and the appetitive parts in an earlier book of the *Republic*.[27] According to Plato, poetry is allied with the lowest (appetitive) part of individuals, rather than with their better (reasoning) one. In his view, drama tends to show the part of human beings that is the least sober and reasonable, either for reasons of artistic convenience or for pleasing the audience. For example, in Plato's view, life teaches us that it is best to bear misfortune patiently,[28] but such a principled attitude towards misfortune would be difficult to represent on stage, and to understand it if represented. Instead, artists are prone to show human beings at moments of deep emotional imbalance, at the heights of incontrollable agitation, and so forth. Plato believes that such a depiction is both easier and more of a crowd-pleaser for the audience than the contrary, sober one. Thus artists who want to remain popular and effective will naturally try to represent these unstable yet effective traits of human personality, and disregard those others which are more reflective and sound, but more difficult to represent, or are less conducive to general applause. This is why, in Plato's view, drama appeals to the appetitive or sentimental element of the human psyche.[29]

Plato's final, and to my mind his most penetrating, critique has to do with the charm and fascination it creates in the audience. As Plato describes: "When we hear Homer or one of the tragic poets representing the sufferings of a hero and making him bewail them at length . . . even the best of us enjoy it and let ourselves be carried away by our feelings; and," he continues, "we are full of praises for the merits of the poet who can most powerfully affect us in this way" (605d).[30] Moreover, "our better nature . . . relaxes its control over these feelings, on the grounds that it is someone else's sufferings it is watching."[31] Yet "very few people are capable of realizing that what we feel for other people must infect what we feel ourselves," and that if let grow too strong, "it will be difficult to restrain these feelings in our own."[32]

The crux of Plato's argument, which I want to unpack slowly, is contained in the paradoxical experience he describes. Despite the fact that most people, he affirms, would be ashamed to be swayed in their real lives by the emotions that tragic heroes display on stage, the very same people enjoy being carried away by these feelings, and even admire the poet who is best able to get them to do so more effectively. How is it then that we submit ourselves to the experience, and praise the poet who subjugates us to experiencing what would otherwise be cause for repudiation? Trying to unravel this paradox is vital, not just because in doing so we may reach the core of Plato's indictment of poetry, but primarily because any eventual return of poetry to the *polis* will ultimately depend upon how well are we able to respond to it.

Consistent with other accounts of the period, Plato too describes (theatrical) audiences as being carried away by their feelings and letting go of their powers of self-control. Unlike those who think that these "feelings" are left behind in the theater, Plato believes that they do in fact permeate and translate into one's actual emotional repertoire, for "what we feel for other people must infect what we feel ourselves." In his view, if audiences see characters expressing themselves in a certain unrestrained way, not only will they adopt the corresponding modes of expressions, but they will no longer be capable of exercising self-restraint in their everyday lives. In a way that is familiar to us by now, Plato warns that such relaxation will become ingrained in the audiences' habits of mind and become second nature to them. What must be noted anew is that, whereas the role models for children were suggested in an open way (i.e. in the form of heroes or characters of high social standing or pedigree ready to be emulated), the self-constituting effect now occurs in a more subtle, almost invisible way, of which most people are not even aware. This in itself is worrisome, for without awareness it is not possible to reflect upon how and in what direction our minds are being constituted. Even those who know that art is pure "illusion" (in the Platonic sense) are dangerously at risk, because believing themselves inoculated against it they let their guards down.

The abandonment of any resistance on the part of the audience entails, significantly for us, the surrender of the capacity of critical judgment. Either because they do not realize it is happening or because they feel at a safe distance from it, members of the audience relinquish their ability to reflect upon what they are seeing and how all this is affecting their habits of perception and character. This guarantees that the constitutive experience of tragedy will take place with the complicity of the mind. The audience accepts and gradually is shaped by what they see, hear, and feel, without ever giving it a further thought. Poetry functions here as a mole in the audience's psyche, not just because of its social prestige, not merely because it is pleasing to the senses, but because it is unmindfully absorbed. From this perspective, then, the fundamental problem is not only that poetry constitutes the self in ways that are at odds with social practices and ideals, but rather that in its silent, imperceptible, and pleasant manner, poetry has many ways in which to succeed without ever being questioned.

Plato seems to leave open the possibility that an adequate mental and intellectual training might help us resist these forces.[33] However, a final and decisive observation renders this sort of intellectual resistance ineffective and somewhat incompatible with the full enjoyment of art. As Plato sees it, the audience comes to the theater with the expectation (implicit in the act of becoming a member of an audience) that the spectacle will be able to charm her in precisely that way. In other words, the relaxation of one's mental resistance is just what tragedy demands from its audience. In Plato's description, one must seemingly submit to the "magic spell" of the theater if it is to be appreciated at all, because refusing to do so is to refuse engaging with it, and consequently, to fail to experience it to its fullest.[34] This relaxation constitutes not just the tragic experience, Plato suggests, but it further defines the "excellence" of art, for "we are full of praises for the merits of the poet who can most powerfully affect us in that way" or, perhaps more accurately, "[we] praise as a good poet [*agathon poieten*] the one who affects us most in this way."[35] Clearly for Plato, this criterion for excellence is indifferent to civic virtue (as understood by philosophy) and often runs contrary to it. In the end, what we call "good" in art – its capacity to move us, to make us feel deeply, to transport us to some other world, and so on – is precisely what Plato fears the most. For what tragedy achieves is not, or not only, the result of the audience's ignorance, carelessness, or even mindless complicity, but rather, the result of what both poet and audience willingly and actively seek out as the proper end of the spectacle, its very *raison d'être*.

What we value in art is therefore the very thing which we ought to fear the most: the magic spell with which the poet is able to transport us into a condition we would be ashamed of, were it to become permanent and were it to rule our lives. And yet, the enjoyment that the general public seems to derive from it is so "exciting," Plato warns us, that very few would consent to forfeit it even though they knew it was harming them, so powerful, that even the best are incapable of resisting it. Perhaps because he has seen art's rare ability to captivate even the most sober of souls, or perhaps because he has experienced it himself, he is led to conclude that art may not be handled safely. The experience it offers and prides itself upon is antagonistic to responsible citizenship.[36]

If up until now Plato had given the impression that art could still be saved – if stories were amended to foster only the highest excellence of character, if role playing was done only for amusement and not too seriously, if exaggerated epistemic claims of poets were cross-examined, if we underwent an adequate mental and intellectual training, and so on – his current realization seems to leave no room for any of that. And thus, considering that the "choice between becoming a good man or a bad" is too important to leave at random, he recommends we "follow the example of the lover who renounces a passion that is doing him no good, however hard it may be to do so" (608a–b). At the end of the day, tragedy can be allowed no safe place within the ideal city.[37]

In effect, Plato takes the politically charged step of banishing the poets from his ideal city, but he does not close all doors to their safe return, provided that someone proves him wrong. He further promises to listen favorably to those who shall defend poetry, for we would have much to gain if someone could show that poetry is a source of lasting benefit and not only of pleasure. In the meantime, he suggests we better keep repeating his warnings "as a charm." Little proof beyond that is necessary to show that it is with the passion of a lover, and the heartrending emotion caused by its loss, that Plato approaches the abandonment of poetry. Among modern readers, there is a tendency to place Plato along with the puritanical and the intolerant, and hence, to miss completely this aspect of his criticism, or worse still, to close the mind to whatever he might say of value. For my part, I cannot help but think that there must be better ways to meet Plato's challenge than disdain. I propose, then, that we take up Plato's challenge and play in his own field, without forcing art to lose its distinctive flavor in the process. How can we say that poetry speaks with *knowledge* and not merely with the untutored tongue of inspiration? Can we say that the passions and emotions it stirs in the audience are not contrary or indifferent to civic virtue? Can the tragic spectacle be absolved from the charge that it lulls the critical capacity? And can tragedy even be said to help us become better and wiser citizens and judges?

My arguments in the sections that follow are cumulative and not conclusive, that is they are not meant to resolve Plato's concerns once and for all (maybe one should not try to "resolve" them at all, but to keep them in mind as a constant reminder). However, I aim these arguments to provide the justification for my claim that undergoing the experience of tragedy can help audiences develop the skills and aptitudes necessary for the practice of legal judgment. I should point out, additionally, that my ultimate target is not Plato himself, but rather the way in which various Platonic arguments are filtered in contemporary legal debates, with the same purpose of excluding the poets and their artistic expressions from having any meaningful place in the political and legal spheres. Consequently if I sometimes give the impression of sidetracking Plato's more subtle criticisms, this is because I aim at a less sophisticated, but no less influential, contemporary target.

5.2 The truth of tragedy: vindicating the tragic experience

The title of this section is bound to raise some skeptical eyebrows, if not the suspicion of a provocation, not only because to speak of truth in the singular appears hopelessly outdated (and for those reading thus far perhaps even incoherent), but also because, of the variety of reasons for which people decide to go to the theater, "truth" may not be the first that comes to mind. If I insist on the word it is because I think it can still be used legitimately in at least two senses. In the first sense, I use truth to mean not incontrovertible knowledge – like mathematical proof – but more or less justified, more or less arguable assertions that populate public debates, e.g. legal arguments, empirical claims, judgments of probability, deep-seated beliefs, moral intuitions, philosophical insights, and so on. The reason to speak of truth [*aleteia*] instead of opinion [*doxa*] is that anyone wishing to bring tragedy back to the *polis* is set on subverting the epistemic hierarchy established by Plato, who debunked poets of their privileged status as "masters of truth."[38] But in a second, more central sense, the truth of tragedy refers not to any propositional content that the tragedy could illuminate, as bits of information regarding a state of affairs that could already be obtained by other means.[39] Rather, this truth refers to the full experience it offers its audience, a demanding and elongated activity that presupposes the willingness to engage with the drama, and that it affects and has effects upon the audience by way of undergoing the modulations, shifts, mediations, rifts, and responses it invites.

This experience cannot be replaced nor made up by any discourse attempting to explain it, but it must be gone through before it can be turned into a competence that one can later rely on in life. This is the "true" experience of tragedy.

In Chapter 1 I have already advanced that the distinction between law and literature cannot rely on the divide between fact and fiction, reality and fantasy, because the work of art constitutes its own reality that must be enjoyed, grasped, and experienced as such. The former does not mean that the play effaces all differences between reality and fiction, because audiences – Athenians included – are still conscious of watching a work of fiction, but still they are captivated (though not captive) and engage with it with the "seriousness of play."[40] Secondly, I have also argued that the emotional and cognitive process that the play generates in the audience – the *experience* of tragedy – is also real and ought to be appreciated in its full capacity to develop the skills and aptitudes necessary for the practice of legal judgment.

Several corollaries follow. The first is that whatever truth may be predicated about the work of art, this has to be measured according to standards set by the play itself, without comparing it with the everyday reality of which the work would be a mere copy. As Gadamer explains, the play possesses the genuine character of a structure or work [*ergon*] and hence it "no longer permits of any comparison with reality as the secret measure of all verisimilitude. It is raised above all such comparisons – and hence also above the question of whether it is all real."[41] Accordingly, one cannot read the *Antigone* as a mere reflection of fifth-century BC attitudes (or legislation) concerning burial and its prohibition. In order to understand the law of the tragedy the interpreter must go back to the tragedy itself and to the world it helps to create, which constructs its own symbolic geography in the audience's imagination. The second corollary is that the tragedy, as an encounter with a thing other than oneself, requires audiences to undergo an experience that may transform the habitual ways in which they are used to seeing or doing things, and hence learn them anew. In this regard, I have already suggested that the experience of judging the tragic conflict – including the critical reflection about what this experience demands and entails – helps to develop the skills and aptitudes necessary for the practice of legal judgment, particularly (but not exclusively) in a hard-case scenario.

All this notwithstanding, if the work of art is indeed a work or "fabrication," that is the deliberate molding into form, then the Platonic critique of the poets' knowledge and claim to truth is still pertinent. Allow me to rehearse Plato's arguments summarily, bringing them to bear on the specific realm of law in the modern context. First, Plato argues that poets are not interested in improving society, or in leaving lasting benefits behind them like the legislative measures of Solon or Lycurgus, but only in perfecting their own make-believe world. That being so, why should we take their work in a way that is not within their original intention? In pushing the analogy between legal adjudication and tragic spectatorship are we not perhaps falling in to what Judge Richard Posner criticizes as "reading *Animal Farm* as a tract on farm management"?[42] Secondly, poets are able to depict more or less credible portrayals of the things they talk about, but this does not entail that they are experts about these things. For example, they may create plausible descriptions of how an arch or bridge is built, without actually knowing how to build them as practitioners do. Therefore, even though poets may write beautifully about legal institutions, their knowledge cannot compare, and must yield, to what a lawyer or judge can learn by practicing the trade. Thirdly and finally, Plato accepts that on occasion poets are divinely inspired by the Muse, who provides them with lucid insights into important aspects of life. However, inspiration is no replacement for method, and falls short of the rigor presiding over critical inquiry. Bringing the criticism to the legal sphere, in what sense are poets entitled to substitute their inspiration for the democratic process of deliberation and decision-making? In sum, anyone who wishes to argue that poetry and the poets have contributions to make to public discourse must find a way to respond to the Platonic critique that the poets lack the *interest*, the *expertise*, and the *entitlement* to do so. In the rest of this section I will try to offer some preliminary arguments as to how one might approach or begin to think about these questions.[43]

The first thing is to make sure we know what to look for or to expect in poetry. Judge Posner is obviously right in that it would be absurd to read *Animal Farm* as providing advice on farm management. At the same time, it is also true that the absurdity would lie only with the reader who was tempted to find it there.[44] Thus, if one wants to learn how to build an arch, one should know better than to rely on Homer's description of it. If truth is to be found in poetry, it is not in practical solutions, policy recommendations, or, perhaps less plainly, in moral lessons, at least when these come in the form of easily discernible and detachable maxims.

This is sometimes not so easy to distinguish. For example, Cornelius Castoriadis argues compellingly that one of the most important political truths of the *Antigone* (not to be confused with the political opinion of the poet) is the denunciation of *monos phronein*, that is the idea that no one is wise alone, leveled by Haemon against his father – but it can also fit other characters in the drama.[45] This may be true, I submit, not because Haemon says it (and of course not just because our modern democratic sensibility or that of the Athenians happen to favor it), but only because in the course of the drama the consequences of Creon's obstinate refusal to listen demonstrate in no uncertain terms the emptiness of he who thinks he alone is wise. The maxim might eventually become part of the larger legal or political *aquis*, which is how Castoriadis advances it, but insofar as it is presented to us in the *Antigone* it remains inextricably linked to its concrete conditions of appearance, embedded in the performance out of which it emerges or manifests itself,[46] and upon which it relies for its full and persuasive force. And this always requires that the audience be made a party to its logic of demonstration.

As a result, more promising is the idea of linking the epistemic value of poetry not to what the poet says or knows, but to what the poetry shows or adumbrates – to what it lets us see that would otherwise remain unseen. What we expect from it is not knowledge in the Cartesian sense, but insight into a hitherto unknown reality, connected to the concrete experience it affords its audience. Here, I believe poets are particularly apt, for as Milan Kundera says, one is bound to learn more of the mood of the bureaucratic state in Kafka than in Weber. Not, of course, that we should disregard Weber, for the only way to contextualize the poet's depiction of the bureaucratic state is precisely by joining forces with the sociologist. As far as I know, however, no scholar in the law and humanities tradition has advocated substituting novels for traditional materials, but only to enrich, and sometimes to question, the way those materials are read.[47]

To be sure, the truth that may be predicated about poetry has to do with the particular *mode of knowing* of literature. This mode is not revelation, such as the messianic utterances of the prophets, or the Decalogues and commands issued by a central authority. Nor is this knowledge in the telling, like the expert who transmits his expertise to those who do not know; if anything, this knowing lies in the ability to elicit, that is to evoke and to bring to light, experiences that may have otherwise eluded the audience, and which presupposes the disposition to participate and engage with it. This may explain the existence of poetic truths that transcend the known subjects of both poet and audience – beyond what they "know." It additionally suggests that whatever knowledge we may gain from it is dependent upon our own submersion and engagement with the experience the work of art offers, thereby stressing our own critical intervention in the process.

For instance, let us concede that there are aspects of life into which tragedy claims to have some insight – to name one, the portrayal of human beings. This can be supported on other experiential grounds, without claiming universal validity for them. For example, it can be argued that tragedy creates a picture of human beings as interdependent and vulnerable, one that I personally find "truer to life" than the autonomous and solipsistic self at the core of modern liberalism. In contrast to the "unencumbered self"[48] of liberalism, tragedy showcases a fragile yet resilient self who is no master of the natural world, but an inhabitant of it, and hence subject to forces that escape individual foresight and control and lay open man's ontological, epistemic, and moral finitude. This self is profoundly historicized and comes encapsulated within an inherited language and *nomos*. Human beings often find themselves within – or thrown into – a universe of unruly, unpredictable, and ultimately unknowable forces which result in the mutability and radical instability of all things human. Still, this world does not eliminate human agency – rather the opposite. It underscores responsibility by stressing that the fundamental question is one precisely of how to live and maintain a sense of worth in it – how to conceive it, how not to lose it, how to face its loss – which often leads to radical self-transformation (as we have seen Antigone do in her last moments among the living). As philosopher and pedagogue Plato might object to this picture on the grounds that human beings are shown at their most vulnerable and weakest – not the best examples for the audience to follow. I would argue, contrarily, that these moments reveal human beings at their most lucid realization of their limits, and thus of who they are and their place in the world that has often ceased to make sense to them. Clearly the "truth-claim" of this argument is not independent from the context in which it figures as polemic (i.e. opposing Plato and the liberal autonomous individual), and hence not universally valid as a true account of human beings, in all times and places, as "knowledge" allegedly derived from tragedy.

The authority of the work of art is therefore to be experienced, not as part of any canon of authoritative sources, but as part of a critical engagement with it. Arguably, such a critical reading can vest poetry with some democratic ascendancy, for it is no longer the working of a single man (the gendered pun is intentional), but a communal activity of reading and re-reading, which requires the active participation of its audience and the contact with other discourses and epistemes. This also gives us a clue as to how the ensuing "knowledge" would be incorporated into the legal setting: not as a "legal implant," "borrowing," or "imposition," but rather as "cross-fertilization," where one idea feeds the next and is translated into a different language through appropriate channels of expression. Contrary to what Plato supposes, poets need not have the intention, or the interest, or the knowledge to make their art exemplary in that fashion. The responsibility of the artist is to their art and to this alone (to make it the best it can possibly be), but their object of creation can be engaged with in a different yet still responsible manner by the audience. Excellence is no longer to be found in whether it offers a more or less accurate portrayal of a given reality (e.g. a particular legal institution), but rather in the ability to call that "given" into question, and maybe even to transform it together with the audience. From this engagement, there springs a reality that is no longer the one which is represented in the work of art, but a different one that is being *enacted* as a result of the complex interplay between poet, text, and audience.

The enactment is crucial for legal judgment in the *Antigone*. Whereas in "the court of King Creon" (the law represented in the drama) Antigone has neither voice nor representation, in the court that is being enacted symbolically by the audience, Antigone has as much a voice and standing as does Creon. For the conflict to be fully deployed, in fact, the audience is to create this triangular structure where Antigone and Creon are the two parties of a trial conducted on a different register, which is where the judgments of the audience take place. Since this stage does not pre-exist the conflict in which Antigone and Creon figure as parties, the audience must carve out the space in which the incommensurable conflict can be properly staged. Notice that this court is neither represented nor performed before the audience, but it is rather *constituted* by the active participation of the audience. As such, the audience acts not as a neutral observer, but as guarantor of the symbolical structure of justice, which is precisely the role and position that Robert Cover reserved for judges when facing a hard case, without relying on the prerogative of jurisdiction as a matter of course, or aligning the jurisdictional office with the powers that be. Therefore the engagement with the incommensurable conflict presented in the *Antigone* brings to consciousness knowledge fundamental to the practice of legal adjudication in a manner that practicing the trade, with all its timely constraints, does not necessarily accomplish. Of course, one should not imagine substituting tragedy for learning the trade, but tragedy does definitely raise the consciousness concerning the problematic of judgment, and this awareness must indeed belong in the education of every judge and lead to a better practice.

5.3 The power of emotions: "education sentimentale"

Martha Nussbaum rightly points out that "a lover of literature who wishes to question Plato's banishment of literary artists from the public realm must, in pleading her case, make some defense of the emotions and their contribution to public rationality."[49] This is so because after Plato associated art with the emotional as opposed to the rational, emotions often followed poetry's cruel fate in philosophy as rivals of reason.[50] I use the term "emotions" (rather than passions or appetites) deliberately: it feels somewhat of a missed opportunity that after Plato's tripartite division of the human psyche into the rational [*to logistikon*], the spirited [*to thumoeides*], and the appetitive [*to epithum¯etikon*] in Book 4 of the *Republic*, he decided to align poetry with the appetitive instead of with the spirited (or should we say, the emotional?). In doing so, he flattened his original tripartite scheme into a much less subtle duality. Had he maintained his original triadic division, there would have been fewer difficulties in realizing that, in Plato's own framework, the spirited (which includes emotions such as anger, indignation (440 a–d), and courage (442c)) is, unlike the appetitive (thirst, hunger, sexual drive (439d)), *a natural ally of reason* (441a).

Nowadays, there is a sufficiently established, growing body of scholarship which has done much to rehabilitate the role of emotions in public discourse.[51] We are taught that emotions such as grief, anger, fear, gratitude, awe, or indignation are not blind bodily responses to external stimuli; rather, they incorporate beliefs and assessments about the situations arousing them, all of which turns them into highly contextual affective and cognitive responses to the social environment. Now we know that emotions are socially constructed and shaped by social expectations and cultural demands, and that the way a person *feels* is often influenced by the way she *thinks* it is appropriate to feel in the particular context.[52]

Not only are emotions imbued with cognitive and evaluative (i.e. "rational") components, but the reverse is also true, for what we call rational thinking is endowed with affective and emotional components. For example, research on individuals with lesions in the frontal lobe has shown that people with otherwise normal motor and intellectual abilities, yet affected by a reduction of emotional reactivity, suffer from an inability to choose a course, foresee consequences, plan for the future, or learn from mistakes, which means that their decision-making landscape is hopelessly flat.[53] As Clifford Geertz explains, the affective disorder that presents itself as a certain affectlessness, shallowness, and detachment, cripples both will and judgment.[54] If emotions are rational and reason is emotional, the once sharp dichotomy between reason and emotions is no longer workable and had better be abandoned. The same conclusion holds true for law as well, which has traditionally given itself the appearance of the dispassionate voice of reason as opposed to emotion. Thus, in a fascinating ethnographic study about emotions in Swedish courtrooms, Leif Dahlberg notes that what is often portrayed as ritualistic and rule-bound rationality does not properly designate an absence of emotion or an emotionless state of mind, but rather a *counter-mood* or resoluteness in the face of certain actions and events.[55]

In the legal scholarship concerned with emotions,[56] the more positive outlook on emotions has been accompanied by appeals to empathy – the ability to place oneself in someone else's shoes – as an adequate virtue of judicial decision-making.[57] This goes hand in hand with the demise of, or the growing discomfort with, formalistic paradigms of law. If, as James Boyd White has suggested, "imagination is at the root of justice,"[58] cultural forms that broaden the student's empathetic abilities such as literature and the arts ought to be incorporated as part of the legal curriculum. This central tenet of the "law and humanities" movement must face, however, Plato's twofold challenge: one, that there may be stories that invite us to participate in emotions that run counter to what is otherwise desirable (for example, expressions of excessive anger and vindictiveness in the courtroom[59]); and, two, that these emotions and the narratives containing them may actually have an adverse constitutive effect upon the listeners (for example, influencing the jurors to impose a harsher sentence than otherwise necessary). Tragedy enters this debate as generating the kind of emotions that, from Plato's perspective, constitute lax and cowardly individuals.

The first person to put these arguments to the test was his disciple, Aristotle. Like his teacher, Aristotle too perceived tragedy as an emotionally charged representation, and singled out two emotions, *eleos* and *phobos* (conventionally translated as pity and fear), as giving us clues to its distinctive quality. Yet, whereas Plato thinks that these emotions are likely to expose us as lax and cowardly individuals, Aristotle embraces them with the argument that tragedy works their *katharsis*.[60] Although Aristotle never explains how it operates, and commentators do not seem to agree as to whether he meant that emotions are *purged* (i.e. extirpated) or *purified* (i.e. cleansed),[61] the relevant point is that after their effective release, the audience does not bring them home: what is experienced in the theater remains in the theater. Aristotle established not so much a spatial distance between the audience and the stage – for him the audience still feels *as* the characters – but a *temporal* one. If we become what we see, as Plato believed, this is so only for a moment. Henceforth, Aristotle encourages audiences to abandon themselves to the pleasures of the spectacle, without fear that it will carry into the real life and cause permanent damage to their psyches. In fact, it has been argued after Aristotle, *katharsis* can improve upon it, for emotions are not bottled up and repressed, but played out and liberated. This could additionally explain the paradox that audiences can feel joy, while watching terrible suffering and extreme sadness: not for what they are watching happening to others (because it happens *to others*), but for what happens to them (because they are relieved of *their own* tensions). Despite its salutary approach, Aristotle's theory of *katharsis* presents several shortcomings.

First, in assuring us that tragedy does not have a negative constitutive effect, Aristotle strips tragedy of its (potentially) educative effects as well. Concerning emotions, *katharsis* is unlikely to bring us closer to knowing how to identify the emotions, how not to mistake one for another, how to know when to display them when needed, and how to correct them when necessary. Aristotle's *katharsis* falls short of such a pedagogic function.[62] Therefore, if there is something to be learned from the (tragic) emotions – not just how to soothe, but to sharpen them – what is most needed (and what the proper vindication of the emotional experience of tragedy requires most) is not their *katharsis*, but the training of our ability to understand and use them well.

Aristotle's theory of *katharsis* presents a second, perhaps more gripping problem, which is that it appears to divorce the *pathos* of tragedy from its *logos* (perhaps because for him tragedy is already more a text than a performance).[63] The audience is moved to tears or awe over what is seen on the stage, but once *katharsis* operates, the members of the audience fall back into shape again, fully restored in their intellectual and mental capacities, and ready to assess the logos of the tragedy, free of its emotional burden. Still, the conditions of the experience of art are indissoluble from its content and can be neither disconnected nor assessed separately, which is what ultimately made Plato shy away from it. For him, the enchanting power of poetry meant that we could not profit from it without simultaneously falling victim to its charm. The same applies to tragedy: there can be no detachable and objective perspective from which to assess it, for even when *reading* it, audiences are required to visualize the play as if it were performed before their eyes, and to jump imaginatively within it, and to assess the words and arguments of the characters, not in isolation, but in the dramatic context in which they appear. Doing otherwise would be an attempt to bring art to the bridle of philosophical discipline. True, Aristotle acknowledges that tragedy is more "philosophical" than history,[64] but the appraisal is made at the cost of depriving poetry of its performative aspects. After Aristotle, philosophy might as well dispense with poetry, for it does not need it any longer.

Finally, there is another reason to go beyond a theory of *katharsis* that does not account for those emotions that are neither purged nor cleansed (and therefore retain their full vigor), and which can potentially clash with citizenship. For example, Aristotle says nothing about emotions such as anguish and despair (by any account part of the tragic experience), which might validate, under Platonic assumptions, passive, despondent, or cynical attitudes. Indeed it is not at all clear why, of the ample elenchus of emotions that may be experienced when watching or reading tragedy – ranging from deep anguish to the awesome realization of cosmic forces, from bottomless despair for human fragility to the proud vindication of human dignity, from guilty pleasures in the realization of poetic justice to the exhilarating joy in transgressions – Aristotle chose to speak of pity and fear as *the* emotions of tragedy, the former for undeserved suffering, the latter because it happens to people like ourselves (*Poetics*, 1453a–4). It is not at all clear to me why modern commentators also continue to refer only to these two to describe *their own* experiences. Consequently, in order to rescue the full range of emotions from the Platonic criticism it is necessary to demonstrate that the tragic experience as such is not just harmless, but actually beneficial, and that it has much to offer the citizen, the statesman, and the judge.

The discussion in the legal arena arises concerning certain emotions (or particular expressions of them) which are not easy to harmonize with the interests of justice. For example, Martha Nussbaum expresses the view that shame and particularly disgust should not, for their complicity in attaching stigma and hierarchy, be utilized as a general basis for legislation, policy, and decision-making.[65] Likewise, Mark Dubber argues that hatred and vindictiveness ought not to have a place in a theory of criminal punishment.[66] Another example can be found in administrative practices or legislative measures based on bigotry and stereotyping.[67] However, the solution is not to create two lists – one for permissible emotions and the other for impermissible ones – for every emotion can send us valuable information to which we should listen.[68] Nor is the debate about whether to empathize or not in general – understanding others is *always* better than not understanding them. But appeals to empathy in decision-making must be accompanied by a reflection of what we are invited to empathize with, and of the kind of person we are invited to become in the process.

One telling and controversial example is that of victim impact statements which are introduced at the sentencing phase of a criminal trial, most often by a family member, in order to describe the effects of the crime on its victims. According to Kenji Yoshino, these kinds of statement "provide a useful starting point for a broader examination of the use of narrative and emotion in legal processes," for they "raise uncomfortable questions about the empathy and narrative movements."[69] In his view, victim impact statements show that "we cannot commit ourselves categorically to narratives on ideological grounds, because narratives can be used to support any ideology."[70] Faced with this kind of narrative, it is tempting to join Plato in the conclusion that the state has the right simply to "exclude" them.[71] Thus it has been argued that victim impact statements ought not be "told" at the sentencing phase of the trial, for they may block the ability of juries to consider extenuating or mitigating circumstances for the crime or defendant.[72] But the argument is not that these narratives are too emotional and hence contrary to public reason. Nor is the objection based on the fact that victim impact statements are difficult to verify, come encapsulated in inflammatory rhetoric, or can be driven by spurious sentiments.[73] More poignantly, the fear is that all this is put to the service of generating a state of mind in the decision-makers (constituting them in a way) that is not conducive to justice, or, still more damagingly, that the narrative is actually *intended to disregard* important interests of justice. Thus, in addition to concern for the worth of what we are to empathize with and for who are we to become in the process, the extent to which incorporating these narratives serves adequately to advance the interests of justice must also be shown. The hurdle according to Plato is that the nature and intensity of certain emotional experiences – i.e. poetry's power to hypnotize us into voluntarily surrendering our critical capacities – may prevent us from precisely that kind of judgment.

Therefore, if we attempt to rescue the experience of tragedy as meaningful for the *polis*, it is necessary to show firstly that tragedy as a genre does not hinder but rather enhances the capacity for judgment; secondly, that exercising this capacity is not incompatible but actually required for the full enjoyment of tragedy; and lastly, that this full experience brings us closer to having a more sensitive appreciation of the parties and their respective positions, and hence nearer also to justice, all of which I will try to show in the sections that follow. In this capacity for judgment lies, in fact, a fundamental difference between tragedy and narratives such as victim impact statements, which are not meant to be thus assessed. Even further, attempting to do so may attract the accusation of being insensitive to the victim or to the family. In other words, one cannot fully remain a critical listener of a victim impact statement without fearing the accusation of cruelty, or worst of all, of "killing the victim a second time." Thus victim impact statements can be influential and persuasive, just like political propaganda can be, but they are not meant to be examined and judged intently. This is what justifies in my view more than an ideological objection to them because, as a *genre*, their audience is deprived altogether of their abilities to reflect critically about what they are being constituted into, and about the kind of (in)justice these statements are inviting its audience to accept.

5.4 A good judge or judging well?

A recurring dilemma facing the student of judgment is whether to create an ideal judge and grant him (or her) the capacities and dispositions deemed good, or whether to focus on the activity of judging and how to perform it well. The first approach aims to improve upon legal standards such as the "reasonable man," which are prone to reproduce gender and racial bias, societal hierarchies, and structures of domination.[74] In this vein, Robin West puts forward the model of "literary woman," whose great empathic competence allows her to access other people's subjectivity, and to make the kind of interpersonal valuations that elude the "economic man."[75] In a similar vein, but more ambitiously, Martha Nussbaum has devised a paradigm of public rationality and judgment in the figure of the "judicious spectator," whose most salient quality is to imagine vividly what it is like to be each of the persons whose situation he or she imagines, and, at the same time, is able to assess externally or from the spectatorial viewpoint the level of empathy it is rational to have in each case.[76]

An alternative approach is to shift the emphasis from the qualities and the person of the judge to the *activity* of judging itself. One of the advantages of this second approach is that, whereas in the former there is a slight danger of homogeneity when people of different races, genders, and backgrounds are made to become the same (ideal) person and share similar attributes, in the latter those same people need only to engage in an (idealized) activity that respects their individuality as people.[77] But a more fundamental reason than this, I think, is that the heterogeneity and captivating force of poetry prevents us from constructing an ideal model of judge who would be able to assess, from an external and fixed position, "the level of empathy it is rational to have."[78] Simply put, there is no spectatorial viewpoint outside the text, nor is it possible to construct one to fit all texts: poetry's ability to drag us into its charm sweeps us along whatever external position we may wish to keep as readers or spectators. This is why, rather than following in the steps of the "good judge," I find it more promising to turn our gaze towards the activity and phenomenology of judging well, a phenomenology that, unlike Duncan Kennedy's model of result-oriented judgment,[79] problematizes its own capacity to judge with justice. This last caveat appears necessary to avoid a common pitfall of the second approach, which consists in offering recommendations that reflect the student's own personal and unfiltered preferences.[80] Instead of criteria of excellence, I try to develop a language for a variety of more or less satisfactory practices of judgment – naturally, this range of "good practices" does not lead to incontrovertible judgments and must be accompanied by the reasons and appreciations that lead us to them. In so doing, I try to discern the kind of competencies and skills demanded for judging legal conflicts, and offer my own acts of reading the *Antigone* as an example. For analogous processes are at work for tragic audiences and for the judge facing a hard case.

5.5 Six spaces of judgment

As I have already suggested, tragedy is woven around a multi-layered web of mediations and motions of a both spatial and temporal nature, which serve simultaneously to constitute the relationship between the audience and the stage and to disavow the uncritical conflation of the two. I will deal with the temporal aspects of judgment – its motions and trajectories – in the final chapter, for the inquiry can only be brought to fruition after the resolution of the play in Chapter 6. Therefore in this section the focus is exclusively on what I call spatial relationships – the distances and mediations – that lie between the subject(s) and object(s) of judgment, which are further enriched in the final part of the book. The analysis now distinguishes six such spatial relationships (*identification*, *separation*, *mediation*, *bifurcation*, *embodiment*, and *disembodiment*) not rooted in preconceived notions of what constitutes "good judgment," but born out of a deliberate attempt to bring to consciousness the kind of activities (both intellectual and emotional) required for a full engagement with the play. To the extent that these spaces for judgment can be shown to emerge as conditions of engagement with the tragedy, this approach can better counteract Plato's critique that the tragic experience lulls or incapacitates judgment. The ability to identify and to understand the way these various spaces are constructed and modulate judgments helps in the legal conflict dramatized in the *Antigone*, but it further sharpens the skills and competences required for judging legal conflicts, I suggest, by bringing awareness of the various kinds of spatial mediations judges face in performing this activity.

5.5.1 *Identification*

The first thing to notice as members of a tragic audience is the presence of characters that speak directly to us. Unlike an omniscient third-person narrator, the theatrical author does not use his own voice, but rather that of multiple characters, each of which speaks in their own voice and language. This narrative construction enables the process I call *identification*, by which the audience enjoys the mimetic experience of getting "under the skin" and inhabiting the world and unique perspectives of each. A second structural device that fosters identification is the sequential or developmental staging of the drama. The interpreter follows the characters through different stages and is able to obtain, more than a snapshot, a view to their evolution and personal transformations. In the process, the audience is able to pierce through the characters' protective shell and to access their inner lives: how each character thinks, values, and perceives things, including the normative world they live in. In other words, identification facilitates the ability to see things from what legal theorists call the "internal point of view," which is essential to understanding the motivations, commitments, and meanings behind every normative action – and law as well.

Identification requires a certain sensitivity and a willingness to listen and to respond to what the characters have to say, without which all efforts will come to nothing. For example, in the first scene the audience hears Antigone complain before her sister about the new evil that comes to her family in the form of Creon's decree. By listening to her claim, the audience is able to empathize with Antigone's suffering, with her terrible family history, with her current misery, and most importantly, with the moral outrage she feels at imagining the body of a loved one being left for birds of prey and dogs, all of which appears to justify her duty to prevent it.

But the fact that we are able to see things from Antigone's perspective (and to that extent to empathize with her) does not mean that we become one with her in any way: identification does not entail identity or fusion between character and audience. Again the first scene is instructive: the dialogical structure of the tragedy puts Antigone face to face with her sister, who has identical relations to the dead and shares the same family history, but who nevertheless reaches an altogether different conclusion about what needs to be done. For Ismene, the new suffering must be endured, as they have learned to do in the past. Faced with two very different appraisals of the very same circumstances, the audience is not ready to take a stand yet. Moreover, Ismene suggests that Antigone is attempting to do something subversive, almost unthinkable, for her time and place, where young women are expected to have neither the strength nor the right to defy those in authority (especially as a niece to her uncle). Having landed in a foreign territory the norms of which we do not know, audiences old and modern must suspend their cultural presuppositions in favor of those enacted in the play – not those in Athens, but in the world of legend – as explained already in Chapter 2. The initial impulse of identification is hence defined by a desire to learn from the characters, their circumstances, and the world they live in, and not to pass the kind of judgments for which the audience is not yet equipped, for example whether a given character follows, bends, twists, breaks, or transcends the societal practices and norms. This attitude leads us to accept as valid, at least for the moment, Ismene's description of the societal norms and cultural expectations concerning women and their role in society.

At the same time, a fundamental bond begins to form already between stage and audience, which has to do with the lens through which the audience accesses the news of the decree. The audience learns about its content from the sisters, not from Creon himself, and filters it through the moral outrage it generates, especially in Antigone. Looking at the decree through the sisters' perspective – focusing on how it affects them and not on the reasons for it – audiences are invited to participate in Antigone's indignation, and to view Creon and his decree in a less than favorable light. The tone of moral offense with which the play begins never leaves the audience, in fact, despite Ismene's timid attempts at calming it down with general appeals to authority and obedience. Without specific reasons to justify obedience in this particular case – e.g. what makes obeying Creon more important than burying one's own brother? – Antigone's sense of offended righteousness seems more attuned to the situation than Ismene's appeals to prudence, which can also be interpreted as fear (or cowardice?) to stand for what she might have otherwise decided to do – implied in the demand for forgiveness from the dead (65–6). Likewise, without the arguments to make Creon's decree more understandable (what reasons can there be, first to prohibit the burial, and then to sentence anyone who tries to carry out the burial to their death?), Creon appears as representative of a distant and impenetrable form of authority. Therefore emotional alignments and sympathies begin to impact the audience's judgments as early as this stage of identification.

5.5.2 Separation

At the other extreme of identification lies a space of separation, for tragedy, like law, comes across invariably as a composition of contrasts and antinomian worldviews. The adversarial and agonistic structure generates a *distancing effect*[81] in the audience, which separates it from one-dimensional and simplistic identifications. Curiously, the effect of separation is often accomplished through the identification of, or with, alternative points of view, which counters affinities that may be running in the opposite direction. For example, when Creon explains that Polyneices came as the head of a foreign army with the intention of ravishing his own country and enslaving its people, the audience does more than learn the motives for the decree. Most importantly, the audience realizes that Polyneices can be accused of wronging the city as much as (Antigone claims) being wronged by it. The information does not change Antigone's stand (for her it is irrelevant what her brother is accused of having done), but the audience's perspective might alter, as the sense of moral outrage and indignation is no longer the same for a person who might not deserve them equally.

Tragedy generates this contrast of sympathies which builds the polyhedral complexity of the conflict. Moreover, each perspective is presented by a party who believes firmly in it and defends it with convincing arguments. None of these perspectives can be faulted a priori, nor attributed to a deficit of rationality, conceptual mistake, or simple error, but the audience must take turns comprehending the rationality embedded in each. Through successive identifications and separations, the audience's preconceptions and standpoints are challenged, for, when holistic forms of life are put face to face with equal verisimilitude, temptations for simple-minded attachments are complicated by the demands of similarly compelling ones. (This suggests that the proper way to counter bias and personal prejudice in matters of judgment is not to pretend not to have any of these, but to oppose them with others.)

The moment of maximum tension arrives when the values, principles, and laws of one side are matched by the values, principles, and laws of an equal though opposite force, as exemplified in the battle between Antigone and Creon. Rather than canceling each other out, tragedy forces us, in an effort as strenuous as it is necessary, to hold them both simultaneously in our minds.

Arguably, this could lead to a situation of impasse, where the audience is unable to decide which of the *nomoi* has a better claim. It is important nonetheless to *stage* this incommensurability – which can be represented as an equidistant angle between the audience and each of the parties – for it assures that the audience understands the conflict prior to delivering any verdicts.

5.5.3 *Mediation*

The audience's relationship with the characters is often indirect or mediated by others, which helps to develop a crispier, wider, or better picture of the object in question. For example, the way a character is perceived by others can reveal a potential disconnect between his or her self-perception and the image he or she projects. This disconnect can lead to charges of self-aggrandizement (as when Antigone compares her situation with Niobe and the Chorus reprimands her for it), or reveal certain shortcomings in their positions (as when Antigone's defense of her family is questioned by her own treatment of Ismene). Mediation thus helps the audience to get a clearer picture than the one that is developed through identification and opposition alone, for example when Haemon's intervention permits us to grasp Creon's inflexible and authoritarian conception of leadership quite conclusively, as seen in Chapter 4.

One of the most important mediating factors in the play is the Chorus of Theban elders, oftentimes directing the audience to issues that may have eluded them or otherwise gone unnoticed. Thus the Chorus often points in the direction of issues that are relevant for the debate and the audience to consider. This is not to say, however, that the Chorus functions as a proxy for the audience on stage, because the elders can also be wrong in their appreciations or provide misleading information, since their impressions are themselves filtered by their own status, gender, age, and personal concerns. As a result, the elders' comments and remarks must always be critically assessed. For instance, after the guard comes to explain that the body of Polyneices has been mysteriously buried, leaving behind no traces of wheels or human tools, the elders wonder whether the task might not have been performed by the gods (278–9). The audience, who unlike the Chorus were aware of Antigone's intentions, are not likely to agree with their hypothesis. Still, their readiness to see the burial as a matter that concerns the gods suggests for the audience that the prohibition of burial has wider implications than the restrictive political considerations of Creon.

Another important mediating factor is the stage-presence of the third actor, a device well analized by Simon Goldhill, which channels some of the audience's judgments.[82] For example, after the exchange between Antigone and Creon, Ismene intervenes briefly to ask Creon whether he will deprive his own son of his beloved bride and to defend the special relationship between the two of them. Bringing the emphasis away from the abstract conflict of principles down to its concrete consequences, Ismene's short interjection reminds the audience that Antigone is not only Creon's niece, but also Haemon's wife-to-be. If Creon takes into effect the threat of killing Antigone, he will not only be punishing his niece but breaking his son's heart.

Sometimes, the intervention of this third actor has a refractory function upon the dramatic action, as the audience's attention is turned towards the manner in which this actor understands or responds to what is happening on the stage. Sometimes this reaction differs from the way the audience is able to perceive the same action, which creates a dissonance between the audience and the character, permitting the audience to see him or her in a different light. For example, the sisters' emotionally charged and beautiful dialogue in which Ismene offers to share the burden of Antigone and the latter refuses and tells her to save herself (536–60) underscores both their closeness and their unbridgeable distance. Such a significant gap between the two completely eludes Creon (but not the audience) who declares both sisters to be equally mad (561–2). Creon's reaction to the earlier dialogue portrays him as insensitive and somewhat obtuse, as he is unable to perceive something that the audience clearly does. Other times, the stage-presence of the third actor can also help to filter information received on the stage and channel the audience's own reactions. For example, as we shall see in the following chapter, Eurydice's presence on the stage when the messenger brings the news of her son's death colors the meaning of the news, as the audience can see in her reactions on stage how they are affecting her.

5.5.4 *Bifurcation*

Bifurcation can be defined as the *caesura* or breaking point of the mimetic connection between character and audience, when the respective experiences of the two part ways and can go in separate directions. This mechanism disrupts the alleged merger of personalities between the audience and the characters that Plato feared could consummate the dissolution of the critical self. The best examples of bifurcation can be found at the point when the characters moan and lament the sad and terrible circumstances they have to endure, and ask for the sympathy of their audience. Plato objects to these demonstrations of weeping and inconsolable lament on account that they offer bad examples, and, although I disagree with his argument, there is something to be said for the prevention of overexposure to human misery. However, to access the emotional entrails of the characters and to encounter their bare and naked truth in all its crudeness does not in itself guarantee pity, for the audience is invited, by the same token, to reflect on what led the characters there, including the role they may have played in it. Bifurcation arises out of this dual relation: on the one hand, the sufferer is able to enlist the audience's sympathy – by which I mean, differently from empathy, not the ability to see things from the character's perspective, but rather the disposition to side with the character or see things favorably to them; on the other hand, the sympathy is not unconditional, for the audience is entitled to wonder what part the characters might have played in sealing their own fate.

Still, the expression of real suffering puts a limit on the kind of judgments that are appropriate at the moment of bifurcation. Arguably, the audience must be receptive to the pain the character is trying to communicate, without rushing yet to express their condemnation. One interesting example can be found in Antigone's last *kommos*, as she tries to enlist the sympathy of the Chorus one last time (806–82). Antigone appeals to the Chorus as witnesses of her suffering – she is being led to her tomb, alone, unmarried, and unwept – but the elders fail to respond as she had hoped, telling her among other things that she has gone to the extreme of daring and stumbled upon the altars of Justice (853–6), and that, having attempted a noble kind of respect, she has shown none in transgressing authority and is now destroyed by her own self-willed passion (872–5). The elders try to offer some words of comfort as well, telling her that it is a great thing to share a fate that is similar to the gods' (836–8), but Antigone is touchy and interprets these words as mockery. However, in comparison with the elders' ability to empathize with her personal suffering, Creon appears decidedly heartless when he interrupts Antigone's lament to say they should rush her to her death (931–2). Exposed to the Chorus' ambivalent expressions of pity (for the person) and mild censure (for the actions), the audience must be careful not to tread heavily on Antigone's pain or reach Creon's insensitive cruelty. Here lies the delicate terrain for the audience to walk on. Hence, to witness Antigone's lament from close quarters does not prevent the consideration of her prior decisions, and in that sense to remark a bifurcation between the experiences of the character and those of the audience. As a result, the spatial relationship that I call bifurcation is a moment of extreme proximity between the character and the audience, and yet there is no total identification between the two positions, as there is still a gap or space reserved for the audience's critical judgment.

5.5.5 *Embodiment*

By embodiment I mean the audience's progressive internalization of the position it is called on to fill in the drama, not externally merely as theater-goers, but internally as members of an audience who must first learn to identify this position, and then perform the role assigned to them. Whereas bifurcation was triggered by the characters' desire to be looked at by the audience, embodiment occurs from the characters' direct demand that the audience look at and fill *their role as audience*. This direct interpellation pushes them to confront their role as members of a dramatic audience and to realize the duties and responsibilities associated with it. Embodiment is the act of responding to that call, embracing these obligations and making them our own, which leaves a wide margin for the audience to fill the space left open.[83]

For example, I have already argued in an earlier chapter that when Haemon brings the report of the "invisible citizens" the audience is not necessarily to conclude that all the citizens favor Antigone. However, Haemon's report compels the audience to retain this new piece of information and to demand an answer to this capital issue, which Creon does not provide. In context, to embody such a position may simply require maintaining this issue in sight and remaining alert to the possibility that Creon's decree may lack the legitimacy he assumes it has.

One of the most interesting examples of what I call "embodiment" occurs in Antigone's long and final speech (or *rhesis*) after the elders have seemingly turned down all her appeals. She had earlier begun her lament by addressing the "citizens of [her] native land" [*patrias politai*] (809) and the "rich men in the city" [*poleôs poluktêmôn andres*] (842–3), presumably hoping to enlist the sympathy of the elders. But after they fail fully to endorse her, she is now led to admit that she may have acted "against the will of the citizens" (*biai politôn*] (907), but that her action is nonetheless right in the eyes of "those who think wisely" [*tois phronousin eu*] (904). Antigone's words open up an intriguing split between the elders of the Chorus and other unspecified "wise citizens" that she hopes will ultimately vindicate her action.

The question is not to take the elders or any other character as representative of those citizens (in fact every character claims to be on the citizens' side[84]), but rather to realize that "citizens" is an oscillatory position that the audience must learn to *embody* in its own readings. Accordingly, Antigone is directly calling on the audience to become the "wise citizens" that can accept her normative claim. To put it differently, Antigone hopes that someone in the audience will be able to see her point of view, namely that it was right and lawful for her to have acted on behalf of Polyneices, even against the citizens. It is up to each member of the audience to enact the role of the "wise citizens" who can understand her rationale and ultimately judge her favorably. Naturally, not everyone is likely to agree with her – not even among those who accept Antigone's invitation and look upon her with sympathy – and the final judgment must rest with every interpreter.

5.5.6 Disembodiment

Disembodiment establishes the farthest distance between audience and stage by inviting audiences to look upon the action, the characters, and their own relative position with an objectifying bird's eye view. Such a view makes possible, for example, the recognition of the device of tragic irony – arisen out of the mismatch between the character's and the audience's respective knowledge – which gives the audience a perspective that is not accessible to the character. I use the word disembodiment because the audience is to take some distance and to detach itself from the dramatic action in order to examine it, as it were from above. Thus, whereas embodiment called on audiences to fill the shoes of their assigned role within the play, disembodiment invites them to view it critically from without (i.e. to "disinhabit" it), by turning it into the object of the audience's critical gaze.

Tragedy creates this disembodied effect mostly through the choral odes, in which the Chorus, leaving behind their role as an ordinary character, takes a more conspicuous and lyrical persona and ponders in rather abstract and general terms about the central issues of the drama. The connection between the odes and the dramatic action is often tenuous (and never unambiguous), but far from being mere fillers or distractions, they allow audiences to observe the issues in their broader moral, political, and metaphysical implications. For instance, after the guard reveals that the burial has been performed despite the death-threat hanging on it, the Chorus sings about the wondrous nature of man, at once terrible and fascinating, equally capable of the greatest accomplishments and of the contrary. The particular act of defiance is thus turned into an ontological reflection about man's potential for transgression, which broadens the audience's horizon and pushes it to wonder whether these words are meant to describe Antigone, Creon, or both. Similarly, after the huge fight between Antigone and Creon and Ismene's vain attempts at saving her sister from certain death, the Chorus sings an ode about the striking forces humans are to stand up against, which nevertheless does not eliminate their moral responsibility. Once again, the audience is invited to step back and imagine how this description reflects on Creon and Antigone's respective situations.

One fascinating example of disembodiment can be found in the fourth *stasimon* which closes Chapter 4, where the chorus mixes mythological stories of diverse progeny, merit, and outcome, which both stimulate the free flow of associations *and* prevent their use as moral compasses for the future. Trapped between the desire to know and the inability to anticipate what the tragedy keeps in store, these two motions define the audience's own location in the drama. Unable to rise above this juncture, and firmly under its grip, the ode becomes the stage on which the audience is located. This provokes an interesting reversal: the audience appears to observe the action and fate of the characters, when in fact it is the former's own position which becomes the *object* of attention. Thus the ode confronts the audience with their own self-reflective regard, that is their own precise location in the drama, which the audience is able to perceive as it were externally.

5.6 The tragic audience and the judge

Whatever additional consequences derive from our necessarily sketchy, stylized account, the stages of identification, separation, mediation, bifurcation, embodiment, and disembodiment demonstrate that tragedy defines its audience as engaged and critical. What is more, being and remaining critically engaged appears necessary not just for understanding the drama, but to experience it to the fullest. Thus there is no need to sever artificially the *pathos* and the *logos* of tragedy in order to enjoy the emotional experience tragedy has to offer, while reflecting simultaneously about the serious issues it presents. This attitude, in fact, contrasts with what is expected from the audience of victim impact statements, constituted as a passive and quiet receptacle of whatever story they are presented with. To be responsive to the tragic performance is not a matter of blind or unchecked reactions, but of judgment, which entails not an attitude of aesthetic contemplation and disinterestedness as in the Kantian tradition, but of concerned reflexivity, where the final aim is to assess the justice of each normative claim.

Tragedy illuminates the legal conflict from many different angles, each of which gives us not just more information, but divergent ways of relating to (and hence of judging) the conflict. In trying to disentangle these various relationships, the audience learns to make progressively better and more nuanced judgments about an issue as complex as the one between Antigone and Creon. For example, we have made some progress after the incommensurable dilemma reached through *identification* (of the precepts, myths, language, and commitments that animate Antigone's and Creon's respective *nomoi*) and *separation* (by putting them face to face and trying to understand the logic of their mutual opposition). Through the *mediation* of both Ismene and Haemon, we may begin to suspect that Creon is not acting in the best interest of his family or of the city, which severely undermines his legitimacy as ruler and the grounds upon which his decree stands. In turn, the audience may empathize with Antigone's suffering yet undergo the *bifurcated* experience of considering her part responsibility for what is happening to her (on account of her prior choices and decisions).[85] Still, if the members of the audience *embody* their position as "wise citizens" there is a way to defend her case as so exceptional that it made it right and lawful to do what she did, even against the citizens. In any case, the audience may still feel the need for certain *disembodiment*, as there are judgments we are not yet ready to make until the end.

Just like the drama presented on a theater stage, the dramatic re-presentation of a hard case requires similar active and participatory imagination on the part of the judge (which is at work also when the judge is a member of a collective body).[86] Imagine, for example, the case of a Jehovah's Witness opposed to a blood transfusion, when this procedure could save his or her life or that of their infant child.[87] The judge would need first to *identify* the perspective of each of the parties and understand them from within, for judges do not have direct and unmediated access to the object of legal controversy. At this stage, the judge must be receptive to the claims and commitments of the parties, without prejudging their validity (i.e. not questioning whether the religion of a Jehovah's Witness effectively prohibits blood transfusions). For the purposes of identification, it is enough that the party presents it as part of the *nomos* for the judge to accept it at face value.

These normative claims are later contrasted with others running in the opposite direction, for example with the normative claims of the hospital trying to save their lives, which fosters the process of *separation*. The *mediation* of expert witnesses or other kinds of testimonies (from family members, friends, employers . . .) can moderate the radical antagonism of each side, enabling a more temperate consideration of the conflict. For example, a cultural anthropologist or an expert in comparative religions can help the judge determine whether the norm prohibiting blood transfusions is more or less dispositive within the normative world being considered (and hence determine the flexibility of the rule or the degree of transgression in breaking it). The judge may also hear testimony about the transfusion procedure and reflect on its risks, necessity, and impact on the life of the individuals. The case may also present an opportunity for *bifurcation*: if the child were to die and the case turn into a charge of wrongful death against the parents for their refusal to allow the blood transfusion, the judge may listen sympathetically to the suffering of the parents who have lost their child, while simultaneously considering their degree of responsibility in causing the child's death. In any event, the judge must learn to *embody* what the case demands from him or her, not only at the moment of determining any eventual responsibility, but much earlier, at the moment in which his or her intervention may become necessary to prevent the death of the child, if the case were to turn to this.[88] Should the judge grant an injunction to order a blood transfusion that could save the child's life? Should the parents' religious views be allowed to prevail instead? Should the judge relieve the parents from making that determination? In embodying this responsibility the judge must respond to the particular demands of the case within the parameters left open by the jurisdictional role (for the case will be framed differently – the questions will be different and differently pursued – before a family law judge than before a criminal court), and answer also to the demands of each individual party. It is important to stress that in doing so the judge is not simply following or relying upon preexistent rules of jurisdiction, but helping to construct it, as it were, creating jurisdiction "as he or she speaks." Finally, the judge must be exposed to a certain *disembodiment*, which allows him or her to view both the case and his or her position in it in a self-critical and reflexive way. For instance, what does the decision entail for the child, the parents, the legal community, and society at large? How does it affect the rights to life, liberty, human dignity, and religious freedom? How do the judge's own views affect these decisions? How should they? In articulating all these judgments, judges are to weave an *interdependent* narrative between their own and each party's *nomos*, away and beyond their original position and prejudices, and towards a more fully developed narrative of justice.

This is certainly no easy task and sometimes the responsibility is agonizing, as exemplified by the British Siamese twins Jodie and Mary.[89] The case involved Siamese twins united by a common aorta that was not expected to sustain their common life longer than three to six months. There was no dispute, on the other hand, that the twins could be surgically separated and that one (Jodie) could lead a normal life, but that the other (Mary) would die in the operation. The issue was whether one should save at least one of the twins even if this meant killing the other, or else refuse to perform the operation to which the parents objected on religious grounds. The hospital could not suffer Jodie's life to be lost and seized the court to allow the operation to be carried out. Lord Justice Ward writing for the Court of Appeal of England and Wales described his responsibility thus: "There is an irreconcilable conflict and the court cannot fully honor its separate duty to each child to do what is best for that child. The Court is placed in an impossible position." He continued, "[a]fter anxious thought I conclude that the court cannot abdicate responsibility and simply say it is too difficult to decide. We are here to make tough decisions," after which he went on to defend his decision to allow the operation as "the least detrimental solution." Despite reaching what he thought was the "best" (i.e. least detrimental) solution, Lord Ward also recognized that his "heart bled," that he had "truly agonized" over the case and that, keeping the "tragedy of this family" constantly in mind, he felt "more sorrow for them today than even . . . when first learning of their plight."[90] My point is not to praise or criticize the decision, or Lord Ward's framing of the dilemma,[91] but solely to illustrate the kind of responsibility judgment sometimes carries with it. In performing this role responsibly the judge and the audience of tragedy are not so far apart from each other as is often thought, and I hope to have shown that there is actually much to benefit from their mutual comparison, enough already to bring tragedy back to the *polis*.

Chapter 6

Antigone, Part III: Realizations

It is time for realizations. Many terrible things will happen: some announced, others unannounced, but all invariably painful. We will hear the fearsome words of the seer who can read the signs of augury and meet, once again, Creon's fierce and obstinate resistance. Then, after a sudden and unexpected reversal, we will pray with the chorus for an act of deliverance. Instead we will find Antigone's body, and a heartbroken Haemon, close to her. We will listen to the news at Eurydice's side, fearing her own silence. Still sadder news will be brought to the stage in the end, with Creon at its center.

6.1 Teiresias: seer and counselor (lines 988–1114)

Aged, blind, and led by a boy, the old seer Teiresias makes a sudden entrance. Since he was not summoned, Creon inquires about the purpose of his visit. Teiresias explains that when he took his place on the seat for bird observation, he heard an indecipherable uproar among the birds, yet he recognized they were tearing each other apart with their claws. Distressed, he then went on to kindle the fire, but the fire would not burn; instead, a dank moisture oozed from the offerings. Such was the utter and absolute failure of the rites. According to the seer, it is Creon's decision [phrenos] which has brought such defilement[1] *upon the city: for the altars are filled with the carrion brought by birds and dogs; the gods no longer accept the offerings; and the birds, having eaten the human flesh of Oedipus' son, no longer give intelligible signs. Teiresias urges Creon to rethink* [phronêson]*: It is human to make mistakes, but foolish to remain inflexible. Creon must give in, for there is no bravery in killing a dead man yet again. Creon should learn from advice that brings him profit* [kerdos].

Creon is furious; to his mind it appears that Teiresias has been bribed by enemies who would not hesitate to engage in seer-craft. He gives a warning: "You {all} shall not hide him in the grave, even if Zeus's eagles should snatch the body and bear the carrion up to their master's throne! Not even then shall I take fright at this pollution [miasma] *and allow him to be buried: for well I know that no mortals have power to pollute the gods." For even those who are clever fall shamefully, he states, when they speak shameful words in pursuit of profit.*

Teiresias cannot believe what he has just heard, and questions Creon's good counsel and understanding [euboulia; phronein]. *Creon accuses the seer of dishonesty. After a heated exchange, Teiresias reveals that Creon will soon exchange corpse for corpse, for sending down to earth a living person belonging to the world above, and keeping a body above – unburied and dishonored – belonging to the world below. As a result, the Erinyes of Hades and of the gods lie in wait for Creon, and soon wailing and lamentations will be heard in his own house.*[2] *Teiresias then asks his young guide to take him home, away from the abuses of Creon.*

Teiresias' exit leaves all petrified, for they all know he has never been proven wrong before. Creon asks for the elders' advice: What should he do? "To yield feels terrible, but to resist heads toward disaster." The Chorus urges a full reversal: release the girl and bury the corpse. Creon agrees: "[O]ne cannot fight against necessity [anagkêi]*." At the chorus's request to act promptly and personally, Creon rushes with his servants to release her whom he imprisoned: it may be better, he concludes, to observe the established laws* [kathestôtas nomous] *throughout one's life to the end* [ton bion telein].

As Karl Reinhardt points out, this scene presents structural parallelisms with that with Haemon.[3] On the one side, Teiresias enters the palace with the halo of venerated seer who appeals to Creon's best interests; when Creon accuses him of personal dishonesty, he gets furious and storms out, but not before leaving a chilling cloud of pending disaster over Creon's head. On the other side, Creon first welcomes Teiresias as the trustworthy counselor and savior of the city, but as soon as his own decision and authority are questioned, he reacts with the same acrimony and arrogance as before. Critics agree in blaming Creon's personal shortcomings and obsessions for failing to appreciate the seer's advice. Such a conclusion, however, hinges on the subtle and progressive shifts in the respective positions of the two men, which enable the audience to reach that understanding with an increased sense of clarity.

The introductory lines are particularly rich in building up Teiresias' personal charisma, known to the audience at least since the *Odyssey*.[4] The sudden and majestic entrance of the blind seer, preceded by a young boy who guides him, conveys an awe-inspiring presence and an air of gravity to the whole scene.[5] The audience is also reminded of Teiresias' past role as savior of the city, which underscores the image of a wise counselor with undoubted loyalty to the city, and proven record on its behalf. Thus, even before opening his mouth, Teiresias' character is granted a voice worthy of respect.

This is not to say that his authority ought to be automatically accepted. Sometimes it is argued that Teiresias' voice is immediately compelling, because, as spokesman of the gods, his word must count.[6] However, it is important to realize that in the art of divination as practiced by Teiresias, the gods do not communicate directly with him, but they do so through signs, which it then becomes the task of the seer to decipher. Historically, the Greeks distinguished two methods of communicating with the gods: one "inspired" or revealed, and the other "inductive" or elicited.[7] In inspired divination, the gods revealed their mind directly and without intermediaries to the chosen person (i.e. the prophet Cassandra, the Pythia at Delphi). In contrast, the inductive method was based not on direct revelation, but on the art of deciphering signs, for example through ornithomancy (the art of observing the voice, flight, and general behavior of birds) and pyromancy (or divination through fire, which consisted of making a pyre with offerings of animals and marking the shape of the flame and manner in which the offerings had burnt). The important thing for us here is not, as Jean Bottéro argues in another context, to be able to read the signs as they did, but to know that they did so in a way that was neither arbitrary nor irrational.[8] Inductive divination was practiced by a professional caste of seers who would collect and classify the omens, read them according to their expertise, and finally render their professional opinion on the object of consultation, as a lawyer might do in front of a client or a doctor in front of a patient. Theirs was, in Jon Mikalson's words, "[a] book-type learning."[9] The fact that Teiresias calls his art a *technê* means that, in his case, divination is not a god-sent gift, but rather a practice that could be learned and taught like every other practical skill. Since this always entails the possibility of error – or bad faith, as Creon will immediately suggest – Teiresias' alleged status as the spokesman of the gods cannot precede the demonstration of his actual ability to read the signs proficiently.

Interestingly, Teiresias acknowledges that his usual methods (the flight of birds, the shapes of the fire, the remains of burnt sacrifices) failed, as he could not obtain any ordinary signs from them – they were "non-signifying" or *asêmôn* (1011–12). However, he interprets this very failure as the most terrifying omen, since the birds killed and tore each other apart with their claws, the fire did not even kindle, and the offerings oozed and were scattered about. In the web of significations that Teiresias masters, these wondrous portents become *symptoms* of a profound cosmic illness: all channels of communication with the gods are broken so that they no longer accept prayers and sacrifices. That the seer is able to offer such diagnosis is not surprising in itself, for, as Bottèro puts it, "it is in face of the unknown that a good seer had to show his 'craft,' just as a good doctor does when he faces a syndrome that has never been described before."[10] As a "doctor" of ritual practice and religion, then, Teiresias suggests an etiology: the material cause is that birds and dogs have brought bits and pieces of Polyneices' corpse to the city's altars and defiled them – his description is quite vivid and gives the audience a sensory feeling of putrefaction. The actual or effective cause is, however, Creon's resolution not to bury him. Teiresias does not phrase the issue in terms of the sacred and inviolable law of burial of which Antigone spoke, but focuses on the physical or outward consequences of allowing birds and dogs to prey on an unburied corpse, visible through his art. Creon's decision has trodden, perhaps unwittingly as the Chorus had forewarned in the Ode on disaster, on a sacred realm and brought impurity and defilement into the city, for the channels of communication with the gods have been disrupted. The vivid and detailed descriptions of Teiresias, coupled with his impressive and authoritative demeanor, leaves in the audience the distinct impression that some terrible disruption has occurred that must be repaired immediately before it is too late.

Teiresias then uses language reminiscent of Haemon when lecturing Creon on the importance of learning, being flexible, and repairing one's mistakes. The seer praises the capacity to reflect [*phronesis*], which in the context lies not in the ability to foresee and avoid error, but rather in the capacity to recognize and rectify an error when it is pointed out to us. *Phronesis* in the sense used by Teiresias entails the willingness to revisit a past decision, even one that the individual thought (and still may think) to be essentially correct, in light of new evidence that shows it to be wrong (or at least to have unforeseen negative consequences). As such, it comprises several intertwined competences and general dispositions, such as the humility to recognize that even one's most cherished decisions might have wrongful consequences; the openness to accept the evidence and the experience of others for whom these consequences are clearly visible, even when they are not to us; and the insight to perceive when the moment to step back or to retract has arrived. By contrast, to remain inflexible in one's original position after the wrongful consequences are revealed is a sign not of determination but of foolishness, no matter how justified or sensible the decision may have seemed at the time, reminding us of the temporal dimension of every judgment.

Teiresias does not tell Creon explicitly what needs to be done, but he seems to have some remedy in mind, namely that Creon must abandon his political resolve and give in to the dead. Teiresias reminds Creon, as Achilles had to be reminded in the end of the *Iliad*, that there is no honor in killing a man a second time and that abusing the body of one's enemy beyond his death brings no further glory. Whether this also means, as Antigone had suggested, that the distinction between friends and enemies is no longer operative after death, Teiresias does not say, but the coincidence in the outcomes of the two arguments is there. Teiresias thus concludes by reassuring Creon of his goodwill and reminds him that following the advice will bring him profit. The seer hopes that if Creon is unable to come to terms with it in terms of "doing the right thing," he will at least be able to understand the language of self-interest. Creon should not see the reversal as giving in to his enemies, but as an act of self-preservation: since he can still use the warning to his advantage, the advice serves Creon's self-interest in a very immediate way. Presented with mounting and persuasive evidence, the audience more easily identifies with the perspective of Teiresias, while distancing itself from Creon's decree.

The fact remains that Teresias' advice is politically charged. Following it would require Creon not only to abandon his cherished and insistently defended resolution, but to relinquish control of an area, that of government, which he considers his own. This feels to Creon like an encroachment and, characteristically, he does not respond favorably. It can be of little surprise, then, to Teiresias. All the same, it is not easy for Creon to discount Teiresias' words, both because the seer has always proven valuable to the city and Creon, and also because his status is not easily amenable to any of the social categories that Creon deems "inferior" (woman, young, subject). Since he cannot conceive that he might be wrong, there *must* be another simple explanation for Teiresias' accusations. Creon now claims to be the target of a broad conspiracy of enemies who do not hesitate to resort to any tactics, including divination, aiming to uproot Teiresias' personal charisma by associating it with people of dubious reputation.[11]

Creon's strategy is interesting, especially when we consider the ways he could have responded but does not. He could have opposed sign-reading in general, that is whether birds or fire can be relevant methods of divination, like the servant of Menelaus in Euripides' *Helen*, when he says: "how worthless and full of lies / the business of seers is. Unsound are / the cries of birds and sacrificial flame."[12] Or he could have argued, differently, that Teiresias' interpretation is incorrect; after all, the seer himself acknowledged that his regular methods did not deliver any clear signs. Creon does neither. Instead, he reacts as if Teiresias' words were pure and simple fabrication, paid for by his enemies: the portents reported by Teiresias never *actually* happened and can be ignored. He warns his enemies that they will never attain their goals, not even if they threaten with pollution on a superlative scale (i.e. should the throne of Zeus be tainted with the body of Polyneices (1041)),[13] which he doesn't believe is actually the case. Consistently with what he said in his inaugural speech (but more vehemently stated than then), fear will not dictate his policies (180f.).

Creon's denials do not do much to strip Teiresias' words of the distinct impression left in the audience – they rather appear oddly out of synch with the scene painted by Teiresias, further underlined by his wrongful attribution, again, to some unnamed "enemies" – nor do they give Creon back the command over the political realm. For this, Creon must positively assert his dominion over the epistemic territory of the seer, and deprive the latter's account of its "appearance" as wisdom. While Creon hopes to reassert his dominion, his words may have the unintended opposite effect. For the sake of argument, Creon is led to argue that even if Teiresias' account were true (the portents had truly happened), and in some obscure sense were bearers of some ominous meaning, the seer's conclusion is not – *cannot* be – right. There is no way in Creon's mind that he or his decision are guilty of any wrongdoing, if for no other reason (and this must be read with caution), that "he knows well enough that no man has the power to pollute the gods" (1043–44).[14] Opinions on this assertion diverge. For Bernard Knox it is a blasphemy unparalleled for its ferocity in all of Greek drama: "[I]f ever a man denied his gods, Creon does here."[15] On the opposing side, Richard Jebb argues that, although the man is certainly wrongheaded, the statement itself is consistent with the most orthodox Greek piety;[16] from yet another angle, George Steiner suggests the possibility of the bleakest of the skepticisms: "the abyss of non-relation between mortal and divine."[17] Differences aside, critics agree that Creon is deluded in the most profound sense of the word, and does not know what he is talking about.[18] The main interpretative difficulty is that Creon combines in a single expression purposes and images contrary to the ones he would like to convey to his audience, which contributes both to the scholarly discrepancies about his actual meaning, and paradoxically to the agreement about Creon's inner state of confusion, further separating him from the audience.

So far Creon has always maintained that he honored the gods and showed them proper reverence, when he forbade the burial of a traitor who came to destroy their temples. Teiresias pushes him to confront the possibility that, by leaving the body exposed, he may have in fact desecrated the city's altars and consequently broken all communications with the gods, which is an objectively worrisome state of affairs. Creon, in turn, wishes to affirm that he has done nothing of the sort and that the connection with the gods remains as strong as ever. However, Creon does more than deny a rupture in the communication with the gods; he further denies that any such thing can ever happen, with the argument that no man has the power to cause it. The problem is that by rejecting not just the occurrence, but the very *possibility* of such an infection, Creon is unwittingly casting doubts on the ordinary channels of communication as well. Instead of insisting that he has not endangered this communication, providing arguments that could put his audience at ease, Creon's words offer a portrayal of discontinuity and severance, as if both realms were disjointed and non-porous entities and no interlocution existed between them.

Second, Creon has consistently defended a relationship of reciprocity and mutual recognition between the city and its gods, where the former pays proper respect to the gods and the latter grant favors and protection in return. Now Creon insinuates that nothing men do can really affect the gods, which suggests a relationship not of reciprocity and mutual concern, but rather one of indifference, perhaps even of contempt.[19] What is more, if there is nothing men can do ever to offend the gods, then they can do absolutely *anything*, without fear that their actions will ever be objected to or assessed negatively – the opposite of what the Chorus had earlier recommended to remain high in the city (368–71). Creon might have hoped to maintain the coincidence in values and the alignment of interests between the *polis* and the gods, but the landscape is one without any such moral order, whence the gods are absent, all of which heightens the anxiety of his audience rather than putting it at ease.

Third, Creon seeks to reinstate a hierarchy between politics and religion, where the political takes pre-eminence over the religious, the king over the seer, in the hope that the audience will still see things from his point of view. If so, his phrasing is bizarre: instead of reaffirming his authority over ritual – which would not surprise an audience who viewed religion as a matter that concerned the state – Creon abjures any position of control, affirming categorically that "no man has that power" [*outis anthrôpôn sthenei*]. Contrary to the image of an autonomous and powerful leader, his utterance puts man (and himself) in an awkward position of servitude and powerlessness – the opposite of what was meant. It appears that Creon's lingering preoccupation with liability pushes him to abdicate any control over the religious sphere, demonstrating to the audience that his mind is not interested in articulating a religious piety, but simply in eluding culpability. The exculpatory nature of his statement is underscored by the fact that, despite its assertive form ("I know well that . . ."), it offers a negative defense based on an ontological impossibility, which is similar to the old legal maxim "the King can do no wrong" but elevated to a broader cosmic scale. Apparently, his desire for immunity is so pervasive that it resurfaces as a presumption of metaphysical insulation, and disguises as a religious truth what is just a denial of political accountability. The audience may be at pains to accept considering that it is he who proclaimed the decree and his rule which was supposed to be under scrutiny (175–7, and accompanying commentary).

Finally, whereas Creon still refuses to believe in the existence of the symptoms, his desire to refute Teiresias' conclusion leads him to take these signs as true, if only discursively, inviting a contrast between Teiresias' vivid description and the general maxim he now presents. The strategy is bound to backfire, because the dangers announced by the seer seemed so vivid and imminent that expecting the audience to take heart instead from the statement of a theoretical impossibility is like telling the passengers of a sinking ship to remain confident in its unbreakable structure. Between Teiresias' holistic description and Creon's empty generalization the choice is already made. Creon does not provide an alternative explanation of the omens and otherwise fails to refute the seer's interpretation. He wants his audience to accept his "knowledge" without explaining how he obtained it – in fact, by implying that he knows what can and cannot offend the gods, he shows the kind of hubristic attitude that is the opposite of knowing – further wishing to impose it in the same authoritarian manner in which he disciplines society. When pushed, Creon lacks real arguments to reaffirm the justness of his position, nor does he give a single reason why Polyneices should remain unburied. After he has spoken, one does not have the impression of understanding him any better. Instead, we are faced with the megalomania of a ruler who believes that he alone is the source of knowledge, but actually manifests the *emptiness* Haemon predicted. Gone are the sympathies in the audience that he may have retained thus far, for from now on he alone is responsible for what may occur as a result of his own failure to listen.

The bitter exchange which ensues illustrates the power battle between the two men, with Creon throwing accusations of bribery, corruption, and personal profiteering in Teiresias' face and the seer pointing out Creon's lack of understanding. Creon's increasingly personal attacks finally provoke the seer into revealing what should perhaps better remain unsaid: that it shall not be long before Creon gives up corpse for corpse – one of his own loins, in return for having lodged one of the living below, while keeping above one who belongs to the gods below. One need not suppose that Teiresias has switched methods of divination here.[20] As Karl Reinhardt points out, "what he prophesies for the future does not differ from the present, but it is only the future shape of what now is."[21] Still, Teiresias' previous account included the symptoms affecting the social body, the causes behind them, a diagnosis of the nature of the illness, and a possible remedy for its cure, but did not contain a *prognosis*, that is a forecast of the future development of "the patient," which his present statement does.[22]

The full extent of his offense is now unfolded: as Steiner writes, "Creon has not committed some local, limited crime [but] has, in a way one might not have deemed possible to a mortal man, inverted the cosmology of life and death."[23] By sending down to earth a living person belonging to the world above, while keeping above a body belonging to the world below, Creon has violated the world's structuring topologies (above/below), hierarchies (mortals/gods), and distributions (Olympian gods/chthonic gods). In this picture, Antigone and Polyneices do not appear as individual characters, but rather as tokens of Creon's all-encompassing transgression. Teiresias warns that such action will cause a reaction that is proportional to the nature of his crime. In the cosmos described by Teiresias, all things exist in a reciprocal state of equilibrium. If this balance is disturbed by an act of injustice, its restoration requires adequate compensation, the measure of which is given by the logic of inverted symmetries. Teiresias presents this as an immanent law of the universe, which resembles Anaximander's dictum about the perennial process of cosmic atonement according to which ". . . things must pay the penalty and make atonement to one another for their injustice according to Time's decree."[24] It also recalls Solon's belief in immanent justice asserting itself in, or through, time [*en dikei chronou*].[25] The kind of universal laws of which Teiresias speaks are not to be equated with Antigone's unwritten laws of burial (they are broader and more general than her particular instantiation), but they confirm at least the existence of an underlying normative structure that, as she claimed, cannot be altered at will.

For his act of transgression, Creon will soon pay his due to the Erinyes "of the gods and of Hades" – an overarching cosmology that underscores its universality. The punishment aims at the restoration of the broken order and is not meant as an act of vengeance or personal retribution. In this light, the action of the Erinyes is better understood in connection to *Dike* (Justice) and its re-establishment, than as a retaliatory response to the calls of the dead as in Aeschylus.[26] Right at this point, Teiresias emphasizes the symmetrical and regulated nature of Creon's punishment: he will give corpse for corpse, "in legal exchange" [*antidous*[27]] for his offenses. In the final analysis, the prophecy about Creon's punishment requires no divine revelation. Rather, it is part of the cosmic process of atonement, the cognizance of which could have allowed

Teiresias to predict (after the ominous signs he observed and Creon's subsequent act of individuation) the timing (1064–5, 1078), magnitude (1067, 1075), and inescapability (1084) of Creon's specific tragedy.

After Teiresias leaves the scene, Creon is willing to accept the suggestion of the elders and reverse his decision. Throughout the entire scene the elders have remained silent, but their advice reveals that they give credit to Teresias over Creon and that, whatever their earlier opinion on the subject of the decree, they cannot support it any longer. To everyone's surprise, Creon agrees to release Antigone and bury Polyneices, and to do it personally. What does this say about Creon? There are those, like C.M. Bowra, who discredit Creon's conversion as "only skin-deep."[28] Quite the opposite, Bernard Knox argues that Creon's capitulation is so unconditional and complete that it is unbecoming of a true Sophoclean hero.[29] On an intermediate position, Griffith suggests that the action itself is that of a well-meaning man wishing to make amends.[30] Perhaps all of these views carry some truth, if not entirely. Creon justifies his reversal on the grounds that one cannot fight against necessity. One can regard this as morally irrelevant, as Bowra does, "for even the gods do not fight against necessity."[31] However, by acknowledging the seer's words as embodying "necessity," this is the first time Creon affirms an opinion other than his own. Still, one cannot avoid the feeling that Creon is overpowered by fear: aware that Teiresias' prophecies have never been proven false before, he loses his nerve and wants out. This shows that, if a threat becomes personal enough to him, fear does in fact dictate his policy. All the same, for once Creon appears willing to accept the Chorus' advice and hold onto good counsel [*eubolia*], precisely what Teiresias has accused him of lacking. Likewise the decision to release Antigone and bury Polyneices, however late, is a step in the right direction, raising the audience's hopes in still a satisfactory resolution. After the elders' suggestion, Creon agrees to take part personally in Antigone's release: "I who imprisoned her shall myself be present to release her." At this point, his words cannot be taken, contrary to what Rebecca Bushnell claims, as an expression of control and willpower.[32] They are, rather, an embryonic assumption of responsibility. The man who denied his imputation vis-à-vis the gods (and Antigone's choice of punishment) is finally led to acknowledge his undeniable role in it all.

In this spirit of acceptance (or resignation) Creon concludes that it may be better to observe the "established laws" [*kathestôtas nomous*] throughout one's life. Does this mean that Creon has finally come to accept Antigone's point of view? Jebb believes that he has.[33] More likely, Creon seems to be referring to the normative order represented by Teiresias.[34] Creon had thought his position of leader in the *polis* entitled him to decide all issues and proclaim all laws, even about matters the ramifications of which he could neither fully anticipate nor comprehend. Now he has been confronted to the borne limits of the normative cosmos, which must be respected as peremptory norms even when their exact content cannot be fully known in advance (consider that even

Teiresias needed to consult the birds of augury before stating they had been broken). More will be said about Teiresias' and Antigone's respective normative universes in the next chapter, but for now it suffices to say that Teiresias' "established order" can include, but is not exhausted by, Antigone's *nomos*.

Teiresias' exit leaves little room for joy, but the elders and Creon seem to believe that there is still a last chance to save the day. If Creon hurries, and does everything he is told, the worst may be averted. Creon agrees to tackle the problem at its roots: if he buries Polyneices and frees Antigone, he may restore the broken order and prevent further ruin. As long as this option remains a possibility, nothing is written in stone. This should not lead us to forget what we already know. Creon refused to relent when he was given the chance, and rose to unimaginable heights of megalomania and insolence. If he was on the edge of the cliff, he may already have gone over it. As Teiresias implied, once the immanent forces are activated they will assert themselves, independent of human intervention: the Erinyes may be late to start, but once in motion they always catch with their prey.

6.2 Fifth *stasimon*: Dionysus, the Chorus Master (lines 1115–54)

The Chorus sings the last choral Ode as a hymn and prayer for Dionysus, god of many names and patron of Thebes. The Ode is composed of two pairs of strophes and antistrophes. The first pair recalls Dionysus's genealogy (son of Semele and Zeus), geographical extension (Italy, Eleusis, the Castalian Waters at Delphi, the hills of Nysa, and Thebes), and the variety of cults associated with him (his association with Apollo at Dephi and his Bacchic side as the god of singing, dancing, and wine). In the next strophe, the Chorus invokes Dionysus as patron of Thebes asking him to come with a cleansing or "cathartic foot" [katharsiôi podi], *to release the city from the grips of its violent disorder* [biaias epi nosou]. *The Chorus ends by hailing Dionysus, as the Chorus Master of the fire-breathing stars, to appear* [prophanethi] *in his capacity as Iacchus, the benefactor.*

Formally, the Ode takes the shape of a hymn or prayer to the god Dionysus, patron saint of the city, with no missing element: "invocation by various names, mention of lineage and haunts, reminder of past help or favor, grounds for present invocation, and specific request."[35] As Albert Heinrichs explains, this is reminiscent of Dionysiac ritual practice, not myth, and is designed precisely to circumvent the more sinister elements highlighted in Dionysiac myth (i.e. the maenadic madness and dismemberment at the core of the Pentheus story).[36] The distinction between myth and cult appears significant, considering the exuberance of the interpretations surrounding the "Dionysiac," too often fixated on the irrational, violent, and destructive aspects of the god.[37] In contrast, Heinrich explains that "cult regards the gods as beneficent and proceeds on the expectation of a mutually beneficial reciprocity between the human and divine realms."[38] Clearly, the Dionysus that the Chorus invokes as "Iacchus, the benefactor" is not the one that has captured the modern imagination from Nietzsche to René Girard, namely the irrational, bloodthirsty, and vengeful god represented in Euripides' *Bacchae*,[39] but the more tamed and civilizing version known in cult. As patron saint of Thebes, the Chorus invokes Dionysus to come and deliver them from the dangers affecting the city, just as in their first entrance they danced and sang in honor of the god after being saved from the war that almost brought the city to the ground.

The Ode has been interpreted as a "hymn of joyful exultation,"[40] and expressive of "true religious fervor."[41] However, the Chorus cannot be expected to ignore the convoluted state of affairs described by Teiresias: his predictions are too precise and fearsome to believe that they can be neatly exorcised with prayer. The very urgency and excitement of their cry betrays some undercurrent of apprehension in their voice:[42] They make appropriate ritual references to Semele, Zeus, and Thebes, as mother, father, and mother city of Dionysus, but they also mention that Semele was struck by lightning by her father Zeus, master of thunder, and that Thebes is erected over the seed provided by a fiery dragon. Continuing with this imagery of lightning, thunder, and fire Dionysus is presiding over a dance of fire-breathing stars, and his followers, the Bacchants, carry smoky torches. Therefore, within the orderly and controlled cultic framework, one can perceive an undercurrent of anxiety, particularly in the prominence of fire metaphors.[43] In addition, the vivid naturalistic imagery of water (the watery flow of Ismenus and the Castalian spring), earth (the land where the tooth of the dragon is planted), rocks (the double-peak rock of Parnassus), mountains (the hills of Nysa and of the vineyards), and the skies underscore the mighty forces they are up against, and the Chorus' correlative powerlessness fully to control them. The act of praying itself entails a certain ambivalence: on the one hand, it presupposes that things are not irreversible and *can* improve; on the other, it acknowledges that it may require the benevolence of one who is not within mortals' reach to make that happen. In sum, whereas Creon's reversal may have infused them with the prospect that there is still time to save the city, the gravity of the situation does not leave much room for optimism, as things may have escalated to the point where nothing can suffice.[44] Still, the Chorus prays for the god to arrive with "kathartic foot" and cleanse or save the city from the gripping disorder that Teiresias has just described.[45]

The Ode seems to call for a sense of shared experience between the Chorus and the audience, where the latter is affected by the same hopes, fears, and uncertainties as the former.[46] Nevertheless, there is a certain disembodiment at the same time, since the audience and the Chorus may be hoping for different things. Whereas the Chorus asks explicitly for the salvation of the *polis*, the audience is also worried for the individual destiny of each character which is too convoluted already. The Ode is therefore suggestive enough for the audience to be carried along with the hopes of the Chorus, and yet to not be caught completely off guard if this does not happen in the form in which it was expected. This poetic construction heightens the emotional *pathos* of the scene in preparation for the final turn of events.

6.3 Tragic news (lines 1155–256)

The messenger, not Dionysus, responds to the Chorus' cry.[47] *He says: "There is no human life that I could blame or approve as though it had come to a stop, for fortune* [tûche] *changes ceaselessly for good or ill. No prophet exists for the things that come to pass to mortals* [mantis oudeis tôn kathestôtôn brotois]*." The messenger explains that Creon once seemed enviable to him, since he saved the land from its enemies and guided it firmly, and it was blooming with his brood of children. But now all pleasure is gone for him, and that is to be next to nothing, a living corpse. "What has happened?" the elders ask; "They are dead," he replies. "Who is the murderer and who lies down?" "Haemon is dead; by his own blood-shedding hand." The elders do not fully understand: "By his father's or his own?" "By his own hand, in anger at his father's own murder." "O old seer," they say, "how true your words have proved to be."*

The elders note Creon's wife Eurydice approaching, who begs the messenger to repeat the news anyway, promising to listen "with ears accustomed to sorrow." The messenger proceeds then to tell the full story: "Why suppress the truth? Truth is always best." He says he accompanied Creon to where the corpse of Polyneices lay unburied, torn apart by the dogs. They washed the body and burned what was left of it. Then, they headed towards the cave of Antigone, where they heard a deep voice wailing from the inside. Creon thought himself to recognize his son's voice and ordered the stones blocking the entrance to be removed. There they saw the young woman hanging by the neck from a piece of linen, and Haemon holding her around the wrist, lamenting the death of his bride and the actions of his father. Creon, with a trembling voice: "Wretch, what have you done?. . . Come out, my son, I entreat you as a suppliant." When Haemon saw his father, he glared at him with furious eyes and spat in his face. He then drew his sword against his father but failed, as Creon jumped to elude the strike. Furious with himself, he threw his own body deeply upon the sword, still having time to embrace Antigone in a last breath.

After the dreadful report of the messenger, Eurydice enters the palace without a word. The elders fear her silence. The messenger fears it too, but expresses the hope that it is only because she wishes to mourn privately. The elders hope that the messenger is right, although they worry she might hide a darker purpose: too much silence is no good, they say.

The messenger's enthralling narrative is framed by a general reflection about the mutability and unpredictability of human life. A person's fortune can change dramatically from one moment to the next and what seemed secure and stable at one moment is utterly destroyed the next. The observation is meant to fit Creon – who has gone from a situation of enviable prosperity to one of absolute misery in the spur of a moment – but the messenger's remarks resemble what the Chorus itself had affirmed generally in the second choral ode. Despite man's apparent control of his own life and destiny there will always be unpredictable circumstances – represented here in the idea of *tyche* (or *tûche*) – that defy all attempts at anticipation and control. Being mortals – and not prophets – human beings are unable to know the future and can only make estimates about what might happen. As a result, the future will be revealed to them only when it has come to pass and is now *established* [*kath-estôtôn*] and thus no longer the future.

If life is essentially unstable and no one can predict what the future shall bring, every judgment about any person's life is radically uncertain, since it always can be proven wrong by later circumstances. According to the messenger, for a judgment *not* to be radically indeterminate it would be necessary for life to stop changing, that is for life to have ceased to be. This does not mean, however, that no judgments can ever be made in life. By all accounts, Creon seemed to enjoy an enviable position, having saved the city from its enemies and guiding it to safety with his noble crop of children. But now, having lost everything, he seems the opposite of enviable. The guard's point is not about the deceptive nature of perceptions – which could be corrected if only we had a better perspective or true knowledge. The point is rather an existential one: when the simple joys of life are gone, or, more accurately, when the joy *in them* is gone, everything else is gone too: without such joy, wealth, prestige and power mean nothing. In saying so, the guard is implicitly valuing the simple pleasures of life – e.g. the enjoyment of one's family – over wealth and power, and additionally suggesting that neither wealth, nor power, nor status can fend off disaster. Creon appeared to have a life that was both enviable and secured; now it looks like the shadow of smoke, miserable and worthless. The judgment of the guard seems accurate and likely to be shared by the audience.

The real focus of the messenger's story is the succinct yet emotionally charged description of Antigone's and Haemon's suicides. One factor that increases the emotional charge of the scene is the arrival of Eurydice, on whom the audience can see reflected the full effects of the messenger's narrative, as already explained when dealing with the spatial relationship of mediation. As Griffith remarks, "the agonized presence of this mother and wife, reacting with gestures and body language – and then with eloquently silent departure (1244–56) – adds another dimension of pathos to the catastrophe."[48] Eurydice is introduced as Creon's wife, but the elders soon mention that she might have arrived on account of her son, revealing once again a tension between a twofold (and eventually incompatible) loyalty. So far this tension remains unresolved, for the audience does not know whether she will show more concern for her husband or her son. Either way, Eurydice's presence assures that the messenger's account shows tangible consequences on the stage, as the audience remains cognizant of the terrible price paid by her and her family. In addition, thanks to Eurydice the audience is sure to hear the full story, as she begs the messenger to spare her no sorrow. Granted permission to speak the truth, the messenger's narrative acquires the unmistakable flavor of an accurate and honest account of pain and misery.

Since the messenger narrates events that are not shown on-stage, the audience is imaginatively carried to the interior of the cave and invited to picture what might have happened there. The device is similar to the one at the very beginning, when the guard reported to Creon that someone had buried Polyneices and the audience had to put together the missing pieces. The difference is that, at that time, the audience was well aware that Antigone intended to bury her brother and was not at all surprised when it happened (even if it was not clear how). Here in contrast we have no similar confirmation that Antigone intended suicide, which makes it harder to recreate. Various different temporalities must in fact be combined to make sense of the scene, as the audience's immediate *perception* of the messenger's narrative – the story he is telling now to Eurydice and the Chorus – is combined with the audience's *visualization* of what might have happened inside the cave, which in turn requires activating (especially in the case of Antigone's suicide) the *recollection* of the characters' last moments.

Antigone's suicide has received almost no attention in the critical literature, which passes lightly over it as a foregone conclusion.[49] This is unfortunate because, as Gerald Else remarks, her suicide appears to be one of Sophocles' personal innovations.[50] To say that Antigone's suicide is "required" to activate the tragic mechanisms says nothing about the way Antigone approaches her own death, which is essential to its interpretation. The text is silent about the exact circumstances surrounding her death (by the time Creon's retinue arrives, Antigone lies hanging from a linen rope), but the emotional pathway that leads her was articulated in her last farewell speech: as Ioannis Panoussis argues, her feelings may have intensified, but not substantially changed.[51] The image evoked in her long and sorrowful march towards her tomb – stressing her sadness, misery, loneliness, and isolation – was unmistakably one of a wretched and almost broken individual, even to the point of questioning the justice of the gods.

The audience does not get to hear her last thoughts in the cave, but it does not take much to fill in these gaps. In her last moments, when everything turns black around her, her hopes of being vindicated, let alone saved, are long gone. The world around her has failed to understand her, to make room for her. She has enough food to survive, Creon informed, but what would be the point? Antigone knows nothing of Haemon's passionate defense of her cause, nothing of the seer's admonition to Creon, nothing of the release force that is coming to set her free. Knowing nothing of these things that could have perhaps given her the strength to resist, she seemingly decides to terminate her misery rather than prolong the agony. Her suicide appears more a cessation of suffering than an act of self-affirmation or genuine desire – even if there is still an element of defiance.[52] Be that as it may, when the messenger gives us a vivid description of her body, hanging by the neck, her death is to be pitied more than celebrated. Her suicide could not be any farther from the description of a "beautiful death."[53]

The situation is a bit different in the case of Haemon, because the messenger reports his actual words and actions immediately prior to taking his own life, even though much needs to be supplied in order to enliven the messenger's sober account of the facts. The messenger says that when they arrived at the cave, they discovered Haemon wailing inconsolably for the death of his bride, his arms around her waist, and lamenting the actions of his father. Whatever Haemon might have intended when heading to Antigone's chamber – whether he was trying to save her, to commit suicide beside her, or just to say a last goodbye – finding her there hanging by the neck fills him with inconsolable grief. Haemon blames his father and is furious with him. His anger does not subside when he hears the voice of his father at the other end of the cave. (What is Creon doing here?) Creon's words do nothing to appease him: "Wretch, what have you done? What was in your mind?" (Does Creon think that Haemon killed Antigone? Or are his words addressed not to Haemon but to Antigone?[54]) "Come out, my son, I entreat you as a suppliant." Creon might want to speak in conciliatory terms, to humble himself before his son, but he does not seem fully to understand his son's pain.[55] Haemon has nothing but contempt for Creon. Looking at him with angry eyes, he spits in his face. Without a word, he draws his sword and directs it at him. His father jumps to one side. Haemon misses. Furious with himself, he turns the sword and presses his body against it, this time without missing.

What makes him turn the sword against himself? Some believe that Haemon is remorseful and ashamed for having attempted to kill his father – or that he did not *really* try to kill him.[56] It is true that he turns his sword against himself with more precision than against Creon[57] – although it is actually easier to let the body fall onto the sword than to strike another person who jumps to elude it. But, as Winnington-Ingram notes, if there is shame and self-loathing in this act it is not for having tried, but for not having succeeded.[58] His father has, once again, escaped unscathed. His failure to kill Creon is but another example of his impotence: unable to do anything for his beloved, he is now incapable of making the guilty party pay.

At the same time, killing his father will not bring Antigone back. Haemon's inability to restore what cannot be restored adds to the pain of having lost what he most loved. Disoriented, his dignity and moral worth shredded to pieces, he can no longer go back to the world of his father, not after what Creon has done to Antigone. His father is already dead for him. Everything he once loved and respected has been destroyed beyond the possibility of repair. There seems to be little left for Haemon in this world.[59] And yet there is still something he *can* do. Whether he may or may not have intended this while pressing his body against the sword, killing himself gets back at his father much more effectively than had he killed him directly. In a last breath he embraces his lover, showing clearly where his loyalty resides. His suicide is his most clear statement.

The messenger concludes with a personal comment in which he states that the narrated events demonstrate how "thoughtlessness" [*aboulia*] is the worst thing among men. It is not clear whose "thoughtlessness" he has in mind and it could be that he refers generally to the case in which a concatenation of bad decisions and judgments has led to a final tragic situation that no one wanted. Notwithstanding, the messenger's denunciation of *aboulia* is clearly reminiscent of Teiresias' identical (albeit inverted) expression used moments earlier to accuse Creon.[60]

As soon as the messenger finishes his report, Eurydice departs abruptly, without uttering a word. Both the messenger and the Chorus speculate about the meaning of her silence: they hope for the best – that she wants to mourn in private – but fear the worst – aware that silence may presage something terrible. What Eurydice might do is not expressed in words, but is left hanging in the air for the audience to ponder, generating the expectation that there will be some kind of reaction. For now it is impossible to know what Eurydice thinks about her son's death and her husband's intervention, but the audience is left with the impression that it will not be long before it becomes clear.

6.4 Final laments (lines 1257–353)

The elders notice Creon's entrance carrying Haemon's body in his arms, bringing the evidence of his own mistakes [autos hamartôn]. *Creon agrees: "Ah, the blunders of my obstinate mind* [phrenon dusphronon hamartemata] . . . *Oh, you witnesses of kindred that have done and suffered murder. Misery caused by my own decisions* [bouleumatôn]. *Ah, my son, you were cut off through my ill-begotten judgment* [dusbouliais], *not your own." The Chorus reprimands: "Alas, you seem to have seen justice only late!" Creon agrees: "I have learned, unhappy as I am!" The messenger rushes back to the front scene bringing more desolate news. "Is there anything worse after these evils?" asks Creon. "Your wife is dead, with wounds newly inflicted." Creon hurts: "Oh, harbor of Hades, never purified. Why do you ruin me?"*

The door of the palace opens and reveals the body of Eurydice. The elders point out that her body can now be seen, no longer indoors. The messenger explains that Eurydice killed herself with a sword, lamenting the empty death of her other son, Megareus,[61] *and that of Haemon as well, and with her last breath of air accused Creon of being a child-slayer. Creon accuses himself too: "Ah me, this can never be transferred to another mortal, acquitting me! For it was I that killed you . . ." Creon wishes his attendants to take him out of the way and wishes death to come, the sooner the better. The elders reply: "That lies in the future and we must attend to present tasks; the future rests where it should rest," and "Utter no prayers now, for there is no releasing mortals from their lots."*[62] *"Lead me out," cries Creon, "I who killed you, my own son and wife . . . I do not know which way to look, or where I should seek support. Everything has gone awry . . . a crushing lot has struck and fallen upon my head."*

Creon exits, and leaves the Chorus alone to utter the last words of the play. Addressing the general public, the elders conclude: "Wisdom is by far the chief part of happiness [pollôi to phronein eudaimonias prôton huparchei]*; and we must not dishonor the gods. Grand words of arrogant men are paid back with great blows in return, and as they grow old they teach wisdom* [phronein]."

Creon is unmistakably the centerpiece of the last scene. He arrives carrying the dead body of Haemon, a broken man, his life close to nothing, having lost all the joys that made it worth living (as the messenger stated). While lamenting the death of his son on the stage, he receives the news that his wife too, in a manner similar to Haemon, has killed herself, blaming him for everything. Unable to cope with the grief (and the guilt), Creon expresses the desire to die, having lost absolutely everything he once loved, and with a dismal future ahead of him. When Creon leaves the stage he is an utterly destroyed individual, less than a man, having been struck hard and brought low by the tragic events. It is often assumed, perhaps by force of habit, that the audience identifies with Creon's suffering and feels pity for him – proverbial tragic emotion after Aristotle. Expressing a common view, Griffith for example writes that "we now share his misery and recognize that such reversal, and degradation, could happen to any of us."[63]

To the contrary I think that the stage is set here not for identifying with Creon, but rather for judging him, and doing so as harshly as he judges himself. In contrast to the ending of *Oedipus Tyrannos* where the audience is indeed terrified at the prospect of realizing that Oedipus could be any one of us, here the audience is not meant to share and identify with Creon's destiny. True, Creon can be the *object* of the audience's pity, for his situation is objectively pitiful (i.e. pathetic). But rather than a feeling of proximity and closeness, the audience is to maintain a certain detachment and pity him "only from a distance." Ultimately it is not Dionysos or the Erinyes or Fate whom the audience finds at the bottom of the tragedy, but a man, and that man is Creon.[64]

During the whole final scene Creon remains at center stage, having the body of his innocent child at his feet. This body, Creon's folly incarnate, remains onstage as visual reminder and indictment against him. The elders point this out as soon as Creon arrives, "carrying the evidence of his own wrongdoings." In contrast to their earlier scrupulously maintained "neutrality," they now openly allow themselves to criticize their King. Creon lays all the blame on himself and attributes it to his "obstinate mind" and his "ill-begotten judgment." But rather than accept Creon's apology, the elders point out that he has come to recognize justice only too late. The elders further refuse to grant him any solace when in the end he wishes only to die. Their sharp responses – "that lies in the future . . . and the future rests with those in whom it rests" (1334–5) and "utter no prayer now!" (1337) – cut the emotional rope that he wishes they would throw to him. The only moment when the elders appear to agree with Creon is when he expresses the wish to be taken out of the way fast. At this point, the elders respond that this would be a gain for him, if there is any gain amidst a sea of troubles. Here again, one of Creon's favorite expressions (*kerdos*: gain, profit, advantage) is tossed back ironically at him.

Eurydice's suicide comes back to haunt Creon as well. Her death does not occur on-stage but is reported by the messenger. This raises a structural similarity with the reports of Haemon's and Antigone's deaths. Just as the audience perceived Antigone's and Haemon's deaths though Eurydice's eyes, now the audience sees Eurydice's death through Creon's eyes. However, the similarity between the two scenes is only apparent. Earlier, the audience was invited to travel imaginatively inside that cave, whereas now the audience's gaze is turned towards the stage where Eurydice's body is visible, no longer hidden indoors. Rather than gathering sympathy for herself, however, Eurydice points her finger back at Creon, who is responsible for "this and the other deaths." Her earlier silence is translated into a clear accusation – even with the use of legal terminology to express it.[65] Now it becomes clear to the audience that, throughout the earlier report of the deaths of Antigone and Haemon, she had been listening with the affection of a mother (and not under the mantle of Creon's authority). Even the manner of her death, replicating that of Haemon, conveys her allegiance. Thus when the messenger refers to Eurydice as Creon's wife, the result is not to accentuate her subordination to him but rather Creon's very responsibility in the death of his wife and "true mother" of his children.[66] In this regard, the emphasis lies not on how Eurydice's death *affects* him (which would at least grant him some measure of sympathy), but on what her death *says about* him (which is not a flattering picture).

Finally, Creon's own reactions do not help lessen the charge. Here, the comparison with Antigone's last march is revelatory. Just like Antigone before him, Creon addresses the whole citizenry of Thebes to witness, to look on him [*ô blepontes*], but the nature of this gaze is completely different. Antigone wanted us to witness what she was suffering as a result of the actions of others, and thus, through her, to actually look at others. In contrast, Creon wants the citizens – and by implication the general audience – to observe what he is suffering as a result of his actions, which accordingly keeps Creon on target. Even though Antigone too wanted us to feel her misery, more importantly she wanted her audience to realize the essentially pious nature of her act and the injustice of those who put her there. In contrast, Creon does not try to persuade his audience that his suffering is undeserved or unjust, nor does he try to deflect the judgment by arguing that other characters may have also contributed to it, or, alternatively, that he is the victim of the kind of errors that can happen to anyone. Thus Creon's lament lacks the self-probing mode that characterizes Antigone's last speech. There is no deep questioning of his actions and no attempt at understanding them. Unlike Antigone, he does not dig into the reasons that led him there.

Nor could we say that, other than lamenting his bad luck, he is expressing any actual "learning" that will enable him to act more wisely in the future. As a result, Creon's acknowledgment of responsibility is not an occasion for the audience to soften and temper this judgment, but rather to agree with him and with his assessment.

All these mediated judgments explain why the Chorus' closing words seem to fit Creon so well, even if he may not be on-stage when uttered. He is a man who has lost all joy in life. His lack of good sense has caused disaster. His arrogance and boasting words come back to haunt him. And we can even doubt whether he has learned anything at all, or is going to in his old age. The Chorus' final words thus resemble the famous Solonian injunction "call no man happy until the end," which is a judgment about the way life has been lived in its totality.[67] Looking back on it, Creon enacted a decree aimed at distinguishing the brother who honored the city from the one who betrayed it, after a war instigated by a family quarrel that almost devastated the land and enslaved its people. In deciding so, he acted not out of personal gain or interest, but consistently to what he thought would better exemplify, preserve, and honor the values of the community. The decree itself was apparently within his purview, not obviously beyond his jurisdiction and authority, and gathered the assent of a representative body of citizens as a way of legitimation. Of course we know now that as a result of defending it Creon has squeezed his family and, the opposite of what he intended, not benefited the city but actually endangered it.

In his way, Creon has shown himself to be an authoritarian and obtuse leader, attributing spurious motives to anyone who disagrees with him and interpreting every contrary opinion as a personal attack, unable to listen to (and of course to accept) anyone's advice. Creon has also remained dangerously oblivious to the way his decisions were affecting other people and callous in their execution. Refusing to back down when errors were pointed out to him, Creon defends his decree like the soldier in the phalanx, lacking the flexibility and suppleness to govern and administer the law in times of peace. It is as if, once proclaimed, Creon concerned himself exclusively with its strict compliance, abdicating the rest of the responsibilities attached to his position and the continued life of the law. In the end, the play shows an empty void of silence around him, from where little by little all his earlier support has evaporated.

This kind of holistic judgment can only be done at the end of the narrative, that is when things acquire the certainty of what has come to pass – as the messenger himself recalled when expressing his inability to judge anything "as if it had come to an end" (1156–7). The end is then the beginning of a different kind of judgment that looks back at the tragedy in its entirety, with the hope of assessing the significance of what we have just witnessed. This is now what remains to be done, particularly in what concerns the legal conflict, beginning with Antigone and her law, which have remained in the audience's line of vision all along.

Chapter 7

The temporalities of judgment: Antigone and law

The developments of the last chapter appear to vindicate Antigone: Creon reverses his decision and Polyneices is finally buried, an outcome that the audience has no problem in accepting. The incommensurable conflict seems finally unblocked, as Creon's law is annulled and the audience confirms that his decree was flawed beyond repair. Ismene may have been right in the beginning to call Antigone's attempt "impossible," but in the end Antigone has managed to demonstrate that her sister (and perhaps the audience too) underestimated her. To call this development remarkable does not begin to describe the radical transformation that has actually happened.

My first question is relatively simple. How has this transformation been made plausible, natural even, for an audience that might easily have shared Ismene's first impressions and reservations about Antigone? This question, which holds the key to the mystery of Antigone (and the play), demands an integral inquiry into the temporal dimensions of law and legal judgment. I will do so here in various steps, beginning with the character of Antigone and her law, and then widening the scope to encompass the law of the *Antigone* and the audience. My final goal is to disentangle the temporal engagements that the audience establishes with the play and permit judging it with increasing proficiency.

7.1 The originality of Antigone

The remarkable thing about Antigone is not, or not only, that she overcomes the enormous gendered and social restrictions in her society to oppose Creon; it is not, or not only, that she escapes the strictly private sphere of domesticity and emerges into the public space of politics; it is not, even, that she decides to honor her dead brother instead of choosing to form a family by marrying and having children. The truly memorable thing about Antigone, the thing that has granted her a place in the pantheon of Western literature and social imaginary, is that she is able to articulate a law that is *not* the one enacted by the *polis* and the main political actors, and, therefore, that she expresses her disobedience in the language of the law. At the end of the play, the stage has been set for her to speak the law on an equal footing with the most powerful men in the *polis*, which in the context of the strongly patriarchal society represented in the play makes her accomplishment all the more remarkable.

Antigone begins her journey as a Homeric warrior fighting for the dead body of her fallen brother, but in the course of arguing and defending her case she acquires the status of a de facto citizen, one who actually promotes the true interests and well-being of the city. No less significantly, in the end she manages to have her determination of law prevail, if not while she is alive, at least after she is dead – i.e. Polyneices is finally buried precisely by the man who had prohibited it. The audience too progressively internalizes Antigone's own perspective, and begins to see things from within her *nomos*. Thus the audience is not at all surprised when Polyneices is finally buried and can even join in celebrating the burial of a "traitor" (unthinkable at the beginning). Thanks to Antigone's intervention, a new and more inclusive understanding of democracy can emerge, as an ideal that recognizes a plurality of voices and actors and leaves a critical space for the contestation of its values and meanings.[1]

The truly radical and transformative experience that Antigone exemplifies, her tremendous social and legal impact, is often hard to realize, perhaps, in part due to her success. Historically we know that the right of burial defended by Antigone became a favorite in Athenian patriotic discourse (e.g. Lysias), and, together with other related legends that portrayed Athenians as champions of freedom and defenders of the oppressed, performed an important ideological function to form their own self-consciousness.[2] Aristotle too, writing a hundred yeas later, cites Antigone in the *Rhetoric* as an example of a kind of law that is common to all men by nature and can be used to counteract the severity of an unjust particular law.[3] Through the ages, Antigone's appeal to the "unwritten laws" and her defiance of a man-made law seeped through the medieval traditions of natural law into the belief that an unjust law is no law at all and could be rightfully disobeyed. Even if the image of Antigone as defender of the divine justice against tyranny no longer remains intact, one could still argue that the right that Antigone defended to bury a family member is "natural" also in the contemporary world, despite its not being explicitly mentioned in any formal declaration of rights or written constitution. As a human right inherent in human dignity, the right of burial could be said to exist implicitly as an "emanation" or "derivation" of certain inalienable rights, which cannot be encroached upon by any government. Here one can do worse than to remember the efforts for the recovery of the bodies of the "disappeared" in countries such as Argentina, Chile, and Spain after their Military Dictatorships.

But there is something not entirely convincing in these attempts to "naturalize" Antigone's law, which can hardly account for the uproar it generates and the disbelief with which it is received, not just by Creon, but also by the elders and, most tellingly, by Ismene. If Antigone were simply reproducing pre-existing norms of her society then there would be no problem, for everyone would immediately recognize them as valid. Instead Ismene, the elders, and Creon are never quite capable of grasping the rationale behind Antigone's act. All react as if Antigone attempted something quite exceptional, almost subversive, and certainly beyond common expectations. Antigone's action is presented as an act out of (her) place and time: a transgression of the norms of decorum and propriety, of social hierarchies and divisions, of the distinction between public and private, of gender expectations, of the rules governing both *oikos* and the *polis*. Antigone confronts men and a world dominated by men; she defies the authority both of her uncle to whom she would owe obedience as the head of both her family (now that her parents are dead) and of the state; she challenges the authority of the elders; and she foregoes marriage and motherhood – as important as anything else for a young woman in Ancient Greece – in order to live out her self-defined career. In addition, she shows a wild and tempestuous temper, defiant and unyielding, and very differently from her sister Ismene, behaves almost like a male.

In this context, attempts to "naturalize" Antigone's act and her law – considering that the two are one and the same – come at the price of a certain *banalization* of both, and Antigone is *anything but* banal. If she were simply relying upon a ready-made social norm that would be obvious to all and with which everyone should agree, then we would have to account not just for the incomprehension she encounters throughout, but for her need to elaborate on a supposedly futile law, which Antigone does not once but twice. Consequently, we should not be satisfied with Aristotle's explanation in the *Rhetoric*. In his reading, Antigone's law becomes a rhetorical instrument that the speaker can use (and abuse) when the legal circumstances are unfavorable; it has nothing to do with the compulsion with which Antigone experiences and expresses it. Likewise, Lysias' later reliance on the funerary *topos* as unabashed Athenian political propaganda – which can be viewed as part of what Nicole Loraux aptly labels "the invention of *Athens*"[4] – ignores the potentially subversive implications underneath her claim, precisely to undermine those very same political structures and institutions. There is something radical in Antigone's original act that cannot be wholly explained as reflecting the rights of the family, the practices of burial, and the rituals for the dead.

Part of the reason why it is hard to do justice to Antigone's originality must be due to the historical divide separating us from the Greeks. Much needs to be supplied to make up for a world that no longer exists and many modern rewritings of the play do not have the strength of the original. Thus Klaas Tindemans notes "the apparent inability of our [modern] theatre to find a stage language that effectively deals with the normative impact of Antigone's claim."[5] In François Ost's excellent modern rewriting, *Antigone Voilée*,[6] Antigone becomes Aïcha, treason becomes terrorism, burial becomes wearing a veil in school in honor of her dead brother, which clashes against the principle of *laicité* that the schoolmaster defends; and the choral odes become the discourses of TV personalities, journalists, and philosophers trying to explain her motivation without fully being able to comprehend it. What Ost captures quite well is how a peaceful act of wearing a veil can be interpreted, from the other side, as an apology for terrorism, and hence how a small and almost insignificant act can acquire a great symbolic and public dimension, difficult to explain in its own terms. It is doubtful, however, whether Ost's modern rewriting has the normative impact and disruptive nature that Tindemans reclaims for the original, for the conflict between Aïcha and the schoolmaster is still framed in terms of the statist categories of freedom of religion and conscience. It seems that not all can be attributed to a historical discontinuity. Even if we could reproduce the world in which Antigone first appeared (either the legendary Thebes, the historical Athens, or a combination of the two), we would still face the problem of the transformative effect that Antigone had upon it, for the normative universe no longer remains the same after her violent irruption.

Attempts to naturalize Antigone's law do not consider the "newness" of Antigone – the fact that her claim was not foreseeable by the previous and antecedent circumstances – nor the novelty that she engenders, forever changing the legal landscape without the possibility of turning back the clock. In a reversal of cause and effect, those readings project *what actually happened* onto *what there was no reason to believe would happen*, as if these two things were linked by causal necessity. The world in which Antigone's law is already created cannot be read back into the situation where it had not yet appeared, nor be logically deduced from it. For Antigone's law to be intelligible and "make sense" at all, it has been necessary for her to create both the language and the context in which that language is to be understood, which is why such a world did not exist prior to Antigone's intervention. Antigone is not merely reproducing the norms of the world as she found it, but defining the language and the norms appropriate for the world she is creating. These two worlds, the world as she found it and the world affected by her action, are incommensurable, in the sense that there is no predetermined, foreseeable, and projectible line crossing from one to the other. To account for Antigone's law is therefore to account for the relation between two heterogeneous worlds – the world *before* and *after* Antigone – *just as this relation is being transformed* precisely by Antigone. In order to do justice to her action we must keep its "newness" alive, without flattening the difference out.

This is easier said than done. Hannah Arendt argues that "whenever something new occurs, it bursts into the context of predictable processes as something unexpected, unpredictable, and ultimately causally inexplicable – just like a miracle."[7] As such, it is difficult both to understand and to assess. How to explain something which defies "rational" explanation? How to assess something unique and radically new? With what standards? For centuries readers have been bewitched by Antigone, trying to understand and yet unable to seize her magnetic power. George Steiner describes how Antigone has been enlisted in the name of many different causes, rewritten many times over, in ways that were never quite able to grasp the enormity and the stature of her original act.[8] For a long time, the image of Antigone has been one of self-sacrifice and heroism, pictured with an almost virginal nature, defending her principles courageously and sacrificing herself on behalf of her loved one, which accords well both with Christian imageries of martyrdom and Romantic ideals about resistance to tyranny. Nowadays, Antigone is more likely greeted with a mixture of detachment and slight apprehension. It is not uncommon to hear that Antigone is both alienated from her society and alienating to her audience, wild and excessive as an animal, estranged from the living and bent on death, unforgiving towards her sister and too attached to her brother, bordering the taboo and the scandal, almost a "symptom" to be diagnosed – which surely must reveal as much about our own shift of sensibilities and presuppositions as about Antigone.

Antigone's legal claim has also been questioned. Is it because she appeals to a law of the gods [*theôn nomima*] that may have lost the immediate and self-evident appeal it once might have had? Is it rather her autarchy, the apparent independence of judgment that leads her to declare a law-unto-herself, which bothers a modern sensibility imbued with a consensual ethos? Or is it rather the uncompromising nature of her claim, unable to recognize her "other"? Or perhaps the apparent contradiction involved in defending her family while rejecting her sister? Or is it that she is unable to maintain the universality of her law when seemingly proclaiming the singularity of Polyneices? Could it be that, in admitting that she would not have done the same for a husband or child, she refuses to utter law at all, in any ordinary, generalizable sense?[9]

There is a risk of pushing these questions too far. Whereas earlier attempts to naturalize Antigone's law could not account for its newness, the opposite tendency to deprive Antigone of legal capability, to regard her as pure aberration, are equally misguided. Whatever misgivings we might have about Antigone must be squared with the fact that her law is finally vindicated: Teireisas says punishing her was part of the transgression Creon committed, the elders argue for her release, her punisher is punished (also) on her account, and Polyneices is finally buried as she always wanted. So, on the one hand, we cannot downplay the newness and radicalism of her claim, and, on the other, we cannot ignore that *legally speaking* her instincts proved to be essentially correct, at least in the world she helped to create.

In between these two poles, I am inclined to believe that Antigone is the normative anomaly that ends up modifying the very concept of normalcy. Her law represents what in the given state of affairs was "impossible" to carry out successfully, but it nevertheless succeeded, and further imposed itself, retrospectively, *as if* it had always been meant to succeed – a fiction that ought not hide the tremendous social fracture and the successive stages entailed by her creation. Thus we have a first moment in which her law was not possible; a final moment when her law has already become acceptable; and another, truly transformative moment where the possibility of her law is created. At its inception, Antigone's law inhabits the region of pure potentiality – the law as it might be – which is actualized in the course of the drama, but can only be assessed after its resolution, once this has ended.

As a legal figure, Antigone has often been invoked in the name of civil disobedience. Within that social imaginary, François Ost reads Antigone as the literary archetype of the person who, in a public and non-violent manner, opposes a law that she or he considers unjust in the name of higher moral or ethical principles.[10] From a slightly different perspective, Klaas Tindemans compares the figure of Antigone with the *parrhesiastes*, the outspoken citizen of Athens analyzed by Michel Foucault as an icon of early free speech activism. He lists five features: outspokenness, truth, risk, critique, and duty, all of which are present in Antigone: "she refers to herself as speaker of (divine) truth and, in doing so, she risks her life. And she considers her act and its verbal confirmation as a duty, acknowledging the political context of its performance."[11] From yet a different angle, Katrin Beushausen has suggested reading Antigone in light of Walter Benjamin's figure of the *great criminal*, who, "in his resistance to violent order, 'however repellent his ends may have been, has aroused the admiration of the public'".[12] In Beushausen's view, "her public resistance appeals to a latent sense of the injustice of the law amongst those who are governed by its order and who are compelled to support the act of opposition to an unjust law regardless of its ends."[13]

There is truth in each of these images of Antigone, but a crucial element seems to be missing: Antigone not only disobeys those in authority in the name of principles not recognized by the political authority and accepts the penalty for it; she not only speaks her mind fearlessly and risks her life in doing so; she not only commits a "crime" for which she may eventually gain the secret admiration of the public. The important thing is that, in doing all that, she is able to *create* a norm that she can communicate to others and that can continue to live even after her death. Like a lawyer in a court of law or a statesman in the Assembly, Antigone defends her action in a public forum, using a creative and rhetorically persuasive language, with reasons that can appeal to the wider audience, relying on principles that prove to be fundamental, even constitutive, both of the *oikos* and of the *polis*. The speaker, the forum, the performance, the language, the social and political implications . . . all about Antigone's law is new. Antigone can therefore be rightly regarded as a true *poet of law*, a *nomos poietes* with the ability to make a whole new legal world before us, using powerful and beautiful language that, in challenging common sensibility and conventional wisdom, re-educates one and redefines the other.

Antigone's genuine act of norm-generation or *nomopoetic act* resembles what Jacques Rancière labels "political act," namely the disruption of the conventionally established order of things by the eruption of something new and unexpected that transforms the public space.[14] The nomopoetic act is always perceived as violent – the violence inherent in every genuine act of law-making as Walter Benjamin observed[15] – and it is for this reason that Antigone's action appears as wild, excessive, irrational, senseless, impossible. But this is only if we look at Antigone's action from the outside, that is from within the logical structure of the conventional legal order, which is the way Ismene, Creon, and the elders see it through much of the drama.[16] However, from within the *nomos* of Antigone, there is nothing more natural than the law she obeys: she carries out her obligation by refusing to obey an order to the contrary (illegal in her view), without causing harm to anyone (other than to Creon's pride). From the perspective of the world that she helps to create, Antigone's action does not appear subversive, but consistent with its underlying values and norms.

7.2 The genealogy of Antigone's law

Once it is recognized that Antigone's law is neither divinely created nor inspired (for she is not endowed with prophetic vision and "no one knows whence such laws came to be"), the question immediately arises as to how her law may have originated. By asking this question, I do not wish to venture into the "dark regions" where her desire has been said to reside,[17] nor do I wish to speculate about the "*unsayable* grounds" upon which it holds sway upon her.[18] My quest is rather a hermeneutical one, wishing to trace the genealogy of Antigone's law in its very trajectory, in the shifting formulations which it is given throughout the play. Such a quest may run against the objection that, at the time the audience first encounters her, Antigone appears already to have made up her mind. This could be interpreted to mean that the norm she presumptively obeys must lie somewhere outside the play, and therefore it is inaccessible and not susceptible to textual analysis. Rebutting this idea, I will argue that Antigone's law is *staged* before our own eyes, starting from an instinctive, almost visceral, reaction of repulse, to a more articulate defense of her norm of action and the illegality of Creon's decree, to a final argument seeking to persuade the citizens of the legitimacy of her disobedience.

The argument relies on two prior assumptions. First, unless she is deceiving us or herself, it is reasonable to suppose that Antigone goes through an internal process similar in kind to the one she lets us glimpse in her public performance. When Antigone learns about Creon's decree, the considerations she later brings to the audience – the story of her family, the mutual death of her brothers, the abuse of Polyneices' body, and so on – may have entered her mind, perhaps in a raw, undiluted, or unconscious manner. But as soon as she contemplates a course of action, she must bring these considerations into the open and put them into (legal) language, particularly when she seeks to enlist the support of her sister. This process of translation continues throughout the play, enabling us to trace the law she claims to obey.

Secondly, there is no realm of pure normativity where norms would lie bare, somewhere out of space and time. Law is necessarily embedded in language and inserted in narratives that give it meaning. Even the Old Testament shows how God's law is created through successive covenants with the people of Israel. The Ten Commandments themselves come after a long and arduous historical development. In fact, before the people of Israel can be bound by the "You shall," they must accept the authority of God as the only God, which is actually questioned as soon as Moses descends from Sinai. Thus it is not the case that first we need to have a law, then it can be used. Antigone and her law exist and grow simultaneously: every time she argues it, she is giving it a slightly different interpretation, and thus refining and adding nuances, as well as modifying the terms of the debate and the law with it. Therefore we should not look for Antigone's law in a singular moment, frozen in time, but rather in a constellation of moments, created through a series of events, personal commitments, and changing formulations that are context-dependent and performative in nature. Seen in this light, Antigone's law is just one claim in an endless spiral of arguments and counter-arguments that is the law.

Antigone enters the stage and asks Ismene whether she has heard the proclamation prohibiting the burial of their brother. Presumably she has not seen the mistreatment of the body, but the mere thought that the brother she once loved must be left to rot in the open, to be abused and torn apart by scavengers, is physically revolting, and not necessarily any less offensive today, I imagine, than it was for Antigone. She tries to enlist Ismene's help, speaking in terms of loyalty and duty, of doing the honorable thing and not betraying him, of performing an obligation born out of their family ties that even the gods honor. Clearly, Antigone is operating under the influence of a norm.

In Chapter 1, we have seen that norms must be accepted subjectively through the personal act of commitment, by which the individual accepts the binding nature of the norm as it applies to her. Through this personal filter, the undiluted normative magma of narratives, images, and myths forming our normative world is turned active. Antigone's commitment binds her to a particular course of action prescribed in the norm she now accepts: she must bury her brother no matter what. As interpreted by Antigone, such a norm agrees with what her family and her dead brother would have wanted and expected in accordance with law and justice, but most importantly, it is in accordance with her sense of self. Antigone would not be able to forgive and to live with herself if she did not carry it out. Antigone does not defend the rights of burial in the abstract, but the particular burial of her brother in a situation in which it has been explicitly prohibited by civil authority. She sees the decree as the last straw in a long history of abuse that her family has endured and she is prepared to put an end to it. To add injury to the offense, Creon's decree prohibits all forms of lamentations and threatens with death anyone who disobeys. Antigone interprets this decision as an intolerable encroachment, and, clearly, as insufficient deterrent to prevent her from doing what she must. As Antigone affirms, Creon has no right to keep her from her own (49).

Antigone's assertion entails a remarkable step not entirely accounted for in the theory of normativity provided thus far. This analysis must be extended to include a different stage, for just as Antigone commits to a norm to which she now feels obligated with the binding force of the law, she simultaneously disengages herself from the normative order that was supposed initially to contain her. We may call that a process of disengagement or "unbinding," which is the condition of possibility for the new commitment.[19] The unbinding marks the separation from the normative order to which Antigone was assigned on account of her age, her gender, and her personal and familial status as an unmarried woman and niece of Creon. A fuller account of normativity must therefore explain how an individual can separate herself from the normative order to which she was originally ascribed.

In Antigone's case, this separation is linked to a sense of gross injustice committed against someone she loved: Creon's decree infringes upon everything she holds sacred: her sense of self, society, family, law, and justice, both mortal and divine. This gross sense of injustice – the last straw in a long succession of family catastrophes – pushes her to the point of fracture with the limits imposed on her on account of her gender, age, and status. Antigone rebels by refusing to be constrained or abide by them anymore. The indignation before an unjustified and unjustifiable prohibition fosters her disengagement from a normative order that no longer represents her and with which she can no longer identify, which is why the unbinding is a certain failure of identification.

When such a failure of identification occurs, the rule emanating from the old order is no longer operative as a norm. At most it becomes an extraneous precept that functions externally; that is, the individual can take notice of it as existing in the outer world, especially insofar as it can be used against him or her in the form of sanctions.[20] But as H. L. A. Hart famously argued, such is a very poor conception of law that does not account for law's capacity to bind.[21] Therefore, when Antigone says that she may be convicted of a crime that is holy (74), she is not actually accepting but rather depriving Creon's decree of something essential for it to function as law. This is the extent of Antigone's acceptance and how Creon's rule will operate from now on: she knows Creon has the power [*potestas*] to put her to death, but she does not recognize that he has authority [*auctoritas*] to dictate norms that bind her.

Disengagement, or rather its absence, can also explain one of the intriguing questions of the play, namely how it is that Ismene, of the same age, gender, and personal status as Antigone, and with equal family history and relations with the dead, is not equally compelled to follow the same course of action as Antigone.[22] Part of the reason is, to be sure, Ismene's timidity, the fact that she does not find in herself the strength to fight against a stronger power. But not everything can be explained by a difference in character. Ismene also has a *disagreement* with Antigone, based on a different normative assessment of the situation.

Here the process of unbinding becomes key, because, whereas Antigone refuses to be constrained by the categories to which she has been ascribed by others, Ismene accepts (normatively) these social and gendered constraints. Ismene defines herself as a woman, which in the patriarchal worldview she accepts means that she *ought not* confront but obey men. Ismene still participates in the system of values and hierarchies represented by Creon. Furthermore, Ismene equates Creon's decree with the law of the citizens (an identification that Antigone severs), making it more difficult for Ismene to disengage herself from an order she still considers binding. Therefore, the same decree is interpreted through a different normative lens: whereas Antigone defends the norm that binds her to burying Polyneices, Ismene weighs such a norm against another set of norms that bind her to Creon (even though this choice may tear her apart). The two sisters part ways: Antigone to perform the burial, which is an action that Ismene may admire from afar but cannot share.

Antigone is caught red-handed performing the burial rites, which provides the occasion for her encounter with Creon. When she speaks before Creon, her commitment goes through a process of *objectification*, by which her initial largely intuitive norm is posited as a legal precept she now claims to obey.[23] Thus, in one of the most cited speeches of all times, Antigone affirms that neither Zeus nor Dike uttered such law to her, aiming to shame Creon into acknowledging that as a mere mortal he has no power to derogate the unwritten and undying laws of the gods, for these are not for now or yesterday but live forever, and no one knows whence first they came to be.

Her words have been rehearsed so many times that it becomes difficult to hear them anew, as if centuries of repeated use have worn out their original freshness. Generally it is assumed that Antigone opposes a man-made law based on a superior divine law, a supposition that rests on a double equivocation. First of all, Antigone nowhere claims that the law *proceeds from* the gods.[24] But even if she had, Antigone would be no more entitled to call her law "divine" than was Creon when he too appealed to Zeus as witness of his decree. Perhaps a better way to understand the expression "laws of the gods," then, would be to say that the gods are *behind* such laws, or even that the gods *sanction* them, in the sense that they both recognize and respect them (just like in modern parliamentary monarchies laws are formally sanctioned by the monarchs, who participate neither in their making nor in their application, and are bound by the laws they sanction). And secondly, the unwritten laws Antigone invokes cannot be represented on top of a Kelsenian pyramidal structure that modern legal theorists fancy. If anything, they are to be imagined like the roots of a tree, providing permanent support and underlying sustenance to the continued life of the *polis*. It is their temporal duration and lastingness, rather than their hierarchical superiority, which Antigone opposes to Creon's ephemeral decree.

My real interest, however, is in the process by which the norm to which Antigone is personally committed is turned into an "external" object of law that she claims to follow. As already noted, Antigone's argument is not a ready-made, conventional rule: culturally, rhetorically, legally, the unwritten law is not "already" there. It is not something that Antigone "finds" lying, waiting for her to be used. (In fact, Antigone may need to transform the social world around her so that it might eventually accommodate her.) Still, the unwritten law is no mere "invention" either; it is not a rhetorical trope Antigone could magically pull out of her bag of tricks. Antigone believes to be faithfully executing her legal obligations, as she renders them as dutifully as she can into language that her audience too might eventually accept as law. At the same time, she makes her action depend upon a law she actually is helping to create as she speaks, even though she was committed to it as soon as she learned of the injustice of Creon and felt the pull of Polyneices' body. Antigone's legal claim is an oral and performative expression of the unwritten law that by this very act ceases to be merely *unwritten*. It becomes posited as an external object of law demanding obedience.

In order to understand this somewhat paradoxical transformation, it is necessary to put her claim in connection with the set of narratives, practices, and institutions that make it meaningful and locate it in history. Thus Antigone's objectification operates (and she sees herself operating) within a set of ritual practices, interpersonal bonds and relationships, and social institutions. Antigone defends her action as consistent with the age-old practices of burial, anchored in timeless memory, unwritten because they exist even before the alphabet was invented. These are customs of time immemorial, from a time before human records and history. Nobody knows when they were established, and surely Antigone cannot "remember" them herself, but they have been passed on from generation to generation and continue to generate obligations in the present. Antigone was compelled, as a result, to defy Creon's law and perform her obligations of *philia*, which does not recognize the distinction between friend and foe upon which Creon's decree stands. Therefore, *philia* – the human tie that connects all brothers and sisters – is both the source of her obligation and the wound within Creon's decree, the scar that makes visible its profoundly discriminatory content (the result of hate according to Antigone). The injustice at the heart of Creon's decree is the reason why it must be invalidated, in accordance with the interpersonal relationships that bind not just her, but all members of the community she envisions as members of the human race.

We can better appreciate Antigone's underlying argument if we compare it with Priam's similar challenge at the end of the *Iliad*, when he attempts to persuade Achilles, enemy and killer of his son, to return Hector's body.[25] Priam could not rely on the existence of a common law of burial, and instead he relies on an argument that stresses their common humanity, to the point where they are no longer Priam and Achilles, Argives and Trojans fighting in a war, but men united in their common experience of pain and death. Antigone too must create a community where there is none, but she does not appeal to the common humanity that unites her with her enemy (Creon), but rather presents a wider and inter-generational community that antecedes and presupposes the existence of the *polis*, namely, the interpersonal bonds of family and human relations which Creon has violated, placing him outside of that eternal community of sentiment that knows no bound, especially after death. It is this community, Antigone argues, from which Creon has *excluded himself voluntarily*.

There can be little doubt that Antigone gives a profound reading of the tradition and dresses it in commanding legal language, appealing to ritual practices that are still observed, on the basis of human relations and bonds that unite all men who have not forgotten their limitations as mortals. This is not to say that her argument is free of problems, beginning with her claim to define the meaning of these traditions and to make them prevail over Creon's explicit law (and the city's control of the practices of burial). In this sense, when she says that she did not think that Creon, being a mortal, had the power to derogate the unfailing laws of the gods, she may want to shame Creon into admitting his puniness and insignificance, but her words become potentially undermining of her own claim to know such laws, herself being a mortal. For how does she know – what assurances can she provide regarding – what the unfailing ordinances of the gods are and require in the present case?

More importantly, her argument does not leave room for Creon, or for the political concerns he has. Unlike Priam, Antigone is not interested in creating a community with his enemy, or in persuading him to change his mind. Antigone has already given up on Creon and does not want to communicate with him, or communicates with him just barely to register her disagreement. Her contempt for Creon is so great that she does not take time to answer some of his most damaging points. Thus Antigone ignores the war that almost devastated her country, and takes no time to defend her brother from the allegations that he came, a traitor to his people, with intentions to burn the city and its temples to the ground.[26] Moreover, Antigone thinks she can afford to be disdainful with Creon on the assumption that the citizens are on her side, but this attitude blinds her to legitimate concerns they may have about the scope and application of her legal claim. For example, her expression about the unwritten laws does not clarify whether the obligations of *philia* trump those owed the city, always and without exception (which is quite an unrestricted claim), or if this only applies in egregious cases such as this one. Without further clarification, her appeal to the unwritten law is hopelessly vague.

Not surprisingly, Antigone's legal claim is not received as well as she had hoped and instead she encounters what she thinks are harsh words from the Chorus. In her last moments, Antigone resents being misrepresented, which motivates a final attempt at self-explanation. In doing so, Antigone harbors the hope that the citizens (if not all, at least those with good judgment) will be able to correct their misconceptions and understand the way she acted. Such a move entails a remarkable opening, as she tries to engage her audience in a re-evaluation of her action. For once Antigone *registers* the notes of disapproval from the elders and can no longer assume uncritically that the citizens are on her side (which she did implicitly in her dialogue with Ismene and explicitly with Creon). For the first time Antigone must entertain the possibility that she may have transgressed, not the arbitrary decree of a tyrant, but a binding "law of the citizens." This time, Antigone must defend her "action against the citizens," which requires her to present her disobedience in light of a norm (or a *nomos*) that her audience may also accept as legitimate.

Antigone produces such a *nomos* with the argument that Polyneices is the last brother she can ever have, and this makes this case unlike any other, including one which would involve the death of a husband and child if she were to form another family. I have suggested that the reason why this case demands especial consideration is that Polyneices embodies the extinction of her whole lineage, which the death of either a child or husband in a second family would not replicate.[27] Regardless of any interpretation, in the process of formulating her *nomos* Antigone's earlier pronouncement about the unwritten law is turned specific, and is now a concrete legal provision designed to govern the case. Therefore the general and abstract "unwritten law" undergoes a process of *singularization* by which it becomes a legal precept fit to apply in the present circumstances. It appears now that in the case of conflict with a *legitimate law of the citizens* (as different from the arbitrary decree of Creon), the obligations of *philia* do not legitimately prevail, always and without exception, but they do in this particular case.[28]

Antigone's *nomos* is thus a fully fledged legal provision susceptible of being accepted in its own right.[29] Contrary to what has been often supposed, Antigone is not withdrawing from her original position, but rather espousing it in all its complexity. For the first time, she recognizes that her society is not a homogeneous entity, and that the opinions of the citizens may reasonably differ. The elders accused Antigone of being *autonomos* (821), but she now defends her original action with an argument that addresses their concerns, showing that she is mindful of both her obligations to her family and to the city. This gesture can be described as the conscientious act of a citizen de facto who wishes to harmonize various conflicting commitments, one of which ties her to the burial, and another to the legitimate laws of the city, towards which she means no general disrespect. In doing so, Antigone shows a political awareness she was lacking before. This is the first time, too, that Antigone acknowledges that the whole legal conflict over the burial of Polyneices is a matter of sensible and wise judgment, and not of self-evident or "higher" truth.

In light of this, the accusation of autonomy leveled against her must be qualified, as it contains both truth and falsity. On the one hand, it is true that her act of norm-generation, as with every act of legal creation, presupposes an authority that it lacks in the moment it is being enacted, and appears to have been created out of nowhere. In this, Antigone behaves no differently than the authors of the American Declaration of Independence, who assumed an authority that did not pre-exist the document on which it is was being founded.[30] On the other hand, Antigone alone – or anyone else for that matter – is not sufficient for her legal claim to become law, which always depends on the interpretations and judgment of different actors – just like the Declaration of Independence depended on many different actors to become a *legal* document. As an essentially social phenomenon, law is immersed in a continuous and historical process of becoming, which demands the participation of a broader audience.

At the end of the day, the genealogy of Antigone's law cannot be represented as a single and isolated moment in space and time, but as a trajectory connecting a broad constellation of spatial and temporal dimensions. What I mean is this: at the outset, Antigone feels the call of the unburied body, urging her to respond. She interprets this call as a demand (in the sense explained in Chapter 1) to bury him despite the prohibition and the death threat hanging on it. Antigone's commitment to burying her brother entails a simultaneous disengagement from the normative order represented by Creon. In addition, Antigone's norm can only be understood within a set of narratives and institutions (of ritual practices, family obligations) that frame it and objectify her norm as a law she must obey. This general law that demands obedience is made specific through a process of singularization by which the general and unspecified unwritten law turns into an applicable legal precept covering this case. The singular provision can thus be subject to further interpretations and give rise to different kinds of judgments, in a never ending process that involves many different actors. Arguably, law is not something that Antigone – or anyone else for that matter – can create on her own.

7.3 The law of the *Antigone* and the experiences of the audience

If Antigone's law is just one claim in a broader context, how is the audience to proceed in the determination of the law of the *Antigone*?[31] One possible method would be to establish the law in Greece and then contrast that determination with what happens in the play. For example, we know from Thucydides that the law of Athens would deny the burial of traitors in Attica, but not altogether, which suggests that Creon's decree goes beyond ordinary legal practices and the audience would see it that way too.[32] Unfortunately, such a distinction between denial of burial altogether or just in a specific location is not a possibility contemplated by anyone in the play and Antigone attacks the rationale behind the prohibition – not just its place of implementation. (Would Antigone be satisfied if she could have buried Polyneices outside of Thebes?) Besides, there is no easy way to determine how the law operated in practice, or to know how long it would have remained unchallenged. Thus the same source that tells us about the law prohibiting the burial of traitors in Attic soil reports about this law in the context of its transgression, when Themistocles' family decided to challenge the law and bury him anyway.[33] Finally, Creon's transgression seems bigger than a mere act of overreaching his jurisdiction (if there is some poetic justice in his punishment his crime must be quite monstrous), and yet at the time he uttered his decree, Beushausen notes, "[it] appears less as an act of transgression into a sphere beyond his authority than a legitimate act of legislation in accordance with the authority granted to him,"[34] and the elders of the Chorus agree. All this suggests that there is no necessary connection between Athenian law and the law of the play. The world of the tragedy inhabits its own specific place in the imagination which creates its own jurisdiction, a symbolic geography that can only be discovered after a full and comprehensive assessment of the play.

A second possible method would be to select one of the characters as the carrier of the play's legal meaning. For a long time, Antigone's law has been thought to occupy such a privileged position (supported by Teiresias' insight into the otherwise inscrutable realm of the gods). But she is not alone. Another likely candidate is Haemon, whose flexible and diplomatic talent brings forward a more democratic understanding of the role of government. Likewise, the elders of the Chorus are able to respect the authority of the *polis* and to show proper reverence to the gods. Even Ismene, in her combination of prudential reasoning and sensible judgment, has been suggested to stand for the law of the *Antigone*.[35]

However, no character can by herself personify the law of the play, even Antigone, and there is something to be learned from (and to criticize in) almost all of them. Ismene's positive role may have been often overlooked, but the fact remains that she submits to a world of men in which women must be subservient and obey them in everything (61–4). Haemon too espouses important political virtues, but if no one is wise alone (as he says to his father), neither is he, and Haemon too may have something to learn even from his father (as the elders suggest). The elders too seem to provide good moral guidance, but on occasion they seem more interested in saving the *polis* (or perhaps their own position within it) than in the genuine justice of the matter. They are also limited by their status, age, and gender, and do not adequately represent the legitimate concerns of the younger generation, or the interests of all the citizens. Teiresias is able to diagnose the legal breach incurred by Creon, but his expertise amounts to a case-by-case interpretation of symptoms and the general inferences drawn from them (a sort of negative knowledge of the limits that must not be transgressed), rather than a positive enactment of the applicable law. The fact of the matter is that there is not one single law in the *Antigone*, but a multiplicity of them, sometimes coexisting peacefully, sometimes clashing irremediably. As a result, any possible answer to the issue of "the law of the *Antigone*" must turn away from readings that privilege a single viewpoint and attend to its multi-voicedness.

We ought not attempt an impossible amalgam or harmonization of all points of view, which would be a third, not wholly satisfactory, method of legal determination: first, because the harmonization of the various competing points of view does not account for those which are mutually exclusive and must be rejected (or, to use Cover's language, "redeemed"); second, because even those laws which are finally invalidated (i.e. Creon's decree in the end), leave some traces behind that must be taken into consideration. The fact that Creon's decree is finally invalidated – i.e. he himself annuls it – does not mean that throughout much of the drama it didn't have the effects of valid law and, misguided as it may have been, functioned as such for Ismene and the Chorus (if not for Antigone). This in itself is not to say much, since, as I have argued in Chapter 1, the important thing is not whether an unjust law can still be valid, but how such perception of injustice affects the continued life of such a law – its reception, dissemination, application, and enforcement.[36]

Departing from previous analyses, I suggest an approach based on the experience that the theatrical audience undergoes throughout the play, now being forced to adopt one legal perspective, now another, leading towards richer and more textured understandings of the multiple issues raised by the burial of Polyneices and its prohibition. In this view, the law of the *Antigone* cannot be determined in the abstract, because such determination is inextricably linked with the shifts and interactions that occur in various successive stages of the performance. As Helene Foley writes, the "dramatic narrative requires its audience (each different member of it) not to uncover a message, not to leave a theater in a state of helpless aporia (inability to make a judgment), but to negotiate among points of view just as it would in a court of law or in the assembly."[37] "Equally important," Foley continues, "is the awareness that tragedy is a complex dialogue that evolves in space and time."[38] Accordingly, any determination of the play's law must comprehend the spatial and temporal dimensions in which its judgment takes place. Through a reflective engagement with the play, the audience learns progressively to make better judgments about its central dilemma: the incommensurable conflict of laws between Antigone and Creon over the burial of Polyneices. Contrary to what Plato feared, the "abandonment" to this experience requires us to activate our critical faculties as audiences, as we learn not only to see the issue from various competing perspectives (which challenges one-sided attachments and identifications), but more importantly to see *our own position* in a critical manner (and thus to rise above our original standpoints and presuppositions).

Progressively, the audience realizes that there are borne limits to the normative cosmos, non-disposable by human will alone. These immanent laws of reality are not knowable in advance, in the sense that individuals may tread on them unknowingly, even when acting consistently in principle with other ethical and social conventions (as Creon). No one can claim to represent them perfectly (not Antigone, not even Teiresias), but at times certain individuals can help to manifest them, i.e. bring them to light, with all the risks of excess and self-aggrandizement this action may entail. For such laws to emerge they have to be recognized and acknowledged by an audience, in stages that are to be constructed, which makes every such law dependent on social processes of verification and collective forms of signification. The manifestation or emergence of law is no mere repetition – the enunciation of a law already in place – but constitutive of the institution whence the normative action issues and potentially transforms – just as the norms and institution of burial are forever changed by Antigone. Every institution is thus open to radical reinterpretation and innovation, just as every new case can potentially alter the direction and trajectory of the law. Ultimately the law of the *Antigone*, which is never fixed or static but constantly in flux, is the law that the audience enacts through its engagement in the activity of judging the play. This activity is performed not according to preconceived notions of good judgment, not as the result of idiosyncratic "judgments of taste," but as the drama itself calls to be judged, through a constellation of engagements with the spatial nature and temporal motions yet to be examined.

7.4 The narrative configuration of time: the temporalities of judgment

Judgment in tragedy operates not from a stable and fixed frame of reference, but from within a narrative that is continuously moving. The same is true in the law. Audiences and judges alike must find their respective positions within the "master narrative" – the tragic play in one case, the legal proceedings in the other – and approach the task of judging from therein. Their respective positions do not remain invariable, but they shift as the play and the legal process advance and new material is introduced.

It is usual to assume that the tragedy advances from beginning, to middle, to end. This is true only in a limited sense, since it gives the false impression of linear progression. Actually the play does *not* advance in a linear fashion, but in many different directions at once, choosing to focalize on certain elements, while holding some others back; disclosing some information, while keeping some hidden; inviting audiences to draw inferences, or else discouraging them; announcing certain developments or foreclosing them; sometimes keeping the ambiguity open, other times closing it up. This is why the framing of the conflict becomes so important – as lawyers know only too well, when they fight to control when to introduce certain evidence, the order in which the witnesses are called to testify, and so on. Hence every judgment operates within such general *fluctuations*, which are the "moving grounds" from where the audience relates to the stage and the judge to the legal conflict. In order to understand how judgments develop over time one must first learn to identify these fluctuations.

Judging in and through time entails more than situating our position within the fluctuations of the play; additionally, it requires a different kind of narrative to describe how and in what direction our relation to the stage is itself moving. Thus every judgment involves not just an appraisal of where we are and how we relate to what is being judged – a sense of spatial location – but a sense of where we and the object of judgment are both going as a result of this interaction – a qualitatively different *temporal* dimension.[39] We might say that whereas spatial relations describe the relationships from the audience to the stage and vice versa as it were internally, temporal motions give these spatial relationships a sense of direction and external trajectory, as it were a *towards*.[40]

In Chapter 5 we spoke about "identification," "separation," "mediation," "bifurcation," "embodiment," and "disembodiment" as ways in which the audience relates spatially to the stage and filters the conflict dramatized on it. In what follows, I shall distinguish six temporal motions or *temporalities* that give a sense of direction and trajectory to the former relationships. These are "immersion," "contention," "prospection," "retrospection," "closing," and "reconstitution," and each represents a different kind of activity or form of judgment with distinct movements and trajectories. Such temporalities must be engaged, in one way or another, *each time* we interpret the play (no matter how many times we have seen or read the play already), for they are indissolubly related to the play as its conditions of intelligibility, no less than are its language and the historical context. In this view, to develop an adequate understanding of the various temporalities engaged in judgment is crucial not only for the incommensurable conflict dramatized in the *Antigone*, but for all kinds of judgment, including conflicts in the law.

7.4.1 *Immersion*

To be willing spectators at a theatrical event entails leaving our own reality behind so that we may imaginatively inhabit a different one constructed before our very eyes. All of a sudden, we are at the gates of the Royal Palace of Thebes, listening to the private conversation of the sisters Antigone and Ismene. In a flash, too, we are to understand that there has been a war, that the Theban side has been victorious, and that two brothers have died, each at the hands of the other, but that only the one will be buried if the new King's decree is to be enforced. Fiction has a strangely captivating power to drag us into its interior, and to bring us in contact with a foreign history and a language, a geographical and moral landscape, a social and legal structure, a political climate, a general atmosphere and mood. The original act of immersion, of plunging into the fictional universe of the play, constitutes us as members of a tragic audience.

Immersion is a mode of relating temporally with the text characterized by the attunement of perspectives and horizons between audience and stage. At the initial stages, the play is perceived as an undifferentiated stream that moves the action forward and carries the unsuspecting audience along.

Unaware of all its twists and turns – of its various rhythms, tempos, pauses, and silences – the audience cannot fathom the overall direction of the play and leans on it as a guide. Immersion is thus a process of blending in with the natural cadence of the play, from where the audience observes the situation, characters, and events with cautious eyes.

As a mode of judgment, immersion invites a certain relinquishment of our independence of judgment to the "sovereignty" of the play. For example, at the early stages we are not to question but rather to assimilate the elements of the story that remain beyond its natural scope (the reasons for fratricidal war between the armies of the two brothers, their mutual deaths at the hands of each other), or that work as premises for it (the burial of a brother who is also a traitor). It is unadvisable, for example, to conclude at this stage that Creon's decree is illegal and void, not only because there are enough dramatic elements to question it, but also because doing otherwise would pre-empt the tragedy from deploying in full. It is safer at this point to defer to the opinion of the elders, who affirm that Creon has the right to do as he pleases. Immersion represents thus an opening towards the play and the world of value presented in it, driven by an attitude of respect and understanding for a world that is not our own.

Immersion occurs not only at the early stages of the play. For example, at the height of the battle between Antigone and Creon, the audience follows the spiral of mutual accusations and reproaches to the point of being lost, unable to stop and think that there are crucial arguments missing in the legal debate.[41] Moreover, immersion can overcome the audience's resistance and operate almost against its will. For example, the Ode on Disaster constitutes an audience that is trapped between its desire to anticipate the future of the characters, and its concurrent inability to predict exactly what will happen next. Like a black hole that impedes the ray of light escaping its gravitational field, the ode disavows any external standpoint to judge it. This does not mean that the audience loses all critical capacities at the time of immersion. In the latter example, the very moral of the song (i.e. the wondrous nature of the things-to-come) invites the audience to have a look at their own act of looking, which grants them a measure of reflexive and self-critical regard.

7.4.2 *Contention*

As the story unfolds, the audience gradually begins to take hold of the play's narrative structure and the direction the play is taking (and the audience with it). The narrative is no longer perceived as an undifferentiated stream, but as an intermittent succession of sequences, halts, and discontinuities. This realization enables the audience to take hold of its own status as an audience and activate the temporality I call *contention*. Contention requires the audience to appraise critically their capacity to make judgments within the boundaries defined by the play. The initial process of assimilation and immersion thus gives way to a more vigilant attitude of the audience's personal jurisdiction. In particular, the audience must retain in the memory the standards of valuation that the play announces but does not yet permit to be answered. For example, when Creon declares that it is impossible to fully know a man until he has proven himself in the art of government, we can appreciate already that this is an important determination to be made in the future, but that in effect one must suspend this judgment until the condition stated in it can be verified, namely until Creon has proven himself in the art of government. Or when, similarly, in the Ode on Man the Chorus links being positioned high in the city and its opposite to the respect paid to the laws of the land and the justice of the gods, the audience is meant to retain that information for when that individuation can be made.

A paradigmatic example of contention occurs at the moment of the incommensurability between Antigone and Creon, where the two parties make equally forceful demands upon the audience, and the latter cannot refuse justice to either of them. If we move in the direction of the normative world represented by either one of the contenders, there is a force of equal magnitude reclaiming us in the opposite direction. Such a battle appears to render time static, as if time had come to a standstill. But more than a time that has ceased to be, it is better to speak of a time that is being pressurized under contrary motions. At this point, contention is experienced precisely as the impossibility of rendering a just verdict which doesn't wrong any party.

Contention also enables us to resist the flow of the play. For example, in the dialogue between Haemon and his father, the former volunteers that, unbeknown to Creon, the citizens are on Antigone's side.[42] The approval of the citizens is not a trivial issue, and was already relevant in the discussion between Antigone and Creon, where each claimed to have the support of the citizens. Creon had argued that the citizens were on his side since no one but Antigone opposed him. Antigone claimed that the citizens were actually on her side, but were afraid of saying so. Surely the audience is intrigued to know what the citizens actually think, for it is crucial in their battle for legitimacy. So when Haemon brings the issue of the citizens again, the revelation cannot go unnoticed. Creon does not follow the argument, and instead accuses his young son of wanting to lecture him, after which the dialogue follows an altogether different route that does not dispel the concern. The play might go in one direction, but the audience does not let go of the issue and keeps it in the back of their mind, showing that the respective temporalities of the stage and the audience may differ.

This does not mean that the audience can render an independent judgment already, however tempting it may be to accept Haemon's report. There might be truth to Haemon's rumors, but this does not grant the conclusion that, at the moment of bringing them, they are as good as verified. As a modality of judgment, contention indicates both the responsibility and the limitations of judgment, activating the retentive qualities of the audience while reminding them of the inability to venture beyond what can be determined in fairness.

7.4.3 *Prospection*

The temporality of judgment I call *prospection* entails a twofold movement from the present towards the future and from the future towards the present. Properly prospection is not a judgment about the future, but about the present in its future form. In this temporality, the audience looks at what is happening on stage through the filter of how it might look in the future, which can happen in either one of these two opposite directions that I call *projection* and *anticipation*. In the former, the audience looks at the present circumstances and projects them onto the future, that is the audience looks at the future through the present. By contrast in the latter the audience brings the expectations about the future to bear on the present situation, that is looks at the present through the future.

An example of projection occurs in the scene with Teiresias. Through the web of significations and inferences of the seer's *techne*, the audience is offered an insight into a world beyond what can ordinarily be seen. The signs, narrated with vivid imagery of failed sacrifices and oozing fat, elicit the perception of a terrible state of affairs and reveal the full extent of Creon's transgression: a full reversal of the cosmology of life and death. In contrast to this vision, Creon's attempts at insulating himself from any wrongdoing diminish him in stature before the audience, who are now able to see him as the plaything of powerful forces that will, more likely than not, catch up with him. Therefore the audience moves along with Teiresias' projection about the future awaiting Creon, which "does not differ from the present, but it is only the future shape of what now is."[43]

An example of anticipation can be observed as the Chorus prays to Dionysus in their last song for a final act of deliverance. Despite the fact that the audience remains cognizant that it may already be too late, its concern for the characters and their well-being lifts the hope that the worst calamity can still be averted. The song is suggestive enough for the audience to be carried along with these hopes, and yet to not be caught completely off guard if they are not fulfilled in the exact form in which they are now anticipated. Thus the kind of expectations and anxieties that the audience harbors about the future affects its judgments of the present.

In the Fourth *Stasimon* we have already seen a combination of both anticipation and projection. We encountered both motions in the attempts of critical readers who anticipate what the destiny of each character will look like by comparing it with the Ode's Omythological stories, and then project the attribution of guilt and innocence found in those stories into Antigone's and Creon's own. In this regard, I have argued that the Ode does not allow prefiguring what the lot of each character will look like with certainty and it additionally frustrates any clear assignment of responsibility.

Consequently, prospection must be carried out with sensibility for our current context and full cognizance of the limitations of not to knowing what only the future can tell.

7.4.4 *Retrospection*

Whereas in prospection the audience judges the present in relation to its future, in retrospection the audience revisits the past with the concerns, worries, and feelings of the present. Retrospection is thus not a judgment about the past as such, but a judgment about the significance of the past in the present. Concerning this kind of judgment, one of the crucial questions is that of remaining *just* to the existential or epistemic conditions of the characters, namely the constraints and limitations that the characters faced at the original time (and which may have disappeared in the present circumstances[44]). To be sure, audiences can criticize the characters for their intransigence, recklessness, or folly, as this is part of the experience of tragedy. Still, this must be done without the arrogance of hindsight, from which retrospection must be clearly distinguished. In cases of hindsight or judgment after the fact, the epistemic conditions of the past are ignored and replaced by contemporary standards. By contrast, retrospection allows us to revisit the past from a different standpoint, but it does not mean to replace it, as both the past and the present moments remain in their interaction.

We have an excellent example of retrospection in the narrative of the guard, when he reports the deaths of Antigone and Haemon in the presence of Eurydice, and the audience's auditive perception, its visual imagination, and its recollection of previous scenes coalesce to make sense of the story. The guard's narrative invites us to visualize what happened in that cave through imaginative reconstruction, but in contrast to the cinematic technique of the flashback, here the theatrical audience still *sees* Eurydice reacting to the news, which assures that such narrative is assessed in her presence. Thus events that occur out of sight are brought back and re-enacted, i.e. *staged* within the audience's field of perception. In this case, Eurydice tells the guard to spare her no sorrow, which colors the deaths of both Antigone and Haemon as moments of profound sadness and pain. Likewise, the worrisome silence of Eurydice at the end assures that the audience does not fall into the temptation to rationalize or "transcend" their deaths as something glorious to celebrate. Thus the current perception of the audience – focused on Eurydice's reaction to the story – filters the way that the past is being assessed.

A similar example occurs when the suicide of Eurydice is recounted in the presence of Creon, when it becomes clear that, throughout the earlier narrative, she had been listening with the affection of a mother – not a wife. At her suicide she could have excused his husband's behavior, for example blaming it on the power of Eros (as the Chorus suggested), or on Antigone (a "bad woman" in her husband's terms), or even on a fateful concatenation of unforeseeable circumstances (as tragic events usually are). By not doing any of the former and instead putting all the blame on Creon, the audience is invited to revisit the earlier scene between father and son with Eurydice's eyes, which reflect poorly on Creon. The adoption of this retrospective interpretive key gives credibility to one version of events according to which Haemon's death is the direct responsibility of Creon.

7.4.5 *Closing*

As the drama begins to close, it settles on one course of action among the potentially infinite, effectively leading the audience in one direction rather than in another. The temporality I call *closing* is characterized by certain stillness in the audience's regard, permitting us to look at the action and the characters from a very close range, as it were putting them under a microscopic lens. For example, when Antigone invites her audience to witness her final march to her tomb, the play comes to a halt so that we may take a better look at her and her predicament. This brings us nearer to the inner depths of the character, which does not entail total identification, since the audience maintains the ability to critically examine her words and actions.

In the case of Antigone, I have already argued that she hopes the audience will embody the role of the "wise citizens" to whom she appeals in her final argument. Implicit in this call is an invitation to judge whether her claim is in fact legitimate, which may not receive a univocal answer from every audience. Thus many commentators have found Antigone's argument excessively cold and rationalistic, improper for this moment of the drama. Others have argued that she illegitimately prioritizes her brother over a husband and family, abandoning her defense of the unwritten law. Differently, I have argued that she is trying to convey the exceptional circumstances of this case – not comparable even to the closest analogy imaginable – with the very practical purpose of justifying her disobedience to the citizens. Whatever the judgment she ultimately deserves, Antigone hopes that, in the very same act of looking at her, the audience will take a good look also at Creon.

During the whole final scene Creon remains at center stage, with the body of his innocent child at his feet. He is lamenting his poor and ill-begotten judgment and the Chorus does not contradict him. All eyes are laid on him when Eurydice's death is reported by the guard. For a moment this seems to deflect the attention, but soon it is brought back, as Eurydice points her finger at her husband as killer of Haemon. Creon does not deny the accusation, nor does he try to offer an alternative explanation that could shift the burden away from him, while inviting us to ponder on different, or at least shared, responsibilities. The unblinking eyes of the audience are all fixed upon him and all the elements on stage – the accusatory body of Haemon, the recriminations of the Chorus, the pointing finger and suicide of Eurydice, and

Creon's own admission of guilt – converge towards a most lucid and clear vision of his responsibility.

7.4.6 *Reconstitution*

Once the curtain falls, the audience is in a position to hold a synchronic vision of the totality of the play as a differentiated unit. The temporality of *reconstitution* takes as its departure the endpoint of the play, and jumps back to its beginning in order to judge the totality or specific parts of it. While being triggered at the completion, the judgment of reconstitution encompasses the whole trajectory of the object under consideration. For example, in this mode I have argued that Antigone is a true poet of law, for she creates a legal language that was not available in her culture before and hands it down to us as her perennial legacy – which has led me through several stages of analysis. Likewise, it can be argued that Creon represents the idea of law's limits, the boundaries that cannot be transgressed, even though they are and remain invisible until someone clashes against them. Thus, the *Antigone* would dramatize the breaking point of law, which is at the same time the birth of something new and unexpected. Note that in these or similar reconstructions, we are no longer bound by the arrangement and order of presentation of the play, but rearrange the events that are relevant for that particular judgment according to a narrative of our own. We might say that, in doing so, we turn into writers ourselves.

At the point of reconstitution, we are no longer *inside* or within the play, but the play becomes rather an object in a larger conversation in which we can engage with our audience. Through reconstitution, we attempt to give an account of the overall meaning of the play in connection with the particular interests of each audience, for example by examining how the play speaks about the issues of legal conflict, gender and family relations, or democratic citizenship, to name a few. In this way, we tend to forget or drop details that we do not consider relevant. Such interpretations may or may not have been shared by the original audience, or intended by the author, but they must be somehow inscribed in the text from its inception, in the sense that we can still say that our account is a fair interpretation of the play. Reconstitution therefore aims at actualizing the several meanings of the play on the basis of the present circumstances of the interpreter.[45]

In doing so, the interpreter, now turned writer, illuminates the play with a particular shade of light – bringing some aspects to the fore while pushing others to the back. This is why reconstitution can also be seen as an exercise in oblivion: the critic begins to leave behind the smallest details and minutiae of the play, to tone down those which are thought less important, and to bring the rest under his or her own vision. Not every interpretation is equally compelling, to be sure, and different interpreters can contest and criticize them, as can my own be, on the grounds that the interpreter has forgotten, missed, or misconstrued other important aspects of the play. This will force each individual to justify his or her particular ways of looking.

In my reading, I have emphasized the incommensurable conflict between Antigone and Creon, and the kinds of judgment that the audience is invited to make about it. Whereas incommensurability can be defined as a moment of impasse for judgment, the play invites many shifts and transformations and, actually, reverses the starting points and positions of the two main characters. Antigone begins from a very fragile position, representing a radical challenge and departure from all rules of convention and propriety, but progressively her position is strengthened and finally she acknowledges the societal implications of her legal claim (what I describe as the progressive humanization of her character). Conversely, Creon begins strongly anchored in his social and political reality, but concludes completely isolated, having lost all the support of family and surroundings. In the end, Antigone's legal instinct turns out to be correct, while Creon is forced to abdicate his decision, bury Polyneices, and liberate Antigone (though he arrives too late). This does not mean that the conflict has been resolved once and for all. If another such conflict were to present itself again, we would have to start all over once more from the beginning with a new immersion – hopefully with the training and added skills of the experience.

In the end, if there is something to be learned from the play it is not in the form of a maxim such as "respect the unwritten law," "everyone has the right to be buried," or any such general statement. The educative strength of the play lies in the experience through which any such clarification can be "staged" by the audience. This requires every member of it to go through many shifts and motions (including an abyssal moment of incommensurability) before making up his or her mind. One cannot go directly to the end and obtain the same "result," or worse still, one cannot mistake this result for the whole experience. The same is true, I want to claim, of legal judgment.

*****

Every legal conflict, in fact, every situation that admits adjudication from a third party, requires one to engage in temporal motions quite similar to those described in this section. First, judging a case requires *immersion* in a conflict that exists prior to the intervention of the judge. Thus the judge must begin by assimilating and becoming familiar with all the particularities of the case before him, gathering as much information as possible about all the relevant details, treating the case as unique and singularly demanding his full and undivided attention. Immersion is thus a motion of *opening towards* the case. If we bring back the case of the Jehovah's Witness faced with a mandatory blood transfusion that could save his or her life,[46] the judge has to encounter a human being whose interpretation of certain biblical narratives (i.e. *Acts* 15: 28–9 and *Genesis* 9: 1–4) prevent them from committing the sin of "eating blood." Whatever the judge's personal opinions, he or she must understand that for the party it is sinful to nourish oneself with the soul of another living being, and that this remains so regardless of whether the "nourishment" comes by way of one's mouth or by transfusion into the person's veins.[47] At the same time, the judge hears also from the doctors who, consistent with a widely held opinion among the medical profession, defend the blood transfusion as a non-invasive treatment that can save the patient immediately without leaving any permanent damage. The judge must tune into the complexities of the case without making interpretive decisions that would foreclose any real consideration of the issues – for example, by treating the Jehova's Witness's belief as "irrational" – which entails presupposing the simultaneous validity of contradictory norms and worldviews.[48] The judge must be pressed to take a decision without delay, but *contention* requires the judge to rein in such an impulse and appraise it critically. Thus the judge's instinctive reaction may be to act immediately for the protection of the life of the person, but the judge cannot confuse the emergency of the situation (and of the decision he must now take) with the decision of the Jehovah's Witness whose belief may have been long meditated in conscience. (This is arguably the mistake that Judge Wright may have committed in the case of *Georgetown*, when the situation in extremis is attributed to the patient, incapacitating her from reaching a "rational" decision.)[49] The temporality of contention thus holds the judge back in a motion *away from* the current flow of the case. Thus through contention, the judge may realize that his own valuation of life need not be commensurate with (and need not be imposed on) that of the Jehovah's Witness, for whom the life that matters is the everlasting one awaiting after death, and prolonging the earthly life is relatively of less consequence.

In the course of the proceedings, different witnesses, testimonies, and points of view can enable the judge to "see beyond" the immediate. These testimonies may allow the judge to put the issue in a broader perspective and to venture *prospective* judgments about its implications, not just for the parties, but for other people concerned. For example, the judge may inquire about the concrete family situation of the person and ask questions such as "Would the children be adequately taken care of if she were permitted to die?" "Do the state's positive obligations towards its citizens compel acting as *parens patriae* to prevent the risk of abandonment?"[50] At the same time, the judge must consider the consequences of the decision on the applicant. For instance, in case the blood transfusion is finally ordered would this be something that the patient could learn to live with and forgive herself (as Ismene hopes), or would it rather be something unforgivable (as Antigone thinks)? On the other hand, the judge would also be asking hard questions of the doctors as well: how necessary really is the transfusion? Can the end of saving life be accomplished by other means? Is in fact blood transfusion as risk-free and non-invasive as the hospital claims? Is the opinion of the medical professional really unanimous?

Fourthly, the judge must look back in *retrospection* at the original decision, in light of the new information that may have surfaced in the course of the proceedings. Having heard the applicant, is there any reason to suspect that the person was coerced into her original decision? Was her demeanor calm and composed? Was her position articulate and credible? Is the Church unduly influencing her in the hope of adding a martyr for the cause? On the other hand, the judge must also ask tough questions of the hospital. What is the hospital's record concerning similar cases? How is this case similar to or different from other cases in which patients are entitled to refuse treatment, even when their life is at risk?

The temporality of *closing* gives the judge the opportunity to focus intently and with higher resolution on the individual applicant. The judge must consider her as a source and depository of distinct values and ends, and treat her not as he would like himself to be treated, but as she herself wants to be treated.[51] This might compel the judge to accept – even if he himself would consider those reasons insufficient – that the state interest in protecting its citizens must yield to the person who decides to sacrifice her life, just as Ismene lets Antigone go in peace once her decision is final. Respecting other people does not mean, however, that they are shielded from all criticism, just as Antigone is not immune from being criticized by Ismene (or the audience). Suppose, for example, that the case is about the child whose life is endangered by the parental refusal to allow the blood transfusion. Here the judge might say that the social interest in protecting the life of those who cannot make decisions on their own outweighs the respect of the religious convictions of the parents – provided he is able to find within his *nomos* compelling arguments for constructing such a redemptive narrative.

Thus when writing the opinion, the judge must *reconstitute* for the audience his understanding of the case and how it needs to be resolved, answering all the questions that have been raised. Here the judge addresses an audience larger than the parties, including the community and the general public that will read and be affected by the decision. Whatever the decision, the judge must live with it. Suppose he grants the wishes of the patient and allows her to die, or else he refuses and orders the blood transfusion. In either case what language shall he use to address the parties, the members of the medical profession, the members of the religious denomination, his own conscience? Imagine, for example, that the judge is able to construct a powerful redemptive narrative against the parents with the argument that no child belongs as property to the parents and that they have no right to make that decision for the child. Regardless of how strongly he felt about his own *nomos*, the judge would still have to face the reproaches of the losing side, the parents, for having stated that they were treating their child as "property." After it is publicized, then, the opinion becomes part of a larger conversation, where it can be read and discussed by different people, commended for the way it has grappled with the hard and complicated issues, or criticized for failing to elaborate such language. In this way, every opinion provides an occasion for new and further immersions.

This is what happened after the original decision in *Georgetown*: the case generated a powerful reaction among Jehovah's Witnesses who launched campaigns of sensitization and education of the medical profession and litigation to make their cases more visible.[52] As a result, they produced a rich hermeneutic process in which their *nomos* was strengthened in opposition to the contrary commitments of the judiciary. Fundamentally, they didn't refuse to engage with the courts and didn't retreat into insularity. Instead, they decided to engage fully in what they saw as the common and interconnected activity of law-making. This demonstrates that the killing of the law is not always the end of the law.

7.5 The experience of judging tragic conflicts: hard cases, anew

At the heart of this book lies the idea that hard cases between conflicting normative universes – of which incommensurable conflicts are one particularly acute manifestation – cannot be resolved by recourse to traditional principles of adjudication (consistency, integrity, coherence). Legal positivists in the tradition of H. L. A. Hart may want to believe that these cases are few and peripheral, but the importance of such cases is not quantitative, for the manner in which a particular legal order responds to these cases illuminates the entirety of cases. It is true that the so-called easy or ordinary cases do not raise the kind of questions analyzed in this book. However, I do not find it prudent or indeed accurate to predicate the existence of two types of judgments, one for easy or ordinary cases and another for hard or difficult cases. The activity is basically the same in both ordinary and extraordinary cases, even though the latter require closer attention to what in ordinary situations simply goes unnoticed (but goes on just the same).

Judgment is never the result of deductive or syllogistic reasoning or of applying the general maxim to the particular case. Every case – no matter how ordinary – requires framing the issues and relevant questions, drawing analogies and distinctions between similar and dissimilar cases, imagining alternative scenarios and outcomes; locating the guiding principles and narratives, translating each into the language of the court, reflecting on the justice or injustice of the result, and bearing in mind the society and the larger culture (legal, sociological, historical) in which the decision shall take place and will affect. All these go beyond what usually is called legal reasoning, for in addition to "rationality" we are dealing with intuition, know-how, imagination, capacity to listen, intellectual honesty, and open-mindedness (or the opposite of all these things). Consequently, simply to say that in hard cases judges must use their discretion – as legal positivists in the tradition of H. L. A. Hart tend to say – does not even attempt to answer the most important question in a theory of legal adjudication (perhaps the only question in need of a real answer), namely how this discretion is to be used in a case of conflict. Certainly in the conflict between Antigone and Creon it does not help much to say that we must adjudicate it merely using our discretion.

Partly as an attempt to find a principled response to this concern, Ronald Dworkin defends a theory of adjudication where judges' discretion is not just severely restricted, but actually denied.[53] In his view of hard cases – which are due not to linguistic ambiguities but to substantive disagreements – adjudication requires judges to find the best law there is, and this demands the reconstruction of the best moral and political principles of the community. It is in such a context that he makes the famous suggestion of the "one right answer" and imagines a Herculean judge tasked with finding it. One way to understand the "one right answer" thesis is to see it as the internal attitude with which judges approach cases (namely, a general aim to find within the confines of the law the legal answer that excludes all others, in light of the most cogent moral and political principles of their community).

Though partially attractive, the blind spots in this picture become clear when transposing it to the task of judging the legal conflict of the *Antigone*. First, Antigone does not represent the best values of the community, for she bursts forth and emerges violently into the public space, transgressing all social conventions. That is, Antigone enacts a social fracture in her community, before her law can even begin to be considered as valid. Secondly, it is not for the audience to find the best law there is to the exclusion of all others: in fact the audience is invited to accept the simultaneous validity of contradictory norms and worldviews, including their respective "correct legal answers," without diluting or resolving their contradictions in an all-embracing principle. Finally, Dworkin's Hercules, like all true heroes, performs a solitary task (despite being surrounded by all the precedents and all the moral and political principles).[54] By contrast, the audience in the *Antigone* cannot proceed in monologic fashion, but must adopt a dialogic and reflexive form of engagement, allowing itself to be illuminated by one party and then by the next, while self-critically examining all these involvements.

Still, the central objection to both Hartian and Dworkinian approaches results from the full recognition of normative pluralism. As Robert Cover has helped us to elucidate, modern pluralistic societies harbor not one single and unifying legal order, but many, each with its own foundational myths and narratives that establish the self-referential priority of their own normative order. In this view hard cases are clashes between holistic normative worlds, that is between the normative filters through which we make sense of the world. Judging in this context cannot be represented as the task of restoring the lost unity or integrity of a legal system believed to be compromised. Rather, the task turns out to be one of deciding which of the worlds in question is to be accepted and which rejected – which excludes an impossible harmonization of all the points of view. This is especially pronounced in conflicts between "redemptive" legal narratives, where the judge must either accept or deny the power of the state to implement such a redemptionist vision, but *cannot fail to do either*. Accordingly, to accept Antigone's right to bury her brother entails necessarily to reject the right of Creon to prohibit his burial and, vice versa, to accept Creon's jurisdiction over the body of a traitor entails that Antigone's right is rejected.

According to Cover, the only possible way to justify this *jurispathic* function is for judges to articulate an independent hermeneutic that would not yield to state power, nor rely on the institutional prerogatives of jurisdiction as a matter of course. (In our case, for example, this begins by refusing to accept Creon's initial claim to exclude Antigone altogether, as his niece and female subject, from the sphere of legitimate legal speech). Within the symbolic triangulation of justice judges may be able to articulate their own independent narratives, including redemptive ones that "crush" one of the laws in conflict as being incompatible with the most fundamental values of society. (This would grant the audience, for example, the right to quash Creon's decree on account of having transgressed the immanent laws of the cosmos). Still, Cover introduces the caveat that these redemptive narratives can only be accepted if there are many groups able and willing to contest them – which presupposes a robust and decidedly egalitarian (understanding of) legal pluralism and democratic politics.

Cover's fruitful insights, expanded with the help of other authors in Chapter 3, have granted us access into the incommensurable conflict of the *Antigone*. First, the analysis brings to the fore the power struggles and structures in which the judge too participates. For example, we are able to realize the inequality of powers between Antigone and Creon, that is the fact that Antigone and Creon are not equal before the law, nor granted equal rights of citizenship. In order for Antigone to challenge Creon, she is first to challenge the power structures upon which Creon's authority lies – based on his age, gender, and status within the polis and the family. Therefore, before the battle between the two main contenders can even be fought, let alone adjudicated, it is necessary to construct the battlefield in which it is to take place, which requires that some sort of leveling or equalizing force be applied by the audience. The audience, like the judge in a legal conflict, is not a detached and impartial observer, but participates in the proper symbolic construction of the conflict.

A second crucial point concerns the inescapability of judgment and its connection with justice. The need to choose, to make decisions, is a permanent condition of the human predicament, not as part of human rationality as Berlin suggested, but, I argued, as part of the pragmatics of action. Not all doors can be kept permanently open, in endless suspension. In one way or another, either by us or for us, *something* will be decided, since both action and omission are in a true sense judgments. Hard cases may yield a situation where judging justly appears impossible, but a refusal to judge is no guarantee that the injustice will be diminished, since every omission has its own unwanted beneficiaries (likely in favor of the status quo). The demands of the parties cannot be ignored, which confront us directly with the personal and ineludible responsibility of judgment. This obligation cannot be discharged, nor shifted away to following commands, abstract rules, or principles. The need to judge, and to judge well, is a demand of justice – or to put it the other way around, without judgment there can be no justice (only power).

This brings us finally to the manner in which judgments are to be performed in a hard case scenario, which is where I find Cover's arguments not entirely satisfactory and in need of further elaboration. First of all, the fact that judges may inflict the "killing of law" does not explain how this activity is meant to happen or to be understood. Just like the origin of law cannot be found in a single and undivided moment in time and space (in the case of Antigone, it has been necessary to follow a long trajectory), the killing of the law is also the result of an elongated engagement and cannot be decreed in an instant. Such a judgment does not happen in a flash, like the falling of an ax. Rather, it occurs in several stages and in more than one trajectory – which paradoxically makes it more easily justifiable, as it relies on thicker and interrelated webs of support and experience. As Charles Sanders Peirce explains it, the image is not one of a logical chain of arguments in which the reasoning is no stronger than its weakest link, but of "a cable whose fibers may be ever so slender, provided they are sufficiently numerous and intimately connected."[55]

Taking Creon's decree as an example, the decision to quash his decree is not an act of judicial fiat, isolated in space and time, but the result of a series of developments and engagements between the audience and the stage, where the audience learns not only from Creon, but also from Ismene, Haemon, Teiresias, the Chorus, the guard and finally from Eurydice that Creon's decree has severely endangered the *polis*. All these lead the audience to a final certainty, impossible to have at the beginning, that Creon's decree is flawed beyond repair. (This is actually compatible with taking Creon's law as valid and his view as politically dominant for much of the play.) More importantly, the killing of Creon's decree does not prevent that, if a similar conflict were ever to arise again between the family and the *polis*, Creon's normative universe could resurface, perhaps in different form, in response to the new context. Finally, it is also important that the decision of killing his law has been inflicted not in the language of Antigone, but in the language that Creon too may understand, that of the city and its well-being. When he is finally able to enunciate the principle that it may be better to observe the "established laws" [*kathestôtas nomous*] (1113), he is not simply being crushed under Antigone's legal position, but reconfiguring his own position in accordance with what Teiresias and subsequently the elders advised. This process of translation is crucial and assures that the decision to crush his decree is not wholly external to his *nomos*.

Secondly, in Cover's analysis, the redemptive narratives of judges are insufficiently protected from their own abuses of power, personal bias, and ideology. As Jeremy Webber argues, such bias need not be based on any feeling of animosity or hatred towards other people; it need not be based on mistaken stereotypical assumptions that can be more or less easily corrected with adequate information. The real concern is one which "results from the judges' *inability to transcend* the attitudes shaped by their gender, class, or culture."[56] What is lacking in Cover, then, is the judges' ability to self-critically appraise their own normative positions and commitments so that the decision itself may have a claim to justice (and not just the symbolical structure in which it is inserted.)

This is what I have tried to show in my own reading of the play, which provides such an experience. The audience is placed in the role of the judge tasked with adjudicating the tragic conflict, not according to idiosyncratic values or notions of justice, but to multiple shifts and engagements with the characters and their worldviews. In doing so, the audience is invited to engage with many different points of view, and to critically examine all of them at various stages of the play. This enables audiences to gain critical self-awareness into their own movements and positioning. Therefore judging tragedy well requires not just the ability to put oneself in someone else's shoes, but also to *see oneself reacting* to these different claims and perspectives, and to explain all these interactions within the constraints of the narrative before us (for example, checking upon judgments of purely speculative nature, or defending the pertinence of some form of temporal contention). Such an experience or phenomenology of judgment inevitably raises the audience from their original standpoint, forcing them to move and to shift positions beyond apparent sympathies and antipathies, assessing how these other voices and perspectives enrich, challenge, undermine, or confirm their initial assessments in a continuous process.

This carries with it a complete reconceptualization of judgment, not as it is often thought to occur in a single point in space and time, the moment of decision, but as temporary assemblages of engagements between subjects and objects in an elongated activity. Not that I judge *this* or *that* (e.g. this is beautiful, that is good, or that other thing is useful), but rather *I relate to this or that in such and such manner*, where all the elements of the relationship are being defined in the motions of judgment. As I have illustrated in several places, the respective positions of the subject and object of judgment are not static, but dynamic, sometimes even reversible, since the stage also has the capacity to interrogate and to "look at" the audience, as the drawing on the cover of this book is intended to suggest, so that the stage stares back at our activity of judgment.

The weaving of a number of spatial and temporal relationships and motions between the judge, the parties, and the object of controversy enable different judgments and narratives. The resulting judgments owe their claim to justice, not to one preconceived notion of what the law or justice require (valid for all times and places), but to the judges' responsibilities towards both parties, their commitment to the excellence of the activity, and their own desire to be just. Here conventional standards such as consistency, coherence, and rational acceptability are not as decisive as submitting to the rigors of the activity and explaining the critical engagements at each step of the way. Even though there will be multiple ways to perform this activity and to perform it well (just like there may be many ways to paint and appreciate good painting), it is also possible to learn to identify when it is done poorly or carelessly. This is why it is important to sharpen our senses and educate our judgments, as we develop the language to express our disagreements.

Some will object that this entails the conflation of aesthetic and hermeneutic categories on the one hand, and legal and political judgments on the other. Indeed, it may be argued that the aim of aesthetic and hermeneutic activity is to increase the appreciation or understanding, whereas the aim of legal adjudication is to do justice. For some, including Robert Cover in *Violence and the Word*, the latter presupposes the political power to implement those decisions in practice, which make law unlike literature. Law and literature are undoubtedly different. But every judgment, in law and tragedy alike, is aesthetic and political at once.[57] Without understanding there can be no justice, and without justice there can be no understanding. And, of course, there can be no politics worthy of the name without understanding and justice.

Appendix

The nature of mythological materials (going back to an untraceable and legendary past) and their mode of cultural transmission (mainly oral) results in their permanent growth and alteration. Each time the rhapsode or the poet shares the story with a different audience, the narrative elements are transformed in the interaction with, and the complicity of, the listeners. Fresh exploits, motives, and characters are added to the old, and novelties are superimposed, which in turn become the engine of ulterior innovation. Even though certain specifics tend to be maintained almost invariably, the fact is that "myths do not have fixed essences,"[1] which means that there is no single "referent" of the stories of Danaë, Lycurgus and Cleopatra against which to read the chorus' stories in the fourth *stasimon*.

With the advent of literacy and written records these tales were eventually imprinted and adopted a quite definite shape.[2] This is the form in which they have arrived with us, mainly through authors such as Apollodorus, Diodorus Syculus, Apollonius of Rhodes, or Pausanias (not to forget relevant information we gather from vase paintings and pictorial representations). Thanks also to the reconstructive efforts of mythographers and historians, we may be closer to drawing the external boundaries defining one myth and distinguishing it from another, and the narrative pieces which are likely to be incorporated into a given myth and its variants. However, such partial achievements must be put in perspective. On the one hand, the principle of consistency could help us exclude pieces of information that are contradictory to the dramatic action, but it does not offer guidance when two pieces are not contradictory yet do not seem to fit together into a coherent storyline, or are otherwise immaterial to the plot. Should we cut "irrelevant pieces" or should we instead make a further attempt to make them coexist? On the other hand, what should we do with incidents of the story that we would expect to hear but don't. In short, how ought we interpret cases of silence? Are we entitled to take unmentioned knowledge for granted, or should we otherwise consider their omission as an intentional (and meaningful) separation from tradition?

These doubts would be less of a problem if we had complete, consistent, and reliable indirect sources. Unfortunately, the sources are anything but complete and often contradict each other. As Dyodorus Syculus acknowledged many centuries ago (precisely after telling the story of Cleopatra's sons and recognizing that his account was not in agreement with what many others had told before him): "[A]s a general thing, we find that the ancient myths do not give us a simple and consistent story; consequently it should occasion no surprise if we find, when we put the ancient accounts together, that in some details they are not in agreement with those given by every poet and historian."[3] Furthermore, the way these stories were collected does not allow us to know the contributions each poet, rhapsode, or mythographer imprinted on each story. Different accounts are glued together in a temporal continuum, forming a big collage or palimpsest without discernible heads or tails. In practical terms, this translates into considerable difficulty distinguishing when a particular story begins or ends, and therefore if it is already *another* story. This fuzzy state of affairs often turns decisions about inclusion, exclusion, relevance, and omission into pure conjecture.

Consider, for instance, Winnington-Ingram's words about the myth alluded to in the third and fourth stanzas:

> It is not that we lack information about Cleopatra and the sons of Phineus: from play fragments, from scholia, from historians and mythographers we have almost too much. We know that Cleopatra was the daughter of Boreas and Oreithyia and that she married the Thracian king Phineus by whom she had two sons *variously named*. After her death, *or while she was still alive*, Phineus married Idaea *or Eidothea*, and, *for one reason or another*, was blinded, and persecuted by the Harpies. The sons of Cleopatra died *or had their sight restored*, by Boreas *or by Asclepius*. *In one version* at any rate Cleopatra lived to triumph over her enemies. *At some stage she or her sons* or *both may have* suffered imprisonment.[4]

And this is when we do have information!

Sometimes it can be fairly assumed that the tragedian alludes to a known variant of the myth, as staged in the City Dionysia either by himself or by one of his predecessors. Unfortunately, only the titles and very scarce fragments of most of these tragedies remain.[5] Attempts have been made to reconstruct these tragedies out of the scattered remaining fragments.[6] However laudable the effort, their outcome cannot but be disappointing, which has nothing to do in principle with the competence of scholars, but with the quixotic nature of the endeavor. Imagine, for instance, that the only remaining information about Ajax was that he was blinded by Athena when he was trying to slaughter the enemies who had deprived him of the armor of Achilles, and that soon after he recovered his senses he committed suicide.[7] Could we ever reconstruct Sophocles' *Ajax* with that? Perhaps the main storyline (mindless of relevant omissions) could be partially sketched. But what could we say about his speech before killing himself? What about his unburied body? What about Teucer and Agamemnon? What about the surprising intervention of his archrival, Odysseus? What, in fact, about the meaning of Sophocles' *Ajax*?

This example illustrates that reconstructing a tragedy – understood now as the poetic treatment of a mythical legend – is much more complex than the mere juxtaposition of facts in an orderly fashion. It is not uncommon that two tragedians depict stories apparently identical but in a diametrically opposite light; or that the same course of action is justified and commendable in one account and utterly vicious and repulsive in another; or that within one same basic storyline, differently stressed incidents, if not different characters, bear the weight of the plot and set the tragedy in motion. Thus, in the context of the dramatic performance, narrative elements become meaningful only in connection to each other and the rest of the surrounding elements. This cannot be provided either, as Christiane Sourvinou-Inwood suggests, by reconstructing the "intertextual frame" of the original audience, that is the assumptions through which a fifth-century audience would have filtered the play.[8] The poet selects, and by doing so modifies, the meaning of the memories he wants to revive in the audience. Therefore not all of the assumptions that the fifth-century audience brought to the theater are relevant for, nor does their meaning remain inalterable by, the specific performance.

The range of issues raised above should be taken rather as a warning against overconfidence than as the radical impossibility of making reasoned inferences and conjectures, provided they are made rigorously.[9] There is perhaps an incurable human urge to make up for the gaps of information, so as to provide for plausible explanations of things uncertain. But this urge should be resisted whenever it runs the risk of becoming the art of tallying unfitting pieces into whatever ready notions of the tragedy, the characters, their principles, and actions. For the good sake of the adventure, the text functions both as the point of departure (for we must necessarily start from somewhere) and as arrival (for we must eventually come back to it).

Notes

Introduction: *Antigone* and the experience of legal judgment

1. H. Arendt, "Introduction into Politics", in *The Promise of Politics*, ed. J. Kohn. New York: Schocken Books, 2005, p. 104.
2. See, however, Milner Ball's seminal study about the parallelisms between legal trials and theatre: M. Ball, "The Play's the Thing: An Unscientific Reflection on Courts Under the Rubric of Theater", *Stanford Law Review*, 1975, 28: 81–115.
3. For example, S. Goldhill, "The Great Dionysia and Civic Ideology", *Journal of Hellenic Studies*, 1987, 107: 58–76, and "Civic Ideology and the Problem of Difference: The Politics of Aeschylean Tragedy, Once Again", *JHS*, 2000, 120: 34–56; S. S. Monoson, "Citizen as Theatēs (Theater-Goer): Performing Unity, Reciprocity and Strong-Mindedness at the City Dionysia," in *Plato's Democratic Entanglements: Athenian Politics and the Practice of Philosophy*. Princeton: Princeton University Press, 2000, pp. 88–110; P. Easterling (ed.), *The Greek Companion to Greek Tragedy*. Cambridge: Cambridge University Press, 1997; J. Peter Euben, *The Tragedy of Political Theory*. Princeton, NJ: Princeton University Press, 1990, and *Corrupting the Youth*. Princeton, NJ: Princeton University Press, 1997; J. Winkler and F. Zeitlin (eds), *Nothing to Do with Dionysos? Athenian Drama in its Social Context*. Princeton, NJ: Princeton University Press, 1990. Even Nicole Loraux, who is highly critical of giving a restrictively ideological and didactic reading to tragedy, accepts the connection between tragedy and *polis*: N. Loraux, *The Mourning Voice: An Essay on Greek Tragedy*, trans. E. Trapnell Rawlings. Ithaca, NY and London: Cornell University Press, 2002, p. 46. Insofar as my view of democratic citizenship does not require but in fact defies consensus or ideological indoctrination, my use of the word "education" is compatible with what Loraux calls "anti-political," that is behavior that challenges the conventional self-understandings of the city-state in order to reclaim or redefine its boundaries (ibid., 26–41).
4. For example, R. Weisberg, *Poethics, and Other Strategies of Law and Literature*. New York: Columbia University Press, 1992; M. Nussbaum, *Poetic Justice: The Literary Imagination and Public Life*. Boston: Beacon Press, 1995; I. Ward, *Law and Literature: Possibilities and Perspectives*. Cambridge: Cambridge University Press, 1995; J. B. White "Review: What Can a Lawyer Learn from Literature?" *Harvard Law Review*, 1989, 102: 2104–47, and *From Expectation to Experience: Essays on Law and Legal Education*. Ann Arbor, MI: University of Michigan Press, 1999.
5. See C. Wells, "Situated Decisionmaking," *Southern California Law Review*, 1990, 63: 1727–46 and "Improving One's Situation: Some Pragmatic Reflections on the Art of Judging," *Washington and Lee Law Review*, 1992, 49(2): 323–38.
6. For more about this conception of time, see Chapter 7.
7. See F. Schauer, "Judging in a Corner of the Law," *Southern California Law Review*, 1988, 61: 1717–34 (arguing that these cases are few and peripheral).

8. For a general overview, see C. D. Kelso and R. Randall Kelso, "Judicial Decision-Making and Judicial Review: The State of the Debate, Circa 2009," *West Virginia Law Review*, 2010, 112: 351–401. For a psychological model of judging, see C. Guthrie, J. J. Rachlinski, and A. J. Wistrich, "Blinking on the Bench: How Judges Decide Cases," *Cornell Law Review*, 2007, 93(1): 1–43. Despite the empirical orientation, their study does not concern the capacity of judging as it is understood and developed here.
9. I think, for example, of writers in the existential tradition of Kierkegaard, Camus, and Sartre.
10. J. Tully, *Strange Multiplicity: Constitutionalism in the Age of Diversity*. Cambridge: Cambridge University Press, 1995. Interestingly, Tully refers to *Antigone* often in the course of this book.
11. See A. Aarnio, *The Rational as Reasonable: A Treatise on Legal Justification*. Dordrecht: Reidel, 1987; M. Atienza, *Las Razones del Derecho: Teoría de la Argumentación Jurídica*. Madrid: Centro de Estudios Constitucionales, 1991. For coherence and consistency, see N. MacCormick, *Legal Reasoning and Legal Theory*. Oxford: Clarendon Press, 1978, and A. Peczenik, "Coherence, Truth and Rightness in the Law," in P. Nerhot (ed.), *Law, Interpretation and Reality*. Dordrecht: Kluwer, 1990.
12. J. Rancière, *Disagreement: Politics and Philosophy*, trans. Julie Rose. Minneapolis, MN and London: University of Minnesota Press, 1999, p. 32.
13. In this I was influenced by Robert Cover's language in *Nomos and Narrative* (see Chapter 1).
14. For a recent critique of this model of reasoning, see S. R. Krause, *Civil Passions: Moral Sentiment and Democratic Deliberation*. Princeton, NJ and Oxford: Princeton University Press, 2008.
15. J. P. Vernant and P. Vidal-Naquet, *Myth and Tragedy in Ancient Greece*, trans. J. Lloyd. New York: Zone Books, 1988, p. 25.
16. Ibid., at 30.
17. Ibid., at 31 and 32.
18. Ibid., at 26.
19. The counter-example of Phrynichus' *Fall of Miletus* is a case in point. According to Herodotus (6.21), the play chronicled the story of Miletus after it was conquered by the Persians, but the event was still too fresh in the Athenians' memory and the audience wept inconsolably. The author was fined and forbidden to stage the play ever again, for it represented calamities that affected them too personally. For an analysis of the theoretical implications, see P. Kottman, *A Politics of the Scene*. Stanford, CA: Stanford University Press, 2008, esp. 116–34.
20. Cf. C. Sourvinou-Inwood, "Assumptions and the Creation of Meaning: Reading Sophocles' Antigone", *Journal of Hellenic Studies*, 1989, 109: 134–48. For a critique of over-reliance on "historical filters," including Sourvinou-Inwood's, see Helene Foley, "Tragedy and Democratic Ideology: The Case of Sophocles' *Antigone*," in B. Goff (ed.), *History, Tragedy, Theory: Dialogues on Athenian Drama*. Austin, TX: University of Texas Press, 1995, pp. 131–50.
21. See P. Holt, "Polis and Tragedy in the Antigone," *Mnemosyne*, 1999, 52: 658–90.
22. About the implied reader see W. Iser, *The Implied Reader: Patterns of Communications in Prose Fiction from Bunyan to Beckett*. Baltimore, MD: John Hopkins University Press, 1974. My own views are closer to James Boyd White's notion of the "ideal reader," constituted by the invited possibilities of perception and response, for feeling and judgment, that every text seeks to realize in its readers. See J. B. White, "Reading Law and Reading Literature," in *Heracles' Bow: Essays on the Rhetoric and Poetics of the Law*. Madison, WI: University of Wisconsin Press, 1985.
23. For example, the European Court of Human Rights decided that the headscarf is not merely a religious and private symbol concerning the individual who decides to wear it. In addition, it has a social and political dimension that concerns other members of society who choose not, but could be pressed, to wear it by those who do (*Leyla Şahin* v. *Turkey*, 10 November 2005, ECHR 2005-IX.).

24. This term is associated with Jerome Frank and employed often derisively against American Legal Realists of the early twentieth century, whose views were never as crude as their detractors made them sound.
25. H. Arendt, *Lectures on Kant's Political Philosophy*, ed. R. Beinerd. Chicago: University of Chicago Press, 1992.
26. Immanuel Kant, *Critique of Judgment*, 1790; see also J.-F. Lyotard, "Sensus Communis", in *Judging Lyotard*, ed. A. Benjamin. London: Routledge, 1992, pp. 14–38.
27. See M. C. Belleau and R. Johnson, "Interdisciplinary Questions about Law, Language and Dissent," in Logan Atkinson and Diana Majury (eds), *Law, Mystery and the Humanities: Collected Essays*. Toronto: University of Toronto Press, 2008, pp. 145–66. The authors borrow the term from A. Amsterdam and J. Brunner, *Minding the Law: How Courts Rely on Storytelling, and How Their Stories Change the Ways We Understand the Law—and Ourselves*. Cambridge, MA: Harvard University Press, 2000.
28. For a recent appraisal of agonism (both modern and ancient), see Andrew Schaap (ed.), *Law and Agonistic Politics*. Aldershot: Ashgate, 2009. Among the writers associated with agonism, political theorist Bonnie Honig has written several lengthy articles on the *Antigone*. See B. Honig, "Antigone's Laments, Creon's Grief: Mourning, Membership, and the Politics of Exception," *Political Theory*, 2009, 37(5): 5–43; "Antigone's Two Laws: Greek Tragedy and the Future of Humanism," *New Literary History*, 2010, 41(1): 1–33; "Ismene's Forced Choice: Sacrifice and Sorority in Sophocles' Antigone," *Arethusa*, 2011, 44(1): 29–68.
29. J. D. Caputo, *Against Ethics: Contributions to a Poetics of Obligation with Constant Reference to Deconstruction* (1993), cited in F. J. Mootz, "Law and Philosophy, Philosophy and Law," *University of Toledo Law Review*, 1994, 26: 142.
30. Luke 6: 37. Actually this maxim does not prohibit judgment, but only that which is rushed, censorious, and done with an exaggerated sense of righteousness or entitlement. The sanction for that kind of "defective" judgment is appropriately a judgment in kind, which suggests a strict rule of reciprocity: to judge is to be ready to be judged.
31. Thus, for example, P. Ricœur, "The Act of Judging", in *The Just*, trans. D. Pellauer. Chicago and London: University of Chicago Press, 2000, pp. 127–32, at p.128. For Ricœur's own analysis of *Antigone*, see P. Ricœur, *Soi-Même Comme une Autre*. Paris: Seuil, 1990, chapter 9.
32. This does not mean that a general rule can be devised to solve the conflict once and for all, for any eventual resolution is indissolubly tied to the concrete conditions of its performance.
33. For a development of the concept of "experience" in fictional texts, including novels and lyric poetry, see J. Phelan, *Experiencing Fiction: Judgments, Progressions, and the Rhetorical Theory of Narrative*. Columbus, OH: Ohio State University Press, 2007.
34. This is how Heidegger and Lacan, for instance, understood it; see C. Douzinas, "Law Deathbound: Antigone and the Dialectics of Nomos and Thanatos," in D. Manderson (ed.), *Courting Death: The Legal Constitution of Mortality*. London: Pluto Press, 1999, pp. 163–80. For a well-argued critique of Lacan, see Judith Butler, *Antigone's Claim*. New York: Columbia University Press, 2000.
35. For a speculative inquiry in Heideggerian fashion about Antigone's hold on the western social imaginary, see G. Steiner, *Antigones*. Oxford: Clarendon Press, 1984, esp. pp. 107–38. About the literature (and fictions) of law's origin, see J. de Ville, "On Law's Origin: Derrida Reading Freud, Kafka, and Levi-Strauss," *Utrecht Law Review*, 2011, 7(2): 77–92.
36. For a different departure based on Aeschylus' *Oresteia*, see B. Bosteels "Force of Non-Law: Alan Badiou's Theory of Justice," *Cardozo Law Review*, 2008, 29(5): 1905–26.

Chapter 1 A window on the normative world

1. Robert M. Cover, "The Supreme Court, 1982 Term – Foreword: Nomos and Narrative," *Harvard Law Review*, 1983, 97: 4–68, at pp. 4–5, footnotes omitted. (Hereinafter Cover, "Nomos and Narrative": all page references are to this article, unless otherwise noted.)

This and the rest of Cover's important law articles can be conveniently found in M. Minow, M. Ryan, and A. Sarat (eds), *Narrative, Violence, and the Law: The Essays of Robert Cover*. Ann Arbor, MA: University of Michigan Press, 1992.

2. For different conceptualizations of the dichotomy, see further Chapter 2.
3. Cover focuses mainly on the law of smallish communities which he then contrasts with the law of the state. I aim differently to provide a phenomenology of law, without distinctions between communities and the state, individuals and groups. Cover's notion of community is not grounded on blood, race, ethnic origin or any other "essentialist" attribute. Rather, it is closer to the idea of a social group bound together by the belief in forming such a group, which includes socially constructed accounts about their own constitution and sets of authoritative texts and values. On how the self-reflective constitution of their collective identity might occur, see Paul Ricœur, *Soi-Même Comme un Autre*. Paris: Seuil, 1990.
4. Cover, "Nomos and Narrative," p. 5.
5. Echoing the language of James Boyd White, Cover affirms that ". . . law is a resource in signification that enables us to submit, rejoice, struggle, pervert, mock, humiliate, or dignify" (at p. 8). See, in particular, White, *The Legal Imagination: Studies in the Nature of Legal Thought and Expression*. Boston: Little, Brown, 1973; Heracles' Bow: Essays on the Rhetoric and Poetics of Law. Madison, WI: University of Wisconsin Press, 1984; and *When Words Lose Their Meaning: Constitutions and Reconstitutions of Language, Character, and Community*. Chicago: University of Chicago Press, 1985).
6. Cover, "Nomos and Narrative," p. 20, citing Deuteronomy 21: 15–17.
7. Cover, "Nomos and Narrative," p. 23; cf. J. Derrida, "Force of Law: The 'Mystical Foundation of Authority,'" *Cardozo Law Review*, 1990, 11: 920–1045, p. 943.
8. Athenians saw themselves as unique among the Greeks because they were sprung from the soil of Attica. See W. Hansen, *Classical Mythology: A Guide to the Mythical World of the Greeks and the Romans*. New York: Oxford University Press, 2005, pp. 102–3.
9. Cf. J. de Ville, "On Law's Origin: Derrida Reading Freud, Kafka, and Levi-Strauss," *Utrecht Law Review*, 2011, 7(2): 77–92.
10. H. White, "The Value of Narrativity in the Representation of Reality," in W. Mitchell (ed.), *On Narrative*. Chicago and London: University of Chicago Press, 1980–1, pp. 1–23, at p. 14. According to White, narrative "is intimately related to, if not a function of, the impulse to moralize reality" and, in fact, "presupposes the existence of a legal [a socialpolitical] system" (ibid., p. 13). Thus the various literary genres – history, fiction, tragedy, comedy – can all be seen as the "imposition of a normative force upon a state of affairs" (ibid., p. 10). This recalls Mikhail Bakhtin's definition of genres not as sets of conventions or instrumental devices, but as fundamental ways of shaping the world or "form-shaping ideologies" (Mikhail Bakhtin, *The Dialogic Imagination: Four Essays*. Austin, TX: University of Texas Press, 1981). The relationship between Cover and Bakhtin has received interesting treatment in Richard Mullender, "Two Nomoi and a Clash of Narratives: The Story of the United Kingdom and the European Union," Berkeley Electronic Press, 2006, at http://www.bepress.com/ils/iss8 (accessed 3 March 2009).
11. For all, H. Kelsen, *Pure Theory of Law*, 2nd rev edn, trans. M. Knight. Berkeley, CA: University of California Press, 1968.
12. The Hartian account followed by many according to which norms are ultimately grounded on social practice (for example recently A. Marmor, "How Law Is Like Chess," *Legal Theory*, 2006, 12: 347–71) not only fails as such (see M. Greenberg, "How Facts Make Law," *Legal Theory*, 2004, 10: 157–98), but it is surprisingly unresponsive to this very dilemma.
13. Cover, "Nomos and Narrative," p. 9.
14. Ibid., p. 10.
15. Despite well-known objections, the Kelsenian metaphor is still a favorite in most legal minds. The Hartian *rule of recognition*, seemingly devised to take over the pyramid, does in fact reproduce the same structure.

16. For an excellent critique, see François Ost and Michel van de Kerchove, *De la pyramide au Réseau? Pour une Théorie Dialectique du Droit*. Brussels: Publications des Facultés Universitaires Saint Louis, 2002.
17. R. Cover, *Justice Accused: Antislavery and the Judicial Process*, New Haven, CT: Yale University Press, 1975, p. 6.
18. For this same possibility of conflicting fundamental norms in the European contexts, see N. W. Barber, "Legal Pluralism and the European Union," *European Law Journal*, 2006, 12: 306–29.
19. In *The Concept of Law* (1961) Hart described the rule of recognition as the secondary rule that permits the identification of the primary rules of the system as belonging to it, and ultimately depends on a social practice or a convention of the officials of that system to follow it. Despite arguments to the contrary, I am not persuaded that the postscript to the 1994 edition (Clarendon Press, 2n rev. edn) altered Hart's original position in a significant way; cf. M. Adler, "Constitutional Fidelity, the Rule of Recognition, and the Communitarian Turn in Contemporary Positivism," *Fordham Law Review*, 2006, 75: 1671–95 (referring to different developments in the works of Andrei Marmor, Scott Shapiro, and Jules Coleman, among others). Hans Kelsen saw the question of validity through the lens of its pyramidal model: a legal rule is valid if it has been habilitated by its immediately superior rule in the ladder, until the final *Grundnorm* which can only be presupposed.
20. Cover, "Nomos and Narrative," p. 31.
21. See Oren Perez, "Law as a Strange Loop," in Gralf-Peter Calliess et al. (eds), *Sociological Jurisprudence: Liber Amicorum Gunther Teubner*. Berlin: de Gruyter, 2009.
22. It is encouraging to hear that self-proclaimed positivists express their discontent with picking sides and advocate to put an end to the hostilities. See, recently, N. MacCormick, *Institutions of Law: An Essay in Legal Theory*. New York: Oxford University Press, 2007, p. 279. (MacCormick defines his position as a "post-positivist" one, though he sees himself as an heir to the works of Kelsen and Hart.)
23. Hart, *The Concept of Law*. Also see his *Law, Liberty, and Morality*. Stanford, CA: Stanford University Press, 1963. The most famous debate about this issue was held between Hart and Lon Fuller, in the pages of the *Harvard Law Review*, 1958, 71. Yet, there are other important actors. Among these, Gustav Radbruch declared that an intolerable law could not be called law. His views have been recently redefined by Robert Alexy ("A defence of Radbruch's Formula," in D. Dyzenhaus (ed.), *Recrafting the Rule of Law: The Limits of Legal Order*. Oxford and Portland, OR: Hart, 1999, pp. 15–39). For a recent appraisal of the position of both Radbruch and Alexy, see B. Bix, *Robert Alexy's Radbruch*, University of Minnesota Law School Legal Studies Research Papers Series No. 06-13, Draft, January 2006.
24. Cover, "Nomos and Narrative," p. 7, emphasis added.
25. Ibid. Certainly, it is not likely that those who enact the law will proclaim it as being unjust and profoundly immoral. This point is taken up by Alexy as a requirement of rationality or correctness ("On Necessary Relations Between Law and Morality," *Ratio Juris*, 1989, 2: 167–83; and again, replying to criticism, in "On the Thesis of a Necessary Connection between Law and Morality: Bulygin's Critique," *Ratio Juris*, 2000, 12: 138–47). But cf. Bix, *Robert Alexy's Radbruch*. Bix presents the hypothetical example of a country that would dismiss concerns of justice from the legal system altogether and substitute them for other kinds of arguments (e.g. efficiency). This case is not unthinkable, and in fact Thucydides reports that, progressively during the course of the Peloponnesian War, Athens abandoned considerations of justice and replaced them with those of expediency and self-interest. Nevertheless, Bix's example appears more the description of an outsider looking in on the system than what the insiders would say about it. (This is the case somewhat with Thucydides too, who was writing after being exiled from Athens.) In fact, Thucydides suggests that the attitude of Athens was not only a complete subversion of what was hitherto the case in the rest of the civilized world, but also that it led directly to and precipitated the political disaster and ultimate downfall of such order. About this inevitable outcome, see

J. B. White, "The Dissolution of Meaning: Thucydides' History of His World," in his *When Words Lose Their Meaning*. Chicago and London: Chicago University Press, 1985, pp. 59–92.

26. About the idea of *tacit knowledge* applied to the realm of science, see M. Polanyi, *Personal Knowledge: Toward a Post-Critical Philosophy*. Chicago: University of Chicago Press, 1974.
27. About this debate, although sometimes dressed in different clothes, see Hart (note 19), at pp. 255–9; R. Dworkin, *Taking Rights Seriously*. Cambridge, MA: Harvard University Press, 1977, pp. 48–58; J. Raz, *The Authority of Law: Essays on Law and Morality*. Oxford and New York: Clarendon and Oxford University Press, 1979, especially chapter 2; see, more recently, M. Greenberg, "How Facts Make Law," arguing that law practices alone cannot determine their own contribution to the content of law. In what follows I shall use the terms "provision" (or to use Cover's words "precept") to refer to the legal utterance deprived of or still lacking in normative force, and the term "norm" to the one that it has already. For the classic distinction between provisions – in Romance languages "dispositions" – and norms, see R. Guastini, *Dalle Fonti Alle Norme* (Torino, 1990) (explained in J. R. Bengoetxea, "Direct Applicability of Effect," in *A True European: Essays for Judge David Edward*. Oxford: Hart, 2003, pp. 353–66).
28. Cover, "Nomos and Narrative," p. 45: "The transformation of interpretation into legal meaning begins when someone accepts the demands of interpretation and, through the personal act of commitment, affirms the position taken" (reference omitted).
29. Hart's "internal point of view" appears to accommodate some of what is being said here, but at the end of the day he still points out that what truly matters is *convention* – practice – and not *conviction* – belief; see Hart's own admission of this point in the Postscript to the 1994 ed. of *The Concept of Law*.
30. *Dredd Scott* v. *Sandford*, 60 U.S. (19 How.) 393, 15 L. Ed. 691 (1857).
31. Cover, "Nomos and Narrative," p. 45: "[T]he community posits a law, external to itself, that it is committed to obeying and that it does obey in dedication to its understanding of that law." This "[f]requently, perhaps always, entails a narrative – a story of how the law, now object, came to be, and more importantly, how it came to be one's own" (ibid.).
32. Most notably, Johan Wolfgang von Goethe (in J. P. Eckerman, *Conversations with Goethe*, trans. J. Oxenford. London: Dent, 1935) and Sir Richard Jebb (ed.) (see Chapter 4).
33. Commentators critical of Antigone interpret her argument before Creon as establishing a demand that obligates her in all cases and circumstances. But this is an *interpretation* of Antigone's utterance and not (necessarily) the norm to which Antigone is committed or the way she herself interprets that demand.
34. Cover locates this never-ending cycle of legal meaning within an organic structure he calls "jurisgenesis" that occurs around two opposite motions, one expansive he calls "paideic" and the other contractive called "imperial." Arguably, the paideic and the imperial are interdependent and mutually effecting synergetic forces, jointly necessary for the healthy functioning of the normative body. See further my article "The Legal Universe After Robert Cover," *Law and Humanities*, 2010, 4(1): 115–47, at p. 129.
35. In the biological sense, the process of mitosis is the process of duplication and reduplication of cells and chromosomes. Cover uses this metaphor to refer to the generative processes of law out of the same "legal DNA."
36. Cover, "Nomos and Narrative," p. 29.
37. "The principle of separateness is constitutive and jurisgenerative" (ibid., p. 29). In other words, "[i]t is not only a principle limiting the [S]tate, but also one constitutive of a distinct *nomos* within the domain left open."
38. This self-referential supremacy is mitigated, however, "by the partly principled, partly prudential rules of deference that each manifests in relation to the other" (ibid., p. 30).
39. Ibid., pp. 31–2, footnotes omitted and emphasis added.
40. Ibid., p. 32, emphasis added. In spite of it, Cover states that it would be absurd not to concede the practical benefits of securing the acquiescence of the State officials (ibid., p. 43).

41. Ibid., p. 30, note 85. This is true of many normative conflicts around the world, for example the constitutional controversy between Basque autonomists and Spanish centralists. The best scholarly exposition of the Basque *nomos* is Miguel Herrero de Miñón, *Derechos Históricos y Constitución*. Madrid: Taurus, 1998.
42. Cover, "Nomos and Narrative," p. 35.
43. Another example Cover analyzes is civil disobedience during the civil rights movement.
44. Cover, "Nomos and Narrative," p. 38, footnote omitted.
45. Ibid., p. 39.
46. To be dismissed as "merely" utopian, Cover says, is the result not of presenting radically different standards of living, but rather of the failure to present them as "real" or "livable," that is, "because they fail to posit alternative lives to which we would commit ourselves by stretching from our reality toward their vision" (ibid., p. 44, footnote omitted).
47. Ibid., p. 39.
48. Certainly, not every group attempting to redeem society may be as commendable as the anti-slavery movement. Thus it may be advisable to grow a healthy skepticism and distrust for groups that want to model the face of the world on their own image (especially when they claim to have a direct – and often exclusive – line to divinity). Notably Cover recommends some attitude of *distrust* in the last paragraph of "Nomos and Narrative," p. 68, but he nonetheless observes that, regardless of what we may think of them, such redemptive groups will continue to exist and try to redeem the world, the law, and us with them.
49. As Cover argues, "just like living in the economic world entails an understanding of price, so living in the normative world entails an understanding of the measures of commitment to norms in the face of contrary commitments of others" (ibid., p. 53).
50. Cover, "Nomos and Narrative," p. 50, quoting J. Bentham's reaction to the *Declaration of Independence*.
51. Ibid. The *Declaration of Independence* may seem at first to confer the inalienable and unencumbered right to resist. Yet, this text concedes to prudence "that we must 'suffer, while evils are sufferable' [and acknowledge] that 'a decent respect to the opinions of mankind' imposes upon us an obligation carefully to recount the reasons that led to the decision to resist" (ibid., p. 49).
52. Ibid., p. 60.
53. Hart, *The Concept of Law*. Further, "because we are men, not gods" (128), Hart thought it inadvisable to try to make rules the application of which would leave no room for further interpretation (128 ff.). Contrary to appearance, his way of pursuing the argument makes it clear to me that he thought this task (almost) *feasible*, if not advisable.
54. R. Dworkin, *Law's Empire*. Cambridge, MA: Harvard University Press, 1986, pp. 350–4.
55. N. MacCormick, *Legal Reasoning and Legal Theory*. Oxford: Clarendon Press, 1978, p. 197 and ff. For different ways to categorize the distinction between easy and hard cases, see J. Bengoetxea, *The Legal Reasoning of the European Court of Justice*. Oxford: Clarendon Press, 1992, p. 183 ff.
56. For *substantive* reasons, see Dworkin, *Law's Empire*; for *pragmatic* reasons, see MacCormick, *Legal Reasoning and Legal Theory* and Bengoetxea, *The Legal Reasoning*. For an interesting *semiotic* interpretation of why cases become hard, see B. Jackson, "Rationalité Consciente et Inconsciente dans la Théorie du Droit et la Science Juridique," *Revue Interdisciplinaire d'Études Juridiques*, 1987, 19: 1–18. Some authors still defend the *semantic* line of argument (see, for example, A. Marmor, *Interpretation and Legal Theory*, 2nd rev. edn. Portland, OR: Hart, 2005; and F. Schauer, *Playing by the Rules: A Philosophical Examination of Rule-Based Decision-Making in Law and in Life*. New York: Clarendon Press and Oxford: Oxford University Press, 1991); and well-taken criticism of these views by F. Atria, *On Law and Legal Reasoning*. Oxford, and Portland, OR: Hart, 2001, pp. 101–22.
57. See Stephen Guest, *Ronald Dworkin*. Edinburgh: Edinburgh University Press, 1992, p. 162.
58. About the *when* and the *why* of hard cases, see Atria, *On Law and Legal Reasoning*, pp. 75–6.

59. This is also the view of J. Raz, who speaks of "regulated" and "unregulated" cases (Raz, *The Authority of Law*, chapter 3).
60. Dworkin, *Taking Rights Seriously*, esp. chapters 4 and 13.
61. Dworkin may criticize Hart's insistence on semantics and discretion, but he still thinks that there is a hard case when and because there is uncertainty or disagreement as to what the law is.
62. Some legal realists also realized that the main issue is the multiplicity of the applicable laws (K. Llewellyn, "Some Realism about Realism," *Harvard Law Review*, 1930–1, 44: 1222–64) or how to choose between different possible major premises (J. Dewey, "Logical Method and the Law," *Cornell Law Quarterly*, 1924, 10: 17–27). However, they never went as far as to speak of inter-systemic normative conflicts.
63. Examples can be multiplied: the issue of deciding which of the laws (mortal or divine) should prevail is at the heart of the conflict between Antigone and Creon in Sophocles' *Antigone* too. On the other hand, the reverse phenomenon of "polynomia" occurs, says Cover, out of the loss or weakness of courts. Cover mentions the Talmudic example of the Court of the Great Sanhedrin, in which, after the destruction of that court, the Law became two laws. Cover, "Nomos and Narrative," p. 41.
64. Cover, "Nomos and Narrative," p. 41, note 118, cites Alexander Hamilton in *The Federalist*, note 22.
65. Ibid., p. 42.
66. As Brian Bix argues, belonging to different *traditions* does not explain why they disagree (see B. Bix, *Law, Language, and Legal Determinacy*. Oxford: Clarendon Press, 1993, p. 55), nor does this necessarily make a disagreement hard. It is then important to stress that, in a hard case situation, groups in conflict are committed to live by and ready to fight for their particular normative determination.
67. Cover, "Nomos and Narrative," p. 44, rejects this dichotomy as false and too easy, in reference to Owen Fiss, "Ojectivity and Interpretation," *Stanford Law Review*, 1982, 34: 739–63.
68. In what concerns the role of the State as adjudicator of conflict, this is to question "the extent to which coercion is necessary to the maintenance of minimum conditions for the creation of meaning" (Cover, "Nomos and Narrative," p. 44).
69. The concern is similar to Nietzsche's attempts at creating value after the death of God (see *Thus Spoke Zarathustra*, 1892).
70. Some of these strategies are analyzed in his book *Justice Accused*; see M. Minow, "Introduction: Robert Cover and Law, Judging, and Violence," in M. Minow, M. Ryan, and A. Sarat (eds), *Narrative, Violence, and the Law: The Essays of Robert Cover*. Ann Arbor, MI: University of Michigan Press, 1993, pp. 1–11, at pp. 2–5.
71. Cover, "Nomos and Narrative," pp. 54–5.
72. Ibid., p. 59, *passim*.
73. Ibid., p. 57, note 158, *in fine*. Cover assures us that his argument does not wish to belittle the "countermajoritarian difficulty," that is the idea that a body of non-democratically elected judges may thwart the will of the political majority. However, he also points out that "majoritarianism" ought not to be our only democratic concern. At the dawn of the century, democracy has come to be identified also with the defense of those values that cannot be frustrated, even in the name of the majority. For a now classical expression of the counter-majoritarian difficulty, see A. Bickel, *The Least Dangerous Branch: The Supreme Court at the Bar of Politics*. Indianapolis, IN: Bobbs-Merrill, 1962. For the view of judicial review as the least intrusive of the alternatives in particularly abhorrent and/or structurally unjust political contexts, see Robert M. Cover, "The Origins of Judicial Activism in the Protection of Minorities," *Yale Law Journal*, 1982, 91: 1287–316.
74. Cover, "Nomos and Narrative," pp. 57–8.
75. Ibid., p. 57, note 158, *in fine*.

76. The structure of adjudication is symbolically constituted by the triadic relationship between the first, second, and third personal perspectives. The first personal perspective is that of the normative universes considered from within; the second personal perspective is that of a plurality of *nomoi* each adopting the perspective of the other looking in (or out). The third personal perspective is constituted by whoever occupies the position of adjudicator, when it articulates an independent hermeneutic that does not collapse upon either the first or second personal perspectives.
77. P. Goodrich, "Satirical Legal Studies: From the Legists to the Lizard," *Michigan Law Review*, 2004, 103: 397–517, at p. 448; the full expression was *theatrum justititia et veritatis* (theater of justice and truth).
78. Plato, *The Laws*, 817b; trans. J. M. Cooper, in J. M. Cooper and D. S. Hutchinson (eds), *Plato: Complete Works*. Indianapolis, IN and Cambridge: Hackett, 1997.
79. Cover, "Nomos and Narrative," p. 35, note 98 and p. 17, note 45.
80. R. M. Cover, "Violence and the Word," *Yale Law Journal*, 1986, 95: 1601 (hereinafter Cover, "Violence and the Word"). Similar arguments can also be found in "The Bonds of Constitutional Interpretation: Of the Word, the Deed, and the Role," *Georgia Law Review*, 1986, 20: 815–33 (hereinafter "The Bonds of Constitutional Interpretation"). In here I will rely on both articles indistinctly, but all parenthetic page references in the text refer to the former essay.
81. Cover is considered one of the "founding fathers" of the movement and there are several reasons for taking this attribution seriously. First, he professes what we may call a literary understanding of law: the fact that narrative and narratives are vital to law and to how it is lived and understood. Thus, even when he takes issue with James Boyd White for underplaying the violent side of law ("Violence and the Word," p. 1601–2, note 2), he does not deny that law is, as White claims, "a set of resources for claiming, resisting, and declaring significance" (ibid.). Secondly, Cover remains sympathetic towards the spirit that animates the so-called "interpretive turn," and fully agrees that "the dominant form of legal thought ought to be interpretive in the extended sense of the term" (p. 1610, note 24). Thirdly, in his scholarship he makes use of literary and humanistic texts that also characterize the movement. Finally, his style of writing is literary to a degree where form and content cannot be separated, itself an important tenet of *law and literature*. All in all, Cover's relationship with the field is productively ambivalent. Thus Cover timidly confesses that he is "still not embarrassed to be counted in the fold of the law and humanities flock" and defines his dissent as a "disagreement among friends engaged in what is, if not a common enterprise, at least a series of enterprises with many commonalities" ("The Bonds of Constitutional Interpretation," p. 815).
82. Herodotus (6.21) recounts the story of a tragedy that so much tore the audience emotionally that the author was fined and the play forbidden from ever being performed again. This episode beautifully illuminates the difficulties of containing *fiction* within the safe haven of the fictional.
83. See Wayne Booth, *The Rhetoric of Fiction*, 2nd edn. Chicago: University of Chicago Press, 1981. For an excellent and condensed study of the constraints and freedoms of the interpretive activity, see Paul Ricœur, "The World of the Text and the World of the Reader," in *Time and Narrative*, vol. 3, trans. Kathleen Blamey and David Pellauer. Chicago and London: University of Chicago Press, 1988, pp. 157–79.
84. For the kinds of constraints faced by literary critics, see S. Fish, *Is There a Text in This Class? The Authority of Interpretive Communities*. Cambridge, MA: Harvard University Press, 1982.
85. H. G. Gadamer, *Truth and Method*, 2nd rev. edn, trans. Joel Weinsheimer and Donald G. Marshall. New York: Continuum, 2004 [1975].
86. Duncan Kennedy, "Freedom and Constraint in Adjudication: A Critical Phenomenology," *Journal of Legal Education*, 1986, 36: 518–62.
87. Cover, "Violence and the Word," p. 1617.

88. For example, John Searle, *Speech Acts: An Essay in the Philosophy of Language*. Cambridge: Cambridge University Press, 1969.
89. See J. Jones, *On Aristotle and Greek Tragedy*. London: Chatto & Windus and New York: Oxford University Press, 1962.
90. Important arguments about this notion are developed in "The Bonds of Constitutional Interpretation."
91. I find it difficult to square with the views of "Nomos and Narrative" that "Violence and the Word" focuses almost exclusively on the work of judges and the officialdom.
92. See S. Skinner, "Stories of Pain and the Pursuit of Justice: Law, Violence, Experience and Jurisprudence," *Law, Culture and the Humanities*, 2009, 5: 131–55.
93. See further J. Etxabe, "A Review of 'Living Speech; Resisting the Empire of Force' by James Boyd White", *Law and Humanities*, 2008, 2(1):138–46.
94. For several examples, see B. Meyler's "Book Review: The Myth of Law and Literature," *Legal Ethics*, 2005, 8(2): 318–25, reviewing Thane Rosenbaum's *The Myth of Moral Justice: Why Our Legal System Fails to Do What's Right*. New York: Harper Collins, 2004; see also, J. Stone Peters, "Law, Literature, and the Vanishing Real: On the Future of an Interdisciplinary Illusion," *PMLA*, 2005, 120(2): 442–52.

Chapter 2 *Antigone*, Part I: Beginnings

1. Considering that the *Antigone* is probably one of the most "loaded" texts in the classical and philosophical tradition, I have found it necessary to begin each scene by setting my own version of the text. In addition, I also provide in square parentheses some of the key terms of value and judgment in the original Greek. The reader is invited to read and keep the text in mind while reading the commentary that follows. For the translation, unless otherwise noted, I rely primarily on H. Lloyd-Jones's edition for Loeb (Cambridge and London: Harvard University Press, 1994). Other recent translations in English are R. Fagles (*Sophocles: The Three Theban Plays*. London: Penguin Classics, 1982), D. Grene (*The Complete Greek Tragedies: Sophocles I*. Chicago: University of Chicago Press, 1991), R. Gibbons and C. Segal (*Sophocles' Antigone*. Oxford: Oxford University Press, 2003). I have also consulted A. Alamillo, *Sófocles: Tragedias*. Madrid: Biblioteca Básica Gredos, 2000 (in Spanish), and P. Mazon, *Sophocle. Antigone*. Paris: Les Belles Lettres, 2002 (with the Greek text in French translation). For the critical editions on *Antigone*, I have relied on M. Griffith (*Sophocles: Antigone*. Cambridge: Cambridge University Press, 1999); J. C. Kamerbeek (*The Plays of Sophocles with Commentaries. Part 3: The Antigone*. Leiden: E. J. Brill, 1978); and R. Jebb (*Sophocles. The Plays and Fragments. Part 3: Antigone*. Cambridge: Cambridge University Press, 1891). The Greek text with English translation and Jebb's critical commentary, with links to the *LSJ* Greek–English dictionary, can be found in the Perseus Classical Library of Tufts University, Medford, MA (see http://www.perseus.tufts.edu).
2. Griffith, *Sophocles: Antigone*, suggests that the accusative neuter *poleis* ("to the city") can also be dative of agent ("by the city"), equating the ruler's will to the city's will (p. 130). This would announce Ismene's words in line 79 [*biai politon*].
3. There's another way to interpret this sentence in the passive tense, as "truly dear to the ones who love you" (e.g. Fagles' trans.).
4. E. Harris, "Antigone the Lawyer, or the Ambiguities of Nomos," in E. Harris and L. Rubinstein (eds), *The Law and the Courts in Ancient Greece*. London: Duckworth, 2004, pp. 19–56; also J. Fletcher "Citing the Law in Sophocles' *Antigone*," *Mosaic*, 2008, 41: 79–96.
5. Griffith, *Sophocles: Antigone*, p. 122.
6. M. Ostwald, "Sophocles' *Antigone*: The Family Collides with the State," in *From Popular Sovereignty to the Sovereignty of Law: Law, Society, and Politics in Fifth-Century Athens*. Berkeley, CA and London: University of California Press, 1986, pp. 148–61, at p. 154 with note 49.

7. Griffith, *Sophocles: Antigone*, p. 122. To be sure war is over, but the decree is the direct consequence of it.
8. These formal attributes of law are mentioned by Edward Harris, who relies on the work of legal anthropologist L. Pospisil (Harris, "Antigone the Lawyer," p. 22).
9. Harris, "Antigone the Lawyer," p. 35.
10. Ibid., p. 22.
11. H. D. F. Kitto, *Form and Meaning in Drama*. London: Methuen, 1964, p. 149.
12. Plato, *Protagoras*, 345d.
13. See H. Foley et al., *Women in the Classical World: Image and Text*. New York: Oxford University Press, 1994.
14. Cf. Xenophon, *Memorabilia*, 1.2.43 (conversation between Alcibiades and Pericles).
15. Griffith, *Sophocles: Antigone*, p. 137.
16. About the latter see P. Holt, "*Polis* and Tragedy in the *Antigone*," *Mnemosyne*, 1999, 52: 658–90.
17. For example, W. B. Tyrrell and L. J. Bennett, *Recapturing Sophocles' 'Antigone'*. Lanham, MD: Rowman & Littlefield, 1998.
18. See V. Rosivach, "On Creon, Antigone, and Not Burying the Dead," in *Rheinisches Museum für Philologie*, 1983, 126: 193–211.
19. Aeschylus wrote a lost tragedy entitled *Eleusinioi*, presumably about the burial of Polyneices and the Seven Argive captains killed at Thebes that were denied burial by the Thebans but were finally buried at Eleusis. (The same material is narrated, with variations, in Euripides' *Suppliants*.) But the tragedies do not offer a uniform picture about the burial and its denial. For example, the story recounted by Lysias conforms better with the Euripidean account than with Aeschylus' lost tragedy, which ended in a truce according to Plutarch, *Life of Theseus*, 29.4. About Aeschylus' and Sophocles' lost *Epigonoi*, see T. Gantz "The Aeschylean Tetralogy: Attested and Conjectured Groups," *American Journal of Philology*, 1980, 101: 133–64, at pp. 158–9, and D. Sutton, *The Lost Sophocles*. Lanham, MA: University Press of America, 1984, pp. 37–40.
20. About the incorporation and ideological significance of this story to Athenian patriotism, see V. J. Rosivach, "Autochtony and the Athenians," *Classical Quarterly*, 1987, 37: 294–306, esp. at pp. 304–5. About Athenian ideology more generally, see Nicole Loraux, *The Divided City: On Memory and Forgetting in Ancient Athens*, trans. Corinne Pache with Jeff Fort. New York: Zone Books, 2002, and *The Invention of Athens: The Funeral Oration in the Classical City*, trans. Alan Sheridan. Cambridge, MA: Harvard University Press, 1986.
21. H. Foley, "Tragedy and Democratic Ideology: The Case of Sophocles' *Antigone*," in B. Goff (ed.), *History, Tragedy, Theory: Dialogue in Athenian Drama*. Austin, TX: University of Texas Press, 1995, pp. 131–50, at pp. 140–1.
22. Christiane Sourvinou-Inwood thinks that Lysias' argument is influenced by the *Antigone* (C., Sourvinou-Inwood, "Assumptions and the Creation of Meaning: Reading Sophocles' *Antigone*," *Journal of Hellenic Studies*, 1989, 109: 134–48, at p. 143.
23. Holt, "Polis and Tragedy in the *Antigone*," pp. 666–7, citing Pindar, *Olympian*, 6.15–17 and *Nemean Odes*, 9.22–4.
24. Foley, "Tragedy and Democratic Ideology," p. 141.
25. Rosivach, "On Not Burying the Dead," p. 201.
26. Thucydides, *History of the Peloponnesian War*, 2.67.
27. Ibid., 1.138 (about Themistocles' body); Xenophon, *Hellenica*, 1.7.22 states the law for traitors in this way: "If anyone shall be a traitor to the state or shall steal sacred property he shall be tried before a court, and if he be convicted, he shall not be buried in Attica, and his property shall be confiscated" (trans. Brownson, Cambridge: Loeb Classical Library, 1918).
28. Lycurgus (*Against Leocrates*, 112–116) reports a public decree by which Phrynichus (who had participated in the Revolution of the Four Hundred in 411 BC) was charged with treason once he was already dead and buried, and after being found guilty, his bones were exhumed from Attica (and even those who dared to defend him verbally were put to death for it!). Lycurgus then goes on to give further examples of similar decrees (ibid., 117 and ff.).

29. See Giovanni Cerri, "Ideologia funeraria nell'*Antigone* di Sofocle," in G. Gnoli and J.-P. Vernant (eds.), *La Mort, les Morts dans les Sociétés Anciennes*. Paris and London: Maison des Sciences de l'Homme and Cambridge University Press, 1982, pp. 121–31.
30. Holt, "*Polis* and Tragedy in the *Antigone*," pp. 664–5 (emphasis in the original).
31. Foley, "Tragedy and Democratic Ideology," p. 137.
32. Without mentioning him by name, the Chorus refers to Capaneus, one of the Argive captains who boasted, even against Zeus, that he would set the city ablaze with fire (Aeschylus, *Seven Against Thebes*, 432 ff.) and had his words imprinted in gold on his shield, as did Polyneices (ibid., 660). While he was trying to climb the walls of the city and make good on his promise, a lightning bolt (symbol of Zeus) struck him dead.
33. For book-length treatments of Sophoclean choruses, see R. Burton, *The Chorus in Sophocles' Tragedies*. Oxford: Clarendon Press, 1980, and I. Errandonea, *Sófocles y la Personalidad de sus Coros: Estudio de Dramática Constructivae*. Madrid: Moneda y Cambio, 1970. For a short, but important essay see G. M. Kirkwood, "The Dramatic Role of the Chorus in Sophocles," *Phoenix*, 1954, 8: 1–22.
34. It is not clear in the text whether the object of comparison with the eagle is Polyneices or the unidentified and abstract "Argive soldier." Griffith argues that the manuscript reading makes Polyneices the object of this comparison, although verses 106 [*leukaspin*] and 114 [*leukês*] require that this should be the Argive man (Griffith, *Sophocles: Antigone*, p.146). It is also possible that Polyneices remains implied in all these symbols, as he is the only person clearly identified by name and singled out as the leader of the invader army.
35. The elders do not specify who was to blame for their quarrel [*neikes*] or what caused it, but the etymological association with *Polyneices* – suggested by Aeschylus in *Seven Against Thebes*, 658–9 – may single him out (Griffith, *Sophocles: Antigone*, p. 146).
36. See Aeschylus, *Seven Against Thebes*, 660.
37. Aeschylus, *Seven Against Thebes*, and Euripides, *Phoenician Women*. The fact that no one in the play mentions this possibility suggests that Sophocles was not following that version or interested in exploring it. See, further, note 86.
38. He is Yocasta's brother and son of Menoeceus (not Laius), and therefore not technically in the same family line as Oedipus and his *oikos*, the Labdacids. This distinction will be important, as I shall suggest when we touch upon the famous lines 904–20 (see Chapter 4).
39. Aristotle, *Nichomachean Ethics*, 1130a1 (the sentence is attributed to Bias of Priene, who lived in the sixth century BC).
40. The origin of the 'ship of the state' metaphor is credited to the sixth-century BC lyric poet Alcaeus and is used by Eteocles in the opening lines of Aeschylus' *Seven Against Thebes*. Cf. Plato, *The Republic*, 488a.
41. See, for instance, A. W. H. Adkins, *Merit and Responsibility: A Study in Greek Values*. Chicago: University of Chicago Press, 1960; K. J. Dover, *Greek Popular Morality in the Time of Plato and Aristotle*. Indianapolis, IN: Hackett, 1994. See also M. Blundell, *Helping Friends and Harming Enemies: A Study in Sophocles and Greek Ethics*. Cambridge and New York: Cambridge University Press, 1989. This author describes Creon's preamble as being "moderate and untyrannical" (p. 116).
42. Thucydides, 2.37–43; and Demosthenes, 19.247 ('On the False Embassy').
43. Kitto, *Form and Meaning*, p. 151.
44. As Bowra explains, Creon's maxims are "innocent enough to be the approved utterance of public men . . . They are the legitimate commonplaces of a patriot and would be accepted as such" (C. M. Bowra, *Sophoclean Tragedy*. Oxford: Clarendon Press, 1944, p. 68).
45. Foley, "Tragedy and Democratic Ideology," p. 138.
46. Simon Goldhill argues that the "viewing, judging spectator" functioned as an "ideal of citizenship" in a city where the theater was such an important institution (S. Goldhill, "Civic Ideology and the Problem of Difference: The Politics of Aeschylean Tragedy, Once Again," *Journal of Hellenic Studies*, 2000, 120: 34–56, at p. 47). As Goldhill describes it, "playing the good democrat, seeing oneself playing the good democrat, enjoying not being

a good democrat, expecting others to be good democrats, and so forth, are all elements of being a citizen in Athens" (ibid.). For a view stressing this educative function of theater-going, see S. Sara Monoson, "Citizen as Theatēs (Theater-Goer): Performing Unity, Reciprocity, and Strong-Mindedness at the City Dionysia," in *Plato's Democratic Entanglements: Athenian Politics and the Practice of Philosophy*. Printon, NJ: Princeton University Press, 2000, pp. 88–110.

47. Cf. Harris, "Antigone the Lawyer," p. 36.
48. See, above, note 37.
49. For example, Thucydides, 1.138; Xenophon, *Hellenica*, 1.7.22. For similar decrees see Lycurgus (see note 27 above). About the issue of burial and its denial in the literature see J. D. Mikalson, *Honor Thy Gods: Popular Religion in Greek Tragedy*. Chapel Hill, NC: University of North Caroline Press, 1991, pp. 122–5, and Rosivach "On not Burying the Dead"; see also D. A. Hester, "Sophocles the Unphilosophical: A Study in the *Antigone*," *Mnemosyne*, 1971, 24 (fourth series): 11–59. Also Cerri, "Ideologia Funeraria."
50. Xenophon mentions the decree of Cannonus (406 BC), according to which those judged guilty of wronging the people of Athens could be cast into a ravine (*Hellenica*, 1.7.20) and presumably left exposed.
51. Plato prescribes this punishment for those convicted of killing mother, father, brethren, or children: "[T]he officers of the judges and magistrates shall kill him and cast him out naked at an appointed cross-roads outside the city; and [they] shall take each a stone and cast it on the head of the corpse . . . and after this they shall carry the corpse to the borders of the land and cast it out (873c) unburied, according to law" (Plato, *The Laws*, 873b–c, trans. R. G. Bury, Loeb Classical edition. Cambridge, MA: Harvard University Press, 1967–8).
52. Even though women would participate in burial ceremonies, the action of burial was essentially a male activity controlled by the state.
53. For example, Tyrrell and Bennett, *Recapturing Sophocles' Antigone*, p. 27.
54. Some critics have observed this fixation with money as being typical of tyrants (e.g. Bowra, *Sophoclean Tragedy*, at p. 72).
55. See Griffith, *Sophocles: Antigone*, p. 174 (citing also Theognis).
56. Among others, B. M.W. Knox, *The Heroic Temper: Studies in Sophoclean Tragedy*. Berkeley, CA and Los Angeles: University of California Press, 1964, at pp. 86 and ff.
57. Bowra, *Sophoclean Tragedy*; R. Scodel, *Sophocles*. Boston: Twayne, 1984.
58. The difference between practical and political arts is that the former were unevenly distributed among different men, but the latter were distributed to all alike, for cities would not come to be if only a few possessed political virtue. Accordingly, Protagoras explains, when people debate about architecture they think that only a few have the right to advise them, but when they debate about political issues, they accept the advice of everyone (Plato, *Protagoras*, 322c–323a). Even though humans are naturally endowed with this political virtue, Protagoras argues that this virtue must be carefully trained and developed, which helps him to justify his own claims to being an expert and teacher of it.
59. C. Segal, *Tragedy and Civilization*. Cambridge, MA: Harvard University Press, 1981, and "Sophocles' Praise of Man and the Conflicts of the *Antigone*," in T. Woodward (ed.), *Sophocles: A Collection of Critical Essays*. Englewood Cliffs, NJ: Prentice Hall, 1966; S. Benardete, *Sacred Transgressions: A Reading of Sophocles' Antigone*. South Bend, IN: St Augustine's Press, 1999.
60. As Heidegger says, "in the first two verses the poet anticipates. He will spend the rest of the poem catching up with himself" (M. Heidegger, "The Ode on Man in Sophocles' *Antigone*," in T. Woodward (ed.), *Sophocles: A Collection of Critical Essays* (1966), pp. 86–100, at p. 88. For a good reading, see J. P. Euben, "*Antigone* and the Languages of Politics," in *Corrupting the Youth: Political Education, Democratic Culture, and Political Theory*. Princeton, NJ: Princeton University Press, 1997, pp. 139–78, esp. pp. 171–6.
61. Bowra, *Sophoclean Tragedy*, p. 85.

62. Plato, *Protagoras*, 320d–323a.
63. Antigone refers here to Creon's law as *nomos* (and also later in 843), which is why there can be no sharp distinction between *nomos* and *kerugma* (see note 4 above and accompanying text).
64. Lloyd-Jones translates: "I have no enemies by birth, but I have friends by birth" (523).
65. Blundell, *Helping Friends and Harming Enemies*, pp. 139–41.
66. In my view, the issue of the double burial should worry the audience no more than do the characters. Cf. Segal, who deems it "one of the most puzzling details of the plot" (*Tragedy and Civilization*, pp. 159–60). For a bibliographical compendium, see Tyrrell and Bennett, *Recapturing Sophocles' Antigone*. See also D. A. Hester, "Sophocles the Unphilosophical."
67. Griffith, *Sophocles: Antigone*, p. 196.
68. About the performative elements of her "refusal to deny," see J. Butler, *Antigone's Claim: Kinship Between Life and Death*. New York: Columbia University Press, 2000; see also S. Gourgouris, "Philosophy's Need for Antigone," in *Does Literature Think? Literature as Theory for an Antimythical Era*. Stanford, CA: Stanford University Press, 2003, pp. 147–8.
69. G. W. F. Hegel, *Phenomenology of Spirit*, trans. A. V. Miller. Oxford: Oxford University Press, 1977.
70. V. Ehrenberg, *Sophocles and Pericles*. Oxford: Basil Blackwell, 1954.
71. Thucydides, 2.37.
72. Aristotle, *Rhetoric*, 1373b, 1375a.
73. F. Ost, "*L'Antigone* de Sophocle: Résistance, apories juridiques et paradoxes politiques," in *Raconter la Loi: Aux Sources de l'Imaginaire Juridique*. Paris: Odile Jacob, 2004, pp. 153–203.
74. J. P. Tomain, "Creon's Ghost," in *Creon's Ghost: Law, Justice, and the Humanities*. New York and Oxford: Oxford University Press, 2009, pp. 1–31.
75. P. Nonet, "Antigone's Law," *Law, Culture, and the Humanities*, 2006, 2: 314–35.
76. Ehrenberg, *Sophocles and Pericles*, pp. 23 and 25.
77. Mikalson, *Honor Thy Gods*, pp. 195 ff; cf. Thucydides, 2.37; Xenophon, *Memorabilia*, 4.4.19–20; Lysias, 6.10 ff.
78. Aristotle, *Rhetoric*, 1373b3.
79. Griffith, *Sophocles: Antigone*, p. 200.
80. Knox, *The Heroic Temper*, p. 97, emphasis added.
81. P. Nonet, "Antigone's Law," *Law, Culture and the Humanities*, 2006, 2: 314–35.
82. See Chapter 1.
83. Her comment "I knew that I would die . . . even if you had made no proclamation" is not to be interpreted as evidence of an alleged "death-wish" in Antigone, but rather as an acknowledgment of her own mortality and limits, which opposes Creon's overstepping his limits as a mortal.
84. Gourgouris, "Philosophy's Need for Antigone," pp. 150–1.
85. The fact that Creon (who does not know what the audience does) misjudges Ismene cannot necessarily be held against him, but it does let the audience realize that Creon is ready to condemn his own niece Ismene without strong evidence of her involvement. This means that Creon is not only harsh in his judgments, but that he *rushes* to them, which cannot be a good quality for a leader (and judge) to have.
86. Antigone's omission may be telling. According to one version, one that Sophocles does not seem to follow, Polyneices came only to enforce an agreement to share the government with his brother Eteocles that the latter had violated (see Aeschylus, *Seven Against Thebes*; Euripides, *Phoenician Women*). The fact that Antigone ignores such an obvious and powerful defense suggests, strongly in my view, that Sophocles wanted his audience to consider Polyneices' treason as a "given." In the hypothesis, Polyneices must be buried not because he is no traitor, but *in spite of* the fact that he is one.
87. This is how Creon's answer to Antigone's question may be interpreted: "Do you want anything beyond my execution?" "Oh, nothing! Once I have that I have everything."

88. Richard Rorty defines *final vocabulary* as the set of words "all human beings carry and employ to justify their actions, their beliefs, their lives. These are the words in which we formulate praise of our friends and contempt of our enemies, our long-term projects, our deepest self-doubts and our highest hopes . . . it is 'final' in the sense that if doubt is cast on the worth of these words, their user has no noncircular recourse. These words are as far as he can go with language; beyond them there is only helpless passivity or a resort to force" (R. Rorty, *Contingency, Irony and Solidarity*. Cambridge: Cambridge University Press, 1989, p. 73).

Chapter 3 Incommensurability and judgment

1. The two most prominent examples are John Rawls' theory of public reason and Jürgen Habermas' theory of communicative action. Other writers in this tradition include Joshua Cohen, Seyla Benhabib, and Amy Gutman.
2. J. Habermas, *Between Facts and Norms: Contributions to a Discourse Theory of Law and Democracy*, trans. W. Rehg. Cambridge, MA: MIT Press, 1996, pp. 310–12.
3. The expression is Habermas', in "Three Normative Models of Democracy," in S. Benhabib (ed.), *Democracy and Difference: Contesting the Boundaries of the Political*. Princeton, NJ: Princeton University Press, 1996, pp. 21–9, at p. 29.
4. For example, Habermas, "'Reasonable' versus 'True,' or the Morality of Worldviews," in *The Inclusion of the Other: Studies in Political Theory*. Cambridge, MA: MIT Press, 1998, pp. 75–101, p. 101.
5. For a more sustained criticism of these models in the context of an alternative tragic conception of democracy, see my article, J. Etxabe "What Do the Poets Know About Democracy? A Case Study in Law and Literature," in B. van Klink and S. Taekema (eds), *Law and Method: Interdisciplinary Research into Law*. Tübingen: Mohr Siebeck, 2011, pp. 341–54.
6. J. Raz, *The Morality of Freedom*. New York: Oxford University Press, 1986.
7. This is the meaning given by John Finnis, "Commensuration and Public Reason," in R. Chang (ed.), *Incommensurability, Incomparability, and Practical Reason*. Cambridge, MA: Harvard University Press, 1997, pp. 215–33; see in the same volume, C. Sunstein, 'Incommensurability and Kinds of Valuation: Some Applications in Law', in Chang, *Incommensurability*, pp. 234–54.
8. This is the sense used, for instance, by philosophers in the tradition of Thomas Kühn and Paul Feyerabend. For an excellent presentation of the problem, see Ruth Chang's "Introduction" in her edition of *Incommensurability, Incomparability, and Practical Reason*, pp. 1–34.
9. This example is developed by Guido Calabresi and Philip Bobbitt in *Tragic Choices*. New York: W. W. Norton, 1978.
10. Some legal theorists deny that the situation in law is ever such: see R. Dworkin, "Moral Pluralism," in *Justice in Robes*. Cambridge, MA: Belknap Press of Harvard University Press, 2006. (This article was originally published as "Do Liberal Values Conflict?" in M. Lilla, R. Dworkin, and R. Silvers (eds), *The Legacy of Isaiah Berlin*. New York: New York Review of Books, 2001.)
11. Berlin's original *Four Essays on Liberty* (1969) are included in the recent volume entitled *Liberty*, ed. H. Hardy. Oxford: Oxford University Press, 2002, which incorporates these and other important essays. All page references are to this edition. The critical commentary on Isaiah Berlin and his work is vast, of which Ian Harris gives a detailed account in an essay entitled "Berlin and His Critics," in Hardy, *Liberty*, pp. 349–66. Personally, I have found enlightening the work of J. Gray, *Isaiah Berlin*. Princeton, NJ: Princeton University Press, 1996; for an application of Berlin's position in the context of legal judgment, see S. Veitch, *Moral Conflict and Legal Reasoning*. Oxford and Portland, OR: Hart, 1999, chapter 3.
12. In philosophy, the view that sees all ends as ultimately compatible extends from the metaphysical realism of Plato to the dialectical Idealism of Hegel. In the area of moral

philosophy, the denial of incommensurability applies both to Kantian morality and to its opponent, utilitarianism. In law, the view that all values are ultimately commensurate is often associated with the movement of law and economics.

13. Berlin, in Hardy, *Liberty*, p. 166.
14. Ibid., p. 42.
15. Ibid., p. 214.
16. The commodification of human life is, for some of us, difficult to accept. This of course does not mean that life is never "traded off." For instance, Guido Calabresi exposes a now classic view that at the heart of the law of accidents and safety regulations there is a tragic clash between the moral commitment to the pricelessness of life – which would require taking every precaution to eliminate risks to it – and the economic or pragmatic rationality that justifies taking only those precautions which are cost-efficient – thus effectively putting a price on human life; see G. Calabresi, *The Cost of Accidents: A Legal and Economic Analysis*. New Haven, CT: Yale University Press, 1970. For a view arguing that "the proposition that life has a value beyond all price might be understood not to forbid all trading off of lives against other goods, but only to forbid trading lives off in accordance with market principles of rationality," see G. Keating, "Pricelessness and Life: An Essay for Guido Calabresi," *Maryland Law Review*, 2005, 64: 159–219, at p. 167.
17. The distinction between "real" and "notional" confrontations belongs to Bernard Williams; see his "The Truth in Relativism," *Proceedings of the Aristotelian Society*, 1974–5, 75: 215–28.
18. This is the usual contention of those who think of incommensurability as incomparability.
19. Berlin, in Hardy, *Liberty*, p. 43.
20. Sometimes Berlin seems to base his argument on purely experiential grounds (ibid., p. 43); at other times he shapes it as a conceptual argument (ibid., pp. 42–3); and at still others, he presents it with the metaphysical undertones of a necessary truth (ibid., p. 215).
21. Perhaps a way to recognize the relative strength of Berlin's position is to question what it would take to deny it. In other words, what kind of evidence (sociological, phenomenological, ethical, political) would you have to disregard, and what grasp of reality would you possibly claim after it?
22. Berlin, in Hardy, *Liberty*, p. 43.
23. Ibid., p. 47.
24. In one sense, rationality is the ability to guide concrete choices; in a second sense, rationality becomes a general capability to make choices, whatever their content; and perhaps in a third sense, on occasions Berlin seems to describe rationality as the ability to recognize one's limitations (cognitive and others) concerning choices.
25. Berlin contrasts the certainty of "single-minded monists, ruthless fanatics, men possessed by an all-embracing coherent vision" to the "doubts and agonies of those who cannot wholly blind themselves to reality" and are "aware of the complex texture of experience" (Berlin, in Hardy, *Liberty*, p. 47).
26. As Berlin puts it, "[I]f rationality entails a normal ability to apprehend the world . . . capacity for choosing is intrinsic to rationality" (ibid., p. 44).
27. J. Raz, *The Morality of Freedom*. New York: Oxford University Press, 1986. For an analysis of Raz's views in connection to Berlin's see Veitch, *Moral Conflict*, pp. 79–82 and 89–95.
28. Raz thinks that statements of incommensurability between two options are denials that their values are comparable.
29. Raz, *The Morality of Freedom*, p. 346.
30. Another example he uses is parenthood and money, where one must refuse to put a monetary value on parenthood in order to successfully engage in it.
31. Raz, *The Morality of Freedom*, p. 350.
32. Ibid., p. 353.
33. Ibid., p. 352.
34. Ibid., p. 353.

35. See Veitch, *Moral Conflict*, p. 92.
36. Raz, *The Morality of Freedom*, p. 334.
37. Ibid., p. 353.
38. Ibid., p. 353.
39. Ibid., p. 340.
40. Ibid., pp. 339, 349
41. Raz does not argue that all people react this way, but that this is a fairly typical reaction, and one that is appropriate within the conventional meaning of marriage. If people were no longer offended by putting an economic price to it, the institution of marriage as we know it would change dramatically.
42. For an account of similar rankings in our everyday experiences, see W. Miller's "Comparing Values and the Ranking Game," in his *Eye for an Eye*. New York: Cambridge University Press, 2006.
43. D. Wiggins, "Incommensurability: Four Proposals," in *Needs, Values, and Truth*, 3rd edn. Oxford: Clarendon Press, 1998 (hereinafter Wiggins, 'Incommensurability'). Wiggins distinguishes four different cases of incommensurability in increasing levels of complexity. For convenience's sake, I will explain without noting these distinctions.
44. Wiggins, "Incommensurability," p. 369. Wiggins remarks that "we deploy these conceptions even as the variety of the contingencies that we actually confront constantly shapes or reshapes the conceptions themselves" (ibid.). A good discussion about how these conceptions are deployed can be found in Charles Taylor, "Leading a Life," in R. Chang (ed.), *Incommensurability, Incomparability, and Practical Reason*, pp. 170–83.
45. Wiggins, "Incommensurability," p. 378.
46. J. P. Sartre, 'Existentialism Is a Humanism', lecture given in 1946, published in W. Kaufman (ed.), *Existentialism From Dostoyevsky To Sartre*. New York: Meridian, 1981. This example is well argued in Veitch, *Moral Conflict*, and criticized by A. MacIntyre, *After Virtue: A Study in Moral Theory*. Notre Dame, IN: University of Notre Dame Press, 1984.
47. Another example of a "tragic dilemma" – an example that will resurface in Chapter 4 – is the choice imposed upon Intaphernes' wife. Herodotus (3.19) recounts the story of the family of Intaphernes all of whom had been sentenced to death by the Persian King Darius. At one point, Darius offers the wife of Intaphernes the choice to save only one. Therefore she is compelled to choose also who is to be put to death.
48. Wiggins, "Incommensurability," p. 378. Wiggins envisions the task of philosophy as continued participation in the critique of reasons, but being "alert to the need to step off the treadmill," and being "prepared for the decision to depend on the exercise of judgment" (ibid.).
49. J. F. Lyotard, *The Differend*, trans. G. Van Den Abbeele. Minneapolis, MN: University of Minnesota Press, 1988. Lyotard thinks of the differend as a kind of incommensurability (e.g. p. 128, notes 178 and 179, and p. 159, note 231).
50. Lyotard, *The Differend*, p. xi, emphasis added.
51. Ibid. Lyotard makes an important distinction between *phrase regimens* (cognitive, descriptive, prescriptive, evaluative) and *genres of discourse* (technical, tragic, comic). Each genre of discourse inspires a mode of "linking" phrases together. By doing so, each genre imprints its own distinctive finality or criteria of success to heterogeneous phrase regimens (to persuade, to convince, to vanquish, to make laugh, to make cry, etc.). Each time that heterogeneous phrase regimens are "linked together," there are other possible linkages that remain neglected, forgotten, or repressed (Lyotard, *The Differend*, p. 136 note 184), which creates the space for the differend. Lyotard argues that this incommensurability may occur both at the level of phrase regimens (because heterogeneous phrase regimens are not translatable into different ones without neutralizing them (ibid., p. 128, note 178)), as well as at the level of genres of discourse (because there is no single, universal genre, to subsume all genres into one that can impose its own finality on the rest (ibid., p. 138, note 189; see also notes 179 and 231).

52. Lyotard, *The Differend*, p. 140, note 195.
53. For further examples, see D. Litowitz, "Lyotard: Just Gaming and a Plurality of Justices," in his *Postmodern Philosophy and Law*. Lawrence, KA: University Press of Kansas, 1997.
54. For an illuminating account of the agent's internal state of mind, as well as for the kind of virtues required to face such situations, see P. Nieuwenburg, "The Agony of Choice: Isaiah Berlin and the Phenomenology of Conflict," *Administration and Society*, 2004, 35(6): 683–700.
55. The transition that I am marking here does not follow Max Weber's well-known distinction between an *ethics of conviction* and an *ethics of responsibility* ("Politics as a Vocation," in *The Vocation Lectures*, eds D. Owen and T. B. Strong. Indianapolis, IN and Cambridge: Hackett, 2004, pp. 32–94, pp. 83 ff. Unlike the ethics of conviction described by Weber, the morality of choice defined here is *responsible* for the consequences of such choices.
56. This position is related to some trends of postmodernism. But consider Derrida: "Without the opening of an absolutely undetermined possible, without the radical abeyance and suspense marking a 'perhaps', there would never be either event or decision. Certainly. But nothing takes place and *nothing is ever decided without suspending the 'perhaps'* while keeping its living possibility in living memory" (J. Derrida, *The Politics of Friendship*, trans. G. Collins. London and New York: Verso, 2005, p. 67, emphasis added.
57. As Scott Veitch bitingly puts it, "the more one hears about 'deferring the undeferrable,' of 'conceiving a justice that cannot but must be conceived,' or of 'saying what cannot be said' and 'listening to what cannot be heard,' the more one is tempted to produce a charge not so much of relativism . . . but of serious fence-sitting" (Veitch, *Moral Conflict*, p. 189).
58. Lyotard acknowledges that the parties must have some sort of "encounter" in order to give rise to the differend and wonders whether it ought not be the case that they must also have some "properties" in common for it to be altogether possible. Lyotard concludes that, in effect, the differend is born out of these encounters, but this is not generated by a prior universe of common properties, but the phrase or sentence in which one presents or articulates this encounter. As Lyotard puts it, "[the encounter] is a transcendental and not an empirical condition" (Lyotard, *The Differend*, p. 28, note 39). However, if the encounter were to take place only in the phrase that explains it, then it would be enough simply not to articulate the phrase for the conflict never to arise. This would make such encounters, contrary to what Lyotard wants to argue, dependent on human will. It is true, as we shall explain in the following section, that the conflict must be "staged" for it to be properly constituted as incommensurable. But this does not make their encounter our exclusive creation, for the parties must meet each other and clash at a certain point for us to be able to describe this encounter at all. This is an empirical and not a transcendental condition.
59. J. Rancière, *Disagreement: Politics and Philosophy*, trans. Julie Rose. Minneapolis, MN and London: University of Minnesota Press, 1999, p. x (hereafter *Disagreement*).
60. Ibid., p. 55.
61. Ibid., p. 55.
62. Ibid., p. 27.
63. Livy, *Livy in Fourteen Vols*, trans. B. O. Foster. Cambridge, MA: Harvard University Press, 1967, Book II, p. xxxii. This passage is also the basis for Shakespeare's *Coriolanus*.
64. Rancière, *Disagreement*, p. 26.
65. Ibid., p. 49.
66. Ibid., p. 50.
67. Ibid., p. 51.
68. Ibid., p. 57.
69. Ibid., p. 52. This entails a second movement: "We are right to argue for our rights and so to posit the existence of a common world of argument. And we are right to do so precisely because those who ought to recognize it do not, because they act as though they are ignorant of the existence of this common world" (ibid., p. 53).
70. Ibid., p. 56.

71. Ibid., p. 58.
72. Ibid., p. 57.
73. Ibid., pp. 47 and 48.
74. According to Rancière, this "they" is not a fixed position external to the discourse, but it alternates and shifts in the interplay between the first, second, and third persons (ibid.).
75. Rancière argues that this appeal to the "they" or to a third person can play a triple role, for example in expressions such as "Workers will not accept . . ." uttered by the workers' representative. First, it designates the other participant as one with whom the situation of the speaker as a speaking being is in question. Second, it addresses a third person at whose door it lays the issue in question. Third, it sets us the first person, the "I" or "we" of the speaker, as representative of a community. According to Rancière, it is this set of interactions that is meant by public opinion: "Not primarily some network of enlightened minds . . . [but] an opinion that evaluates the manner in which people speak to each other" (ibid., p. 48).
76. Ibid., p. 48.
77. See note 58.
78. Rancière, *Disagreement*, p. 27.
79. This is the first time to our knowledge that this expression was ever used [V. Ehrenberg, *Sophocles and Pericles*. Oxford: Blackwell, 1954, pp. 23, 25), but certainly not the last, for it became popularized as a cultural commonplace in the Aristotelian and later traditions of natural law.

Chapter 4 *Antigone*, Part II: Transitions

1. Some editors attribute this line to Ismene (Lloyd-Jones, Gibbons and Segal), others to the Chorus (Fagles). The latter scenario seems more in tune with Creon's response to the effect that her death had been decided jointly with the elders, as he has believed throughout. Attributing this line to the Chorus is also consistent with the elders' surprise in 770 after hearing that the death sentence still hangs on both sisters, and Creon's immediate rectification in 771.
2. Aristotle, *Poetics*, 1449a–15.
3. Simon Goldhill has recently shown that Sophocles uses the third actor as a way of creating a space for the audience to discover its own critical distance from what is happening on the stage. See S. Goldhill, "The Audience on the Stage: Rhetoric, Emotion, and Judgment in Sophoclean Theatre," in S. Goldhill and E. Hall (eds), *Sophocles and the Greek Tragic Tradition*. Cambridge: Cambridge University Press, 2009, pp. 27–47.
4. Most commentators see Ismene as the shadow that makes the hero's radiance shine brighter (e.g. H. D. F. Kitto, *Form and Meaning in Drama*, 2nd edn. London: Methuen, 1964, p. 163). This view is progressively shifting. See, for example, Jill Frank, "The *Antigone*'s Law," *Law, Culture, and the Humanities*, 2006, 2: 336–40, arguing that Ismene stands for the human practice of justice, respectful of what is, and appropriate to the world of plurality that is the *polis* (p. 339). Tyrrel and Bennett claim that for the original Athenian audience, Ismene would be a paradigm of how an Athenian woman should act (W. B. Tyrrel and L. J. Bennett, *Recapturing Sophocles' Antigone*. Lanham, MD: Rowman & Littlefield, 1998, pp. 76 and ff.).
5. This appears to be Sophocles' own version (M. Griffith (ed.), *Sophocles: Antigone*. Cambridge: Cambridge University Press, 1999, p. 9).
6. In context, I think it makes more sense to read Ismene's defense of their fitting relationship from an affective side (i.e. a relationship that is "well-suited") than from a patrimonial side (a relationship that is "appropriate" in terms of the Greek laws of marriage and inheritance). According to the latter, the marriage between first cousins is considered highly desirable when the girl's father has died without male heirs so that the inherited property may remain in the family (R. Gibbons and C. Segal, *Sophocles' Antigone*. Oxford: Oxford University Press, 2003, pp. 137–8). About the laws of inheritance and the family, see W. K. Lacey, *The Family in Classical Greece*. Ithaca, NY: Cornell University Press, 1968, esp. chapters 5 and 6.

7. In addition to the usual, I have benefited from H. D. F. Kitto's beautiful translation (*Form and Meaning*, pp. 165–6).
8. I follow Kitto's reading (ibid.) (also Lloyd-Jones). Some editors read not ax [*kopis*], but dust [*konis*] as "the blood-stained dust of the gods . . ." (Jebb, Griffith, Gibbons and Segal), which is reminiscent of Aeschylus' *Seven Against Thebes* (734–7).
9. Griffith, *Sophocles: Antigone*, p. 218.
10. For these mechanisms of zooming in and out, see C. Sourvinou-Inwood, "Assumptions and the Creation of Meaning: Reading Sophocles' *Antigone*," *Journal of Hellenic Studies*, 1989, 109: 134–48.
11. For example, Aeschylus, *Seven Against Thebes* (740–4).
12. The Erinyes or Furies are often represented as the avenging deities of the lower world who typically punish the crime of bloodshed within the family [cf. Aeschylus, *Eumenides*]. Here, however, the fury seems to exist in the *phren* or the mind of individuals. See G. Else, *The Madness of Antigone*. Heidelberg: Carl Winter Universitätsverlag, 1976, pp. 73–4. For an exhaustive analysis of the *phren* and its cognates, see S. Sullivan, *Sophocles' Use of Psychological Terminology*. Canada: Carleton University Press, 1999.
13. See W. Jaeger, *The Theology of the Early Greek Philosophers*, trans. E. Robinson. Eugene, OR: Wipf & Stock, 2003, pp. 34–7.
14. Ibid. See also W. Jaeger, *Paideia: The Ideals of Greek Culture*, 3 vols, trans. Gilbert Highet. New York: Oxford University Press, 1933, 1943 and 1944, vol. 1, chapter 8.
15. According to some commentators, hope "is more commonly pictured as a flattering phantom – an illusion born of an uncertain future. It is a mocking goddess who tempts man to forget the limits of the possible" (J. Opstelten, *Sophocles and Greek Pessimism*. Amsterdam: North-Holland, 1952, pp. 204–6). However, hope can also have comforting value, depending on the circumstances. As Kenneth Dover explains, "it was commonly realized that in adversity from which we have not yet found an escape [hope] keeps us going . . . [but requires] reasons justifying such hope" (K. Dover, *Greek Popular Morality in the Age of Plato and Aristotle*. Indianapolis, IN and Cambridge: Hackett, 1994, p. 132).
16. P. Gerard, "Domination, Résistance et Démocratie de Contestation" (available by courtesy of author); see also C. Meier, *The Political Art of Greek Tragedy*, trans. A. Webber. Oxford: Polity, 1993.
17. M. Bowra, *Sophoclean Tragedy*. Oxford: Clarendon Press, p. 74.
18. Griffith, *Sophocles: Antigone*, p. 247.
19. J. Fletcher, "Citing the Law in Sophocles' *Antigone*," *Mosaic*, 2008, 41(3): 79–96, at p. 85.
20. The reliability of Haemon's report is defended by A. van Erp Taalman Kipp, "Truth in Tragedy: When Are We Entitled to Doubt a Character's Words?" *American Journal of Philology*, 1996, 117: 517–36.
21. Aristotle, *Rhetoric*, 1418b *in fine*.
22. See Else, *The Madness of Antigone*, p. 56. Kamerbeek explains the diction in 699–700 [*ouk hêde chrusês axia times lachein / toiade . . . phatis*]: "for a moment Haemon seems to speak his own mind, but he immediately corrects himself" (J. C. Kamerbeek (ed.), *The Plays of Sophocles with Commentaries. Part 3: The Antigone*, E. J. Brill, 1978, p. 133).
23. This had already been suggested earlier (577) (see, above, note 1).
24. Jebb says that it is justified by a simple wish to avoid physical violence; Bowra (*Sophoclean Tragedy*) that Creon hopes to avert the anger of the gods and yet save his own dignity; Kitto (*Form and Meaning*) that Creon avoids public stoning, the only form of execution in which the whole community could actively take part. M. Blundell (in *Helping Friends and Harming Enemies: A Study in Sophocles and Greek Ethics*. Cambridge and New York: Cambridge University Press, 1989) argues that Creon is afraid of insurrection and popular dissent.
25. The *miasma* from which Creon wants to protect the polis remains puzzling. As Eric Dodds explains, *miasma* "is the automatic consequence of an action, belongs to the world of external events, and operates with the same ruthless indifference to motive as a typhoid germ"

(E. R. Dodds, *The Greeks and the Irrational*. Berkeley, CA and Los Angeles: University of California Press, 1951, p. 36). However, "the 'polluted' man is dangerous, and must be treated as such" (A. W. H. Adkins, *Merit and Responsibility: A Study in Greek Values*. Chicago: Chicago University Press, 1960, chapter 5).

26. I follow the sense of Griffith (". . . you who make assaults upon herds") and not of Lloyd-Jones ("you would fall upon men's property"), for "it is conventional to specify that Desire affects animals, humans and gods (Griffith, *Sophocles: Antigone*, p. 257).
27. See especially the dialogue between Aphrodite and Hera in *Iliad*, 14.198–9 and 216–17, ideas also present in the dialogues between Paris and Helen (*Iliad.*, 3.442) and Zeus and Hera (*Iliad.*, 14.294).
28. For example, Kitto, *Form and Meaning*, p. 167 and ff. For some critics, the love-motivation *must* be excluded because "any intrusion of Haemon's personal feelings would obscure the issue, which is the rightness of Antigone's principles and her act" (K. von Fritz, *Haimons Liebe zu Antigone*, quoted by Else, *The Madness of Antigone*, p. 53). Another *strategy of denial* is to exorcise the maddening power of Eros and turn it into a sort of "beneficial" Platonic Love (Else, *The Madness of Antigone*, pp. 54–5).
29. I am following Lloyd-Jones's "you are not crowned by glory," not necessarily uttered as a sign of reproach, but as a matter of fact. Kamerbeek and Griffith translate it as interrogative: "Well, are you not dying a glorious death?" The meaning would not change much if understood as the elders' sensitivity to Antigone's own sentiments. The affirmative, "certainly, you are crowned with glory" (Jebb) does not seem warranted by the tenor of the conversation. But cf. 836–8 (referring to the glory of suffering the same fate as the gods).
30. The word is "thesmoi" and it denotes the power and authority of convention and tradition.
31. Goldhill, "The Audience on the Stage," p. 45.
32. For an attempt see my article, "Antigone's *Nomos*," in *Animus: The Canadian Journal of Philosophy and Humanities*, 2009, 13: 60–73. Good analyses are offered in H. Foley, "Antigone as a Moral Agent," in M. Silk (ed.), *Tragedy and the Tragic: Greek Theatre and Beyond*. New York and Oxford: Clarendon Press, 1996, pp. 49–73; and M. Cropp, "Antigone's Final Speech: Sophocles' 'Antigone' 891–928," *Greece and Rome*, 1997, 44(2): 137–60. See also M. Nieburg, "How Like a Woman: Antigone's 'Inconsistency,'" *Classical Quarterly*, 1990, 40(1): 54–76.
33. Jebb, p. 259.
34. Herodotus, *The Histories*, 3.119. About this borrowing (of which I am not entirely persuaded), see S. West "Sophocles' Antigone and Herodotus Book Three," in J. Griffin (ed.), *Sophocles Revisited*. Oxford: Oxford University Press, 1999, pp. 109–36.
35. The elders of the chorus do *not* represent all the citizens, but it is not unreasonable to take their opinion as a more or less reliable (though contestable) barometer of the values of the play's community. For they have been prominent actors in Theban politics for quite a long time, not just after the arrival of Creon, but much before. They first honored the throne of Laius, then that of Oedipus at his height, and after his death, they were also loyal to his children (164–9).
36. On his treatise on persuasive argument, Aristotle says that when the speaker makes a claim that is unbelievable [*apiston*], she should give reasons to support it, as Sophocles does in this passage of the Antigone (Aristotle, *Rhetoric*, 1416a–1417b). This suggests that the argument, though unconventional, is itself reasonable. Cf. Sourvinou-Inwood, arguing that the passage is "explicitly and unambiguously and emphatically wrong, in ways that cannot be explained away" ("Sophocles' *Antigone* 904-20: A Reading", *AION*, 1987–8, ix–x: 19–35, at p. 32.
37. S. Murnaghan, "Antigone 904–20 and the Institution of Marriage," *American Journal of Philology*, 1986, 107(2): 192–207.
38. Generally see Walter Lacey, *The Family in Classical Greece*. This rooting out could be prevented by the institution of the *epiklerate*, by which the girl who had no brothers would

marry her nearest agnatic relative (i.e. relative on the father's side) and continue the father's *oikos*. However, such a marriage is not possible in this case, because there are no extant family members on Oedipus' side (if Antigone were to marry Haemon, she would be incorporated into the *oikos* of Creon, her uncle on her mother's side). Another legal measure would be the adoption of a male heir from a different family, but the death of the parents precludes this possibility too. Without surviving male relatives on the father's side and no more brothers to be had (either naturally or via adoption), all measures for the continuation of the house of Oedipus are now exhausted. The survival of Ismene does not necessarily alter this fact, for she would most likely join the *oikos* (family house) of her husband after marriage rather than continue the *oikos* of her father.

39. Antigone is definitely *not* a citizen, but she acts like one. Josiah Ober argues that performing a speech-act that the speaker knows is not generally accepted in the larger culture can be read as an "intentional act of resistance." See J. Ober, "How to Criticize Democracy," in J. P. Euben, J. R. Wallach, and J. Ober (eds), *Athenian Political Thought and the Reconstruction of American Democracy*. Ithaca, NY and London: Cornell University Press, 1994, p. 163. In this case, Antigone's act of resistance seeks to transform the (socio-political) norms of the entire society.
40. See N. Loraux, *The Mourning Voice: An Essay on Greek Tragedy*, trans. E. Trapnell Rawlings. Ithaca, NY: Cornell University Press, 2002, pp. 21–3. Loraux associates this odd feminine use with what she calls "anti-politics," that is "the other of politics," or "another politics" (p. 23).
41. I. Errandonea, *Sófocles y la Personalidad de sus Coros: Estudio de Dramática Constructiva*. Madrid: Moneda y Cambio, 1970, p. 95.
42. About these difficulties in the context of this Ode, see Appendix.
43. R. F. Goheen, *The Imagery of Sophocles' Antigone: A Study on Poetic Language and Structure*. Princeton, NJ: Princeton University Press, 1951, p. 64.
44. Apollodorus, *The Library*, 2.4.1. According to some versions of the myth, Danaë's son Perseus killed his grandfather accidentally with a quoit in his adult life (Pausanias, *Description of Greece*, 2.23.7).
45. While in prison, Danaë was visited by Zeus in the form of a stream of gold pouring from the roof into her lap, and was impregnated with a son (Perseus).
46. R. Goheen, *The Imagery of Sophocles' Antigone*, p. 65; also, I. Errandonea, *Sófocles y la Personalidad de sus Coros*, p. 98.
47. Kamerbeek, p. 24; see also Goheen, *The Imagery of Sophocles' Antigone*, p. 70.
48. Among many, see Goheen, *The Imagery of Sophocles' Antigone*, p. 70; see, also, R. P. Winnington-Ingram, *Sophocles: An Interpretation*. Cambridge: Cambridge University Press, 1980, p. 103.
49. In Apollodorus' version, Dionysus retaliated by driving Lycurgus mad and in this state of madness he killed his son with an axe imagining that he was a branch of vine (Apollodorus, *The Library*, 2.4.4.). By contrast, the Chorus tells us that Lycurgus was already mad when he opposed Dionysus and that he was punished not with madness but with imprisonment, after which his madness drained away.
50. C. Sourvinou-Inwood, "The Fourth Stasimon of Sophocles' 'Antigone,'" in *Bulletin of the Institute of Classical Studies of the University of London* (*BICS*), 1989, 36: 141–65, at p. 141.
51. For example, Jebb and Kamerbeek. The story mostly correlates with Apollodorus, *The Library*, 3.15.3. The scholiast commenting on *Antigone*, 981, provides a version of the story in which Cleopatra, as a new Medea, blinded her own sons as revenge on their father. According to Sourvinou-Inwood, "Sophocles left the identity of the blinding wife ambiguous, undecided between the stepmother and the mother" ("The Fourth Stasimon," p. 157).
52. Winnington-Ingram, *Sophocles: An Interpretation*, pp. 105–8.
53. As Griffith puts it, "with so much uncertain and open to disputed interpretation, any links we make must be tentative: and we cannot tell whether this uncertainty was shared by the original audience" Griffith, *Sophocles: Antigone*, p. 292.

54. Even if Cleopatra had been the "cruel wife" who blinded her own children out of spite as Sourvinou-Inwood argues, the story would still be one of extreme suffering and pain.
55. For example, Jebb, Kamerbeek, Goheen, Winnington-Ingram.
56. Sourvinou-Inwood, *The Fourth Stasimon of Sophocles Antigone*.
57. *Iliad*, 5.385–404.
58. The repetition of the formula "oh, my child" twice, once in the beginning (948) and the other as the last word of the stasimon (987), also calls for a parental relation between the Chorus and Antigone similar to that between Dione and Aphrodite.
59. R. Burton, *The Chorus in Sophocles' Tragedies*. Oxford: Clarendon Press, 1980, p. 128. Another example he mentions is Aeschylus' *Agamemnon*, 1040 f.
60. ". . . Moridia tis dunasis deina" (951). As Jebb notes, the strange position of the enclitic form *tis* [whatever, anything] that functions as a parenthetic thought gives the sentence its full expressive form.
61. As Michael Ewans puts it, the ancient Greeks lived "in a world which lacked any concept of predestination or a mechanistic fate" (M. Ewans, "Patterns of Tragedy in Sophocles and Shakespeare," in M. S. Silk (ed.), *Tragedy and the Tragic: Greek Theatre and Beyond*. Oxford: Clarendon Press, 1996, pp. 438–56, at p. 441.
62. Vivasvan Sony rightly points out that "there has been much confusion in the study of tragedy because the concept of fate has been understood as necessity (*ananke*) rather than as eventuality (*moira* – what has befallen or fallen to one's lot)" (V. Sony, "Trial and Tragedies: The Literature of Unhappiness (A Model for Reading Narratives of Suffering)," *Comparative Literature*, 2007, 59(2): 119–39, at p. 132, note 21.

Chapter 5 Acts of reading, acts of judgment

1. Plato, *The Republic*, trans. Desmond Lee, 2nd edn, reprinted in Penguin Classics, 1987. Another edition that I have relied on is *Plato: Complete Works*, eds J. M. Cooper and D. S. Hutchinson. Indianapolis, IN: Hackett, 1997.
2. See H.-G. Gadamer, *Truth and Method*, trans. revised J. Weinsheimer and D. G. Marshall, 2nd revised edn. New York and London: Continuum, 2004 [1975], pp. 324–46. Gadamer's analysis of legal interpretation aims to show that every interpreter is part of the text he tries to apprehend – so that understanding a text always and necessarily involves an instance of "application," just as for the judge or legal interpreter wishing to understand/apply a piece of legislation or a contract. This argument is directed against those social scientists (specifically historians) who would deny the former by claiming that they are able to step outside the text and remain neutral and objective. However insightful Gadamer's arguments are in the context of historical interpretation (which I do not wish to question), Gadamer does not claim originality for his analysis of legal interpretation that remains conventional in many ways. This is why we must move beyond Gadamer's analysis of legal interpretation.
3. For the ways in which legal trials and the courtroom itself are meant and designed to generate performative experiences of this kind, see M. Ball, "The Play's the Thing: An Unscientific Reflection on Courts Under the Rubric of Theater," *Stanford Law Review*, 1975–6, 28: 81–115.
4. For an excellent analysis and development of this question, see J. Webber, "A Judicial Ethic for a Pluralistic Age," in Omid Payrow Shabani (ed.), *Multiculturalism and Law: A Critical Debate*. Cardiff: University of Wales Press, 2007, pp. 67–100.
5. James Boyd White compares the activity of reading with learning to live in a different city: the experience is of necessity somewhat different for everyone who does it, but there are nonetheless accounts of the text, as there are accounts of Paris or Chicago, that are illuminating and others that are less so. See J. B. White, "Reading Law and Reading Literature: Law as Language," in *Heracles' Bow: Essays on the Rhetoric and Poetics of the Law*. Madison, WI: University of Wisconsin Press, 1985, pp. 77–106, at p. 90.

6. About the concept and dangers of aestheticization, see W. Benjamin, "Critique of Violence," in P. Demetz (ed.), *Reflections: Essays, Aphorisms, Autobiographical Writings*, trans. E. Jephcott. New York: Schocken Books, 1986, pp. 277–300. About how to counteract these dangers by constantly keeping them in mind, see the incisive essay by R. Shusterman, "Aesthetic Ideology, Aesthetic Education, and Art's Value in Critique," in *Pragmatist Aesthetics: Living Beauty, Rethinking Art*, 2nd edn. Lanham, MD: Rowman & Littlefield, 2000, pp. 139–68.
7. See R. Posner, *Law and Literature: A Misunderstood Relation*. Cambridge, MA: Harvard University Press, 1988, reviewed by J. B. White, "What Can a Lawyer Learn from Literature?" *Harvard Law Review*, 1989, 102: 2014– 47.
8. Plato's relationship with poetry (and with all that stands for it against his philosophy) is immensely rich and features as a topic in many of his dialogues (e.g. *Phaedrus*, *Ion*, *Protagoras*, *Gorgias* . . .). However, I focus on the *Republic* which provides the most frontal and sustained attack. For a different analysis based on the *Symposium*, see F. Rokem "The First Encounter: Plato's *Symposium* and the Ancient Quarrel between Philosophy and Poetry," *Philosophers and Thespians. Thinking Performance*. Stanford CA: Stanford University Press, 2009, pp. 21–58.
9. See W. Jaeger, *Paideia*: *The Ideals of Greek Culture*, 3 vols, trans. Gilbert Highet. New York: Oxford University Press, 1933, pp. 43–4. See also E. Havelock, *Preface to Plato*. Oxford: Basil Blackwell, 1963.
10. See, for example, G. R. F. Ferrari, "Plato on Poetry," in G. A. Kennedy (ed.), *The Cambridge History of Literary Criticism*, vol. 1. Cambridge: Cambridge University Press, 1989, pp. 45–78; see also Havelock, *Preface to Plato*. See also the collection of essays J. Moravcsik and P. Temko (eds), *Plato on Beauty, Wisdom, and the Arts*. Totowa, NJ: Rowman & Littlefield, 1982. For a short general overview, see Elizabeth Amis, "Plato on Poetic Creativity," in R. Kraut (ed.), *The Cambridge Companion to Plato*. Cambridge: Cambridge University Press, 1992, pp. 338–64.
11. See M. Edmundson, *Literature Against Philosophy, Plato to Derrida: A Defence of Poetry*. Cambridge: Cambridge University Press, 1995. More recently, see Rokem, *Philosophers and Thespians*.
12. R. Nadaff, *Exiling the Poets: The Production of Censorship in Plato's Republic*. Chicago and London: University of Chicago Press, 2002.
13. Plato speaks of mimetic art in general, and I will make liberal use of terms such as literature, poetry, story-telling and so on, but my real concern is with tragedy, i.e. poetry that requires being acted and enacted, as well as received by an audience that engages with it.
14. Plato, *Republic*, 378e.
15. Ibid., 378b.
16. Ibid., 392.
17. There is perhaps a fundamental difference between Plato and the modern censor. Contrary to the modern moralist, Plato's objection is not based on prudish objections to the nature of certain words, acts, images, or language which would be offensive (immoral, blasphemous) *per se*. When he objects to the depiction of Kronos' physical castration of Ouranos, for instance, it is not to uphold religious orthodoxy, but rather to warn of potential transfers into children's own future lives by offering a "(bad) example."
18. In a fascinating aside, Plato contrasts the good doctor and the good judge: unlike the good doctor, who may know and experience illness in his own body, the good judge is a person to whom knowledge of wickedness must come late in life, not as a feature he perceives in his own character, but as an evil whose nature he has learned to discern in other people after long practice (Plato, *Republic*, 409).
19. Plato, *Republic*, 401c and 396e.
20. See H.-G. Gadamer, "Plato and the Poets," in *Dialogue and Dialectic: Eight Hermeneutical Studies on Plato*. New Haven, CT and London: Yale University Press, 1980, pp. 39–72, esp. pp. 64–5.

21. For the difference between the moral and the ethical, see A. MacIntyre, *After Virtue: A Study in Moral Theory*. Notre Dame, IN: University of Notre Dame Press, 1984, pp. 118–19 (arguing about Nietzsche's remark).
22. See, explicitly, Plato, *Republic*, 602b. Moreover, Plato attacks Homer on his capacity as "the first and foremost tragedian" (595c, 598d–601; also 607). As observed in *The Laws* (817b), Plato considers that tragedians and statesmen are engaged in the same "genre," but the former must be subordinated to the latter, whose tragedy is "the finest and best." See full citation in Chapter 1, section 1.5.
23. According to prominent ideas at the time, poets provided models of human excellence that one should study in order to become knowledgeable on matters of justice and injustice, good and bad, right or wrong. For one, the sophists claimed to be the heirs of Homer and Hesiod and grounded their educational curriculum in an incisive and deft interpretation of myths and poetry. See, for example, Plato's *Protagoras*. See also Jaeger, *Paideia*, and Havelock, *Preface to Plato*.
24. Furthermore, the *reality* that poets imitate is the phenomenological one, which in Plato's ontology holds a status inferior to that of the rational forms (*eidea*). This could explain Plato's often misunderstood dictum of poets being "at three removes from reality" (*Republic*, 597e). The theory of forms notwithstanding, Plato's present point is plain enough: poets *do not create, but only imitate*, and this remains so, irrespective of the ontological status of that which is imitated.
25. According to Plato, the expertise of the flute player on the sound of his own instrument may enable him to give directions to the flute maker on how to build a better flute. This is not so for the poets, who have neither the kind of knowledge that a maker of an object does, nor that of a competent practitioner (Plato, *Republic*, 602a).
26. Plato, *Republic*, 599c.
27. Ibid., Book 4.
28. Plato gives several reasons for bearing misfortune patiently (ibid., 604c): because we cannot tell in advance whether a given circumstance will turn out well or ill; because nothing is gained by impatience; because nothing in human life is of such great importance; and because grieving excessively prevents us from getting the help we need.
29. Judging from the modern entertainment industry, Plato's critique that art appeals to the lowest common denominator and to the easy and sentimental appears almost prophetic. Though well regarded, this is but an objection to "bad art," which needs to worry us in a measure inversely proportional to the seriousness with which we take these products. More worth considering is the idea that in its association with the emotional, art – all art – is somewhat opposed to rational thinking.
30. In Cooper's translation the last part reads, perhaps more accurately: "And [we] praise as a good poet [*agathon poieten*] the one who affects us most in this way" (Plato, *Republic*, 605d).
31. Plato, *Republic*, 606a–b.
32. Ibid.
33. Ibid., 606b, *a sensu contrario*
34. According to Plato, only Socrates among the whole audience seemed unaffected by this tragic spell. What Plato does not tell us, although he must have suspected it, is that Socrates may not have been able to entirely appreciate tragedy either. Socrates' relative "deafness" to *musike* (a deafness that one could never accuse Plato of experiencing) is suggestively described in the *Phaedo* as something of a longing in Socrates' life, and therefore missing.
35. Plato, *Republic*, 605d (trans. by Cooper).
36. See S. Halliwell, "Plato's Repudiation of the Tragic," in M. S. Silk (ed.), *Tragedy and the Tragic: Greek Theatre and Beyond*. Oxford: Clarendon Press, 1996, pp. 332–49.
37. For an enlightening study of this move, see Nadaff, *Exiling the Poets*.
38. See M. Detienne, *The Masters of Truth in Archaic Greece*, trans. Janet Lloyd. New York: Zone Books, 1996.

39. According to Gianni Vattimo, if the work of art is taken as the manifestation of a truth in such a sense, once I obtain that piece of information then the work no longer means anything to me. He refers to this as the error of thinking of the relationship between art and truth metaphysically; see G. Vattimo, *Art's Claim to Truth*, ed. Santiago Zabala, trans. Luca D'Isanto, New York: Columbia University Press, 2010, p. 153. For an excellent criticism of that kind of attitude towards literature, see White, "What Can a Lawyer Learn from Literature?"
40. In *Truth and Method*, Gadamer has explored the ontology of the work of art with the help of the concept of *Play* [*Spiel*]. According to Gadamer, the player knows that the play is not serious – this is why he plays – but at the same time "seriousness in playing is necessary to make the play wholly play. Someone who doesn't take the game seriously is a spoilsport" (*Truth and Method*, p. 102). Thus the "[p]lay fulfills its purpose only if the player loses himself in play" (ibid.), or, as Johann Huizinga puts it, in the concept of play "the difference between belief and pretense is dissolved" (cited in Gadamer, *Truth and Method*, p. 104). In this way, play transcends the behavior and consciousness of the individual player and becomes an activity that absorbs the player's full attention. Furthermore, the play is understood as a whole, not by the players performing their roles, but by the audience, in front of whom the play is presented (ibid., p 109).
41. Gadamer, *Truth and Method*, p. 112.
42. Richard A. Posner, "The Ethical Significance of Free Choice: A Reply to Professor West," *Harvard Law Review*, 1986, 99: 1431–48, at p. 1433.
43. Some of these arguments can be found, with a shift of focus towards democracy and political conflict, in my essay J. Etxabe, "What Do the Poets Know About Democracy: A Case Study in Law and Literature," in B. van Klink and S Taekema (eds), *Law and Method: Interdisciplinary Research into Law*. Tübingen: Mohr Siebeck, 2011, pp. 341–54.
44. K. Yoshino, "The City and the Poet," *Yale Law Journal*, 2005, 114: 1835–96, at pp. 1865–6.
45. C. Castoriadis, "The Greek Polis and the Creation of Democracy," in D. Ames Curtis (ed.), *Philosophy, Politics, Autonomy: Essays in Political Philosophy*. New York and Oxford: Oxford University Press, 1991, pp. 81–123, at p. 120.
46. This is what Statis Gourgouris refers to as literature's "explicitly constitutive performativity" (p. 8) and is linked to its distinctive ways of "thinking". See S. Gourgouris, *Does Literature Think? Literature as Theory for an Antimythical Era*. Stanford, CA: Stanford University Press, 2003, reviewed by C. Altieri in *Comparative Literature Studies*, 2004, 41: 436–40.
47. J. Gaakeer, "Law, Language and Literature: Their Interrelations in *Law and Literature*," in B. van Klink and S. Taekema (eds), *Law and Method: Interdisciplinary Research into Law*. Tübingen: Mohr Siebeck, 2011, pp. 215–35. For an exemplary kind of what a "humanistic reading" might bring forth to law, see G. Watt, *Equity Stirring: The Story of Justice Beyond Law*. Oxford and Portland, OR: Hart, 2009.
48. M. Sandel, "The Procedural Republic and the Unencumbered Self," *Political Theory*, 1984, 12: 81–96.
49. M. C. Nussbaum, *Poetic Justice: The Literary Imagination and Public Life*. Boston: Beacon Press, 1995, p. 54. See also Nussbaum, *Upheavals of Thought: The Intelligence of Emotions*. New York: Cambridge University Press, 2001.
50. There are also notable exceptions, for instance David Hume and his followers. For a recent reappraisal of Hume in relation to judgment and deliberation, see S. Krause, *Civil Passions: Moral Sentiment and Democratic Deliberation*. Princeton, NJ and Oxford: Princeton University Press, 2008.
51. Without being exhaustive one can refer to the works of Daniel Goleman, Jerome Bruner, and Carol Gilligan (moral and developmental psychology); Bill Miller and Clifford Geertz (cultural history and anthropology); Alasdair MacIntyre, John McDowell, and Martha Nussbaum (ethics and philosophy); Lynne Henderson, Martha Minow and Elisabeth Spellman (law and decision-making), among others.

52. The study of the social norms that regulate the appropriate display of emotions has been called "emotionology" by historians of emotion Peter Stearns and Carole Stearns in *American Cool: Constructing a Twentieth-Century Emotional Style*. New York: New York University Press, 1994. For "emotionology" applied to the judicial context, see M. L. Schuster and A. Propen, "Degrees of Emotion: Judicial Responses to Victim Impact Statements," *Law, Culture and the Humanities*, 2010, 6: 75–104.
53. Antonio Damasio (in *Descartes' Error: Emotion, Reason, and the Human Brain*. New York: Putnam, 1994), explained in Clifford Geertz, *Available Light*. Princeton, NJ: Princeton University Press, 2000, pp. 213–14. For a recent review on the research and literature on emotions, see Sharon S. Krause, 'Recent Alternatives to Rationalism', in *Civil Passions: Moral Sentiment and Democratic Deliberation*. Princeton, NJ and Oxford: Princeton University Press, 2008, pp. 48–76.
54. Geertz, *Available Light*, p. 213.
55. L. Dahlberg, "Emotional Tropes in the Courtroom: On Representation of Affect and Emotion in Legal Court Proceedings," *Law and Humanities*, 2009, 3(2): 175–205, at p. 204. Dahlberg finds that judges, legal parties, and other legal actors often refrain from expressing certain emotions, even though these can "show through: in posture, glances, timbre of voice, silences, flushes, crying, outbursts of laughter, and the smell of sweat" (ibid., p. 183). These affects and emotions do not often get into the transcripts of the trial and the decisions of judges, Dahlberg argues, not because they were not there to begin with, but because they have been "silenced" and rendered invisible "as imperceptible sediments of human life" (ibid., p. 184).
56. For a well-documented survey of the study of law and emotions, with extensive bibliography, see Terry A. Maroney, "Law and Emotion: A Proposed Taxonomy of an Emerging Field," *Law and Human Behavior*, 2006, 30(2): 119–42.
57. For example, L. Henderson, "Legality and Empathy," *Michigan Law Review*, 1986–7, 85: 1574–653. She defines empathy as a form of affective as well as cognitive elements, comprising: (1) *feeling* the emotion of another; (2) *understanding* it; and (3) *acting* upon it (ibid., p. 1579). Here I only refer to the second of these.
58. J. B. White, *Living Speech: Resisting the Empire of Force*. Princeton, NJ and Oxford: Princeton University Press, 2006, p. 90.
59. Schuster and Propen, "Degrees of Emotion."
60. According to Walter Kaufmann, Aristotle's theory of *katharsis* might have been developed precisely to meet this point. See W. Kaufmann, *Tragedy and Philosophy*. Princeton, NJ: Princeton University Press, 1979, p. 22.
61. For a classic but still excellent account of Aristotle's theory of *katharsis*, see P. Laín Entralgo, *La Curación por la Palabra en la Antigüedad Clásica*. Madrid: Revista de Occidente, 1958, esp. pp. 261–333; there is an English translation published by Yale University Press (1970). In English, the classical work is Gerald Else's monumental *Aristotle's Poetics: The Argument*. Cambridge, MA: Harvard University Press, 1957. For a more recent appraisal, see Amélie Oksenberg Rorty (ed.), *Essays on Aristotle's Poetics*. Princeton, NJ: Princeton University Press, 1992.
62. For an argument along these lines, see J. Lear, "Katharsis," in Oksenberg Rorty, *Essays on Aristotle's Poetics*, pp. 315–40.
63. As Aristotle puts it, the quality of tragedy can be gauged by reading it aloud (*Poetics*, 1462–a8).
64. This is so because art speaks of the general or of what might have happened, whereas history speaks of the particular or of what did happen (*Poetics*, 1451b).
65. M. Nussbaum, *Hiding From Humanity: Disgust, Shame, and the Law*. Princeton, NJ: Princeton University Press, 2004; see, however, W. I. Miller, *Anatomy of Disgust*. Cambridge, MA: Harvard University Press, 1997 (arguing that disgust fulfills important societal and moral, including democratizing, functions).

66. M. Dubber, *The Sense of Justice: Empathy in Law and Punishment*. New York: New York University Press, 2006; cf. W. I. Miller, *Eye for an Eye*. New York: Cambridge University Press, 2006 (explaining that vengeance is a deeply ingrained habit of mind and offers a measure of justice).
67. Interestingly, Lynne Henderson argues that neither of these responses rely on empathy, but actually disavow it, for emotional responses based solely on stereotypy and irrational prejudice block the ability to understand ("Legality and Empathy," p. 1641).
68. D. Welch, "Ruling with the Heart: Emotion-Based Public Policy," *Southern California Interdisciplinary Law Journal*, 1997, 6: 55–87, at p. 76.
69. Yoshino, "The City and the Poet," p. 1883.
70. Ibid.
71. Yoshino, who advocates the adoption of a Platonic solution, rejects the admissibility of victim impact statements in cases of capital trial because "the function of sentencing is to permit the defendant to tell her story untrammeled by other voices" (ibid., p. 1884). See also K. Bilz, "We Don't Want to Hear it: Psychology, Literature and the Narrative Model of Judging," *University of Illinois Law Review*, 2010, 2: 101–55 (arguing for an "exclusionary model" of judging, where the law limits on normative grounds the sort of stories parties are allowed to tell).
72. S. Bandes, "Empathy, Narrative, and Victim Impact Statements," *University of Chicago Law Review*, 1996, 63: 362–412.
73. See *Booth* v. *Maryland* 482 U.S. 496 (1987) (opinion written by Justice Powell), overruled by *Payne* v. *Tennessee*, 501 U.S. 808 (1991).
74. The "reasonable man" has been rightly criticized as tending to reproduce the mental and socio-economic assets of the white/male/middle-aged/upper-class suburbanite; see C. MacKinnon, *Feminism Unmodified: Discourses on Life and Law*. Cambridge, MA: Harvard University Press, 1987. For an excellent analysis, see M. Minow, "Foreword: Justice Engendered," *Harvard Law Review*, 1987–8, 101: 10–95.
75. R. West, "Economic Man and Literary Woman: One Contrast," in *Narrative, Authority, and Law*. Ann Arbor, MI: University of Michigan Press, 1993, pp. 251–63.
76. Nussbaum, *Poetic Justice*.
77. Does talking about the activity of judging not involve certain homogeneity? Not in the same way. To be able to delineate the contours of the activity of judging – and to contrast it with others, e.g. playing the piano or swimming – does not mean that there are not potentially infinite contrasting styles, personalities, and philosophies for performing it proficiently, like there are multiple satisfactory, and even contrasting, ways of swimming or playing the piano.
78. Despite my overall appreciation of Nussbaum's project, I wonder whether her judicious reader goes too far in the direction of denaturalizing the gripping emotional experience that both Plato and Aristotle observed is proper to tragedy (and which eluded Socrates). See also note 34.
79. See, for example, D. Kennedy, "Freedom and Constraint in Adjudication: A Critical Phenomenology," *Journal of Legal Education*, 1986, 36: 518–62.
80. Martha Minow and Elizabeth Spelman propose several criteria of judicial excellence aimed at heightening the judge's sensitivity to the human beings affected by the decision; see M. Minow and E. Spelman, "Passion for Justice," *Cardozo Law Review*, 1988, 10: 37–76. Although I agree mostly with their suggestions – e.g. that the judge should take the perspective of all parties before the decision, and develop the kind of arguments that the party whose position he rejects would consider fair – their method for reaching at them is liable to the criticism raised above.
81. This effect is altogether different from Bertold Brecht's alienation-effect (*Verfremdungseffect*), which is meant to make the familiar strange and push the audience away from the theatricality of the experience. In contrast, here the audience is still implicated with the dramatic

action and shares in the experience of the theater, even though it distances itself from one-sided and facile identifications. On Brecht's views on theater, see Rokem, *Philosophers and Thespians*, chapters 4 and 5.

82. See S. Goldhill, "The Audience on the Stage: Rhetoric, Emotion, and Judgment in Sophoclean Theatre," in S. Goldhill and E. Hall (eds), *Sophocles and the Greek Tradition*. Cambridge: Cambridge University Press, 2009, pp. 27–47.
83. For further elaboration of what I have elsewhere labeled a "space of silence," see Etxabe, "What Do the Poets Know About Democracy?" esp. pp. 349–52.
84. All characters appeal to the citizens at one point of another of the drama: Ismene to justify her passivity, Creon his decree, Antigone her disobedience, and Haemon his defense of Antigone.
85. To be able to empathize with the plights of the tragic characters does not mean that we feel as they do, because the feeling of pity for those who suffer is different from the suffering of those we pity. In fact, the content of our empathy does not properly target our own feelings, but our understanding of theirs.
86. See Dahlberg, "Emotional Tropes," finding many points of intersection between the courtroom and the stage. Concerning imagination, Hannah Arendt, following Kant, defines it as the faculty of making present or bringing to mind what is absent (H. Arendt, *Lectures on Kant's Political Philosophy*, ed. Ronald Beiner. Chicago: University of Chicago Press, 1992.
87. For a case in which a single appellate judge (without the proper quorum and without following procedure) decided to order a blood transfusion against the patient's will in order to preserve her life, see *Application of the President and Directors of Georgetown College, Inc.* 331 F.2d 1010 (D.C. Cir. 1964), as analyzed by J. B. White, *The Legal Imagination: Studies in the Nature of Legal Thought and Expression*. Boston: Little, Brown, 1973, pp. 84–9. I introduce this case here merely as an illustration, but will elaborate on it further in the closing chapter, after we speak about the temporal motions of judgment.
88. See note 87.
89. *Re A (Children) (Conjoined Twins: Surgical Separation)* [2001] Fam 147, Court of Appeal.
90. The news report about the case, as well as the Lord Justice's unprecedented public statement for the BBC, can be accessed in http://news.bbc.co.uk/2/hi/health/937586.stm.
91. For a well-argued critique of the way Lord Justice Ward framed and articulated both the issue and his decision, see G. Watt, "The Case of Conjoined Twins: Medical Dilemma in Law and Literature," in Daniela Carpi (ed.), *Bioethics and Biolaw Through Literature*. Berlin and New York: De Gruyter, 2011, pp. 93–107.

Chapter 6 *Antigone*, Part III: Realizations

1. The word used by Teiresias is *nosei* (malady, illness), which some translate as plague (usually *miasma* – as Creon will say in 1042–4, though in order to deny it). Yet Teiresias' description is not one of a general plague like in *Oedipus Tyrannos*, but rather one of impurity and desecration, which is why I prefer to render it as a "defilement" affecting the city's altars and communication with the gods.
2. I skip here any reference to lines 1080–3, the authenticity and understanding of which are disputed among scholars.
3. See K. Reinhardt, *Sophocles*, trans. H. Harvey and D. Harvey. New York: Harper & Row, 1979, pp. 87 and ff.
4. About the depiction of Teiresias in the mythological tradition, see C. García Gual, "Tiresias o el Adivino como Mediador," *Emérita*, 1975, 43: 107–32.
5. Although arguments about appearance are largely speculative, Teiresias' overall presence in the *Antigone* must have been more authoritative, for example, than in Euripides' *Bacchae*.
6. For example, C. Bowra, *Sophoclean Tragedy*. Oxford: Clarendon Press, 1944, p. 107.

7. About this distinction, see R. Flacelière, *Greek Oracles*, trans. D. Garman. London: Elek Book, 1965.
8. J. Bottéro, "Symptômes, Signes, Écritures en Mésopotamie Ancienne," in J. P. Vernant et al. (eds), *Divination et Rationalité*. Paris: Seuil, 1974, pp. 70–197.
9. J. D. Mikalson, *Honor Thy Gods: Popular Religion in Greek Tragedy*. Chapel Hill, NC: University of North Caroline Press, 1991, p. 93.
10. Bottéro, "Symtômes," p. 132 (my translation). The comparison is not coincidental, as seers might be seen as doctors of ritual and religion.
11. Although seers and soothsayers still played an important role in Athenian social and political life during the fifth century, a growing attitude of skepticism had taken over the blind confidence of the old days. The proliferation of rogues, frauds, and unscrupulous charlatans may have contributed to this shift (Flacelière, *Greek Oracles*, pp. 61–6).
12. Euripides, *Helen*, 744–7 (trans. by Mikalson, *Honor Thy Gods*, p. 96).
13. The statement *per se* involves neither impiety nor religious skepticism. The immediately following sentence ("not for the dread of *that* defilement [*oud' hôs miasma touto*]") allows us to infer that, had the eagles transported Polyneices' remains to Zeus' throne, such occurrence would in principle qualify as "pollution." But Creon does not believe in actual pollution because he doubts the veracity of the seer's account.
14. *Eu gar oid' hoti theous miainein outis anthrôpôn sthenei.*
15. B. Knox, *The Heroic Temper: Studies in Sophoclean Tragedy*. Berkeley, CA and Los Angeles: University of California Press, 1964, pp. 108–9.
16. R. Jebb (trans. and ed.), *Sophocles. The Plays and Fragments. Part 3: Antigone*. Cambridge: Cambridge University Press, 1891, pp. 186–7, citing Euripides, *Heracles* (1232); cf. J. C. Kamerbeek (ed.), *The Plays of Sophocles with Commentaries. Part 3: The Antigone*. Leiden: Brill, 1978, p. 178.
17. G. Steiner, *Antigones*. Oxford: Clarendon Press, 1984, p. 275 (resuscitating the ideas first expressed by Lewis Campbell in his edition of *Antigone*, 1879, v. 1).
18. Despite his sympathy for the man, even Jebb admits that Creon's "religious sense is temporarily confused by his anger" (p. 187).
19. Perhaps Creon intends to argue solely that the gods are above mundane trifles (i.e. the spurious motives and intrigues of the seer), but the distance is easily crossed from a world where the gods are not so concerned to another in which they simply *don't care*.
20. Cf. Bushnell, who argues that Teiresias is now possessed with the truth of Apollo and is answerable to him alone (R. Bushnell, "Speech and Authority: *Antigone*," in *Prophesying Tragedy: Sign and Voice in Sophocles' Theban Plays*. Ithaca, NY: Cornell University Press, 1988, pp. 55 and 60.
21. Reinhardt, *Sophocles*, p. 89.
22. One may speculate about the reasons why Teiresias did not reveal this earlier. One possible explanation is that seers show reluctance to speak in front of the person affected by their prophecies, either because it is cruel (e.g. Teiresias in front of Oedipus in *Oedipus Tyrannus* (324 ff.); Menoeceus in Euripides' *Phoenician Women* (891–5)), or else because they fear for their own physical safety. Another, more suggestive, interpretation is that the future elicited by divination presents an array of undifferentiated possibilities which are individuated only by the subsequent choices of the person affected, just as the prognosis of a doctor varies depending on the level of compliance of the patient. Only after Creon refuses to listen does the worst case scenario begin actually to materialize. From the failure of the signs Teiresias could perceive that Creon was on the edge of a precipice, but it is Creon's current behavior which pushes him over it.
23. Steiner, *Antigones*, p. 287.
24. Anaximander, A 9 (as read in Werner Jaeger, *The Theology of the Early Greek Philosophers*, trans. E. Robinson. Eugene, OR: Wipf & Stock, 2003, pp. 34–7). Other famous interpretations of Anaximander's fragment include Nietzsche and Heidegger. See recently J. de Ville,

"Rethinking the Notion of a 'Higher Law': Heidegger and Derrida on the Anaximander Fragment," *Law and Critique*, 2009, 20: 59–78.

25. Solon believed that time would always discover and set right an act of injustice, even without human cooperation, as a norm inherent in reality; see W. Jaeger, *The Theology of the Early Greek Philosophers*, p. 35 with notes.
26. H. D. F. Kitto, *Form and Meaning in Drama*. London: Metheun, 1964, p. 174; Reinhardt, *Sophocles*, p. 90; cf. Steiner, *Antigones*, pp. 287–9. About the relation between the Erinyes and Dike, consider these words by Werner Jaeger: "Anaximander's symbolic interpretation of the cosmic process as a trial or legal contest (*dikē*) is also a forerunner, to which Heraclitus himself reverts when, for instance, he writes: 'The sun will not overstep his measures; for otherwise the Erinyes, Dike's deputies, will find him out' (B 94). Here Dike serves as an embodiment of the inviolable order of nature" (Jaeger, *Early Philosophers*, pp. 115–16). There is also a literary precedent of this usage in the *Iliad*, 19.418.
27. *Antidosis* was an Athenian legal procedure concerning the exchange of estates between two parties. When a wealthy person was tasked with the obligation to perform a public liturgy he could nominate a richer man to take his place. If this second man disagreed, their entire estates would be exchanged.
28. Bowra, *Sophoclean Tragedy*, p. 110; see also Bushnell, *Prophesying Tragedy*, p. 62.
29. See, paradigmatically, Knox (*The Heroic Temper*, pp. 74–5 and pp. 109–10), who emphasizes the "uniqueness" of such a reversal in Sophoclean drama. For a view qualifying this assertion, see A. Machin, *Cohérence et Continuité dans le Théâtre de Sophocle*. Québec: Serge Fleury, 1981, pp. 303–7.
30. M. Griffith (ed.), *Sophocles: Antigone*. Cambridge: Cambridge University Press, 1999, at p. 310.
31. Bowra, *Sophoclean Tragedy*, p. 110.
32. Bushnell, *Prophesying Tragedy*, p. 61.
33. According to Jebb, p. 98, these "established laws" refer to Antigone's "unwritten laws" [*agrapta nomima*]; cf. Gibbons and Segal, p. 166.
34. Oudemans and Lardinois argue that Creon refers to Teiresias' "cosmic laws" (T. C. W. Oudemans and A. P. M. H. Lardinois, *Tragic Ambiguity: Anthropology, Philosophy and Sophocles' Antigone*. Leiden: E. J. Brill, 1987, p. 198).
35. Elizabeth van Nes Ditmars, *Sophocles' Antigone: Lyric Shape and Meaning*. Pisa: Giardani Editori, 1992, p. 155.
36. A. Henrichs, "Between Country and City: Cultic Dimensions of Dionysus in Athens and Attica," in M. Griffith and D. Mastronarde (eds), *Cabinet of the Muses*. Atlanta, GA: Scholars Press, 1990, pp. 257–8.
37. For a sobering account, see R. Friedrich, "Everything to Do with Dionysos? Ritualism, the Dionysiac, and the Tragic," in M. S. Silk (ed.), *Tragedy and the Tragic: Greek Theatre and Beyond*. Oxford: Clarendon Press, 1996, pp. 257–83. Friedrich argues that "the one-sidedly primitivist, irrationalist, and savage image of Dionysos in many modern theories about him [are] academic constructs deriving ultimately from a poetic construct – namely Euripides' representation of Dionysos and maenadism in the Bacchae" (p. 259).
38. Heinrichs, "Between Country and City."
39. See A. Heinrichs, "Loss of Self, Suffering, Violence: The Modern View of Dionysus from Nietzsche to Girard," *Harvard Studies in Classical Philology*, 1984, 88: 205–40.
40. I. Errandonea, *Sófocles y la Personalidad de sus Coros*. Madrid: Moneda y Cambio, 1970, p. 106; see also A. Henrichs, "Why Should I Dance? Choral Self-Referentiality in Greek Tragedy," *ARION*, 1994–5, 3(1): 56-111, at p. 73.
41. Ditmars, *Sophocles' Antigone*, p. 157.
42. See R. W. B. Burton, *The Chorus in Sophocles' Tragedies*. Oxford: Clarendon Press, p. 132.
43. Winnington-Ingram reads sinister hints in these allusions to the murky light of the torches and the fire-breathing stars (R. P. Winnington-Ingram, *Sophocles: An Interpretation*.

Cambridge: Cambridge University Press, pp. 113–14); but see Charles Segal, who notes that this fire breathed by the stars "is not the totally destructive fire which Polyneices brings against his city" (C. Segal, *Tragedy and Civilization: An Interpretation of Sophocles*. Cambridge, MA: Harvard University Press, 1981, p. 204).

44. There are those who argue that Dionysus in fact "appears" and delivers destruction (e.g. R. Seaford, "Something to Do with Dionysos – Tragedy and the Dionysiac: Response to Friedrich," in M. S. Silk (ed.), *Tragedy and the Tragic: Greek Theatre and Beyond*. Oxford: Clarendon Press, 1996, pp. 284–94; see also Winnington-Ingram, *Sophocles: An Introduction*). Most commentators, however, deny that the result can be attributed to the god: see, for example, R. Burton, *The Chorus in Sophocles' Tragedies*; R. F. Goheen, *The Imagery of Sophocles' Antigone: A Study of Poetic Language and Structure*. Princeton, NJ: Princeton University Press, 1951; Oudemans and Lardinois, *Tragic Ambiguity*; N. Loraux, *The Mourning Voice: An Essay on Greek Tragedy*. Ithaca, NY and London: Cornell University Press, 2002. Such an epiphany would be contrary to the human focus of the Sophoclean stage, where human beings and not gods are ultimately responsible.
45. For different interpretations about the nature of this catharsis, see S. Scullion, "Dionysus and Katharsis in the *Antigone*," *Classical Antiquity*, 1998, 17(1): 96–122; cf. Loraux, *The Mourning Voice*, pp. 92–3.
46. Burton, *The Chorus in Sophocles' Tragedies*, p. 134; Errandonea, *Sófocles y la Personalidad de sus Coros*, p. 107; see also M. Nussbaum, "Sophocles' Antigone: Conflict, Vision, and Simplification," *The Fragility of Goodness: Luck and Ethics in Greek Tragedy and Philosophy*, rev. edn. New York: Cambridge University Press, 2001, p. 82.
47. Burton, *The Chorus in Sophocles' Tragedies*, p. 133.
48. Griffith, *Sophocles: Antigone*, p. 326.
49. The most detailed and attentive analysis is that of Ioannis Panoussis in *Crainte et Violence dans le Théâtre de Sophocle*. Villeneuve d'Ascq: Presses Universitaires du Septentrion, 2002. For a sociologically oriented reading of suicide in drama, see Elise P. Garrison, *Groaning Tears: Ethical and Dramatic Aspects of Suicide in Greek Tragedy*, Leiden: E. J. Brill, 1995; See also, Jan Kott "Why Did Antigone Kill Herself?" *New Theater Quarterly*, 1993, 9(34): 107–10, contrasting Antigone with other protagonists from the Greeks to Shakespeare and Racine.
50. G. Else, *The Madness of Antigone*. Heidelberg: Carl Winter Universitätsverlag, 1976, p. 86.
51. See Panoussis, *Crainte et Violence*, p. 144.
52. Some argue that she at least has the solace in knowing that she has done the right thing by her loved ones, and that they, at least, will understand her action and welcome her by their side (897–9). But this is little consolation for one who thought her action was absolutely right in the world of the living as well.
53. Panoussis, *Crainte et Violence*.
54. For a good discussion of the implications of the various readings suggested, see Griffith, *Sophocles: Antigone*, pp. 336–7.
55. Seth Benardete argues that Creon's questions are calculated to enrage Haemon (S. Benardete, *Sacred Transgressions: A Reading of Sophocles' Antigone*. South Bend, IN: St Augustine's Press, 1999, p. 138). This appears inconsistent with Creon's pleading in supplication.
56. Jebb; Garrison, *Groaning Tears*; see also G. H. Gellie, "*Antigone*," in *Sophocles: A Reading*. Melbourne: Melbourne University Press, 1972, pp. 29–52, at p. 51. Gellie speaks of the "remorse," "self-disgust," and "shame" that is to be expected in the son we have met earlier in the play. The problem is, in my view, that Haemon is *not* the son we met earlier in the play.
57. Panoussis, *Crainte et Violence*, p. 141 and notes.
58. Winnington-Ingram, *Sophocles: An interpretation*, p. 94.
59. Haemon still has his mother Eurydice to count on, but he does not seem to consider her here.
60. Teiresias praises good counsel [*eubolia*] as the best of all possessions, in order to denounce its lack in Creon.

61. Little is known about Megareus. In Aeschylus' *Seven Against Thebes* he is one of the warriors keeping one of the Seven Gates, who must either die and pay the earth for his nurture, or capture two men and adorn his father's house with the spoils (474–9). In Euripides' *Phoenicians* (930–1018), one of Creon's sons must be sacrificed to appease Ares for the slayer of the dragon, and since Haemon is married, it falls upon the other son, Menoeceus, who kills himself against his father's will. According to Paul Mazon there is no reason to identify Megareus with Menoeceus (see also Kamerbeek, *The Plays of Sophocles*; cf. Jebb, *Sophocles*, referencing Statitus, *The Thebaid*, 10.589–782). All we know for certain is that Megareus is dead, and that Eurydice laments his death together with that of Haemon.
62. I resist translating *peprômenês* as "fated" (Lloyd-Jones) or "destined" (Jebb), because the agency of these happenings is unclear and, therefore, better left under-determined. This under-determination is well expressed by the Chorus in the sentence, "the future rests where or with whom it should rest" (1334–5) and by Creon, when he responds that he does not know what (lot/fate) struck him so hard (1345–6).
63. Griffith, *Sophocles: Antigone*, p. 342.
64. This is not incompatible with fearing that we, too, can become victims of tragedy. As the Chorus had sung in the second choral ode, the fact that anyone can become a victim of disaster does not eliminate the possibility of (and need for) moral judgments.
65. Griffith, *Sophocles: Antigone*, p. 352, explains that the words *episkeptô/omai* and *episkepsis* (cf. 1312–13) are legal terms in Athens for the first stage of the prosecution.
66. The messenger refers to Eurydice in her twofold status as "wife" [*gunê*] and "true mother" [*pammêtôr*] (1282).
67. For an excellent article explaining the significance of the Solonian injunction for tragedy, see Vivasvan Sony, "Trials and Tragedies: The Literature of Unhappiness (A Model for Reading Narratives of Suffering)," in *Comparative Literature*, 2007, 59(2): 119–39.

Chapter 7 The temporalities of judgment: Antigone and law

1. For this conception of democracy, see S. Goldhill, "Civic Ideology and the Problem of Difference: The Politics of Aeschylean Tragedy, Once Again," *Journal of Hellenic Studies*, 2000, 120: 34–56. Antigone may appeal to *Themis* or to other ancient forms of justice, but her position is not reactionary or backward looking, for it opens new forms of legal and political participation (see K. Tindemans, "Antigone and the Law: Legal Theory and the Ambiguities," in S.E. Wilmer and Audrone Zukauskaite (eds), *Interrogating Antigone in Postmodern Philosophy and Criticism*. Oxford: Oxford University Press, 2010, pp. 185–96; see also J. Frank, "The Antigone's Law," *Law, Culture, and the Humanities*, 2006, 2: 336–40). For a different view of Antigone as defending aristocratic, i.e. non-democratic, ideals, see B. Honig, "Antigone's Laments, Creon's Grief: Mourning, Membership, and the Politics of Exception," *Political Theory*, 2009, 37(1): 5–43.
2. V. Rosivach, "Autochthony and the Athenians," *Classical Quarterly*, 1987, 37(2): 294–306; Nicole Loraux, *The Invention of Athens: The Funeral Oration in the Classical City*, trans. Alan Sheridan. Cambridge, MA: Harvard University Press, 1986.
3. Aristotle, *Rhetorics*, 1373b3 and 1375b.
4. Loraux, *The Invention of Athens*.
5. Tindemans, "Antigone and the Law", p. 192.
6. F. Ost, *Antigone Voilée*. Brussels: Larcier, 2004.
7. H. Arendt, *The Promise of Politics*. New York: Schocken Books, 2005, pp. 111–12. Impossible things can and do happen, Arendt argues, but they require the mediation of human agency and action (pp. 113–14).
8. G. Steiner, *Antigones*. Oxford: Clarendon Press, 1984. For a recent review of the multiple literary metamorphoses of Antigone in the second half of the twentieth century, see Moira

Fradinger, "Nomadic Antigone," in F. Söderbäck (ed.), *Feminist Readings of Antigone*. New York: SUNY Press, 2010.

9. This problematic is well analyzed by J. Butler, *Antigone's Claim: Kinship between Life and Death*. New York: Columbia University Press, 2000.
10. F. Ost, *Raconter la Loi*. Paris: Odile Jacob, 2004, pp. 196–9.
11. Tindemans, "*Antigone* and the Law," p. 187.
12. K. Beushausen, "Dangerous Fracture: Undermining the Order of the Law in Sophocles' *Antigone*," *Mosaic*, 2008, 41(3): 15–30, at p. 22 (the internal citations are to Benjamin's "Critique of Violence").
13. Ibid.
14. Among many, see J. Rancière, *Disagreement: Politics and Philosophy*, trans. Julie Rose. Minneapolis, MN and London: University of Minnesota Press, 1999.
15. W. Benjamin, "Critique of Violence," in P. Demetz (ed.), *Reflections: Essays, Aphorisms, Autobiographical Writings*, trans. E. Jephcott. New York: Schocken Books, 1986, pp. 277–300. Writing several centuries earlier, Jewish codifier and mystic Joseph Caro made a similar observation concerning the distinction between law-creating "strong" forces and law-maintaining "weak" forces (see R. Cover, "The Supreme Court 1982 Terms – Foreword: Nomos and Narrative," *Harvard Law Review*, 1983, 97: 4–68, at p. 12).
16. These perceptions do not remain invariable: Ismene ends up accepting Antigone's choice and the elders, after Teiresias' explanations, argue for Antigone's release and the burial of Polyneices.
17. See C. Douzinas and R. Warrington, "Antigone's *Dike*," in *Justice Miscarried: Ethics, Aesthetics and the Law*. Hemel Hempstead: Harvester Wheatsheaf, 1994, pp. 25–92, especially pp. 79–80.
18. See P. Nonet, "Antigone's Law," *Law, Culture and the Humanities*, 2006, 2: 314–35.
19. These two stages (of commitment and disengagement) are two distinct and logically differentiated processes, even though in Antigone's case they happen simultaneously. Antigone's commitment to burying her brother entails, at the same time, a disengagement from the order of Creon.
20. Here we are reminded of Oliver Wendell Holmes' figure of the "bad man," which has sufficient knowledge of the law so that he can avoid being affected negatively (O. Wendell Holmes Jr, "The Path of the Law," in *Collected Legal Papers*. New York: Harcourt Brace, 1920, pp.167–202, originally published in 1897). The difference between Holmes' "bad man" and Antigone is that she does not want to avoid the negative consequences, but to endure them and to make them known to the public.
21. H. L. A. Hart, *The Concept of Law*, 2nd edn. Oxford: Oxford University Press, 1994.
22. This is intriguing because Ismene asks forgiveness from the dead, suggesting that she too feels the pull of the norm that binds her to burying them, and further, that the course followed by Antigone expresses proper love for her family.
23. As explained in Chapter 1, objectification is the process of positing an external "object of law" (often in the form of a legal text) to which the individual owes obedience as a "faithful other." Once the norm is objectified, it becomes part of the language-games that can be played with the law, enabling different actors to reinterpret and employ it in other circumstances and contexts.
24. As Phillippe Nonet comments on this: "since this law 'always ever lives, and no one knows whence it came to light,' it cannot be thought to *proceed from* any determinate god or groups of gods, either above or below" (Nonet, "Antigone's Law," p. 327, emphasis in the original).
25. Homer, *The Iliad*, Book 24.
26. See page 209, note 86.
27. This second family would not be extinguished if some of its members were to die (the death of a spouse could be cured by marriage, the death of a child by a new birth), but the death of the last male in the line means the extinction of the family line, which is an entirely different situation and demands special reverence. For the full argument, see also J. Etxabe, "Antigone's *Nomos*," *Animus: The Canadian Journal of Philosophy and Humanities*, 2009, 13: 60–73.

28. Sometimes it has been objected that Antigone's argument cannot constitute a law in a proper sense, because it seems to be exhausted in its very utterance (the problem is well stated by J. Butler, *Antigone's Claim: Kinship Between Life and Death*. New York: Columbia University Press, 2000, p. 10). Nevertheless, the fact that Antigone may use this argument just this once does not mean that her *nomos* cannot apply in other cases as well. This possibility is in fact demonstrated by the use of Intaphernes' wife in Herodotus' story (Herodotus, 3.119), who was able to rely on it, and with great success, in a very different context.
29. To be sure, this is only half of the equation: the rest lies on those on whose door the legal claim is presented, namely on the shoulders and interpretations of the citizens who must accept such a claim if the law is to continue to live.
30. For a brilliant analysis of how the Declaration of Independence accomplishes this in its very performance, see James Boyd White, *When Words Lose Their Meaning: Constitutions and Reconstitutions of Language, Character, and Community*. Chicago: University of Chicago Press, 1984.
31. See Jill Frank, "The Antigone's Law," (making a distinction between "the law of Antigone" and "the *Antigone*'s law").
32. See E. Harris, "Antigone the Lawyer, or the Ambiguities of Nomos," in E. Harris and L. Rubinstein (eds), *The Law and the Courts in Ancient Greece*. London: Duckworth, 2004, pp. 19–56; see also W. B. Tyrrell and L. J. Bennett, *Recapturing Sophocles' Antigone*. Lanham, MD: Rowman & Littlefield, 1998.
33. Thucydides, 1.138.
34. Beushausen, "Dangerous Fracture," p. 17.
35. Frank, "The Antigone's Law," p. 340 (also mentioning Teiresias, the Chorus, and Haemon).
36. For an analysis of the decree's trajectory, see J. Fletcher, "Citing the Law in Sophocles' *Antigone*," *Mosaic*, 2008, 41(3): 79–96.
37. H. Foley, "Tragedy and Democratic Ideology: The Case of Sophocles' *Antigone*," in Barbara Goff (ed.), *History, Tragedy, Theory: Dialogues on Athenian Drama*. Austin, TX: University of Texas Press, 1995, p. 144. The comparison between these three institutions is not accidental. As Simon Goldhill argues, "the theatre, the law-court and the assembly [are] the three great institutions for the display of *logoi* in the city of words" (Goldhill, "Civic Ideology and the Problem of Difference," p. 35).
38. Foley, "Tragedy and Democratic Ideology," p. 145.
39. For a phenomenological distinction between space and time, see H. Bergson, *Time and Free Will: An Essay on the Immediate Data of Consciousness*, trans. F. L. Pogson. New York: Dover, 2001 [1913]. See, further, *La Pensée et le Mouvant*. Geneva: Albert Skira, 1946. For a general representation of time in tragedy, see J. de Romilly, *Time in Greek Tragedy*. Ithaca, NY: Cornell University Press, 1968.
40. Clearly, by temporality I do not mean the historical chronology of events or the cosmological movement of the planets. The time I have in mind is a *narrative motion* through and through (cf. P. Ricœur, *Time and Narrative*, 3 vols, trans. K. Blamey and D. Pellauer. Chicago: University of Chicago Press, 1988). For the interconnections of time and law, see François Ost, *Le Temps du Droit*. Paris: Odile Jacob, 1999.
41. See, however, the moment of incommensurability, which I analyze within the temporality of *contention*.
42. I have already analyzed this in Chapter 5 within the spatial relationship I called "embodiment." Now I add a temporal dimension to it, which shows the outward trajectory of the former relationship.
43. K. Reinhardt, *Sophocles*. New York: Harper & Row, 1979, p. 89.
44. In Chapter 5 we saw that this generates a "mediation" with the audience.
45. This is what Gadamer refers to as the question of "application," in *Truth and Method*, 2nd revised edn, trans. Joel Weinsheimer and Donald G. Marshall. New York: Continuum, 2004 [1975].

46. See *Application of the President and Directors of Georgetown College, Inc.* 331 F. 2d 1010 (D.C. Cir 1964). For a highly informative article on the evolution of the jurisprudence since *Georgetown* and the problems of litigation in the US context, see Charles H. Baron, "Blood Transfusions, Jehovah's Witnesses, and the American Patients' Rights Movement," in Alice Maniatis, Phillipe van der Linden, and Jean-François Hardy (eds), *Alternatives to Blood Transfusion Medicine*. Chichester: Wiley-Blackwell, 2010, pp. 529–53.
47. Ibid., p. 530.
48. According to Baron, the decision of Judge Wright in *Georgetown* (to order the blood transfusion against the patient's expressed wishes) seems ultimately to have been based on a certain inability to understand her reasons and treating them as irrational: believing that Mrs Jones' life was being thrown away for no good reason, he considered that the extreme situation she faced made her somewhat less than competent to decide for herself (ibid., p. 532).
49. See note 47.
50. All these questions were influential in *Georgetown*, which concerned a 25-year-old mother who, it was argued, would be "abandoning" her seven-year-old son if her decision were to prevail.
51. For the problem of treating the self and not the other as the basis for applying the Golden Rule, see M. Minow, "The Supreme Court 1986 Term, Foreword: Justice Engendered," *Harvard Law Review*, 1987, 101: 10–95, esp. pp. 77–8. This might be the fundamental distinction between an "ethics of care" and an "ethics of otherness" – see Mónica López Lerma, "Law in High Heels: Performativity, Alterity, and Aesthetics," *Southern California Interdisciplinary Law Journal*, 2011, 20: 289–324.
52. Baron, "Blood Transfusions."
53. See R. Dworkin, *Taking Rights Seriously* and *Law's Empire*, both at Cambridge, MA: Harvard University Press, 1977 and 1986 respectively. In his principled approach, Dworkin opposes not just Hartian positivism, but legal pragmatism of the kind defended, notably, by Richard Posner (see, more recently, R. Dworkin, *Justice in Robes*. Cambridge: Harvard University Press, 2006).
54. Dworkin's metaphor of the "chain novel" does not necessarily alter this picture. Although the novel itself is a collaborative effort, each judge faces his or her own task individually ("Law as Interpretation," *Texas Law Review*, 1982, 60: 527).
55. C. S. Peirce, "Some Consequences of Four Incapacities," as cited in M. Minow "Justice Engendered," p. 77.
56. J. Webber, "A Judicial Ethic for a Pluralistic Age," in O. Payrow Shabani (ed.), *Multiculturalism and Law: A Critical Debate*. Cardiff: University of Wales Press, 2007, pp. 67–100, at p. 72, emphasis added.
57. See, D. Manderson, "Judgment in Law and the Humanities," in A. Sarat, M. Anderson and C. O. Frank (eds), *Law and the Humanities: An Introduction*, Cambridge: Cambridge University Press, 2010, pp. 496–516. See, also, Manderson, *Songs Without Music: Aesthetic Dimensions of Law and Justice*, Berkeley and Los Angeles: University of California Press, 2000.

Appendix

1. C. Sourvinou-Inwood, "The Fourth Stasimon of Sophocles' 'Antigone,'" *Bulletin of the Institute of Classical Studies*, 1989, 36: 141–66, at p. 142.
2. About this process, see J. Wise, *Dyonisus Writes: The Invention of Theatre in Ancient Greece*. Ithaca, NY: Cornell University Press, 1998.
3. Diodorus Syculus, 4.44, trans. C. Oldfather, Loeb Classical Library. Cambridge, MA: Harvard University Press, 1935.
4. R. P. Winnington-Ingram, *Sophocles: An Interpretation*. Cambridge: Cambridge University Press, 1980, p. 105, emphasis added.

5. We know that the three great tragedians wrote different plays concerning the myths of this Ode and that Sophocles alone wrote two or three about Phineus and another about Danaë (and her father Acrisius). These fragments are collected by A. C. Pearson, *The Fragments of Sophocles*, 3 vols. Cambridge: Cambridge University Press, 1917; see also S. Radt, *Tragicorum Graecorum Fragmenta*, vol. 4. Göttingen: Vadenhoeck & Ruprecht, 1977; more recently, see H. Lloyd-Jones, *Sophocles III: Fragments*, Loeb Classical Library. Cambridge, MA and London: Harvard University Press,1996.
6. For example, see M. L. West, in "Tragica VI", *Bulletin of the Institute of Classical Studies*, 1983, 30: 63–82, tries to reconstruct Aeschylus' lost trilogy about Lycurgus which may have some bearings on our ode.
7. This resembles, by the way, the extent of our knowledge about Lycurgus' myth.
8. See also C. Sourvinou-Inwood, "Assumptions and the Creation of Meaning: Reading Sophocles' Antigone," *Journal of Hellenic Studies*, 1989, 109: 134–48.
9. In his commentary to this *stasimon* the otherwise punctilious Richard Jebb says that although the Chorus never mentions Cleopatra's imprisonment we should take it for granted, using Diodorus Syculus' account as his authority. However, if we are going to believe Diodorus about the imprisonment, we should also believe him when, immediately afterwards, he denies that the blinding of the sons ever occurred (Diodorus Syculus, 4.43–4). Jebb does not explain how he resolves this contradiction.

Works cited

Translations and critical editions of Sophocles' *Antigone*

Alamillo, A., *Sófocles: Tragedias*. Madrid: Biblioteca Básica Gredos, 2000.

Fagles, R. *Sophocles: The Three Theban Plays*. London: Penguin Classics, 1982.

Gibbons, R. and Segal, C., *Sophocles' Antigone*. Oxford: Oxford University Press, 2003.

Grene, D., *The Complete Greek Tragedies: Sophocles I*. Chicago: University of Press, 1991.

Griffith, M. (ed.), *Sophocles: Antigone*. Cambridge: Cambridge University Press, 1999.

Jebb, R. (trans. and ed.), *Sophocles. The Plays and Fragments. Part 3: Antigone*. Cambridge: Cambridge University Press, 1891.

Kamerbeek, J. C. (ed.), *The Plays of Sophocles with Commentaries. Part 3: The Antigone*. Leiden: E. J. Brill, 1978.

Lloyd-Jones, H., *Sophocles: Antigone*, Loeb Classical Library. Cambridge, MA and London: Harvard University Press, 1994.

Mazon, P., *Sophocle, Antigone*. Paris: Les Belles Lettres, 2002.

Classical sources

Aeschylus, *Seven Against Thebes*, in *Aeschylus* in two vols, vol. 1, H. W. Smyth, Loeb Classical Library. Cambridge, MA and London: Harvard University Press and William Heinemann, 1926.

Aeschylus, *The Oresteia*, trans. R. Fagles. London: Penguin Classics, 1979.

Anaximander, fragment A9 [DK 12A9, B1], in H.Diels and W.Kranz (eds), *Die Fragmente der Vorsokratiker*. Berlin: Weidmannsche Verlagsbuchhandlung, 1960.

Apollodorus, *The Library*, trans. Sir J. G. Frazer, Loeb Classical Library. Cambridge, MA and London: Harvard University Press and William Heinemann, 1921.

Aristotle, *Nichomachean Ethics*, trans. H. Rackham, Loeb Classical Library. Cambridge, MA and London: Harvard University Press and William Heinemann, 1934.

Aristotle, *Poetics*, trans. W. H. Fyfe, Loeb Classical Library. Cambridge, MA and London: Harvard University Press and William Heinemann, 1932.

Aristotle, *Rhetoric*, trans. J. H. Freese, Loeb Classical Library. Cambridge, MA and London: Harvard University Press and William Heinemann, 1926.

Demosthenes, *On the False Embassy*, trans. C. A. Vince and J. H. Vince, Loeb Classical Library. Cambridge, MA and London: Harvard University Press and William Heinemann, 1926.

Diodorus Siculus, *Diodorus of Sicily*, 12 vols, trans. C. H. Oldfather, Loeb Classical Library. Cambridge, MA and London: Harvard University Press and William Heinemann, 1935.

Euripides, *Helen*, in *The Complete Greek Drama*, eds W. J. Oates and E. O'Neill, in 2 vols, vol. 2, trans. E. P. Coleridge. New York: Random House, 1938.

Euripides, *Phoenician Women*, in *The Complete Greek Drama*, eds W. J. Oates and E. O'Neill, in 2 vols, vol. 2, trans. E. P. Coleridge. New York: Random House, 1938.

Euripides, *The Suppliants*, in *The Complete Greek Drama*, eds W. J.Oates and E.O'Neill, in 2 vols, vol. 1, trans. E. P. Coleridge. New York: Random House, 1938.

Herodotus, *The Histories*, trans. A. D. Godley, Loeb Classical Library. Cambridge, MA and London: Harvard University Press and William Heinemann, 1920.

Homer, *The Iliad*, trans. R. Fitzgerald. Oxford: Oxford University Press, 1998.

Isocrates, *Panathenaicus*, in *Isocrates with an English Translation in Three Vols*, trans. G. Norlin. London: William Heinemann, 1980.

Livy, *Livy in Fourteen Vols*, trans. B. O. Foster. Cambridge, MA: Harvard University Press, 1967.

Lycurgus, *Against Leocrates*, in *Minor Attic Orators* in two vols, trans. J. O. Burtt, Loeb Classical Library. Cambridge, MA: Harvard University Press, 1962.

Lysias, *Lysias. With an English Trans. by W. R. M. Lamb*, Loeb Classical Library. Cambridge, MA and London: Harvard University Press and William Heinemann, 1930.

Pausanias, *Description of Greece*, trans. W. H. S. Jones, Loeb Classical Library. Cambridge, MA and London: Harvard University Press and William Heinemann, 1921.

Pindar, *Nemean Odes*, ed. and trans. Diane Arnson Svarlien, available in the Perseus Classical Library of Tufts University, Medford, MA (see http://www.perseus.tufts.edu).

Pindar, *Olympian Odes*, in *Pindar in 2 vols*, ed. and trans. William H. Race, Loeb Classical Library. Cambridge, MA: Harvard University Press, 1997.

Pindar, *Pythian Odes*, in *Pindar in 2 vols*, ed. and trans. William H. Race, Loeb Classical Library. Cambridge, MA: Harvard University Press, 1997.

Plato, *Protagoras*, in J. M. Cooper and D. S. Hutchinson (eds), *Plato: Complete Works*. Indianapolis, IN: Hackett, 1997.

Plato, *The Republic*, trans. Desmond Lee, 2nd edn, in J. M. Cooper and D. S. Hutchinson (eds), *Plato: Complete Works*. Indianapolis, IN: Hackett, 1997.

Plato, *The Laws*, trans. R. G. Bury, Loeb Classical Library. Cambridge, MA: Harvard University Press and William Heinemann, 1967–8.

Plutarch, *Life of Theseus*, in *Plutarch's Lives*, trans. B. Perrin, Loeb Classical Library. Cambridge, MA and London: Harvard University Press and William Heinemann, 1914.

Thucydides, *History of the Peloponnesian War*, rev. edn, trans. R. Warner. London: Penguin, 1972.

Xenophon, *Hellenica*, in *Xenophon in Seven Vols*, vols 1 and 2, trans. C. L. Brownson, Loeb Classical Library. Cambridge, MA and London: Harvard University Press and William Heinemann, 1918 and 1921.

Xenophon, *Memorabilia*, in *Xenophon in Seven Vols*, trans. E. C. Marchant, Loeb Classical Library. Cambridge, MA and London: Harvard University Press and William Heinemann, 1923.

Secondary literature

Aarnio, A., *The Rational as Reasonable: A Treatise on Legal Justification*. Dordrecht: Reidel, 1987.

Adkins, A., *Merit and Responsibility: A Study in Greek Values*. Chicago: University of Chicago Press, 1960.

Adler, M., "Constitutional Fidelity, the Rule of Recognition, and the Communitarian Turn in Contemporary Positivism," *Fordham Law Review*, 2006, 75: 1671–95.

Alexy, R., "On Necessary Relations Between Law and Morality," *Ratio Iuris*, 1989, 2: 167–83.

Alexy, R., "A Defence of Radbruch's Formula," in D. Dyzenhaus (ed.), *Recrafting the Rule of Law: The Limits of Legal Order*. Oxford and Portland, OR: Hart, 1999, pp. 15–39.

Alexy, R., "On the Thesis of a Necessary Connection between Law and Morality: Bulygin's Critique," *Ratio Iuris*, 2000, 12: 138–47.

Amis, E., "Plato on Poetic Creativity," in R. Kraut (ed.), *The Cambridge Companion to Plato*. Cambridge: Cambridge University Press, 1992, pp. 338–64.

Amsterdam, A. and Brunner, J., *Minding the Law: How Courts Rely on Storytelling, and How Their Stories Change the Ways We Understand the Law – and Ourselves*. Cambridge, MA: Harvard University Press, 2000.

Arendt, H., *Lectures on Kant's Political Philosophy*, ed. R. Beiner. Chicago: University of Chicago Press, 1992.

Arendt, H., *The Promise of Politics*, ed. J. Kohn. New York: Schocken Books, 2005.

Atienza, M., *Las Razones del Derecho: Teoría de la Argumentación Jurídica*. Madrid: Centro de Estudios Constitucionales, 1991.

Atria, F., *On Law and Legal Reasoning*. Oxford and Portland, OR: Hart, 2001.

Bakhtin, M., *The Dialogic Imagination: Four Essays*. Austin, TX: University of Texas Press, 1981.

Ball, M. S., "The Play's the Thing: An Unscientific Reflection on Courts Under the Rubric of Theater," *Stanford Law Review*, 1975, 28: 81–115.

Bandes, S., "Empathy, Narrative, and Victim Impact Statements," *University of Chicago Law Review*, 1996, 63: 362–412.

Barber, N. W., "Legal Pluralism and the European Union," *European Law Journal*, 2006, 12: 306 29.

Baron, C. H., "Blood Transfusions, Jehovah's Witnesses, and the American Patients' Rights Movement," in Alice Maniatis, Phillipe van der Linden, and Jean-François Hardy (eds), *Alternatives to Blood Transfusion Medicine*. Chichester: Wiley-Blackwell, 2010, pp. 529–53.

Belleau, M. C. and Johnson, R., "Interdisciplinary Questions about Law, Language and Dissent," in L. Atkinson and D. Majury (eds), *Law, Mystery and the Humanities: Collected Essays*. Toronto: University of Toronto Press, 2008, pp. 145–66.

Benardete, S., *Sacred Transgressions: A Reading of Sophocles' Antigone*. South Bend, IN: St Augustine's Press, 1999.

Bengoetxea, J. R., *The Legal Reasoning of the European Court of Justice*. Oxford: Clarendon Press, 1992.

Bengoetxea, J. R., "Direct Applicability of Effect," in M. Hoskins and W.Robinson (eds), *A True European: Essays for Judge David Edward*. Oxford: Hart, 2003, pp. 353–66.

Benjamin, W., "Critique of Violence," in P. Demetz (ed.), *Reflections: Essays, Aphorisms, Autobiographical Writings*, trans. E. Jephcott. New York: Schocken Books, 1986, pp. 277–300.

Bergson, H., *La Pensée et le Mouvant*. Geneva: Albert Skira, 1946.

Bergson, H., *Time and Free Will: An Essay on the Immediate Data of Consciousness*, trans. F. L. Pogson. New York: Dover, 2001 [1913].

Berlin, I., *Liberty*, ed. H. Hardy. Oxford: Oxford University Press, 2002.

Beushausen, K., "Dangerous Fracture: Undermining the Order of the Law in Sophocles' *Antigone*," *Mosaic*, 2008, 41(3): 15–30.

Bickel, A., *The Least Dangerous Branch: The Supreme Court at the Bar of Politics*. Indianapolis, IN: Bobbs-Merrill, 1962.

Bilz, K., "We Don't Want to Hear it: Psychology, Literature and the Narrative Model of Judging," *University of Illinois Law Review*, 2010, 2: 101–55.

Bix, B., *Law, Language, and Legal Determinacy*. Oxford: Clarendon Press, 1993.

Bix, B., *Robert Alexy's Radbruch*, University of Minnesota Law School Legal Studies Research Papers Series No. 06-13, Draft, January 2006.

Blundell, M. W., *Helping Friends and Harming Enemies: A Study in Sophocles and Greek Ethics*. Cambridge and New York: Cambridge University Press, 1989.

Booth, W., *The Rhetoric of Fiction*, 2nd edn. Chicago: University of Chicago Press, 1981.

Bosteels, B., "Force of NonLaw: Alan Badiou's Theory of Justice," *Cardozo Law Review*, 2008, 29(5): 1905–26.

Bottéro, J., "Symptômes, Signes, Écritures en Mésoptamie Ancienne," in J. P. Vernant et al. (eds), *Divination et Rationalité*. Paris: Seuil, 1974, pp. 70–197.

Bowra, C. M., *Sophoclean Tragedy*. Oxford: Clarendon Press, 1944.

Burton, W. B., *The Chorus in Sophocles' Tragedies*. Oxford: Clarendon Press, 1980.

Bushnell, R. B., *Prophesying Tragedy: Sign and Voice in Sophocles' Theban Plays*. Ithaca, NY: Cornell University Press, 1988.

Butler, J., *Antigone's Claim: Kinship Between Life and Death*. New York: Columbia University Press, 2000.

Calabresi, G., *The Cost of Accidents: A Legal and Economic Analysis*. New Haven, CT: Yale University Press, 1970.

Calabresi, G. and Bobbitt, P., *Tragic Choices*. New York: W. W. Norton, 1978.

Castoriadis, C., "The Greek Polis and the Creation of Democracy," in D. Ames Curtis (ed.), *Philosophy, Politics, Autonomy: Essays in Political Philosophy*. New York and Oxford: Oxford University Press, 1991, pp. 81–123.

Cerri, G., "Ideologia funeraria nell'*Antigone* di Sofocle," in G. Gnoli and J.-P. Vernant (eds), *La Mort, les morts dans les sociétés anciennes*, Paris and London: Maison des Sciences de l'Homme and Cambridge University Press, 1982, pp. 121–31.

Chang, R. (ed.). *Incommensurability, Incomparability, and Practical Reason*. Cambridge, MA: Harvard University Press, 1997.

Cover, R., *Justice Accused: Antislavery and the Judicial Process*. New Haven, CT: Yale University Press, 1975.

Cover, R., "The Origins of Judicial Activism in the Protection of Minorities," *Yale Law Journal*, 1982, 91: 1287–316.

Cover, R., "The Supreme Court, 1982 Term – Foreword: Nomos and Narrative," *Harvard Law Review*, 1983, 97: 4–68.

Cover, R., "The Bonds of Constitutional Interpretation: Of the Word, the Deed, and the Role," *Georgia Law Review*, 1986, 20: 815–33.

Cover, R., "Violence and the Word," *Yale Law Journal*, 1986, 95: 1601.

Cropp, M., "Antigone's Final Speech: Sophocles' 'Antigone' 891–928," *Greece and Rome*, 1997, 44(2): 137–60.

Dahlberg, L. "Emotional Tropes in the Courtroom: On Representation of Affect and Emotion in Legal Court Proceedings," *Law and Humanities*, 2009, 3(2): 175–205.

Derrida, J., "Force of Law: The 'Mystical Foundation of Authority,'" trans. Mary Quaintance, *Cardozo Law Review*, 1990, 11: 920–1045.

Derrida, J., *The Politics of Friendship*, trans. G. Collins. London and New York: Verso, 2005.

Detienne, M., *The Masters of Truth in Archaic Greece*, trans. Janet Lloyd. New York: Zone Books, 1996.

Dewey, J., "Logical Method and the Law," *Cornell Law Quarterly*, 1927, 10: 17–27.

Ditmars, E. van Nes, *Sophocles' Antigone: Lyric Shape and Meaning*. Pisa: Giardani Editori, 1992.

Dodds, E. R., *The Greeks and the Irrational*. Berkeley, CA and Los Angeles: University of California Press, 1951.

Douzinas, C., "Law Deathbound: Antigone and the Dialectics of Nomos and Thanatos," in D. Manderson (ed.), *Courting Death: The Legal Constitution of Mortality*. London: Pluto Press, 1999, pp. 163–80.

Douzinas, C., with Warrington, R., "Antigone's Dikē," in *Justice Miscarried: Ethics, Aesthetics and the Law*. Hemel Hempstead: Harvester Wheatsheaf, 1994, pp. 25–92.

Dover, K. J., *Greek Popular Morality in the Time of Plato and Aristotle*. Indianapolis, IN and Cambridge: Hackett, 1974.

Dubber, M., *The Sense of Justice: Empathy in Law and Punishment*. New York and London: New York University Press, 2006.

Dworkin, R., *Taking Rights Seriously*. Cambridge, MA: Harvard University Press, 1977.

Dworkin, R., "Law as Interpretation," *Texas Law Review*, 1982, 60: 527.

Dworkin, R., *Law's Empire*. Cambridge, MA: Harvard University Press, 1986.

Dworkin, R., *Justice in Robes*. Cambridge, MA: Belknap Press of Harvard University Press, 2006.

Easterling, P. (ed.), *The Greek Companion to Greek Tragedy*. Cambridge: Cambridge University Press, 1997.

Eckerman, J. P., *Conversations with Goethe*, trans. J. Oxenford. London: Dent, 1935.

Edmundson, M., *Literature Against Philosophy, Plato to Derrida: A Defence of Poetry*. Cambridge: Cambridge University Press, 1995.

Ehrenberg, V., *Sophocles and Pericles*. Oxford: Basil Blackwell, 1954.

Else, G. F., *Aristotle's Poetics: The Argument*, Cambridge: Harvard University Press, 1957.

Else, G. F., *The Madness of Antigone*. Heidelberg: Carl Winter Universitätsverlag, 1976.

Erp Taalman Kipp, A. van, "Truth in Tragedy: When We Are Entitled to Doubt a Character's Words?" *American Journal of Philology*, 1996, 117: 517–36.

Errandonea, I., *Sófocles y la Personalidad de sus Coros*. Madrid: Moneda y Cambio, 1970.

Etxabe, J., "A Review of 'Living Speech: Resisting the Empire of Force' by James Boyd White," *Law and Humanities*, 2008, 2(1): 138–46.

Etxabe, J., "Antigone's *Nomos*," *Animus: The Canadian Journal of Philosophy and Humanities*, 2009, 13: 60–73.

Etxabe, J., "The Legal Universe After Robert Cover," *Law and Humanities*, 2010, 4(1): 115–47.

Etxabe, J., "What Do the Poets Know About Democracy? A Case Study in Law and Literature," in B. van Klink and S.Taekema (eds), *Law and Method: Interdisciplinary Research into Law*. Tübingen: Mohr Siebeck, 2011, pp. 341–54.

Euben, J. P., *The Tragedy of Political Theory*. Princeton, NJ: Princeton University Press, 1990.

Euben, J. P., "*Antigone* and the Languages of Politics," in *Corrupting the Youth: Political Education, Democratic Culture, and Political Theory*. Princeton, NJ: Princeton University Press, 1997, pp. 139–78.

Ewans, M., "Patterns of Tragedy in Sophocles and Shakespeare," in M. S. Silk (ed.), *Tragedy and the Tragic: Greek Theatre and Beyond*. Oxford: Clarendon Press, 1996, pp. 438–56.

Ferrari, G. R. F., "Plato on Poetry," in G. A. Kennedy (ed.), *The Cambridge History of Literary Criticism*, Vol. 1. Cambridge: Cambridge University Press, 1989, pp. 45–78.

Finnis, J., "Commensuration and Public Reason," in R. Chang (ed.), *Incommensurability, Incomparability, and Political Reason*. Cambridge, MA: Harvard University Press, 1997.

Fiss, O., "Objectivity and Interpretation," *Stanford Law Review*, 1982, 34: 739–63.

Flacelière, R., *Greek Oracles*, trans. D. Garman. London: Elek Books, 1965.

Fletcher, J., "Citing the Law in Sophocles' *Antigone*," *Mosaic*, 2008, 41(3): 79–96.

Foley, H. P., "Tragedy and Democratic Ideology: The Case of Sophocles' *Antigone*," in B.Goff (ed.), *History, Tragedy, Theory: Dialogue in Athenian Drama*. Austin, TX: University of Texas Press, 1995, pp. 131–50.

Foley, H. P., "Antigone as a Moral Agent," in M. Silk (ed.), *Tragedy and the Tragic: Greek Theatre and Beyond*. New York and Oxford: Clarendon Press, 1996, pp. 49–73.

Foley, H. P., *Female Acts in Greek Tragedy*. Princeton, NJ: Princeton University Press, 2001.

Foley, H. P., with Fantham, E., Kampen, N. B., Pomeroy, S. B. and Shapiro, H. A., *Women in the Classical World: Image and Text*. New York: Oxford University Press, 1994.

Fradinger, M., "Nomadic Antigone," in F. Söderbäck (ed.), *Feminist Readings of Antigone*. New York: SUNY Press, 2010, pp. 15–23.

Frank, J., "The Antigone's Law," *Law, Culture, and the Humanities*, 2006, 2: 336–40.

Friedrich, R., "Everything to Do with Dionysos? Ritualism, the Dionysiac, and the Tragic," in M. S. Silk (ed.), *Tragedy and the Tragic: Greek Theatre and Beyond*. Oxford: Clarendon Press, 1996, pp. 257–83.

Gaakeer, J., "Law, Language and Literature: Their Interrelations in *Law and Literature*," in B. van Klink and S.Taekema (eds), *Law and Method:* Interdisciplinary Research into Law. Tübingen: Mohr Siebeck, 2011, pp. 215–35.

Gadamer, H. G., "Plato and the Poets," in *Dialogue and Dialectic: Eight Hermeneutical Studies on Plato*. New Haven, CT and London: Yale University Press, 1980, pp. 39–72.

Gadamer, H. G., *Truth and Method*, revised trans. J. Weinsheimer and D. G. Marshall, 2nd revised edn. New York and London: Continuum, 2004 [1975].

Gantz, T., "The Aeschylean Tetralogy: Attested and Conjectured Groups," in *American Journal of Philology*, 1980, 101(2): 133–64.

García Gual, C., "Tiresias o el Adivino como Mediador," *Emérita*, 1975, 43: 107–32.

Garrison, E. P., *Groaning Tears: Ethical and Dramatic Aspects of Suicide in Greek Tragedy*. Leiden: E. J. Brill, 1995.

Geertz, C., *Available Light*. Princeton, NJ: Princeton University Press, 2000.

Gellie, G. H., "*Antigone*," in *Sophocles: A Reading*. Melbourne: Melbourne University Press, 1972, pp. 29–52.

Gerard, P., *Domination, résistance et démocratie de contestation. Les enjeux politiques de L'Antigone de Sophocle*. Paper delivered during the colloquium "Antigone et la Resistance Civile," Brussels, 10 November 2000 (available by courtesy of the author).

Gewirtz, P., "Aeschylus' Law," *Harvard Law Review*, 1988, 101: 1043–55.

Goheen, R. F., *The Imagery of Sophocles' Antigone: A Study of Poetic Language and Structure*. Princeton, NJ: Princeton University Press, 1951.

Goldhill, S., "The Great Dionysia and Civic Ideology," *Journal of Hellenic Studies*, 1987, 107: 58–76.

Goldhill, S., "Civic Ideology and the Problem of Difference: The Politics of Aeschylean Tragedy, Once Again," *Journal of Hellenic Studies*, 2000, 120: 34–56.

Goldhill, S., "The Audience on the Stage: Rhetoric, Emotion, and Judgment in Sophoclean Theatre," in S. Goldhill and E. Hall (eds), *Sophocles and the Greek Tragic Tradition*. Cambridge: Cambridge University Press, 2009, pp. 27–47.

Goodrich, P., "Satirical Legal Studies: From the Legists to the Lizard," *Michigan Law Review*, 2004, 103: 397–517.

Gourgouris, S., "Philosophy's Need for Antigone," in *Does Literature Think? Literature as Theory for an Antimythical Era*. Stanford, CA: Stanford University Press, 2003, pp. 116–57.

Gray, J., *Isaiah Berlin*. Princeton, NJ: Princeton University Press, 1996.

Greenberg, M., "How Facts Make Law," *Legal Theory*, 2004, 10(3): 158–98.

Guest, S., *Ronald Dworkin*. Edinburgh: Edinburgh University Press, 1992.

Guthrie, C., Rachlinski, J. J. and Wistrich, A. J., "Blinking on the Bench: How Judges Decide Cases," *Cornell Law Review*, 2007, 93(1): 1–43.

Habermas, J., *Between Facts and Norms: Contributions to a Discourse Theory of Law and Democracy*, trans. W. Rehg. Cambridge, MA: MIT Press, 1996.

Habermas, J., "Three Normative Models of Democracy," in S. Benhabib (ed.), *Democracy and Difference: Contesting the Boundaries of the Political*. Princeton, NJ: Princeton University Press, 1996, pp. 21–9.

Habermas, J., *The Inclusion of the Other: Studies in Political Theory*. Cambridge, MA: MIT Press, 1998.

Halliwell, S., "Plato's Repudiation of the Tragic," in M. S. Silk (ed.), *Tragedy and the Tragic: Greek Theatre and Beyond*. Oxford: Clarendon Press, 1996, pp. 332–49.

Hansen, W., *Classical Mythology: A Guide to the Mythical World of the Greeks and the Romans*. New York: Oxford University Press, 2005.

Harris, E., "Antigone the Lawyer, or the Ambiguities of Nomos," in E. Harris and L. Rubinstein (eds), *The Law and the Courts in Ancient Greece*. London: Duckworth, 2004, pp. 19–56.

Hart, H. L. A., *Law, Liberty, and Morality*. Stanford, CA: Stanford University Press, 1963.

Hart, H. L. A., *The Concept of Law*, 2nd edn, with an added Postcript by A. Bulloch and J. Raz. Oxford: Oxford University Press, 1994 [1961].

Havelock, E., *Preface to Plato*. Oxford: Basil Blackwell, 1963.

Hegel, G. W. F., *The Phenomenology of Spirit*, trans. A. V. Miller. Oxford: Oxford University Press, 1977.

Heidegger, M., "The Ode on Man in Sophocles' Antigone," in T. Woodward (ed.), *Sophocles: A Collection of Critical Essays*. Englewood, NJ: Prentice Hall, 1966, pp. 86–100.

Heinrichs, A., "Loss of Self, Suffering, Violence: The Modern View of Dionysus from Nietzsche to Girard," *Harvard Studies in Classical Philology*, 1984, 88: 205–40.

Heinrichs, A., "Between Country and City: Cultic Dimensions of Dionysus in Athens and Attica," in M. Griffith and D. Mastronarde (eds), *Cabinet of the Muses*. Atlanta, GA: Scholars Press, 1990, pp. 257–77.

Heinrichs, A., "Why Should I Dance? Choral Self-Referentiality in Greek Tragedy," *ARION*, 1994–5, 3(1): 56–111.

Henderson, L., "Legality and Empathy," *Michigan Law Review*, 1986–7, 85(6): 1574–653.

Herrero de Miñón, M., *Derechos Históricos y Constitución*. Madrid: Taurus, 1998.

Hester, D. A., "Sophocles the Unphilosophical: A Study in the Antigone," *Mnemosyne*, 1971, 24 (Fourth Series): 11–59.

Holmes, O. Wendell Jr, "The Path of the Law," in *Collected Legal Papers*, New York: Harcourt Brace, 1920, pp. 167–202.

Holt, P., "Polis and Tragedy in the Antigone," *Mnemosyne* 52, 1999, 658–90.

Honig, B., "Antigone's Laments, Creon's Grief: Mourning, Membership, and the Politics of Exception," *Political Theory*, 2009, 37(1): 5–43.

Honig, B., "Antigone's Two Laws: Greek Tragedy and the Future of Humanism," *New Literary History*, 2010, 41(1): 1–33.

Honig, B., "Ismene's Forced Choice: Sacrifice and Sorority in Sophocles' *Antigone*," *Arethusa*, 2011, 44(1): 29–68.

Iser, W., *The Implied Reader: Patterns of Communications in Prose Fiction from Bunyan to Beckett*. Baltimore, MD: Johns Hopkins University Press, 1974.

Jackson, B., "Rationalité consciente et inconsciente dans la théorie du droit et la science juridique," *Revue Interdisciplinaire d'Études Juridiques*, 1987, 19: 1–18.

Jaeger, W., *Paideia: The Ideals of Greek Culture*, trans. Gilbert Highet, 3 vols. New York: Oxford University Press, 1933, 1943 and 1944.

Jaeger, W., "Praise of Law: The Origins of Legal Philosophy and the Greeks," in *Interpretations of Modern Legal Philosophies*. New York: Oxford University Press, 1947, pp. 352–75.

Jaeger, W., *The Theology of the Early Greek Philosophers*, trans. E. Robinson. Eugene, OR: Wipf & Stock, 2003.

Jones, J., *On Aristotle and Greek Tragedy*. London: Chatto & Windus and New York: Oxford University Press, 1962.

Kant, I., *Critique of Judgement*, trans. J. Creed Meredith. Oxford: Clarendon, 1973 [1790].

Kaufmann, W., *Tragedy and Philosophy*. Princeton, NJ: Princeton University Press, 1979.

Keating, G., "Pricelessness and Life: An Essay for Guido Calabresi," *Maryland Law Review*, 2005, 64: 159–219.

Kelsen, H., *Pure Theory of Law*, trans. M. Knight, 2nd rev. edn. Berkeley, CA: University of California Press, 1968.

Kelso, C. D. and Kelso, R. R., "Judicial Decision-Making and Judicial Review: The State of the Debate, Circa 2009," *West Virginia Law Review*, 2010, 112: 351–401.

Kennedy, D., "Freedom and Constraint in Adjudication: A Critical Phenomenology," *Journal of Legal Education*, 1986, 36: 518–62.

Kirkwood, G. M., "The Dramatic Role of the Chorus in Sophocles," *Phoenix*, 1954, 8: 1–22.

Kitto, H. D. F., *Form and Meaning in Drama*, 2nd edn. London: Methuen, 1964, pp. 139–78.

Knox, B., *The Heroic Temper: Studies in Sophoclean Tragedy*. Berkeley, CA and Los Angeles: University of California Press, 1964.

Kott, J., "Why Did Antigone Kill Herself?," *New Theatre Quarterly*, 1993, 9(34): 107–10.

Kottman, P., *A Politics of the Scene*. Stanford, CA: Stanford University Press, 2008.

Krause, S. R., *Civil Passions: Moral Sentiment and Democratic Deliberation*. Princeton, NJ and Oxford: Princeton University Press, 2008.

Lacey, W. K., *The Family in Classical Greece*. Ithaca, NY: Cornell University Press, 1968.

Laín Entralgo, P., *La Curación por la Palabra en la Antigüedad Clásica*. Madrid: Revista de Occidente, 1958.

Litowitz, D., *Postmodern Philosophy and Law*. Lawrence, KS: University Press of Kansas, 1997.

Llewellyn, K., "Some Realism about Realism: Responding to Dean Pound," *Harvard Law Review*, 1930–1, 44: 1222–64.

Lloyd-Jones, H., *Sophocles III: Fragments*, Loeb Classical Library. Cambridge, MA and London: Harvard University Press, 1996.

López Lerma, M. "Law in High Heels: Performativity, Alterity, and Aesthetics," *Southern California Interdisciplinary Law Journal*, 2011, 20: 289–324.

Loraux, N., *The Invention of Athens: The Funeral Oration in the Classical City*, trans. Alan Sheridan. Cambridge, MA: Harvard University Press, 1986.

Loraux, N., *The Divided City: On Memory and Forgetting in Ancient Athens*, trans. Corinne Pache with Jeff Fort. New York: Zone Books, 2002.

Loraux, N., *The Mourning Voice: An Essay on Greek Tragedy*, trans. E. Trapnell Rawlings. Ithaca, NY: Cornell University Press, 2002.

Lyotard, J. F., *The Differend*, trans. G. Van Den Abbeele. Minneapolis, MN: University of Minnesota Press, 1988.

Lyotard, J. F., "Sensus Communis," in *Judging Lyotard*, ed. A. Benjamin. London: Routledge, 1992, pp. 14–38.

MacCormick, N., *Legal Reasoning and Legal Theory*. Oxford: Clarendon Press, 1978.

MacCormick, N., *Institutions of Law: An Essay in Legal Theory*. New York: Oxford University Press, 2007.

Machin, A., *Cohérence et Continuité dans le Théâtre de Sophocle*. Québec: Serge Fleury, 1981.

MacIntyre, A., *After Virtue: A Study in Moral Theory*. Notre Dame, IN: University of Notre Dame Press, 1984.

MacKinnon, K., *Feminism Unmodified: Discourses on Life and Law*. Cambridge, MA: Harvard University Press, 1987.

Manderson, D., "Judgment in Law and the Humanities," in A. Sarat, M. Anderson and C. O. Frank (eds), *Law and the Humanities: An Introduction*, Cambridge: Cambridge University Press, 2010, pp. 496–516.

Manderson, D., *Songs Without Music: Aesthetic Dimensions of Law and Justice*, Berkeley and Los Angeles: University of California Press, 2000.

Marmor, A., *Interpretation and Legal Theory*, 2nd rev. edn. Oxford and Portland, OR: Hart, 2005.

Marmor, A., "How Law Is Like Chess," *Legal Theory*, 2006, 12: 347–71.

Maroney, T. A., "Law and Emotion: A Proposed Taxonomy of an Emerging Field," *Law and Human Behavior*, 2006, 30(2): 119–42.

Mazon, P., *Sophocle, Antigone*. Paris: Les Belles Lettres, 2002.

Meier, C., *The Political Art of Greek Tragedy*, trans. A. Webber. Oxford: Polity, 1993.

Meyler, B., "Book Review: The Myth of Law and Literature" [reviewing Thane Rosenbaum, *The Myth of Moral Justice: Why Our Legal System Fails to Do What's Right*. New York: Harper Collins, 2004], *Legal Ethics*, 2005, 8: 318–25.

Mikalson, J. D., *Honor Thy Gods: Popular Religion in Greek Tragedy*. Chapel Hill, NC: University of North Carolina Press, 1991.

Miller, W. I., *The Anatomy of Disgust*. Cambridge, MA: Harvard University Press, 1997.

Miller, W. I., *Eye for an Eye*. New York: Cambridge University Press, 2006.

Minow, M., "The Supreme Court 1986 Term, Foreword: Justice Engendered," *Harvard Law Review*, 1987, 101: 10–95.

Minow, M. and Spelman, E., "Passion for Justice," *Cardozo Law Review*, 1988, 10: 37–76.

Minow, M., Ryan, M., and Sarat, A. (eds), *Narrative, Violence, and the Law: The Essays of Robert Cover*. Ann Arbor, MI: University of Michigan Press, 1992.

Monoson, S., "Citizen as Theatēs (Theater-Goer): Performing Unity, Reciprocity, and Strong-Mindedness at the City Dionysia," in *Plato's Democractic Entanglements: Athenian Politics and the Practice of Philosophy*. Princeton, NJ: Princeton University Press, 2000, pp. 88–110.

Mootz, F. J., "Law and Philosophy, Philosophy and Law," *University of Toledo Law Review*, 1994, 26: 127–46.

Moravcsik, J. and Temko, P. (eds), *Plato on Beauty, Wisdom, and the Arts*. Totowa, NJ: Rowman & Littlefield, 1982.

Mullender, R., "Two Nomoi and a Clash of Narratives: The Story of the United Kingdom and the European Union," *Berkeley Electronic Press*, 2006; online at http://www.bepress.com/ils/iss8/.

Murnaghan, S., "Antigone 904–20 and the Institution of Marriage," *American Journal of Philology*, 1986, 107: 192–207.

Nadaff, R., *Exiling the Poets: The Production of Censorship in Plato's Republic*. Chicago and London: University of Chicago Press, 2002.

Nieburg, M., "How Like a Woman: Antigone's 'Inconsistency,'" *Classical Quarterly*, 1990, 40(1): 54–76.

Nietzsche, F., *Thus Spoke Zarathustra*, ed. R. Pippin, trans. A. del Caro. Cambridge: Cambridge University Press, 2006 [1892].

Nieuwenburg, P., "The Agony of Choice: Isaiah Berlin and the Phenomenology of Conflict," *Administration and Society*, 2004, 35: 683–700.

Nonet, P., "Antigone's Law," *Law, Culture, and the Humanities*, 2006, 2: 314–35.

Nussbaum, M., *Poetic Justice: The Literary Imagination and Public Life*. Boston: Beacon Press, 1995.

Nussbaum, M., "Sophocles' 'Antigone': Conflict, Vision, and Simplification," in *The Fragility of Goodness: Luck and Ethics in Greek Tragedy and Philosophy*, rev. edn. New York: Cambridge University Press, 2001, pp. 51–82.

Nussbaum, M., *Upheavals of Thought: The Intelligence of Emotions*. New York: Cambridge University Press, 2001.

Nussbaum, M., *Hiding From Humanity: Disgust, Shame, and the Law*. Princeton, NJ: Princeton University Press, 2004.

Ober, J., "How to Criticize Democracy," in J. P. Euben, J. R. Wallach, and J. Ober (eds), *Athenian Political Thought and the Reconstruction of American Democracy*. Ithaca, NY and London: Cornell University Press, 1994, pp. 149–71.

Oksenberg Rorty, A. (ed.), *Essays on Aristotle's Poetics*. Princeton, NJ: Princeton University Press, 1992.

Opstelten, J. C., *Sophocles and Greek Pessimism*. Amsterdam: North-Holland, 1952.

Ost, F., *Le Temps du Droit*. Paris: Odile Jacob, 1999.

Ost, F., "*L'Antigone* de Sophocle: Résistance, apories juridiques et paradoxes politiques," in *Raconter la Loi: Aux Sources de l'Imaginaire Juridique*. Paris: Odile Jacob, 2004, pp. 153–203.

Ost, F., *Antigone Voilé*. Brussels: Larcier, 2004.

Ost, F., *Raconter la Loi: Aux Sources de l'Imaginaire Juridique*, Paris: Odile Jacob, 2004.

Ost, F., with Kerchove, M. van de, *De la Pyramide au Réseau? Pour une Théorie Dialectique du Droit*. Brussels: Publications des Facultés Universitaires Saint Louis, 2002.

Ostwald, M., "Sophocles' Antigone: The Family Collides with the State," in *From Popular Sovereignty to the Sovereignty of Law: Law, Society, and Politics in Fifth*-Century Athens. Berkeley, CA and London: University of California Press, 1986, pp. 148–61.

Oudemans, T. C. W. and Lardinois, A. P. M. H., *Tragic Ambiguity: Anthropology, Philosophy and Sophocles' Antigone*. Leiden: E. J. Brill, 1987.

Panoussis, I., *Crainte et violence dans le théâtre de Sophocle*. Villeneuve d'Ascq: Villeneuve d'Ascq Presses Universitaires Septentrion, 2002.

Pearson, A. C., *The Fragments of Sophocles*, 3 vols. Cambridge: Cambridge University Press, 1917.

Peczenik, A., "Coherence, Truth, and Rigthness in the Law," in P. Nerhot (ed.), *Law, Interpretation and Reality*. Dordrecht: Kluwer, 1990.

Perez, O. "Law as a Strange Loop," in Gralf Peter Callies et al. (eds), *Sociological Jurisprudence: Liber Amicorum Gunther Teubner*. Berlin: De Gruyter, 2009.

Phelan, J., *Experiencing Fiction: Judgments, Progressions, and the Rhetorical Theory of Narrative*. Columbus, OH: Ohio University Press, 2007.

Polanyi, M., *Personal Knowledge: Towards a Post-Critical Philosophy*. Chicago: University of Chicago Press, 1974.

Posner, R., "The Ethical Significance of Free Choice: A Reply to Professor West," *Harvard Law Review*, 1985–6, 99: 1431–48.

Posner, R., *Law and Literature: A Misunderstood Relation*. Cambridge, MA: Harvard University Press, 1988.

Radt, S., *Tragicorum Graecorum Fragmenta*, vol. 4. Göttingen: Vadenhoeck & Ruprecht, 1977.

Rancière, J., *Disagreement: Politics and Philosophy*, trans. Julie Rose. Minneapolis, MN and London: University of Minnesota Press, 1999.

Raz, J., *The Authority of Law: Essays on Law and Morality*. Oxford and New York: Clarendon Press, 1979.

Raz, J., *The Morality of Freedom*. New York: Oxford University Press, 1986.

Reinhardt, K., *Sophocles*, trans. H. Harvey and D. Harvey, NY: Harper & Row, 1979.

Ricœur, P., *Time and Narrative*, trans. K. Blamey and D. Pellauer, 3 vols. Chicago: University of Chicago Press, 1988.

Ricœur, P., *Soi-Même Comme un Autre*. Paris: Seuil, 1990.

Ricœur, P., "The Act of Judging," in *The Just*, trans. D. Pellauer. Chicago and London: University of Chicago Press, 2000, pp. 127–32.

Rokem, F., *Philosophers and Thespians. Thinking Performance*. Stanford, CA: Stanford University Press, 2009.

Romilly, J., *Time in Greek Tragedy*. Ithaca, NY: Cornell University Press, 1968.

Rorty, R., *Contingency, Irony, and Solidarity*. Cambridge and New York: Cambridge University Press, 1989.

Rosivach, V., "On Creon, Antigone, and not Burying the Dead," *Rheinisches Museum Philologie*, 1983, 126: 193–211.

Rosivach, V., "Autochthony and the Athenians," *Classical Quarterly*, 1987, 37(2): 294–306.

Sandel, M., "The Procedural Republic and the Unencumbered Self," *Political Theory*, 1984, 12: 81–96.

Sartre, J. P., "Existentialism Is a Humanism," in W. Kaufman (ed.), *Existentialism from Dostoyevsky to Sartre*. New York: Meridian, 1981.

Schaap, A. (ed.), *Law and Agonistic Politics*. Aldershot: Ashgate, 2009.

Schauer, F., "Judging in a Corner of the Law," *Southern California Law Review*, 1988, 61: 1717–34.

Schauer, F., *Playing by the Rules: A Philosophical Examination of Rule-Based Decision-Making in Law and in Life*. Oxford: Oxford University Press, 1991.

Schmidt, D., "Can Law Survive? On Incommensurability and the Idea of Law," *University Toledo Law Review*, 1994, 26: 147–58.

Schuster, M. L. and Propen, A., "Degrees of Emotion: Judicial Responses to Victim Impact Statements," *Law, Culture and Humanities*, 2010, 6: 75–104.

Scodel, R., *Sophocles*. Boston: Twayne, 1984

Scullion, S., "Dionysos and Katharsis in Antigone," *Classical Antiquity*, 1986, 17(1): 96–122.

Seaford, R., "Something to do with Dionysos – Tragedy and the Dionysiac: Response to Friedrich," in M. S. Silk (ed.), *Tragedy and the Tragic: Greek Theatre and Beyond*. Oxford: Clarendon Press, 1996, pp. 284–94.

Searle, J., *Speech Acts: An Essay in the Philosophy of Language*. Cambridge: Cambridge University Press, 1969.

Segal, C., "Sophocles' Praise of Man and the Conflicts of the Antigone," in T. Woodward (ed.), *Sophocles: A Collection of Critical Essays*. Englewood Cliffs, NJ: Prentice Hall, 1966, pp. 62–85.

Segal, C., *Tragedy and Civilization: An Interpretation of Sophocles*. Cambridge, MA: Harvard University Press, 1981.

Shusterman, R., "Aesthetic Ideology, Aesthetic Education, and Art's Value in Critique," in *Pragmatist Aesthetics: Living Beauty, Rethinking Art*, 2nd edn. Lanham, MD: Rowman & Littlefield, 2000, pp. 139–68.

Silk, M. (ed.), *Tragedy and the Tragic: Greek Theatre and Beyond*. Oxford: Clarendon Press, 1996.

Skinner, S., "Stories of Pain and the Pursuit of Justice: Law, Violence, Experience and Jurisprudence," in *Law, Culture and the Humanities*, 2009, 5: 131–55.

Sony, V., "Trial and Tragedies: The Literature of Unhappiness (A Model for Reading Narratives of Suffering)," in *Comparative Literature*, 2007, 59(2): 119–39.

Sourvinou-Inwood, C., "Sophocles' Antigone 904–20: A Reading," *AION* (*Annali dell'Istituto Universitario Orientale di Napoli*), 1987–8, IX–X: 19–35.

Sourvinou-Inwood, C., "Assumptions and the Creation of Meaning: Reading Sophocles' Antigone," *Journal of Hellenic Studies*, 1989, 109: 134–48.

Sourvinou-Inwood, C., "The Fourth Stasimon of Sophocles 'Antigone," *Bulletin of the Institute of Classical Studies*, 1989, 36: 141–65.

Stearns, P. and Stearns, C., *American Cool: Constructing a Twentieth-Century Emotional Style*. New York: New York University Press, 1994.

Steiner, G., *Antigones*. Oxford and New York: Clarendon Press, 1984.

Steiner, G., "Tragedy, Pure and Simple," in M. S. Silk (ed.), *Tragedy and the Tragic: Greek Theatre and Beyond*. Oxford: Clarendon Press, 1996, pp. 534–53.

Stone Peters, J., "Law, Literature, and the Vanishing Real: On the Future of an Interdisciplinary Illusion," *Publications of the Modern Language Association of America*, 2005, 120: 442–52.

Sullivan, S., *Sophocles' Use of Psychological Terminology*. Ottawa: Carleton University Press, 1999.

Sunstein, C., "Incommensurability and Kinds of Valuation: Some Applications in Law," in R. Chang (ed.), *Incommensurability, Incomparability, and Political Reason*. Cambridge, MA: Harvard University Press, 1997, pp. 234–54.

Sutton, D., *The Lost Sophocles*, Lanham, MA and London: University Press of America, 1984.

Taylor, C., "Leading a Life," in R. Chang (ed.), *Incommensurability, Incomparability, and Practical Reason*. Cambridge, MA: Harvard University Press, 1997, pp. 170–83.

Tindemans, K., "Antigone and the Law: Legal Theory and the Ambiguities of Performance," in S. E. Wilmer and A. Zukauskaite (eds), *Interrogating Antigone in Postmodern Philosophy and Criticism*. Oxford: Oxford University Press, 2010, pp. 185–96.

Tomain, J. P., *Creon's Ghost: Law, Justice, and the Humanities*. New York and Oxford: Oxford University Press, 2009.

Tully, J., *Strange Multiplicity: Constitutionalism in the Age of Diversitity*. Cambridge: Cambridge University Press, 1995.

Tyrrell, W.B. and Bennett, L. J., *Recapturing Sophocles' Antigone*. Lanham, MD: Rowman & Littlefield, 1998.

Ugartemendia, J. I., *La Desobediencia Civil en el Estado Constitucional Democrático*. Basque Country, Spain: Instituto Vasco de Administración Pública, 1999.

Van Erp Taalman Kip, M. A., "Truth in Tragedy: When Are We Entitled to Doubt a Character's Words?" *American Journal of Philology*, 1996, 117: 517–36.

Vattimo, G., *Art's Claim to Truth*, ed. Santiago Zabala, trans. Luca D'Isanto. New York: Columbia University Press, 2010.

Veitch, S., *Moral Conflict and Legal Reasoning*. Oxford and Portland, OR: Hart, 1999.

Vernant, J. P. and Vidal-Naquet, P., *Myth and Tragedy in Ancient Greece*, trans. Janet Lloyd. New York: Zone Books, 1988.

Ville, J. de, "Rethinking the Notion of a 'Higher Law': Heidegger and Derrida on the Anaximander Fragment," *Law and Critique*, 2009, 20: 59–78.

Ville, J. de, "On Law's Origin: Derrida Reading Freud, Kafka, and Levi-Strauss," *Utrecht Law Review*, 2011, 7: 77–92.

Ward, I., *Law and Literature: Possibilities and Perspectives*. Cambridge: Cambridge University Press, 1995.

Watt, G., *Equity Stirring: The Story of Justice Beyond Law*. Oxford and Portland, OR: Hart, 2009.

Watt, G., "The Case of Conjoined Twins: Medical Dilemma in Law and Literature," in Daniela Carpi (ed.), *Bioethics and Biolaw Through Literature*. Berlin and New York: De Gruyter, 2011, pp. 93–107.

Webber, J., "A Judicial Ethic for a Pluralistic Age," in *Multiculturalism and Law: A Critical Debate*, ed. Omid Payrow Shabani. Cardiff: University of Wales Press, 2007, pp. 67–100.

Weber, M., "Politics as a Vocation," in D. Owen and T. B. Strong (eds), *The Vocation Lectures*. Indianapolis, IN and Cambridge: Hackett, 2004, pp. 32–94.

Weisberg, R., *Poethics, and Other Strategies of Law and Literature*. New York: Columbia University Press, 1992.

Welch, D., "Ruling with the Heart: Emotion-Based Public Policy," *Southern California Interdisciplinary Law Journal*, 1997, 6: 55–88.

Wells, C. P., "Situated Decisionmaking," *Southern California Law Review*, 1990, 63: 1728–46.

Wells, C. P., "Improving One's Situation: Some Pragmatic Reflections on the Art of Judging," *Washington and Lee Law Review*, 1992, 49: 323–38.

West, M. L., "Tragic VI," *Bulletin of the Institute of Classical Studies*, 1983, 30: 63–82.

West, R., "Economic Man and Literary Woman: One Contrast," in *Narrative, Authority, and Law*. Ann Arbor, MI: University of Michigan Press, 1993, pp. 251–63.

West, S., *Sophocles' Antigone and Herodotus' Book Three*, in J. Griffin (ed.), *Sophocles Revisited*. Oxford: Oxford University Press, 1999, pp. 109–36.

White, H., "The Value of Narrativity in the Representation of Reality," in W. Mitchell (ed.), *On Narrative*. Chicago and London: University of Chicago Press, 1980–1, pp. 1–23.

White, J. B., *The Legal Imagination: Studies in the Nature of Legal Thought and Expression*. Boston: Little, Brown, 1973.

White, J. B., *When Words Lose Their Meaning: Constitutions and Reconstitutions of Language, Character, and Community*. Chicago: University of Chicago Press, 1984.

White, J. B., *Heracles' Bow: Essays on the Rhetoric and Poetics of Law*. Madison, WI: University of Wisconsin Press, 1985.

White, J. B., "What Can A Lawyer Learn from Literature?" *Harvard Law Review*, 1989, 102: 2104–47.

White, J. B., *From Expectation to Experience: Essays on Law and Legal Education*. Ann Arbor, MI: University of Michigan Press, 1999.

White, J. B., "Legal Knowledge," *Harvard Law Review*, 2002, 115: 1396–431.

White, J. B., *Living Speech: Resisting the Empire of Force*. Princeton, NJ: Princeton University Press, 2006.

Wiggins, D., *Needs, Values, Truth*, 3rd edn. Oxford: Clarendon Press, 1998.

Williams, B., "The Truth in Relativism," *Proceedings of the Aristotelian Society*, 1974–5, 75: 215–28.

Winkler J. and Zeitlin, F. (eds), *Nothing to Do with Dionysos? Athenian Drama in its Social Context*. Princeton, NJ: Princeton University Press, 1990.

Winnington-Ingram, R. P., *Sophocles: An Interpretation*. Cambridge: Cambridge University Press, 1980.

Wise, J., *Dionysus Writes: The Invention of Theatre in Ancient Greece*. Ithaca, NY: Cornell University Press, 1998.

Yoshino, K., "The City and the Poet," *Yale Law Journal*, 2005, 114: 1835–96.

Index

For Product Safety Concerns and Information please contact our EU representative GPSR@taylorandfrancis.com
Taylor & Francis Verlag GmbH, Kaufingerstraße 24, 80331 München, Germany

www.ingramcontent.com/pod-product-compliance
Ingram Content Group UK Ltd.
Pitfield, Milton Keynes, MK11 3LW, UK
UKHW011000180926
475701UK00004B/475
* 9 7 8 0 4 1 5 6 5 7 1 8 1 *